THE STRUCTURED ESSAY: A Formula for Writing

Second Edition

Mary S. Spangler
Rita R. Werner
Los Angeles Valley College

Resource *Publications*
An imprint of *Wipf and Stock Publishers*
199 West 8th Avenue • Eugene OR 97401

Resource *Publications*
an imprint of Wipf and Stock Publishers
199 West 8th Avenue, Suite 3
Eugene, Oregon 97401

The Structured Essay
A Formula for Writing
By Spangler, Mary and Werner, Rita

ISBN: 1-57910-920-9
Publication Date: March, 2002
Previously published by Kendall/Hunt Publishing Company, 1986.

Contents

Preface

The Structured Essay: A Formula for Writing, 2nd ed., is a systematic approach to college-level writing. In this updated version we have incorporated suggestions made by colleagues and students across the country. The most notable changes are the addition of twelve professionally written essays and the term paper chapter revision which reflects the 1984 Modern Language Association guidelines. In addition, the physical layout has been improved for easier reading of the pages. The chapter on expository paragraph and essay writing has been separated into two chapters. The chapter on analysis has also been separated so that each of the three types of analysis is presented in its own chapter. The text relies on practical formulas that can be adapted to writing assignments in other subjects. It progresses from simple exercises to longer and more difficult analytical evaluations. It includes items most frequently cited by our students as being helpful in their learning to write.

The Structured Essay: A Formula for Writing, 2nd ed., contains the following features. It is rhetorically organized, beginning with an overview of the writing process. The book moves to description, narration, and exposition, where paragraph and essay writing are examined. A detailed treatment of each of the expository patterns of development is followed by argumentation. The book next includes sections on nonfiction prose analysis and the term paper. It ends with a brief handbook that focuses on sentence writing, combining, and correcting.

Each rhetorical method includes a brief discussion, an organizational pattern, a writing sample analyzed for parts, samples with discovery exercises, additional samples including professionally written essays, suggested writing topics, a worksheet, and a cover grading sheet. The sample essays written by our students at Los Angeles Valley College are practical and realistic models for beginners who often have difficulty adapting the techniques of professional writers.

The Structured Essay: A Formula for Writing, 2nd ed., can be adapted to several different teaching approaches. It is well suited for use in the traditional lecture method because it provides many specific models and a consistent system. It is also suited for individualized instruction because it is structured. Its regular pattern provides the support that enables students to work independently. The text incorporates elements of mastery learning because each writing assignment is designed to be completed in a sequence of steps. Students choose their subject, write their thesis statement, and obtain the instructor's approval on their worksheet. Then they develop their outline during a laboratory session. Only after these steps are completed do the students write the essay. The sequence ends with an opportunity to rewrite and improve their final draft. The worksheets and cover sheets can be detached from the book and submitted with the student's essay. Because the text is consistent and carefully structured, students develop competence in writing logical, well-organized essays.

Optional exercises include

- journal writing
- peer evaluations of essays
- three types of expository analysis, including analysis of advertisements
- analysis of nonfiction prose, including a professional essay and a book
- numerous short "discovery exercises"

We wish to thank the many people who have helped us in developing this textbook. In particular, we appreciate the help of our copyeditor, Marymargaret Parker. We are grateful to our colleagues—Thomas Clayton, Stephen Statham, Paige Wilson, and Marvin Zuckerman—who have class tested the material and our students who have contributed their essays and suggestions over the years.

Mary Spangler and Rita Werner

CHAPTER 1

The Writing Process: An Overview

The purpose of this textbook is to help you express in writing your ideas, attitudes, beliefs, and feelings in order to communicate them to other people. Acquiring this skill requires time, effort, and practice. The structured approach used here is designed to help you develop this skill. You will find that a carefully planned, structured essay enables your audience to better understand and remember your ideas. Thus, organization in writing is a means to the goal of effective communication. Using the patterns presented in this text allows you to focus your creative efforts on content.

Preliminary to using specific patterns in writing is learning the three stages in the writing process: prewriting, writing, and rewriting. This chapter introduces you to the requirements of these stages that are further separated into nine steps. Later chapters explore them in greater detail and provide specific examples to guide you through the actual process. Chapter 1 also presents the basic concepts of writing, which include structure, unity, and order. In addition, this section discusses the stylistic aspects of good writing by examining tone, diction, sentence structure, and coherence. Charts and lists present in detail these important concepts in forms that are easy to understand and to use. For easy reference, these resources are indexed on the inside back cover of the text.

Refer to this chapter throughout the course, before beginning each assignment and during the actual writing process. Read it carefully in order to become familiar with the sequence of steps and with the specific resources that are referred to regularly in the rest of the text.

PREWRITING—THE INVENTING STAGE

Step 1: Choose a subject
Step 2: Focus the subject
Step 3: Frame the main idea and supports
Step 4: Sketch an outline

Step 1: Choose a Subject

The goal is to find a subject that you can develop adequately in the time and space allotted. You will need to select either a subject with which you are personally familiar or one about which you can easily find information.

Sources for ideas

Personal experience is an obvious and rich source for concrete details. Specific subjects include your job, trips you have taken, your leisure interests, skills, or hobbies, likes and dislikes, childhood moments, and happy or sad times.

Objective material provides ideas from newspapers, magazines, anthologies, or courses in other disciplines.

Journal writing on a regular basis is a good habit to develop for several reasons. You are expressing yourself and practicing writing free of negative judgments from others and free of the necessity for logical and polished work. You are also sharpening your powers of observation and your senses.

Write at least a paragraph for each journal entry but preferably one page. In addition to the written entry, you might also include nonverbal material such as drawings, doodles, photos, or bars of music. Try out different forms and styles of writing by following these suggestions for journal entries:

- a vivid and detailed description of someone or something you know
- a narration of a significant event or occurrence that happened to you or to someone you know
- a personal reaction or feeling or attitude that you experienced and what caused it
- an interpretation or analysis of some idea or concept discussed in one of your classes
- an argument, objection, or disagreement with someone, with the explanation and defense of your argument
- a problem you have encountered and possible solutions to it
- a discussion of goals, dreams, or disappointments
- poems, sentences, paragraphs, sayings that you heard or read which appealed to you
- anything else that you can express in words

Using the sources

Having decided on the general area, subject, or topic for your assignment, you now use one or two of these techniques to develop the material to write about. **Free writing** is usually most effective with personal experience or journal entries. This technique involves jotting down at least a page of notes on as many specific details, facts, ideas, or associations you can recall about your subject. List these items in whatever sequence they occur to you, without worrying about their relative importance. Since this is just a starting point, allow your imagination and memory free rein.

Questioning is useful with personal experience, objective material, or journal entries. This technique involves asking questions about your subject. The questions provide a systematic way to probe your topic because they reflect the way you think. While not every question is appropriate for every subject, the answers that you discover can become material for your assignment.

What happened?
When did it happen?
Where did it happen?
What does it look like?
What are its characteristics?
What are some typical cases or examples of it?
How did it happen?
What makes it work?
How is it made?
Why did it happen?
What caused it?
What does it cause?
What are its effects?
How is it related to something else?
How is it like other things?
How is it different from other things?
What are its parts or types?
How can its parts or types be separated or grouped?
Do its parts or types fit into a logical order?
Into what categories can its parts or types be arranged?
On what basis can it be categorized?
What is it?
How does it resemble other members of its class?
How does it differ from other members of its class?
What are its limits?

By answering just a few of these questions, you can begin to see the possibilities of your subject. For example, by using this technique with a broad topic like "the Titanic," you can develop many approaches.

What did it look like? A description of the Titanic

How did it differ from other members of its class? A contrast of the Titanic with other luxury liners of its period

What happened? A short narration of the sinking of the Titanic

How did it happen? An analysis of the stages in its sinking

Why did it happen? An analysis of the causes that led to its sinking

What were its effects? An analysis of the consequences that followed its sinking

Note taking is especially appropriate with objective material and also with journal writing. This technique involves taking at least a page of notes on some major aspects of the subject you think you might want to write about. Whenever possible, take notes in your own words rather than copy from your source. If you do use someone else's words, you should put them within quotation marks and later give credit to the author.

With any of these techniques, the main concerns are creativity and originality of thought and content. You should not worry about such matters as mechanics and usage, order and coherence, at this point. In addition, these approaches will help you to choose a topic about which you have enough information. If your topic is still too broad, you can try narrowing it and apply these techniques again. Once you have developed several topics, select the one that interests you or that is within your scope of knowledge or that is appropriate to the limits of the assignment. As you gain experience in choosing a subject, you will most likely discover the combination of these techniques that is most successful for you.

Step 2: Focus the Subject

The goal is to limit and shape the subject you choose by making decisions about the paper's purpose, audience, tone, and diction.

Decide on the purpose

A clear decision about the purpose of your paper will sharpen your thinking and give focus and consistency to your writing. You should have one main purpose predominate even though other reasons for writing may be included. For example, your purpose may be to describe a picturesque landscape, or you may want to relate a frightening experience you had last week. Other purposes are to explain how a camera works or to inform the reader about the similarities between two jobs. A description of the camera or an anecdote about a job could be secondary purposes for the writing. You may also choose to argue about a particular measure passed by your local government. Your decision about the purpose then determines the form or structure of your essay. Later chapters discuss each of these forms in detail.

Purpose →	**Form/Structure**
to describe or show	Description
to relate or tell	Narration
to inform or explain	Exposition
to argue or persuade	Argumentation

Decide on the audience

You must always be aware of the individual or group to whom you are addressing your writing. That audience determines the kinds of information and words you use.

For your college writing you should assume that your readers have some college education, many interests, some large gaps in knowledge, and a few prejudices. They do not want to read seriously flawed, poorly organized, dull, wordy material, but they enjoy humor, concrete details, and meaningful information.

Much of the communicating that you will do in the near future—such as writing letters, reports, or memos—will be directed at a specialized audience. It is important that you have a clear notion of the characteristics of the particular individual or group. For help in defining the specialized audience, refer to Chapter 14, p. 305.

Decide on the tone

Tone is your attitude as a writer primarily toward your subject or material but also toward your audience and yourself. Tone is revealed through the entire piece of writing rather than in a single sentence or word. Your essay may have more than one tone, but multiple tones must complement and support each other. Your attitude as a writer is conveyed by your choice of words (diction) and by the way you use them (sentence structure).

Therefore, always choose your tone carefully and use it consistently. Make sure it is in harmony with your subject, purpose, and audience. The following chart defines some effective and ineffective tones and identifies diction appropriate to them.

How to Use the Tone Chart—*as a writer*

1. Select from the first column of alphabetized terms an **effective** tone for your essay. The second column briefly describes each tone. For example, if your subject is home remodeling and your purpose is to explain some of the hazards to a general audience, you might select a humorous or a serious tone. A humorous tone is described on the chart as "funny; laughable; comic; witty; amusing; playful." A serious tone is described as "thoughtful; sober; grave; earnest; weighty; not joking or jesting."
2. Note in the third column the types of diction that usually contribute to and develop that tone. For instance, if you choose the humorous tone, you might use diction that is "alliterative, concrete, connotative, subjective, figurative." If you choose a serious tone, your diction could be "concise, concrete, denotative, literal, objective, technical."
3. Next, take the suggested diction, and check the Diction Chart in the next section to find the descriptions and examples of vocabulary you can use in your essay. For example, a humorous tone often uses connotative diction which is described as "suggesting negative or positive emotional feelings in addition to the literal meaning of the word; colored or colorful words." A serious tone would use concise diction which is described as "expressing much in few words; compact; economical; no unnecessary words."
4. Avoid the tones described as ineffective.

How to Use the Tone Chart—*as a reader of the writings of others*

1. Select representative or characteristic vocabulary samples from the passage you are reading.
2. Check the Diction Chart in the next section to help you identify the examples you have chosen. The chart will describe the types of diction that the passage is using.
3. Take the diction terms and locate them in the third column of the Tone Chart.
4. Find the tone or tones that include most of the types of diction you have identified in the passage you are reading.

EFFECTIVE TONE CHART

Term	Description	Suggested Diction
admiring	worshipping; approving; respectful	connotative, slanted, subjective
aggressive	powerful; energetic; forceful, bold, vigorously active; assertive	connotative, slanted
angry	indignant; outraged; inflamed	connotative, slanted, subjective
argumentative	quarrelsome; debating; combative; controversial	abstract, connotative, slanted
anxious	troubled; upset; uneasy	connotative, slanted, subjective
bitter	disagreeable; distasteful; showing resentment; painful	connotative, figurative, subjective
caustic	stinging; sharp; sarcastic; biting	concrete, connotative, slanted
concerned	interested; involved	concise, subjective, literal
disinterested	impersonal; impartial; objective; weighing all sides	concise, denotative, objective
disliking	hostile; abhorring; attacking; antagonistic; disapproving	connotative, slanted, subjective
elevated	grand; lofty; eminent; noble; imposing	abstract, formal, technical
facetious	lightly joking; not seriously believing what one is saying; jesting; flippantly humorous; clever	alliterative, connotative, figurative, subjective, overstated, understated
farcical	ridiculous; absurd; exaggerated; joking; ludicrous; using derisive remarks	alliterative, connotative, figurative, subjective, overstated
friendly	good-natured; jovial; jolly	concrete, semiformal, subjective, informal
grim	stern; forbidding; terrifying; relentless; fierce; uncompromising	concise, connotative, subjective
humorous	funny; laughable; comic; witty; amusing; playful	alliterative, concrete, connotative, subjective, figurative
ironic	using sarcasm or humor to literally say the opposite of what is meant; resulting in the reverse of what is expected	connotative, figurative
nostalgic	longing for familiar circumstances or for the faraway or long ago	abstract, subjective, connotative, figurative, slanted, euphemistic
reverential	expressing profound respect, often with awe and affection; showing courtesy, homage, deference	abstract, subjective, slanted
romantic	imaginary; fictitious; sensuous; not based on fact	connotative, subjective
sarcastic	scornful; contemptuous, taunting; cutting; biting; a **spoken** tone	connotative, subjective, slanted, figurative, overstated, understated
sardonic	cynical; sneering; mocking; derisive	connotative, subjective, slanted, figurative, overstated, understated

EFFECTIVE TONE CHART—Continued

Term	Description	Suggested Diction
satiric	ridiculing; ironic; witty; used to expose or attack abuses, vices, follies, and stupidities; a **written** literary form; may be lightly and gently mocking or harshly and cruelly mocking	connotative, subjective, slanted, figurative, overstated, understated
serious	thoughtful; sober; grave; earnest; weighty; not joking or jesting	concise, concrete, denotative, literal, objective, technical
sorrowful	mournful; sad; unhappy; woeful; painful; distressed	connotative, subjective, slanted, abstract
straight-forward	direct; honest; frank	concise, concrete, denotative, literal, objective
subdued	restrained; moderate; controlled	concise, denotative, literal
sympathetic	compassionate; pitying; congenial; agreeable	connotative, slanted, subjective
terse	free from superfluous words; to the point; pithy; succinct	concise, concrete, denotative, literal, objective, technical
whimsical	oddly out of the ordinary; capricious; fanciful; quaint; fantastic; eccentric	abstract, connotative, subjective, figurative

INEFFECTIVE TONE CHART

Term	Description	Suggested Diction
arrogant	unnecessarily or excessively proud; overbearing; haughty; insolent	connotative, formal, jargonistic, overstated, understated
bombastic	high-flown; verbose; wordy	connotative, wordy, padded, euphemistic, formal, abstract
colloquial	informal and conversational (can be used effectively in limited contexts)	cliché, informal, jargonistic, slang, trite
condescending	patronizing; talking down to the audience	connotative, jargonistic, formal
dull	tedious; unclear; exciting little interest; lifeless; tiresome; boring; apathetic; indifferent; unconcerned	repetitious, vague, trite, wordy, understated
familiar	unnecessarily, intimate, forward, informal, or personal	informal, subjective, slang
indecisive	hesitant; irresolute; having more than one interpretation; evasive; indirect	ambiguous, abstract, euphemistic, understated
pompous	exaggerated in self-importance and dignity; pretentious; flowery; overbearing	overstated, abstract, formal, wordy, padded, subjective
preaching	heavily moralizing or sermonizing; meddlesome	euphemistic, slanted, overstated, subjective
strident	harsh; shrill; grating	overstated, subjective, slanted

Decide on the diction

Semantics is the study of the development and changes in the meaning of words. One area of semantics involves diction. Diction is your conscious choice of words or vocabulary within an essay. Using a dictionary can help you select the best words for your ideas. However, your diction must be suited to the subject, purpose, audience, and tone you have chosen. When chosen carefully, diction makes ideas clearer. There are three levels of language or diction: formal, semiformal, and informal. In general, college-level writing is semiformal. The following chart defines and illustrates both effective and ineffective diction.

How to Use the Diction Chart—*as a writer*

1. Select an appropriate tone or tones from the Tone Chart in the previous section. Note the suggested diction listed in the third column.
2. Look up each suggested type of diction in the alphabetized first column of the Diction Chart. The second column briefly describes each kind of diction. The third column gives a typical example.
3. Use those kinds of vocabulary in writing your paper. Consult a dictionary and thesaurus to help you choose words with precise shades of meaning.
4. Avoid ineffective diction.
5. Study the following examples to see how differences in tone require different types of diction.

Subject: remodeling

Tone: humorous

Diction	Example
alliterative	dusty, dirty, and dingy
concrete	eating cheese and crackers for breakfast, lunch, and dinner
connotative	interminable, aggravating delays
figurative	mountains of plaster and nails
subjective	the most educational experience of my life

Tone: serious

Diction	Example
concise	two-week demolition period
concrete	walls eight feet high
literal, denotative, objective	high-gloss green paint in the den
technical	200 linear feet of flex conduit

How to Use the Diction Chart—*as a reader of the writings of others*

1. Select representative or characteristic vocabulary samples from the passage you are reading.
2. Check the Diction Chart to help you identify the examples you have chosen. The chart will describe the types of diction that the passage is using.
3. Take the diction terms and locate them in the third column of the Tone Chart in the previous section.
4. Find the tone or tones that include most of the types of diction you have identified in the passage you are reading.

EFFECTIVE DICTION CHART

Term	Description	Example
abstract	expressing a quality that is separate from a specific object or particular instance; qualitative; not detailed or precise; general; the reverse of concrete	The horse's strength was amazing.
alliterative	repeating the same initial letter or sound of two or more words in close succession	Snide remarks filtered through the sideline spectators.
concise	expressing much in few words; compact; economical; no unnecessary words	"To be or not to be, that is the question." (Hamlet)
concrete	expressing a particular or specific entity that can be perceived by the senses; objectively real; specific; the reverse of abstract	On the wood-ribbed deck, a dirty white, weather beaten 5/25 inch-cannon points at the horizon.
connotative	suggesting negative or positive emotional feelings in addition to the literal meaning of the word	
types: colorful	conveying sense details and images; especially descriptive and vivid; loud and noisy words, rather than quiet and soft	The battered, soiled muddy-brown coat hung loosely on his small bent shoulders.
purr	arousing positive feelings; colored in a positive manner	The slender young woman glided gracefully into the gourmet restaurant.
snarl	arousing negative feelings; colored in a negative manner	The skinny adolescent strutted awkwardly into the fast-food eating place.
denotative	conveying the actual, explicit, or specific meaning or object identified by a word, as opposed to what it suggests (connotation)	The dog ate the bone.
figurative	using words in a nonliteral way to create a vivid image; associating two ordinarily separate items or ideas; the reverse of literal	
common figures of speech: simile	comparing two items unlike in most respects but similar in others and introduced by "like," "as," or "than"	The evening felt like butterflies and green grass.
metaphor	comparing one item to another by speaking of it as if it were that other	The Alpine peak was a frosted cake.
analogy	comparing generally dissimilar items in an extended manner	(comparing an electric current to the flow of a river)
allusion	making an indirect reference to persons, places, or objects that are commonly known; drawn from history, literature, the Bible, current events among others	This singing group is the Beatles of the 1980's.
personification	bestowing human qualities on objects or ideas	The sky wept uncontrollably.

EFFECTIVE DICTION CHART—Continued

Term	Description	Example
formal	expressing ideas in a more elaborate, complex vocabulary and sentence structure than everyday writing	"We hold these truths to be self-evident; that all men are created equal; that they are endowed by their creator with certain inalienable rights; that among these are life, liberty, and the pursuit of happiness." (Declaration of Independence)
literal	expressing the exact stated meaning; factual; free from figurative language	Columbus arrived in America in 1492.
objective	treating ideas without including personal feelings, opinions, prejudices; detached; unbiased; the reverse of subjective	A balanced diet includes some fruit.
semiformal	expressing ideas on a level that most educated people use; precise vocabulary and tight sentence structure of moderate length; no contractions	Picasso turned to a historical event, the destruction by the Germans of Guernica, Spain, to inspire his powerful mural.
slanted	expressing a special attitude, bias, or opinion; using charged words with positive or negative emotional feelings	The author of the best-selling potboiler is a creative genius. (positive) The author of the best-selling potboiler is a prosperous hack. (negative)
subjective	treating ideas from a personal, inner perspective; including one's beliefs, ideals, impressions, prejudices, emotions; the reverse of objective	That movie was fantastic and enjoyable.
technical	using words dealing with a particular art, science, or trade; referring to specialized skill or knowledge, especially mechanical or scientific	In many ganoid fishes, the fulcrums are the rows of spinlike scales along the forward edge of the median and paired fins.

INEFFECTIVE DICTION CHART

Term	Description	Example
ambiguous	giving several simultaneous meanings; not precise; doubtful or uncertain	Pain is a feeling which can totally change the perspective of one's life.
cliché	using a worn-out or overused phrase	I was busy night and day for hours on end working my fingers to the bone.
euphemistic	substituting a mild or agreeable word or phrase for a realistic description of a disagreeable topic	He passed on to his eternal reward.
*informal	expressing ideas in the language of ordinary conversation or familiar, common writing; colloquial	It's obvious that Jane never got out of this nasty habit.
jargonistic	using specialized or technical language of a particular group; using confused or meaningless language	The party of the first part herein agrees to render payment to the party of the second part.
*overstated	exaggerating the importance of; expressing in too strong terms; may be used effectively for ironic tone	Our first kiss has been the most unbelievably wonderful moment of my entire life.

Term	Description	Example
padded	adding unnecessary material in order to make the passage longer	In my opinion, I believe that students when they are writing shouldn't get into the habit of using too many unnecessary words that they don't need in order to convey their idea.
repetitious	restating the same idea or using the same words excessively; redundant; monotonous; dull; unvaried	The differences between the women lie in their attitudes toward childrearing, their attitudes toward marriage, and their attitudes toward working.
slang	using stale language that is inexpressive because it wears out quickly	The guy went bananas when his old man was bumped off.
trite	lacking freshness or originality; worn out by repetition	In today's society, pollution is a big problem.
*understated	being unemphatic and restrained; saying with less force than the subject requires; may be used effectively for ironic tone as a contrast to point up the importance of the content	Napoleon in a letter to Josephine: "Things did not go so well for us at Waterloo."
vague	stating an idea unclearly, obscurely, indefinitely, indistinctly; colorless	The things I bought awhile ago were very nice.
wordy	using an unnecessary number of words	Believe it or not, the movie of the book was better than that of the play, to me.

*May be used effectively on certain occasions.

Dictionaries

A dictionary, which describes rather than dictates meanings, is a useful tool in helping you to select the best words to express your ideas. A reliable dictionary contains the following information:

- spelling, capitalization, syllabication, pronunciation
- parts of speech and inflected forms (word changes and endings)
- definitions and examples of usage
- synonyms (words with similar meanings), antonyms (words with opposite meanings), and idioms (expressions developed by convention)
- origin (etymology)

A brief sampling of types of dictionaries includes

1. Scholarly and historical:

   The Oxford English Dictionary (OED) in 12 volumes and supplement traces the progressive history and meanings of words in British English.

   A Dictionary of American English on Historical Principles does the same for American English.

2. Unabridged (includes the half million words in the English language):

   The Random House Dictionary of the English Language

   Webster's Third New International Dictionary

3. Abridged and collegiate:

   American Heritage Dictionary of the English Language

   Funk & Wagnalls Standard College Dictionary

   Webster's New Collegiate Dictionary

4. Specialized:
   Roget's International Thesaurus (a dictionary of synonyms and antonyms)
   Dictionary of American Slang

Step 3: Frame the Main Idea and Supports

One goal is to reach a conclusion about your subject so that you can express this conclusion as the main idea of your essay. A second goal is to select the major ideas which support your conclusion. Every form of writing, except description and narration, contains a stated or implied main idea.

Levels of generality

As you look over the notes you collect prior to writing the actual essay, you should notice that some ideas are more general and some are more specific than others. The words **general** and **specific** are relative terms which express a relationship between two or more items. For example, going from the most general to the most specific, the word *fruit* is more general than *apple* and more specific than *food*. The relationship between these levels is that of **subordination** since the items are not equally general or specific. You can visualize this relationship by indenting each new subordinate level of generality several spaces to the right. This approach will help you to evaluate the range of your ideas more easily.

```
1 food
   2 fruit
      3 apple
         4 Pippin
```

We can discuss this relationship by using the concept of **levels of generality.** The most general level, which includes all other levels, is labeled **level 1.** All items directly subordinate to level 1 are **level 2.** All items directly subordinate to level 2 are **level 3** and so on.

Another relationship that exists in these levels is that of **coordination.** Here two or more items are on the same level of generality. You can visualize this relationship by listing all items on the same level underneath each other. This approach will help you to determine whether you have enough supporting details at each level. For example, all types of food are level 2. All types of fruit are level 3. All types of apples are level 4.

```
1 food
   2 fruit
      3 apple
         4 Pippin
         4 Rome
      3 pear
         4 Anjou
         4 Bartlett
   2 meat
```

The relationship between levels 1, 2, 3, and 4 is subordinate. The relationship within a level (between Pippin and Rome, for example) is coordinate.

Unity

Unity is the most fundamental element of good writing. It exists when all of the details and supports within a piece of writing are clearly related to the main idea. From your notes, you will have decided on your subject and all major supporting ideas. These supports lead to a conclusion about the subject. This conclusion is the controlling idea of your essay. The subject and controlling idea together form the **thesis statement,** which is the one main idea of the essay. An essay can have only one thesis statement, which is labeled level 1. It can best be expressed as a formula:

Thesis statement = subject + verb + controlling idea

From your list of notes, you will choose **three** major supports, the level 2's, to use in your essay. If these supports reinforce the thesis statement, the essay will have unity.

Point of view and verb tense

After you have chosen your thesis statement and major supports, you must decide on the point of view and verb tense. In writing, point of view does not refer to your opinion or attitude about a subject. A more precise way to identify your opinion is to call it your viewpoint. Instead, you should reserve the phrase **point of view** to indicate the position from which the details of the essay are being presented. This position is determined by your choice of pronoun for the point of view. There are three possible choices.

first person	I	we
second person	you	you
third person	he, she, it, everyone, somebody	they all

It is best to avoid the second-person pronoun *you* because it can be monotonous and convey a preaching tone. However, it is appropriate to use the second person when giving directions or commands. In these cases, the pronoun *you* is not stated but implied, and the sentence usually begins with the verb. An example is, "Change the water in the tank every three days."

You also must decide how you will use time (which verb tense you will select) in writing your essay. You will probably choose present or past tense rather than future tense. The present tense gives the reader a feeling of immediacy and closeness to the subject. The past tense puts more distance between the reader and the subject. To some degree the subject will help to determine your verb tense. Be sure to follow consistently the choices you make about point of view and verb tense in order to avoid unnecessary and distracting shifts within the paper.

Step 4: Sketch an Outline

The goal is to develop each of the major supports more specifically by dividing them into subcategories that include concrete examples, details, definitions, and experiences.

Order

Order refers to the sequence in which something is presented. You will begin by selecting an order for your major supports. There are five ways of ordering these supports within an essay. This chart indicates where you can find a more detailed discussion of each order.

Order	Where Used	Definition
Space	Description, Ch. 2	Identifies person, place, or object in relationship to a physical area Proceeds from left↔to right, top bottom, inside↔outside, foreground background, clockwise or counterclockwise
Time/ Chronological	Narration, Ch. 3 Illustration, Ch. 6 Process Analysis, Ch. 9 Causal Analysis, Ch. 10	Identifies an event in the sequence in which it occurred Proceeds chronologically from beginning → middle → end

Order	Where Used	Definition
General to Particular	Illustration, Ch. 6 Classification, Ch. 7 Functional Analysis, Ch. 8 Comparison, Analogy, Ch. 11 Contrast, Ch. 11 Definition, Ch. 12 Argumentation, Ch. 13	Moves from a main or central idea to the specific instances or details which support it
Climactic	Illustration, Ch. 6 Classification, Ch. 7 Functional Analysis, Ch. 8 Comparison, Analogy, Ch. 11 Contrast, Ch. 11 Definition, Ch. 12 Argumentation, Ch. 13	Moves from the least important to the most important statement or detail Expresses the intended scale of importance within a larger idea
Alternating	Comparison, Ch. 11 Analogy, Ch. 11 Contrast, Ch. 11	Systematically shifts from one item to another within a paragraph in order to show the relationship between the items

After you have chosen the order of your major supports, you can begin to make an outline. Next, you will select supporting details, examples, and definitions of your level 2 major supports. Because unity is the most fundamental aspect of good writing, these supporting levels (3, 4, 5) must follow from their respective level 2 major supports.

Forms of outlines

An outline may take one of two forms. Both forms begin with the thesis statement written as a complete sentence. In both, supporting details are indented to express coordinate and subordinate relationships. The **conventional outline** uses numbered and lettered breakdowns. Each breakdown must include at least two items. Examples of this form are included with the five-paragraph essay in Chapter 5 and the term paper in Chapter 15. The **worksheet** uses levels of generality. It records prewriting decisions on source of material, subject, controlling idea, order of subtopics, point of view, verb tense, tone, and diction. As you make decisions in each of these areas, enter them in the appropriate place on the worksheet. Completed worksheets for description, narration, the paragraph, exposition, and argumentation illustrate the planning for those types of writing.

The outline or worksheet has a number of significant features:

- It is easier to make changes at this stage rather than later.
- It is easier to see gaps in material, and so you can check for unity before you develop ideas.
- It is easier to see inconsistencies in the development of an idea.
- It saves time in later revisions.

Either the phrase or sentence outline is acceptable. Whichever form you use, be consistent in using it. Remember that the thesis statement is always written as a sentence.

The outline is only a preliminary or working plan of your ideas. The more complete and detailed it is, the easier it will be to write the essay. However, the outline is subject to modification during the constructing stage, which occurs next.

WRITING—THE CONSTRUCTING STAGE

Step 5: Develop the body paragraphs Step 6: Write the introductory paragraph Step 7: Write the concluding paragraph

Step 5: Develop the Body Paragraphs

The goal is to build the body of the essay by showing the relationship of the ideas that have been sketched in the outline.

Paragraph

A **paragraph** is a group of related sentences. It contains one main idea which is called the **topic sentence.** Although this sentence may be positioned anywhere in the paragraph, it is best to place it first for clarity. For the paragraph to have unity, all of the sentences within it must follow from the topic sentence. You will write the paragraph (in complete sentences) from the outline. You must include concrete details, examples, and definitions in developing your ideas.

Methods of development

Even though each paragraph has one main method of development, there may be others within it. Discussion and examples of each of these methods occur later in the text.

Description presents the impressions that a physical, concrete subject makes on one's senses.

Narration relates actions and events by telling a story.

Exposition informs or explains about ideas in the following different ways:

- **Illustration** uses concrete, specific examples to represent and clarify a general idea.
- **Classification** divides a group of items into the types or kinds of members which comprise it.
- **Functional analysis** shows what the individual parts of a structure are in their relation to each other and to the whole.
- **Process analysis** shows how the steps or stages of an event occur.
- **Causal analysis** explains why events are related to each other.
- **Comparison** examines the similarities between two or more items which share a basic kinship.
- **Analogy** examines the similarities between two items which do not share a basic kinship.
- **Contrast** examines the differences between two or more items which share a basic kinship.
- **Definition** sets limits on a term by telling how it is being used.

Argumentation aims through the presentation of evidence to gain acceptance of an opinion.

Miscellaneous serves several different functions:

- **Summary** condenses the important ideas of a longer passage.
- **Evaluation** judges the significance or worth of a person, place, thing, or idea.
- **Transition** indicates the shift from one part of a discussion to the next.

Coherence

After you have developed the body paragraphs, you must move smoothly from one idea to another. Transitions will tie the parts of your structure together. Several devices help to achieve this coherence.

Transitional expressions are words or phrases that signal specific relationships. A complete list is included in the Handbook in Chapter 16, pp. 374–376.

Parallel structures are two or more grammatical constructions (words, phrases, or clauses) that express equal ideas in similar patterns. The Handbook discusses these structures.

Pronoun reference is the use of a pronoun to replace a noun (antecedent) mentioned previously.

Repetition of key terms is the use of the same word or a synonym to emphasize the term; use a thesaurus to find synonyms.

Step 6: Write the Title and the Introductory Paragraph

The goal is to select an inventive title and interesting introductory material to catch the reader's attention. Background information is necessary for an understanding of the subject. You should present the main idea or thesis that the essay will treat in the body paragraphs and then enumerate the major supporting ideas (not necessary in description and narration). Use one of the good beginnings from this list in your introduction.

Beginnings

Good

1. Present a brief dramatic incident, anecdote, or experience.
2. Ask a question which leads directly to the thesis. Limit the question to one that is answered in the thesis statement.
3. Make a statement to startle or attract attention or to provoke curiosity. For example, surprise the reader with frank or unusual information; deliberately misquote a famous saying or create some sort of pun.
4. Relate the subject to a topic of current interest.
5. Give a quotation appropriate to the subject or purpose of the essay. (Use a book of quotations.)
6. Make a statement which anticipates the reader's possible objections.
7. Mention the limits in your essay of the discussion of the subject; then give the thesis statement.
8. State the occasion or reason which led you to pick this subject and thesis.
9. State the belief or argument you intend to disprove in your essay.
10. Present a contrast which emphasizes the thesis.
11. Cite the opposing arguments and then your thesis or conclusion.
12. Give the necessary special information for an understanding of your subject.
13. List the various ways in which the subject might be discussed, and then state your method.
14. Give some background of your subject—historical, psychological, social, legal—whichever applies.
15. Mention the difficulties that exist in discussing the subject.

Bad

1. Do not apologize, for instance, for your lack of knowledge or ability or for the length of the paper.
2. Do not begin with a sentence which repeats the title or depends upon the title to be understood.
3. Do not begin with the dull pronouncement of what the paper is going to do or say.
4. Do not give a meaningless question for which there is no answer.
5. Do not begin with a dictionary definition except in an extended definition essay.
6. Do not begin by pompously stating an obvious idea.

Step 7: Write the Concluding Paragraph

The goal is to leave the reader with a general idea of the subject and its complexities. One of the good endings from this list will make your conclusion effective.

Endings

Good

1. In a long essay, sum up the major points.
2. Give a significant quotation which supports the thesis. (Use a book of quotations.)
3. Relate an anecdote or story which illustrates the thesis.
4. Suggest solutions to the problem presented in the essay.
5. Present a statement designed to make the reader think or act upon the problem suggested by the paper.
6. Show that the solution of some problems may lead to new problems.

7. Offer a final evaluation or judgment or interpretation of the subject matter.
8. Note the significance or value of the thesis and/or subject matter to the writer, the reader, society.
9. Offer some predictions of what might happen if the thesis or solutions you propose are not followed.
10. Use figurative diction to capture the essay's feeling or thought.

Bad

1. Do not present new information or new problems not covered in the paper itself.
2. Do not use a preaching tone.
3. Do not trail off weakly or end abruptly.

REWRITING—THE POLISHING STAGE

Step 8: Revise for structure, ideas, logic, and style Step 9: Revise and correct mechanics and usage

Step 8: Revise for Structure, Ideas, Logic, and Style

The goal is to evaluate and improve the content and method of presentation before submitting the essay. You will read the paper to insure that the content is directly related to the main idea.

Structure refers to the organizational pattern of the paragraphs as part of the essay and the sentences as part of the paragraphs.

Ideas refer to the quality of the thesis statement and the quality and quantity of the supporting material.

Logic refers to the correctness of the reasoning. Chapter 13 identifies common flaws in reasoning.

Style refers to the quality of the expression of the ideas. It is how you say what you say. Style must be appropriate to the subject and the audience. An effective style combines the elements of tone, diction, sentence structure, and coherence.

- **Tone** is your attitude toward the subject, the reader, and yourself.
- **Diction** is the conscious selection of words or vocabulary within the essay.
- **Sentence structure** is the kind and variety of grammatical patterns you use to express your ideas. The Handbook in Chapter 16 identifies ways to expand the basic sentence pattern by modifying, coordinating, and subordinating ideas.
- **Coherence** is the smooth transition from one idea to another.

Style = tone + diction + sentence structure + coherence

Step 9: Revise and Correct Mechanics and Usage

The goal is to submit an essay free from mechanical and usage errors. If possible, you should wait about 24 hours before revising an essay. This time lapse will make errors more noticeable. Reference materials such as a dictionary, thesaurus, and handbook will help you to revise. If spelling is a special problem for you, one helpful suggestion is to read your paper backwards slowly. In that way you will see each word separately and be more likely to notice spelling errors.

If your instructor permits or requires you to rewrite your graded essay, you will repeat steps 8 and 9. These steps are discussed in greater detail in Chapter 5.

STANDARDS FOR ENGLISH ESSAYS

To the student: the main purpose of this textbook is to help you learn to write nonfiction prose in such a way that a thoughtful, mature, educated reader will pay respectful attention to your ideas. The following criteria are concerned only with measurable achievement, not with the amount of effort that goes into writing the essay.

	Ideas	**Supporting Details**	**Reasoning**
Superior	unusually significant original perceptive ingenious	abundant exceptionally vivid strikingly appropriate, very well chosen	logical convincing worth considering extremely effective structure
Above average	less original and perceptive than the superior essay more mature than the average essay	sufficient vivid appropriate well chosen	logical convincing worth considering effective structure
Average	not particularly original but more than just commonplace clearly stated main idea appropriate for length neither too broad nor too narrow	adequately developed clearly related to main idea sufficient factual evidence	generally clear thinking free from errors adequate structure
Below average	trite insufficiently explored	too narrow too broad inappropriate for subject underdeveloped poorly chosen	insufficient evidence for ideas errors in thinking unclear structure
Inferior	trivial poorly explored not responsive to assignment	collection of loosely related opinions too many generalizations without specifics inappropriate for subject	serious errors in thinking poor grasp of structure

Diction and Tone	Sentence Structure and Coherence	Mechanics/Usage
skillful use of language awareness of exact meaning and flavor of words use of figures of speech	special fluency, force, elegance skillful combination of coordination, subordination, parallelism, emphasis effective variety of sentence structure effective use of transitional expressions	very few errors in spelling, punctuation, capitalization no errors in sentence or paragraph construction
accurate economical use of language use of some figures of speech effective choice of tone	competent combination of coordination, subordination, parallelism, emphasis use of transitional expressions	few errors in spelling, punctuation, capitalization few errors in sentence or paragraph construction
average use of language generally free from slang adequate choice of tone	less variety in sentence structure some use of transitional expressions	mastery of basic grammar no incomplete or run together sentences few or no dangling or misplaced modifiers clear pronoun reference to and agreement with antecedents subjects and verbs agree no careless shifts generally correct spelling and punctuation
clichés slang limited vocabulary weak use of language ineffective or inconsistent tone	lack of variety in sentence structure awkward use of language excessive repetition of words and phrases inadequate use or absence of transitional expressions	fragmentary or run-on sentences references of pronouns often unclear several errors in spelling and punctuation
extremely limited vocabulary ineffective use of language ineffective or inconsistent tone	excessive awkwardness in sentence structure excessive use of simple and compound sentence patterns little use of modifiers incorrect use or absence of transitional expressions	many fragmentary or run-on sentences showing lack of understanding of what a sentence is many disagreements between nouns and pronouns or between subjects and verbs showing no mastery of concept of agreement many errors in spelling and punctuation

CHAPTER 2
Description

You are often asked to describe what others have not seen, for example, the place where you spent your vacation, a new friend you have made, or an object you have recently acquired. Being able to re-create this place, person, or object so that your listener can picture it is a demanding task which requires you to use all your senses and powers of observation. Description creates a picture of a subject rather than explains or tells about it.

This type of writing rarely occurs independently; it is usually a subordinate part of some other form. Description conveys the qualities of a subject—person, place, or object—by focusing on concrete sensory details of sight, sound, touch, taste, and smell.

Unity is achieved in description by creating a **dominant impression** of the subject. All aspects that are described should directly relate to and help to develop the dominant impression or major effect you wish to convey. The way you respond to a subject determines the tone of the passage. For example, a student sample in this chapter, "A Second Chance," describes an abandoned Victorian house. The dominant impression the essay conveys is that the house is lonely and abandoned. All of the details the writer selected reinforce this impression and develop the nostalgic tone.

Order is achieved in description by means of **spatial relationship,** the way items are physically arranged in space and linked to each other. For example, the order in "A Second Chance" moves from top (the roof of the house) to bottom (its porch). The careful writer indicates and controls these relationships by using transitional expressions that identify space order. A passage may contain several spatial arrangements:

top ↔ bottom
inside ↔ outside
foreground ↔ background
left ↔ right
clockwise or counterclockwise

Types of Description

There are two types of descriptive writing distinguished by the extent to which the writer's personal attitudes, opinions, or emotions enter into them. **Objective** description is impersonal and concerned almost entirely with factual, external details. It emphasizes the subject being written about and is used primarily in scientific and journalistic writing. **Subjective** description, on the other hand, is personalized and more expressive of the writer's personal beliefs, feelings, or impressions. It emphasizes how the writer sees and interprets the subject. For example, the author of "The Greasy Spoon" includes only those details that convey his subjective, negative impression of a restaurant. Which type of description you use—objective or subjective—depends on your purpose and audience.

Descriptive Language

Good description requires sharp powers of observation and discrimination. In order to describe subjects accurately, you must be receptive to and concentrate on the impressions made on all of the senses: sight, sound, smell, taste, touch (wetness, coldness), internal sensation (nausea, hunger), and movement or tension in muscles or joints. For example, "A Second Chance" appeals to the senses of touch, taste, sound, and smell, as well as sight.

Careful observation, however, must be accompanied by discrimination in selecting the most important and vivid of the sensory details. This critical judgment also involves choosing precise words and avoiding vague and colorless diction. In general, descriptive language uses concrete nouns, action verbs, and limiting modifiers (for example, instead of "brightly colored car" write "candy-apple red convertible"). Note that "A Second Chance" uses concrete, figurative words to create a focused picture of the old house. The skills developed in the writing of description are basic to all effective writing. The ability to focus sharply on a person, place, or object enables you to explain ideas more clearly in larger or more complex papers.

Objective description requires language that is impersonal, unbiased, and unambiguous. Since it has a rational appeal, it uses neutrally slanted and heavily denotative words and phrases. The student sample "Prepare to Dive" is an example of objective description.

On the other hand, subjective description appeals to the emotions and so relies on language that is connotative, positively or negatively slanted. It is often poetic because it uses figures of speech like the simile, metaphor, and personification. (Examples of these descriptive devices are included in the Diction Chart in Chapter 1 under "figurative.")

Elements of Descriptive Writing

- a dominant impression which determines the major aspects of the subject
- sharp, concrete, graphic details that appeal to the reader's senses of sight, sound, touch, taste, and smell
- spatial order of the major aspects
- diction that is connotative, denotative, concrete, and figurative (see Chapter 1)
- consistent physical relationship or position of the writer with the subject (point of view)
- setting (place and time), if relevant

Problems to Avoid

First, avoid using excessively vague, abstract words, like *beautiful, nice, exciting,* and *wonderful,* when focusing on the general qualities. Second, you should rarely use the linking verb *to be* and the passive voice because they contribute to weak and unclear writing. Third, in a purely descriptive passage de-emphasize both the story element and an explanation of the subject. Consequently, highly concentrated descriptions are usually short. Finally, once you decide on the point of view, verb tense, and tone of the descriptive passage, use these consistently.

STUDENT SAMPLE—Objective Description

Prepare to Dive

Berthed in the crystal blue waters of Pearl Harbor, Hawaii, an old World War II submarine proudly displays combat scars permanently imprinted on its slightly rusted steel exterior. Strung along the perimeter of the freshly painted wooden deck are two life lines made of stranded hemp rope. On the wood-ribbed deck of this war patrol submarine, a dirty white, weather beaten 5/25-inch cannon points directly at the horizon. The armored conning tower still supports the long tubular periscope, the football-shaped early warning radar dish, and the communications antenna. Below the tower, in the submarine's interior, is the engine room which houses two colossal and fully operational 16-cylinder, 1,600-horsepower combustion engines. Each engine is connected to a separate electric generator for maximum starting power. The nerve center, the control room, is filled with large-faced gauges encased in highly polished brass shells. Overhead hang clusters of gauze-wrapped tubing and fittings. Projecting outward from the bulkheads are red, white, and blue color-coded valve knobs. Securely cradled in the impeccably clean forward torpedo tubes rest six brass-nosed torpedoes that once sank many ships. The smell of diesel fuel and hot bearing grease still lingers while the aroma of gunpowder is gone. The old submarine will never again participate in combat, but its preserved condition memorializes its victorious mission and the heroic deeds of the men who served on it.

Discovery Exercise

1. List examples of neutral concrete details.

______________________ ______________________

______________________ ______________________

______________________ ______________________

______________________ ______________________

______________________ ______________________

2. What is the dominant impression? ______________________

____

STUDENT SAMPLE—Subjective Description

Illusion of a Culinary Masterpiece

Instead of "visions of sugarplums dancing in my head," an illusion of a luscious strawberry whipped cream cake sometimes magically appears before my eyes and tantalizes my taste buds. This delectable apparition contains four round layers of lightly textured yellow cake thinly coated with sweet, flavorful strawberry jelly. An exquisite mouth-watering creamy custard resembling liquid gold nestles between each layer. Piped columns of whipped cream gracefully ascend the sides of the cake, simulating white gloved fingers with fingertips gracefully arched over the top edge. Ripe juicy red strawberries stand proudly on top like sparkling rubies set in a crown. A glistening strawberry glaze gently engulfs the fruit like a transluscent sea of molten lava. A delicate pattern of red glaze and whipped cream encircles this fabulous culinary fantasy.

Discovery Exercise

1. List examples of connotative language.

2. Identify examples of figures of speech.

3. To which senses is the description appealing?

4. What is the dominant impression?

Discovery Exercises for Descriptive Writing

1. One way to make descriptive writing vivid is to use concrete and specific words. In the passage below the colorless, vague words are boldface. For each boldface word, list three words that are **more** concrete and specific in the spaces under the word. Try to use single words rather than phrases. Do not merely list synonyms.

   It was a **hot** afternoon as the **man walked** down the street and

   Example: **muggy**

   looked at the **things** in the window. It was not often, he thought,

   that he felt so **uncomfortable** in his **clothes** or that the **surroundings**

   looked so **unattractive.** Just then the **sound** of a **car** interrupted his thoughts. **Someone sitting** in the car **called to** him, so he **went**

__________ __________ __________ __________

__________ __________ __________ __________

__________ __________ __________ __________

across the street to get a ride home.

2. Select a dominant impression for the passage you have just completed, and enter it in the appropriate space. Then fill in the remaining blank spaces in the passage below with words from the previous exercise that consistently support that impression.

Dominant Impression: ____________________

It was a(n) __________ afternoon as the __________ __________ down the street and __________ the __________ in the window. It was not often, he thought, that he felt so __________ in his __________ or that the __________ looked so __________ . Just then the __________ of a(n) __________ interrupted his thoughts. __________ __________ in the car __________ him, so he __________ across the street to get a ride home.

3. Another way to make descriptive writing vivid is to use figures of speech to create visual pictures for the reader. For the following boldfaced words, construct similes or metaphors to describe the idea.

Example: He felt **uncomfortable.**
He felt as uncomfortable as a 250-pound football player in a size 10 jersey.

It was a **hot** afternoon. ____________________

____

The man **walked** down the street ____________________

____

The surroundings looked **unattractive.** ____________________

____

Organizational Pattern for Descriptive Writing

Study this blueprint so that you can see and better understand the elements necessary for descriptive writing. Then use the pattern as a guide in assembling your own passage. Note that all the student samples in the chapter use this organizational pattern.

Introduction

Concrete identification of subject to be described

Establishment of point of view
verb tense
tone
diction
setting (place and time) if relevant

Body

Presentation of at least three major aspects of the subject

A major aspect identifies a shift in spatial position, indicated either by a transitional expression or by a different part of the object.

Sufficient development of concrete, specific details of the subject so that the reader can visualize it

Spatial order of the three major aspects (more than one order possible):

____ top ↔ bottom

____ inside ↔ outside

____ foreground ↔ background

____ left ↔ right

____ clockwise or counterclockwise

Transitional expressions to indicate progression of spatial order:

above	in the background, center, foreground
around	next to
at one end	on the inside, outside
behind	on the one (other) side
below	on the right, left
closer	on the top, bottom, side
further	to the right, left, side, center
in front of	under

Conclusion

Presentation of dominant impression

SAMPLE WORKSHEET FOR DESCRIPTIVE WRITING

1. Select a subject to describe.
2. List 25 concrete details about the subject.
3. Get approval from your instructor after completing the preliminary information.
4. Complete the remainder of the worksheet **before** writing the passage.
5. Attach the worksheet to the finished passage.
6. Attach the Descriptive Writing Cover Sheet to the finished passage.

Subject to be described: *a Victorian house*

Concrete details:

vacant, 2-story house	*sticky tar paper showing*
steep, angled roof	*oily, fishy railroad ties*
"no Trespassing" sign	*looks like "Lincoln Logs"*
overgrown chapparal weeds	*wooden wall splintering*
missing floorboards	*covered with worn paint*
rooster weathervane	*once white with blue trim*
rusty	*6 rusty, corroded pipes*
spinning slowly	*2 chimneys at either end*
raised above ground	*stones of football size*
front door covered with plywood	*broken windows in rotted frames*
old, uneven boards	*plywood covers large windows*
dangling telephone cables	*collapsing picket fence*
brick-faced porch	

Preliminary information

Dominant impression: *The house is lonely and abandoned.*

Spatial order: *top → bottom → right*

Point of view: *third person*

Verb tense: *present*

Tone: *nostalgic*

Diction: *concrete, figurative*

Setting (place and time), if relevant: *on neglected property*

MS/RW

(instructor approval)

At least three major aspects of subject in spatial order:

1. roof

concrete details: ① steep, shingled roof- Victorian style
② metallic rooster weather vane
rusted, spinning sluggishly
③ 2 chimneys - one at either end of roof
made of football-sized smooth stones

2. front of house

concrete details: ① greasy, staggered planks of old plywood
② "No Trespassing" sign - gold and black
③ brick-faced porch showing sticky tar paper
④ rock-shattered windows in rotted frames
⑤ plywood protects larger windows

3. right side of house

concrete details: ① black telephone cables like licorice
syncopated, tapping sounds
dangling limply
② splintered wooden wall - weather-worn paint
③ 6 rusty, corroded pipes for water.

STUDENT SAMPLE—Descriptive Writing—Analyzed for Parts

Observe that elements of structure and content are labeled on the left while elements of style are identified on the right. This detailed analysis will help you plan your own passage.

A Second Chance

[Introduction — Place; Subject to be described]

Foot-high chaparral weeds grow abundantly on the neglected property. The cold vacantness of the old two-story home ominously looms in their midst. The house, elevated off the ground, gives the eerie impression of a magician's levitation act. Ten individual stacks of oily, fishy-smelling railroad ties, each interlocked like a child's "Lincoln Logs," support the listless weight of this immense home. This now lifeless abode, ripped from its foundation, waits for removal to a new location.

[Verb tense: present; Point of view: Third person; Diction: figurative (metaphor); Diction: concrete (touch, smell); Diction: figurative (simile); Sentence Structure: Verbal phrase]

[Body — 1st Major Aspect; 2nd Major Aspect]

On the steep, sparsely shingled Victorian-style roof perches a rusted, rooster-shaped weather vane. The metallic rooster spins sluggishly as if a motor is propelling it from within the garret. Projecting upward from each end of the acutely angled roof are two chimneys constructed of smooth, football-sized stones. Below the roof, the most noticeable aspect of the front of the house is the greasy, staggered planks of over-used plywood

[Diction: concrete; A Sentence Structure: coordinate adjectives; Diction: figurative (simile); Diction: figurative (metaphor); Diction: concrete (touch)]

☆Coherence: transitional expressions circled

which bar unauthorized admission to the front entrance. Posted on this hastily fashioned barricade is a gold and black "No Trespassing" sign. The porch shows sporadic patches of sun-bleached brick facing. The aged bricks cling precariously to a base of sticky, black tar paper. The jagged edges of the rock-shattered porch windows miraculously hold fast in their rotted frames. Misshapen cuts of filthy plywood protect the larger, unbroken windows. On the right side of the house, syncopated tapping emanates from licorice-like strands of black telephone cables dangling limply from their powerless terminals. The weather-worn paint on the splintered wooden wall looks like a half-erased blackboard. Finally, jutting out from the same wall are six rusty pipes whose corroded threads will never again couple with the property's water supply.

Diction: concrete (touch)

Diction: concrete (sight)

3rd Major Aspect

Diction: concrete (sound)

Diction: figurative (simile, taste)

Sentence Structure: Verbal phrase

Diction: figurative (simile)

The house in full perspective with its barren, dilapidated appearance paints a lonely picture. Perhaps after its move and renovation, it will have a second chance to attract admiring glances from passers-by.

B Sentence Structure: coordinate adjectives

Dominant impression

Conclusion

STUDENT SAMPLE—Descriptive Writing

The Ambulance

Sounds and images swim in my mind: a flash of green light, an accelerating forward motion, screeching tires, a crunching jolt, the scream of buckling metal, and the tinkling of broken glass. After the wail of a siren stops, I am moving from the intensity of daylight into the luminescence of fluorescent lighting on a white-on-white ceiling. The sting of alcohol and disinfectant assaults my nostrils.

A clear plastic bag dangles from a hook above me, and from this bag, carrying a watery fluid, descends a tube which disappears into a patch of tape on my arm. A pale translucent-green tube clings to my face and hisses into my nose. On my left a ghostly silhouette, backlit by the smokey glass of a long window, floats back and forth. The orange vinyl bench upon which my nameless co-inhabitant sits is shared by a medical bag and a radio. Into the handset of the radio he speaks the gobbledygook of medicine and from the bag withdraws syringes, needles, and tiny glass bottles. To my right is a formica wall of imitation woodgrain. Plastic sliding doors hold captive on the shelves bottles, skinny boxes with names like epinephrine and dopamine, linens, tubes with rubber stoppers, and bandages of all shapes and sizes. Within a cubby hole of this miniature hospital supply, plopped like unmolded gelatin, lie bags of fluid like the one above me. Within the milky outer coverings, partially obscured labels stutter the contents of --actated --ngers, 5% dex-- in wat--, and normal salin--. Through a small door above my head the cacophony of another radio crackles addresses and medical problems.

As numbness spreads through me, to the beginnings of motion and the banshee scream of a siren, I abandon the ambulance and surrender to the inky blackness and twinkling stars of unconsciousness.

Discovery Exercise

1. Identify the subject being described: ______________________________
2. Identify the direction of the spatial orders used:

   ____ top↔bottom ____ left↔right

   ____ inside↔outside ____ foreground↔background

   ____ clockwise or counterclockwise
3. Identify the point of view: ____________ person
4. Identify the verb tense: ____________
5. Circle transitional expressions indicating spatial movement or direction.

6. List the figures of speech used in the description:

7. Underline all concrete nouns.
8. Choose terms from the diction chart that characterize the diction:
9. Choose terms from the tone chart that describe the tone:

10. After reviewing Chapter 16, bracket **five** verbal phrases, one type of grammatical structure used in this passage.
11. Identify the dominant impression:

STUDENT SAMPLE—Descriptive Writing

The Greasy Spoon

I enjoy traveling by car. But after several hours of nonstop driving, my stomach grumbles loudly that it is time to locate a roadside cafe, a usually depressing place. I try to find one with the least amount of peeling paint and the parking lot most free of debris with no vicious dogs loitering outside. I finally choose, park, plunge, and enter the door.

The depressing exterior is just an introduction to the delights of the interior. The first detail to assail my senses is the aroma of burned eggs and toast, greasy meat, and overly strong coffee vying with each other for recognition in a room that manages to be too hot and stuffy even in contrast with the frigid outside air. I look past the booths of ripped naugahyde and the tables covered by ketchup-stained tablecloths with dark, sticky circles left from the previous customer's coffee cup, over the dirty, unswept floor to the counter. At the counter, smudged girlie calendars nestle among neon beer signs; menus look as if they had been there for years, and a thin layer of dust coats little boxes of cereals.

I sit down and open the least sticky menu in the receptacle attached to the left side of the table. The slatternly waitress, her dirty uniform unbuttoned to the third buttonhole, ambles over to take my order. I request eggs, hash-brown potatoes, toast, and orange juice. As I wait, I notice that the other customer is a "gentleman" nursing a coffee cup in the corner booth. The same smells which first assaulted my senses herald the arrival of my food a long thirty minutes later. The lukewarm, greasy eggs and potatoes and the cold, burnt toast are inoffensive compared to the fly casually swimming in my orange juice. My disgust dies as I look through the kitchen door and see the dirty, unshaven, muscle-bound cook responsible for the disaster on my plate. Leaving the food uneaten, I storm out, slam the door, and drive away.

Discovery Exercise

1. Identify the subject being described: ____________________
2. Identify the direction of the spatial orders used:

   ____ top↔bottom ____ left↔right ____ clockwise or counterclockwise

   ____ inside↔outside ____ foreground↔background

3. Identify the point of view: __________ person
4. Identify the verb tense: __________
5. List vivid, specific adjectives and adverbs:

   ____________________ ____________________

   ____________________ ____________________

   ____________________ ____________________

   ____________________ ____________________

6. Underline all action verbs.
7. Circle transitional expressions indicating spatial movement or direction.
8. Choose terms from the diction chart that characterize the diction: ____________________
9. Choose terms from the tone chart that describe the tone:

   ____

10. After reviewing Chapter 16, bracket **five** examples of items in a series, one type of grammatical structure used in this passage.
11. Identify the dominant impression: ____________________

    ____

STUDENT SAMPLE—Descriptive Writing

Ready to Fire

A thick gray fog creeps softly over the battle-scarred field, like a cat stalking its prey. In spite of its denseness, the fog cannot conceal the ashen faces of the eighty soldiers in the Twenty-Third regiment. The shivering men huddle closer to one another, forming a rough-edged rectangle which writhes and trembles as the distant thunder of cannons grows ever closer.

Four rows of twenty make up the regiment. At its front stands a rigid line of young boys in brightly colored uniforms of scarlet and gold. Their locked fists cling to long-barreled rifles which they hold firmly against their chests. Knuckles, blanched by the unyielding grasp of stiffened fingers, seem to jut out like snow-capped peaks over a steel blue river of frozen metal. Streaming from wide-open eyes, tears turn petrified cheeks to glistening alabaster. On the regiment's right side, chocolate brown horses scream and rear in terror as a bolt of lightning cuts through the clouds like the thrust of a silver sword. Drenched with sweat and flecked with dots of foamy white froth, their dark coats shimmer during the brief burst of light. Pulling frantically against their short leather ties, the equine marionettes seem to dance to the cadence of the cannons' booming drumbeat. A flaming ball traces an arc of gilded orange across the gloomy purple sky. Eighty pairs of spellbound eyes follow its path. Even the older soldiers in the last row twitch as the bomb explodes behind the regiment. The acrid scent of burning sulfur stings their nostrils; a milky gray smoke burns their eyes. Tense fingers play a nervous melody on lips grown suddenly pale. The men, like actors in a silent movie, softly mouth the words of last minute prayers. Under deeply furrowed foreheads, their eyes stare forward, mesmerized by the swaying of the approaching scarlet-clad silhouettes whose stiff, mechanical motions mimic the movements of wooden toy soldiers. The men of the Twenty-Third regiment wait as though held in place by a tightly wound key.

The swirling mist of smoke-laden fog frames an eerie portrait of frightened faces. Fear is a soldier's greatest enemy. It paralyzes his body and breeds thoughts which cloud his mind. A soldier's first battle lies within himself. Only after he conquers his fear can he be ready to fire.

PROFESSIONAL SAMPLES—Descriptive Writing

Read these short samples to see how two professional writers have used the technique of description. Then answer the discovery questions which focus on the major elements of descriptive writing.

Roger Ascham (1515–1568), an Englishman educated at Cambridge University, was private tutor to Queen Elizabeth. He wrote a treatise on archery, stressing the importance of physical training in school, as well as a book on the education of boys and men of position both in and out of school. He contributed to the development of a simple English prose style.

The Wind

1 [It is impossible for a man to see the wind with his eyes;] the nature of it is so fine and subtile; yet this experience of the wind had I once myself, and that was in the great snow that fell four years ago. I rode in the high way betwixt Topcliff-upon-Swale and Borough-bridge, the way being somewhat trodden before, by wayfaring men; the fields on both sides were plain, and lay almost yard-deep with snow; the night afore had been a little frost, so that the snow was hard and crusted above; that morning the sun shone bright and clear, the wind was whistling aloft, and sharp, according to the time of the year; the snow in the high way lay loose and trodden with horses' feet; so as the wind blew, it took the loose snow with it, and made it so slide upon the snow in the field, which was hard and crusted by reason of the frost over night, that thereby I might see very well the whole nature of the wind as it blew that day. And I had a great delight and pleasure to mark it, which maketh me now far better to remember it. Sometime the wind would be not past two yards broad, and so it would carry the snow as far as I could see. Another time the snow would blow over half the field at once. Sometime the snow would tumble softly; by and by it would fly wonderful fast. And this I perceived also, that the wind goeth by streams, and not whole together. For I should

see one stream within a score on me; then the space of two score, no snow would stir; but, after so much quantity of ground, another stream of snow, at the same very time, should be carried likewise, but not equally, for the one would stand still, when the other flew apace and so continue sometime swiftlier, sometime slowlier, sometime broader, sometime narrower, as far as I could see. Nor it flew not straight, but sometime it crooked this way, sometime that way, and sometime it ran round about in a compass. And sometime the snow would be lift clean from the ground up to the air, and by and by it would be all clapt to the ground, as though there had been no wind at all, straightway it would rise and fly again. And that which was the most marvel of all, at one time two drifts of snow flew, the one out of the west into the east, the other out of the north into the east. And I saw two winds, by reason of the snow, the one cross over the other, as it had been two high ways. And, again, I should hear the wind blow in the air, when nothing was stirred at the ground. And when all was still where I rode, not very far from me the snow should be lifted wonderfully. This experience made me more marvel at the nature of the wind, than it made me cunning in the knowledge of the wind; but yet thereby I learned perfectly that it is no marvel at all though men in wind lose their length in shooting, seeing so many ways the wind is so variable in blowing.

Discovery Questions

1. Ascham describes a climatic condition that is experienced but not really seen. How does he make the reader see the wind?
2. Identify at least five different ways in which the wind changes the appearance of the snow.
3. What is the dominant impression about the wind that Ascham conveys?

Rachel Carson (1907–1964), an American naturalist and conservationist, worked as a marine biologist for the U.S. Fish and Wildlife Service. She wrote several books on nature along the Atlantic Coast and waters, including *The Edge of the Sea* from which the following descriptive passage is taken; *The Sea Around Us* and *Silent Spring* are her most famous books.

Walking to the Seacoast

1 One of my own favorite approaches to a rocky seacoast is by a rough path through an evergreen forest that has its own peculiar enchantment. It is usually an early morning tide that takes me along that forest path, so that the light is still pale and fog drifts in from the sea beyond. It is almost a ghost forest, for among the living spruce and balsam are many dead trees—some still erect, some sagging earthward, some lying on the floor of the forest. All the trees, the living and the dead, are clothed with green and silver crusts of lichens. Tufts of the bearded lichen or old man's beard hang from the branches like bits of sea mist tangled there. Green woodland mosses and a yielding carpet of reindeer moss cover the ground. In the quiet of that place even the voice of the surf is reduced to a whispered echo and the sounds of the forest are but the ghosts of sound—the faint sighing of evergreen needles in the moving air; the creaks and heavier groans of half-fallen trees resting against their neighbors and rubbing bark against bark; the light rattling fall of a dead branch broken under the feet of a squirrel and sent bounding and ricocheting earthward.

2 But finally the path emerges from the dimness of the deeper forest and comes to a place where the sound of surf rises above the forest sounds—the hollow boom of the sea, rhythmic and insistent, striking against the rocks, falling away, rising again.

3 Up and down the coast the line of the forest is drawn sharp and clean on the edge of a seascape of surf and sky and rocks. The softness of the sea fog blurs the contours of the rocks; gray water and gray mists merge offshore in a dim and vaporous world that might be a world of creation, stirring with new life.

Discovery Questions

1. Carson describes a walk to the seacoast by appealing to what senses?
2. What are the different sounds she describes?
3. What is the dominant impression about the walk that Carson conveys?

Suggested Subjects to Describe

Select one of the following or similar subjects that you have studied closely in the past or are able to observe carefully now:

Describe any place or object by telling how it looks, smells, feels, tastes, sounds. Possible topics might include the interior of a car (new, wrecked, abandoned), a ship's cabin, a junkyard and some object in it, a bar, a plant, a bedroom, a beauty shop or barber shop, a deserted stage, a kitchen, a barracks, an office, an alley, a dressing table.

Use the description of a place or object to reveal the personality, character, or interests of a person related to that place or object: for example, the van of a twenty-one-year-old person or the bedroom of an invalid.

Describe the physical appearance and character traits of a person, real or imaginary, unusual, offensive, memorable.

Select a particularly striking natural scene and describe it in detail: for example, a dawn or a sunset, the Grand Canyon, underground caves.

Describe the scene of a disaster: for example, a fire, an earthquake, a storm.

Describe a fascinating man-made place: for example, the Mayan ruins of Mexico, Hoover Dam, Mt. Rushmore, the Golden Gate Bridge, the Empire State Building, Independence Hall.

Select an architecturally unusual building within a 35-mile area to describe.

Select from your journal one person, place, or object that you have observed and recorded. Describe it in concrete detail.

Review Roger Ascham's description, "The Wind," and describe some other type of climatic condition: for example, a rain or sand storm, a heat wave, a hurricane.

Review Rachel Carson's description, "Walking to the Seacoast," and describe a special walk you have taken somewhere: for example, in the mountains, on the beach, in the woods. Select details to create a dominant impression and appeal to several senses as Carson does.

WORKSHEET FOR DESCRIPTIVE WRITING

1. Select a subject to describe.
2. List 25 concrete details about the subject.
3. Get approval from your instructor after completing the preliminary information.
4. Complete the remainder of the worksheet before writing the passage.
5. Attach the worksheet to the finished passage.
6. Attach the Descriptive Writing Cover Sheet to the finished passage.

Subject to be described: ______________________________

Concrete details:

______________________ ______________________
______________________ ______________________
______________________ ______________________
______________________ ______________________
______________________ ______________________
______________________ ______________________
______________________ ______________________
______________________ ______________________
______________________ ______________________
______________________ ______________________
______________________ ______________________
______________________ ______________________

Preliminary information

Dominant impression: ______________________________

Spatial order: ______________________________

Point of view: ______________________________

Verb tense: ______________________________

Tone: ______________________________

Diction: ______________________________

Setting (place and time), if relevant: ______________________________

____
(instructor approval)

At least three major aspects of subject in spatial order:

1. ______________________________

concrete details: ______________________________

____

____

____

____

2. ______________________________

concrete details: ______________________________

____

____

____

____

3. ______________________________

concrete details: ______________________________

____

____

____

____

Name: ____________________

Date: ____________ Class: ________

DESCRIPTIVE WRITING COVER SHEET		
Structure/Ideas	+	______
Usage Mechanics	−	______
Total		______
Rewrite points	+	______
TOTAL		______

Structure and Ideas **(50 points)**	**Original**		**Rewrite**
INTRODUCTION: concrete identification of subject	5______		______
BODY: three aspects of subject	5______		______
concrete, sufficient development of details	30______		______
spatial order with transitional expressions	5______		______
CONCLUSION: dominant impression	5______		______
Total	50______	+	______

The points in this section reflect your score for structure and ideas. If you have received fewer than 50 points, you may rewrite your paper to earn them. Use the numbers as a guide to what areas need revision.

Usage and Mechanics (minus points). See Correction Symbol chart.			
You **may** earn these points in revision:			
Usage: adj; adv; agr; awk; col; dm; frag; mm; ref; rep; shift; verb ww; / /; ¶	−3 ea. ______		______
You **may not** earn these points in revision, but you must correct the errors:			
Mechanics: abbr; apos; cap; lc; p; ro; sp; ∧	−1 ea. ______		______
Total	− ______	+	______

CHAPTER 3
Narration

You probably find yourself frequently recounting stories of incidents that you have witnessed or experienced. The usual events of having car trouble or being incorrectly billed by the department store or attending a party all provide material for personal stories. When you talk about these experiences, you are using the process of narration.

The purpose of narration is to tell a story, to relate a physical or psychological action so that the reader can experience it without actually having lived through it. Narration allows the reader to project himself or herself into the action as a living participant or witness. Narration is used primarily in the fictional forms of the short story and novel to share an experience. It is also incorporated into other types of writing, as an anecdote, to explain an idea.

Unity is achieved in narration by establishing a central action that has a point and selecting specific incidents and details that support the point. In an essay that explains an idea, unity results when every segment of the narrative illustrates that idea. In a story that recreates an experience, unity is the result of a central action that focuses on the theme (the story's insight into life), or the plot (the sequence of the events themselves), or the character (the traits of the central figure). This central action determines the selection of the specific scenes or details.

For example, the first student sample in this chapter, "The Evening of the Second First Kiss," humorously relates the sequence of events leading up to the central action, the kiss. Only those details that develop the action are recorded.

Order is achieved in narration by means of time relationship. You may choose chronological or artistic time. **Chronological time** recreates the sequence of events as they actually occurred: beginning → middle → end. For example, the same student sample follows this time pattern. **Artistic time,** on the other hand, is the arrangement of time for a special dramatic effect. You may begin with the end of the story and then flash-back to the beginning and middle. Or you may begin in the middle, flash back to the beginning, and finish with the end. For example, the essay, "The Evening of the Second 'First Kiss' " might have begun with the woman and man kissing at the front door and then flashed back to the incidents that led up to that moment. Regardless of pattern, transition expressions indicate changing time.

Types of Narration

Narrative writing, then, relates a sequence of events about someone (character) somewhere (setting) doing something (action). There are two types of narrative writing. **Expository narration** tells a story (anecdote) to clarify, support, or emphasize an idea. It may be used in various patterns of exposition, including illustration, process analysis, and causal analysis. Expository narration relies on well-paced, appropriate details to make a point quickly. In addition, it is characterized by compressed action, simplified details, and occasional dialogue (conversational passages). For instance, the illustration essay entitled "Facing Up to Failure" in Chapter 6 contains expository narration.

Fictional narration tells a story to allow the reader to share the happenings of human experience. It appeals to the imagination by addressing the issues of how and why an event occurred. This type of narration often suggests deeper meanings. One of the student samples in this chapter, "The Sled's First

Run," is an example of fictional narration because sleds, of course, do not talk. However, by personifying an inanimate object, the writer can offer an unusual perspective.

Stages of Action in Narration

Narrative writing includes three stages of action. The **beginning** stage presents information necessary to the understanding of the action. It identifies the setting (place or time) and introduces the conflict of forces, attitudes, beliefs, or individual characters. The **middle** stage develops the conflict through a series of complications that alter the direction of the action. This stage conveys tension, excitement, suspense, or surprise. It creates a sense of forward movement and builds toward the **climax** or point of greatest intensity. The **end** stage resolves the action in one of the following ways: (1) a physical victory of one set of forces over another, (2) the reconciliation of forces, (3) the fusion of previously opposing forces to create new ones, or (4) a new awareness on the part of the character involved. This stage reveals the meaning of what has gone before.

Narrative Language

A unique feature of narration is dialogue, the actual words of speakers talking to each other. Correct usage requires that each person's speech, even if the speech is short, must begin a new paragraph. Included in the paragraph along with the conversation are expository references and verbs of saying.

Dialogue is identified with quotation marks around the spoken word. Commas set off such expressions as *he stated* and *she added* unless a question mark or exclamation point is used. The first word in dialogue is capitalized. For example, "He always wants to go first!" whines the little girl. If the dialogue is broken up by verbs of saying, then quotation marks enclose the separated parts of the conversation. For example, "Now, children," the mother interrupts, "stop fighting. We'll all have a chance to use the sled."

Another feature of narration is point of view that refers to the position from which you relate the events. It should be selected to convey most appropriately the main action of the story. In addition, it must be used consistently; that is, you should not shift from one point-of-view character to another in a short work without a justifiable reason.

The two most commonly used points of view are first person and omniscient. **First person** focuses on the narrator's personal feelings, experiences, thought processes, and dreams. Three of the student samples in this chapter are first-person narratives. **Omniscient** (all-knowing) uses the third-person pronoun to relate the events of the story impersonally with no intrusion from the narrator or reporter. Short stories and novels often use this point of view. The student sample "An Unexpected Maneuver," uses this point of view. There are more complicated points of view, such as third-person limited which is restricted to one character's knowledge instead of being omniscient.

Elements of Narrative Writing

- a central action with a point
- incidents, dialogue, and vivid details relevant to the point of the central action
- appropriate order to show the passage of time and convey a sense of forward movement
- appropriate point of view

Problems to Avoid

First, include only that information which is relevant to the central action. In addition, you should show, not explain or discuss, the action. Incidents and details should dramatize the action rather than generalize about it. Finally, once you decide on the point of view and tone of the narrative passage, use these consistently.

Organizational Pattern for Narrative Writing

Study this blueprint so that you can see and better understand elements necessary for narrative writing. Then use the pattern as a guide in assembling your own passage. Note that all the student samples in the chapter use this organizational pattern.

Introduction

Identification of central action and nature of conflict

Establishment of point of view
- verb tense
- tone
- diction
- setting (place and time), if relevant

Body

Presentation of at least three major segments of the action leading to and including the climax

A major segment identifies a development in the action, indicated either by a transitional expression or by a time change.

Sufficient development of the complications of the action so that the reader can develop a sense of witnessing the event

Time order of the three major segments of the action:

_____ chronological

_____ artistic

Transitional expressions to indicate change in time:

after	now
before	suddenly
finally	then
first	until
immediately	when
next	

Conclusion

Presentation of the resolution of the action by means of one of the four types of narrative endings

Optional presentation of meaning of or opinion about action

SAMPLE WORKSHEET FOR NARRATIVE WRITING

1. Select an action to narrate.
2. Get approval from your instructor after completing the information for the introduction.
3. Complete the remainder of the worksheet **before** writing the passage.
4. Attach the worksheet to the finished passage.
5. Attach the Narrative Writing Cover Sheet to the finished passage.

INTRODUCTION

Central action and nature of conflict: a first goodnight kiss from a male friend

Order: chronological

Point of view: first person

Verb tense: past

Tone: humorous, whimsical

Diction: concrete, connotative

Setting (place and time), if relevant: evening at home

MS/RW
(instructor approval)

BODY

At least three major segments of action leading to climax:

1. dinner in the kitchen
   wet carpets
   children and dogs
2. conversation after children go to bed
   funny smells
   self-conscious talk
3. walking to the door
   excited dogs
   awkward moment

Climax: off-center kiss

CONCLUSION

Resolution of action: friend returns and kisses improve

STUDENT SAMPLE—Narrative Writing—Analyzed for Parts

Observe that elements of structure and content are labeled on the left while elements of style are identified on the right. This detailed analysis will help you plan your own passage.

The Evening of the Second "First Kiss"

Introduction (Beginning of Action) | Central action to be narrated

There I was, a thirty-one-year-old woman, anxious and nervous again about a first kiss. I had anticipated for several days that he was going to kiss me that night. It had been twenty-one years ago that I had had my "first kiss" from a whiskerless nineteen-year-old boy. My second "first kiss" would be from a forty-year-old man with a mustache. What took place that night was not the candle-and-roses love scene that I had hoped for but rather a warm and tender love scene from a comedy.

Point of view: first person | *Verb tense: past* | *Time* | *Conflict*

1st Major Segment | Complication | Complication

Dinner that night was not quite perfect. I had won his praise with the exotic flavor of my teriyaki steak served with steaming rice. The scene, however, was not so successful. In my preparations for the evening I had ordered my carpets cleaned. Clean they were but soaking wet. We were forced to remain in the kitchen and climb over the living-room furniture which was crowded in with us. He was sweet. I was trying to remain calm. My three children and two dogs loved the cozy atmosphere.

Diction: concrete (taste, smell) | *Sentence Structure: unusual order*

★Coherence: transitional expressions circled

2nd Major Segment

Complication

Body (Middle of Action)

Finally, the children's bed time arrived. I was hoping they wouldn't notice that it was actually one-half hour earlier than usual. I tried to feign sorrow as I whisked them off to sleep. Now we were alone at last, except for the two faithful dogs. The air was filled with the aroma of the gingery teriyaki sauce mixed with rug shampoo and wet carpet. It was so romantic. The conversation was lively but self-conscious. We talked of motorcycles, his divorce, my husband's death from cancer, children, school, and any other subject we could think of as the time for that kiss drew nearer. I tried not to notice him staring when I was talking, and he tried not to notice when I lost my place.

Diction: concrete (smell)

Diction: connotative

A Sentence Structure: items in a series

B Sentence Structure: parallelism and repetition

3rd Major Segment

Complication

The climactic moment arrived promptly at the perfect time--eleven-thirty. He would not be leaving too early just for that kiss, nor would he be staying too late for a gentleman. We walked to the door with the ever-loyal dogs jumping up and down excitedly. He was going slowly, hoping I would catch up. I was staying a discreet distance behind. I'm not sure how many times he opened and shut the door, but each time he turned toward it, I edged closer. On the last close of the door he

Sentence Structure: noun clause

Climax

had but two choices: either kiss me or go home unkissed. He chose the kiss and put his arms around me. It was about three quarters of an inch off center, but he was too embarrassed to relocate, and I was too kind to let him know I noticed. After a decent length of time for a kiss, he held me tightly. I didn't want him to ever let go, and I could tell he felt the same way.

C Sentence Structure: parallelism

Conclusion *(End of Action)*

Resolution of action

I'm not sure how long we stood there. Eventually, he did go home. Love has a way of overcoming blunders, for the evening felt like butterflies and green grass and blue skies. And the man still comes back. And the kisses have improved, yet none has been so tingling and exciting as that second "first kiss."

Diction: figurative (simile)

Diction: concrete (touch)

STUDENT SAMPLE—Narrative Writing

The Sled's First Run

I've been sitting here in this muggy ski shop for so many months now that my once shiny runners are rotting with rust and my stiff backboard creaks like an old wooden stair. My life as a sled has not been very consistently rewarding. All through the spring, summer, and fall I anxiously await winter's first snowfall which brings with it the much appreciated influx of tourists. Now, at last, I will be free to feel and smell the gusts of raw winter air, hear the cacophony of winter sounds, and explore the hills and valleys shimmering with winter's white crown.

Early one morning my dreams finally materialize when a family of two children and their parents rent me for the day. When we first reach the slopes, my freshly waxed runners receive a startling awakening as I am set down in a chilly snowbank. A sharp gust of wind causes the family to snuggle more tightly into their parkas; it freezes the moisture on my body into a thin layer of ice. The blast of wind brings with it that fresh aroma of newly fallen snow mingled with the tangy scent wafting from the pine trees. By tomorrow a new scent will be added--the smell of civilization splattered onto the snow by numberless boots, skis, and sleds.

The family is thoroughly involved in the serious matter of who will be the first to ride me. The sounds of their argument contrast sharply with the joyous laughter of another couple swooshing by on a toboggan.

The boy insists, "Me first; Mommy promised."

"He always wants to go first!" whines the little girl.

"Now, children," the mother interrupts, "stop fighting. We'll all have a chance to use the sled. We've rented it for the whole day."

"Daddy, you decide," agree the children.

I impatiently wait for his decision as my runners get colder. Finally, he says that the boy can go first and then the little girl. As the boy pulls down his cap and tucks in his scarf, I can hear the light snow being crunched into a hard pack by other sleds and can hardly wait for my turn. The wind is still rushing past us, whining through the pine needles and brushing the snow from the tree limbs. The clumps of snow falling from the branches sound like animals moving through the woods and startle the boy into jumping on the sled.

After some jiggling and twisting around, he at last lies prone on my strong backboard and grips my frosty handlebars. As we push off down the hill, the magnificent landscape before me is draped in a coat of white. The purity of the white is broken by the greens and browns of the pines standing on each side of the run, the frigid blue of the lake far below, and the bright hues added by the scattered parkas. Suddenly, the colors rush into one great kaleidoscope as we gain momentum in our descent. The speed, the colors, and the cold exhilarate me, but the boy's high-pitched screams interrupt the thrill of the run. And then only one object is clearly in sight, and we are headed straight for it--a tree! I hold my breath in anticipation and fear that this will be my first and last run of the season. I can feel the boy frantically twisting my frame until finally he turns me back onto the proper path and we slow to a stop.

I am drained for a moment, but I have time to contemplate my life as I am dragged back up the icy slope. I think that although I am only useful for a few months out of the year and despite some occupational hazards, the ecstasy and beauty experienced from the winter are definitely worth the dangers.

Discovery Exercise

1. Identify the action being narrated: ____________________________________

____

2. Identify the setting (place and time): ____

____

3. Identify the time order used:

   ____ chronological

   ____ artistic

4. Identify the point of view: ____________ person
5. Identify the verb tense: ____________
6. Circle transitional expressions indicating time movement or direction.
7. Identify the climax of the story: ____

____

8. Identify two techniques that make this story effective: ____________________
9. Choose terms from the diction chart that characterize the diction: ____________________
10. Choose terms from the tone chart that describe the tone:

____

11. After reviewing Chapter 16, bracket **four** compound sentences, one type of grammatical structure used in this essay.

STUDENT SAMPLE—Narrative Writing

An Unexpected Maneuver

For a full week the soldiers had done nothing but prepare for their scheduled trek into Ranger Swamp. The 60 men who comprised A Company's Third Platoon practiced minor navigation exercises continuously for that notorious maneuver. The platoon was divided into eight squads; Lopez was the squad leader for one of them. So there they were, eight of them, standing at the edge of a southern swamp, on an early evening in May.

The leader rechecked their compass heading, took the point, and led the men into the swamp in a northwesterly direction. Holding their weapons up out of the waist-deep water wasn't too difficult, but carrying 60-pound packs and having to consciously yank their booted feet out of the muck every step reminded Lopez of Merrill's Marauders' Mission in Burma. He had noticed from the start of the mission that there was a lot of talk in the squad about snakes and other swamp creatures. The soldiers had been assured by their superiors that the swamp had been thoroughly dynamited the previous day, but the men's talk had aroused Lopez's apprehension. With every purposeful step, he became more and more aware of little sneaky splashes and slithering sounds. The chirping and cooing of this junglelike place steadily grew louder. The rising steam seemed as if it were straight out of Hell. How it stank!

The group had been driving themselves on relentlessly for the third and fourth hours. The leader decided that the squad needed a rest, so the platoon stopped alongside a peat shoal. Lopez sat on a dead cypress root resembling a serpent's hump sticking out of the water. He told the squad that they had five minutes to eat, sleep, or do whatever. Five sat near Lopez while the other two investigated the surrounding terrain. Suddenly a horrified scream tore through their ears. It was Smith. He came leaping off the shoal with no weapon and no pack. No sooner had he landed in the swamp than Jones came jumping in. The unmistakable effluvium of an encounter with a skunk immediately followed them. Smith and Jones both yelled at the same time. Lopez finally gathered that when Smith had reached down to pick up his weapon, a skunk was nearby. He must have startled it. The skunk bit Smith's hand and then sprayed Jones who was standing behind them.

Harper, the first-aid man, started to tend to Smith's injured hand which was bleeding quite freely, as all could see by flashlight. Meanwhile, Lopez climbed onto the shoal, with a weapon which was useless since there were no live rounds, to search for the possibly rabid skunk. There it was, a few feet away from the leader, hissing. The air smelled horrible. Not one to fool around, Lopez threw his M-16 at it. Direct hit! It was injured. On its side, it sprayed and struggled. Lopez took off his pack and swung it from a shoulder strap. He hit it again. The skunk no longer moved. He picked up his weapon and smashed the butt into the animal's head. Quite sure it was dead, the leader slid back into the water. Moments later he quickly put a plan into effect. Jones stripped and tried to deodorize himself. All the men remained in the swamp while Johnson and Lopez left to get medical help. They ran and swam for what seemed like hours, periodically checking their course. The humming of strange insects filled their ears. They saw one water moccasin, but it slithered away.

Forty-five minutes and one mile later, Johnson and Lopez arrived at the commanding officer's tent and explained the situation. A chopper was dispatched to pick up the remaining squad members. The chopper crew was instructed to bring back the dead skunk for tests. The skunk was rabid, so Smith and Jones had to undergo rabies treatment, but they both completed their training with A Company's Third Platoon.

Discovery Exercise

1. Identify the action being narrated: ____

   ____

2. Identify the setting (place and time): ____

   ____

3. Identify the time order used:

   ____ chronological

   ____ artistic

4. Identify point of view: ____________ person

5. Identify verb tense: ____________

6. List the major segments of the action:

7. Identify the climax of the story:

8. Circle transitional expressions indicating time movement or direction.

9. Choose terms from the diction chart that characterize the diction:

10. Choose terms from the tone chart that describe tone:

11. After reviewing Chapter 16, bracket **five** sets of dependent clauses, one type of grammatical structure used in this essay.

STUDENT SAMPLE—Narrative Writing

The Open Door

My family moved into the house on Denver Street when I was eight years old. My brother and I played with the children from the house down the street, and because their mother, Sheila, and my mother were good friends, our families spent a lot of time together. Many experiences from that period of time are etched in my mind, but the one I most vividly remember is the day I entered Sheila's house and found that it had been burglarized.

As a favor, she had asked me to care for her dog while she and her family went on a vacation. It was a very hot summer afternoon the first time I went to check on the house. As I approached the steps, I noticed that the front door was wide open, exposing the entry and part of the living room. Sheila must have been in a hurry to leave, I thought; yet when I walked inside, I doubted myself. With a child's imagination, I thought of some possibilities. Of course, the wind could have blown the door open, or another neighbor could have been inside and had simply forgotten to close it. A strange, eerie feeling crept over me. I somehow knew that someone had broken into the house, and worse, I sensed that this "someone" was still hiding in the shadows of the house.

Frantically, I searched for something with which to protect myself. It did not occur to me to leave the house. My eyes fell on a rolled-up newspaper. Arming myself with my "weapon," I peeked into the kitchen, but nothing was out of place. I then crept into the living room, but again, nothing was amiss. He must be in one of the bedrooms, I decided.

Summoning all of my courage, I cautiously walked down the hall to the master bedroom. Standing in the doorway, I discovered the beginnings of the burglary. Drawers had been pulled from the dresser, clothes snatched from them and spread throughout the room. Jewelry boxes, robbed of their valuable contents, had been thrown onto the unmade bed. I noticed that the closet door stood open, a perfect hiding place, I thought, for the dangerous criminal. Because of my position in the doorway and the shape of the room, I could not see inside the closet. Fearing someone remained in its depths, I whirled around and ran to the phone in the kitchen. I immediately called my mother and told her that Sheila's house had been robbed and that I thought the man was still in the house. Before she could tell me what to do, I heard a loud SMASH! from outside. He was coming back for more! Shaking with fear, I pulled the curtain aside and looked out. The newspaper boy had simply thrown the paper onto the porch and into a pot. I also saw, however, that the burglar had torn the screen out of the window and forced it open in order to get inside. Crying now, I heard my mother tell me to get out of the house. I ran out the front door, fervently hoping that no one would follow me.

Ten minutes later, which felt like ten hours to me, my mother drove up with the police. After I had calmed down enough to explain, the police searched the entire house. They did not find the dangerous criminal hiding in the closet, waiting for me to get close enough to grab me. Yet to this day I am certain he was there. The police said I had scared away the burglar. He did not return to the house. Neither did I, unless I was with someone or I knew that Sheila was there waiting for me. That was the most frightening experience of my life, and I was not taking any chances for it to happen again.

PROFESSIONAL SAMPLE—Narrative Writing

Read the following sample to see how a professional writer has used the technique of narration. Then answer the discovery questions which focus on the major elements of narrative writing.

Virginia Woolf (1882–1941), a British novelist and essayist, is considered one of the most important modern English novelists. Her superb use of language and her delving into her characters' states of consciousness were significant literary contributions. Her two most admired novels are *Mrs. Dalloway* and *To the Lighthouse.* This selection is taken from *The Death of the Moth and Other Essays.*

The Death of the Moth

1 Moths that fly by day are not properly to be called moths; they do not excite that pleasant sense of dark autumn nights and ivy-blossom which the commonest yellow underwing asleep in the shadow of the curtain never fails to rouse in us. They are hybrid creatures, neither gay like butterflies nor sombre like their own species. Nevertheless, the present specimen, with his narrow hay-coloured wings, fringed with a tassle of the same colour, seemed to be content with life. It was a pleasant morning, mid-September, mild, benignant, yet with a keener breath than that of the summer months. The plough was already scoring the field opposite the window, and where the share had been, the earth was pressed flat and gleamed with

moisture. Such vigour came rolling in from the fields and down beyond that it was difficult to keep the eyes strictly turned upon the book. The rooks too were keeping one of their annual festivities; soaring round the tree-tops until it looked as if a vast net with thousands of black knots in it had been cast up into the air; which, after a few moments sank slowly down upon the trees until every twig seemed to have a knot at the end of it. Then, suddenly, the net would be thrown into the air again in a wider circle this time, with the utmost clamour and vociferation, as though to be thrown into the air and settle slowly down upon the tree-tops were a tremendously exciting experience.

2 The same energy which inspired the rooks, the ploughmen, the horses, and even, it seemed, the lean bare-backed downs, sent the moth fluttering from side to side of his square of the window-pane. One could not help watching him. One was, indeed, conscious of a queer feeling of pity for him. The possibilities of pleasure seemed that morning so enormous and so various that to have only a moth's part in life, and a day moth's at that, appeared a hard fate, and his zest in enjoying his meagre opportunities to the full, pathetic. He flew vigorously to one corner of his compartment, and, after waiting there a second, flew across to the other. What remained for him but to fly to a third corner and then to a fourth? That was all he could do, in spite of the size of the downs, the width of the sky, the far-off smoke of houses, and the romantic voice, now and then, of a steamer out at sea. What he could do he did. Watching him, it seemed as if a fibre, very thin but pure, of the enormous energy of the world had been thrust into his frail and diminutive body. As often as he crossed the pane, I could fancy that a thread of vital light became visible. He was little or nothing but life.

3 Yet, because he was so small, and so simple a form of the energy that was rolling in at the open window and driving its way through so many narrow and intricate corridors in my own brain and in those of other human beings, there was something marvelous as well as pathetic about him. It was as if someone had taken a tiny bead of pure life and decking it as lightly as possible with down and feathers, had set it dancing and zigzagging to show us the true nature of life. Thus displayed one could not get over the strangeness of it. One is apt to forget all about life, seeing it humped and bossed and garnished and cumbered so that it has to move with the greatest circumspection and dignity. Again, the thought of all that life might have been had he been born in any other shape caused one to view his simple activities with a kind of pity.

4 After a time, tired by his dancing apparently, he settled on the window ledge in the sun, and the queer spectacle being at an end, I forgot about him. Then, looking up, my eye was caught by him. He was trying to resume his dancing, but seemed either so stiff or so awkward that he could only flutter to the bottom of the window-pane; and when he tried to fly across it he failed. Being intent on other matters I watched these futile attempts for a time without thinking, unconsciously waiting for him to resume his flight, as one waits for a machine, that has stopped momentarily, to start again without considering the reason for its failure. After perhaps a seventh attempt he slipped from the wooden ledge and fell, fluttering his wings, on to his back on the windowsill. The helplessness of his attitude roused me. It flashed upon me that he was in difficulties; he could no longer raise himself; his legs struggled vainly. But, as I stretched out a pencil, meaning to help him to right himself, it came over me that the failure and awkwardness were the approach of death. I laid the pencil down again.

5 The legs agitated themselves once more. I looked as if for the enemy against which he struggled. I looked out of doors. What had happened there? Presumably it was midday, and work in the fields had stopped. Stillness and quiet had replaced the previous animation. The birds had taken themselves off to feed in the brooks. The horses stood still. Yet the power was there all the same, massed outside indifferent, impersonal, not attending to anything in particular. Somehow it was opposed to the little hay-coloured moth. It was useless to try to do anything. One could only watch the extraordinary efforts made by those tiny legs against an oncoming doom which could, had it chosen, have submerged an entire city, not merely a city, but masses of human beings; nothing, I knew, had any chance against death. Nevertheless, after a pause of exhaustion the legs fluttered again. It was superb this last protest, and so frantic that he succeeded at last in righting himself. One's sympathies, of course, were all on the side of life. Also, when there was nobody to care or to know, this gigantic effort on the part of an insignificant little moth, against a power of such magnitude, to retain what no one else valued or desired to keep, moved one strangely. Again, somehow, one saw life, a pure bead. I lifted the pencil again, useless though I knew it to be. But even as I did so, the unmistakable tokens of death showed

themselves. The body relaxed, and instantly grew stiff. The struggle was over. The insignificant little creature now knew death. As I looked at the dead moth, this minute wayside triumph of so great a force over so mean an antagonist filled me with wonder. Just as life had been strange a few minutes before, so death was now as strange. The moth having righted himself now lay most decently and uncomplainingly composed. O yes, he seemed to say, death is stronger than I am.

Discovery Questions

1. What are the major segments of the action in the death of the moth?
2. Identify several of the complications in the narrative.
3. Which one of the four possible narrative endings does Virginia Woolf use to resolve the action?

Suggested Events to Narrate

Select one the following or similar events that you remember vividly and in great detail:

If you have ever been extremely frightened, give an account of the experience.

It is important and often exciting to be away from home at a certain age. It can also be lonely. Narrate your most exciting or loneliest experience.

Many writers have written of their happy childhoods. But for other writers, childhood was a time of misery and horror. Narrate a happy childhood experience. Or narrate an unpleasant experience that you were glad to outgrow or escape.

Narrate the experiences you had before, during, and/or after your first job interview.

Narrate a frustrating experience you have had; for example, getting your car repaired, buying some item, waiting for someone.

Narrate the events of your first date.

Narrate the first time you had a crush on a person of the opposite sex.

Narrate how someone helped you through a trying time.

Narrate a situation in which you were extremely jealous of someone for a very insignificant reason.

Narrate what happened when you found yourself a complete stranger in a new place; for example, new school, new place of work.

Narrate any of the above topics using the third-person point of view.

Narrate a story from your imagination.

Review Virginia Woolf's narration, "The Death of the Moth," and narrate some event you have closely observed in nature: for example, birds building a nest, fish swimming upstream, bees gathering honey, two animals fighting.

WORKSHEET FOR NARRATIVE WRITING

1. Select an action to narrate.
2. Get approval from your instructor after completing the information for the introduction.
3. Complete the remainder of the worksheet **before** writing the passage.
4. Attach the worksheet to the finished passage.
5. Attach the Narrative Writing Cover Sheet to the finished passage.

Title: ______________________________

INTRODUCTION

Central action and nature of conflict: ______________________________

____

Order: ______________________________

Point of view: ______________________________

Verb tense: ______________________________

Tone: ______________________________

Diction: ______________________________

Setting (place and time), if relevant: ______________________________

____

____
(instructor approval)

BODY

At least three major segments of action leading to climax:

1. ______________________________
____
____

2. ______________________________
____
____

3. ______________________________
____
____

Climax ______________________________

CONCLUSION

Resolution of action: ______________________________

____

Name: ____________________
Date: ____________ Class: ________

NARRATIVE WRITING COVER SHEET		
Structure/Ideas	+	______
Usage/Mechanics	−	______
Total		______
Rewrite points	+	______
TOTAL		______

Structure and Ideas (100 points)		**Original**	**Rewrite**
INTRODUCTION: title, at least five sentences including action to be narrated	20	______	______
BODY: three important segments of action leading to the climax	15	______	______
concrete, sufficient development of complications of the action	45	______	______
time order with transitional expression	10	______	______
CONCLUSION: resolution of action; meaning or opinions (optional)	10	______	______
Total	100	______	+ ______

The points in this section reflect your score for structure and ideas. If you have received fewer than 100 points, you may rewrite your paper to earn them. Use the numbers as a guide to what areas need revision.

Usage and Mechanics (minus points). See Correction Symbol Chart.			
You **may** earn these points in revision:			
Usage: adj; adv; agr; awk; col; dm; frag; mm; ref; rep; shift; verb; ww; //; ¶	−3 ea.	______	______
You **may not** earn these points in revision, but you must correct the errors:			
Mechanics: abbr; apos; cap; lc; p; ro; sp; ∧	−1 ea.	______	______
Total	−	______	+ ______

CHAPTER 4
Exposition—The Paragraph

If you want to be successful in the writing that you do, you will have to master the elements of expository writing. Whether you are taking an examination, applying for a position, preparing a memo, writing a letter, or filing a complaint, all of these tasks require skill in organizing and presenting information. This chapter will introduce you to the paragraph, the basic structure of informative writing.

The purpose of exposition is to explain an idea or make a concept understandable. Exposition accomplishes its purpose in a number of ways: by giving an example, by sorting into types, by identifying parts, by explaining how an object or process works, by giving reasons or results, by showing similarities or differences, and by giving the limits or the meaning of a word or concept.

Unity is achieved in expository writing by establishing one main idea called a topic sentence or thesis statement. All supporting details must follow from and directly relate to the topic sentence or thesis statement. For example, the first student sample in this chapter states in the topic sentence the paragraph's main idea: "The children on a television program react in three different ways." All the supporting details discuss and give examples of the three different reactions. Another student example, "The Land of the Strauss Waltzes," presents in the thesis statement the essay's main idea: "Visiting Austria offered many new cultural experiences." All the supporting details develop and exemplify these experiences.

Order is achieved in expository writing by the logical pattern you choose to develop the topic sentence or thesis statement. Logical order is the way ideas and details are arranged in a rational, systematic sequence to convey a general concept. There are four main types of logical order. (1) **Time or chronological order** is discussed in Chapter 3. (2) **General to particular** moves from the main idea to the specific details which support and explain it. An example of this order is shown in "How Color Affects Our Lives." (3) **Climactic order** moves from the least important support to the most important one. An example of this order appears in "Coming to America," where religion, the most important reason, is discussed last. (4) **Alternating order** moves back and forth between two subjects and is most commonly used in comparison-contrast essays such as "The Lady and the Libber," in Chapter 11, which contrasts traditional and liberated women.

EXPOSITORY PARAGRAPH WRITING

A paragraph is a group of related sentences containing one main idea called the **topic sentence** (level 1) and supporting details (levels 2, 3, 4). The topic sentence is often, but not always, the first sentence of a paragraph. For example, in all of the samples except the last one in this section, the topic sentence is the first in the paragraph. However, in that sample, the topic sentence is the fourth one, following some introductory material.

As a unit of thought, the paragraph stands midway between the sentence and the essay. A paragraph may appear by itself, but in groups paragraphs are often used to develop a larger idea. Consequently, mastery of the paragraph is preliminary to handling larger blocks of related ideas in the essay.

Elements of Paragraph Writing

- topic sentence (level 1) presenting a main idea
- sufficient and unified development of the topic sentence by means of supporting details (levels 2, 3, 4)
- logical order of ideas
- effective style
- consistent point of view, verb tense, and tone

Problems to Avoid

First, you should try not to begin the topic sentence with "there is" or "there are" because these phrases are weak and wordy. For example, "There are several primary advantages to using the college library" can be more precisely stated as "The college library offers students several primary advantages." Second, you should avoid using irrelevant material that strays from the main idea and thus weakens the paragraph. Finally, once you decide on the point of view, verb tense, and tone of the paragraph, use these consistently.

How to Prepare Your Paragraph

One way to develop skill in paragraph writing is to use a carefully structured model. The model presented in this section is an 11-sentence form. Since it contains all the elements of the five-paragraph essay in condensed form, it is an easy transition to the full-length essay—the major focus of a writing course.

The section which follows is an exercise preliminary to the essay. The 11-sentence paragraph is a good tool because, once the paragraph is mastered, you can more easily respond to the writing assignments later in the text. This 11-sentence paragraph form may seem rigid; however, it is highly flexible in practice. Its flexibility comes from the fact that it expands and contracts according to the number of supporting details (levels 2 and 3) needed. The last sample paragraph in this section shows one such expansion; it contains fifteen sentences.

Your information will come from personal experience or objective sources. There is a place on the worksheet to indicate the source of the material. (See Chapter 1 under "Selecting Your Subject.") The topic sentence is the key to the paragraph. You are given a formula to help you construct the sentence and write a good paragraph from it. This formula states that the topic sentence is composed of the following elements: subject, verb, and controlling idea. These may be rearranged within the sentence. Because the controlling idea focuses the subject, you will need to select a control that is clear and precise. Therefore, the controlling idea formula is suggested to you as a way of forming an effective topic sentence. This formula states that the controlling idea contains three elements: a number, an adjective, and a noun. The chart following shows the possibilities for creating this idea.

Topic Sentence—*the key to the paragraph*

A **paragraph** is a group of related ideas that begins with a clearly stated topic sentence. This sentence is composed of a subject (area of discussion), a verb, and a controlling idea (how the subject will be developed). Stated as a formula:

TOPIC SENTENCE = SUBJECT + VERB + CONTROLLING IDEA

A strong controlling idea is composed of three distinct items. They are a number (how many major subtopics or supporting points), an adjective (the predominant attitude), and a noun (the general emphasis). Stated as a formula:

CONTROLLING IDEA = NUMBER + ADJECTIVE + NOUN

Controlling Idea Chart

To compose a controlling idea, you can choose **one** item from **each** of the three columns.

Number	**Adjective***		**Noun**	
three	basic	main	advantages	groups
a few	beneficial	major	areas	ideas
several	best	necessary	aspects	illustrations
many	chief	positive	benefits	kinds
a variety of	dangerous	primary	categories	parts
numerous	different	principal	causes	problems
any of three	essential	serious	characteristics	proofs
various	humorous	useful	concepts	qualities
certain	important	separate	details	reasons
	distinct		effects	responsibilities
			elements	results
			examples	stages
			factors	steps
			facts	tests
	*can be a prepositional phrase (ex. "three problems with teenagers")		forms	types

Discovery Exercise for the Topic Sentence

Each of these items can now be combined to create several topic sentences—the starting place of a well-written paragraph.

Transform the following fragments into topic sentences by adding a verb and controlling idea.

Use the formulas: TOPIC SENTENCE = SUBJECT + VERB + CONTROLLING IDEA
CONTROLLING IDEA = NUMBER + ADJECTIVE + NOUN

Do not begin your sentences with "there is" or "there are."

Example: `Grooming a dog for show`

TS: Grooming a miniature poodle for show (Subject) + requires (Verb) + several (Number) + important (Adjective) + steps (Noun). [Controlling Idea]

1. The serious college student ______________________________

2. Learning how to write ______________________________

3. The safety of one's home ______________________________

4. To prepare for major surgery ______________________________

5. The most successful parties ______________________________

Organizational Pattern for the Expository Paragraph

Study this blueprint so that you can see and better understand the elements necessary for paragraph writing. Then use the pattern as a guide in assembling your own paragraph. Note that most of the student samples in the chapter use this organizational pattern.

Topic sentence (level 1)

Identification of main idea to be developed (subject, verb, controlling idea)

Establishment of order of subtopics
- point of view
- verb tense
- tone
- diction

Three major subtopics and supporting details (levels 2, 3, 4)

Presentation of three major subtopics (level 2)

Sufficient development of subtopics by means of supporting details such as specific examples, facts, illustrations, anecdotes (levels 3 and 4)

Logical order of three major subtopics

____ time/chronological
____ general to particular
____ climactic
____ alternating

**Level 2:* Transitional expression + reference to topic sentence + subtopic 1

Level 3 / Level 3 or 4 } Optional transitional expression + at least two supports for subtopic 1

**Level 2:* Transitional expression + reference to topic sentence + subtopic 2

Level 3 / Level 3 or 4 } Optional transitional expression + at least two supports for subtopic 2

**Level 2:* Transitional expression + reference to topic sentence + subtopic 3

Level 3 / Level 3 or 4 } Optional transitional expression + at least two supports for subtopic 3

Transitional expressions: see Handbook.

Concluding sentence (level 1)

Optional transitional expression + restatement of topic sentence in different words with no new information

*These elements may be rearranged within the sentence.

SAMPLE WORKSHEET FOR EXPOSITORY PARAGRAPH 1

1. Complete the worksheet **before** writing the paragraph.
2. Attach the worksheet to the finished paragraph.
3. Attach the Paragraph Cover Sheet to the finished paragraph.

Source of material: textbook from class in child development

Subject to be discussed: children's reaction to being on television

Controlling idea: three (number) + different (adjective) + ways (noun)

Order of major subtopics: general to particular

List three subtopics: inhibition due to fright
complete extroversion
neutral manner

Point of view: third person

Verb tense: present

Tone: serious

Diction: abstract, concrete, objective

Level 1, topic sentence in sentence form: The children on a television program react in three different ways.

MS/RW
(instructor approval)

Level 2, first major subtopic: inhibition due to fright

Level 3, support for subtopic: ex: shying away from the camera

Level 3 or 4: ex: paralyzed in one position

Level 2, second major subtopic: complete extroversion

Level 3, support for subtopic: other children want to avoid

Level 3 or 4: rambunctious behavior – examples

Level 2, third major subtopic: neutral manner

Level 3, support for subtopic: ex: remain calm, forget camera

Level 3 or 4: easy to handle

Level 1, concluding sentence: easy to notice varying reactions

STUDENT SAMPLE—Expository Paragraph 1—Analyzed for Parts

Observe that elements of structure and content are labeled on the left while elements of style are identified on the right. This detailed analysis will help you plan your own paragraph.

When they first realize that the camera is on, the children on a television show react in three different ways. One such reaction from the children is inhibition due to fright. An example of this behavior is a child's shying away from the camera by seeking refuge behind the other children. Another example is the child who becomes so inhibited as to appear almost paralyzed in one position and unaware of the surroundings. A second way in which children react is complete extroversion, a contrast to the first way. Such extroverts are those pre-schoolers whom the other more composed children attempt to avoid. More often than not, these active children force their presence upon others through rambunctious behavior: making faces at the camera, pushing others, and talking constantly. Children reacting in a rather neutral manner is the third way. To illustrate, because they are neither shy nor boisterous, they remain calm and act as if the television camera does not exist. In many respects, these children are easiest to handle because they are pleasant, obedient, and observant when compared to the

Topic Sentence Level 1
Level 2
Level 3
Level 3
Level 2
Level 3
Level 4
Level 2
Level 3
Level 3
3 major subtopics with supporting details

Subject + Verb + Controlling Idea
\# adj N.
Transitional expression + Reference to Topic Sentence + Subtopic 1
Transitional expression + Reference to Topic Sentence + Subtopic 2
Reference to Topic Sentence + Subtopic 3 + Transitional expression

others. Undoubtedly, when youngsters are placed in front of the television camera, their varying reactions are easily noticed.

Concluding Sentence Level 1

Transitional expression + Restatement of Topic Sentence

STUDENT SAMPLE—Expository Paragraph 2

Source of material: personal experience

Before catching a plane departing from any major airport, the traveler must take care of a few aggravating problems. The first wave of irritation breaks as one enters the access street to all the different terminals and faces the difficulty of parking. A constant stream of cars usually floods an already full parking lot. To illustrate, people often rush to catch their plane; as a result, tempers fly, brakes screech, and horns blast as the traveler drives in circles until someone vacates a parking space. The second aggravation is transporting one's luggage from the parking lot to the correct air terminal. The amount of luggage depends upon the length of the trip. For example, two suitcases, a handbag, a coat or sweater, airline tickets, and possibly a small child all needing to be lugged across the airport make the check-in quite complicated. Once the passenger is inside the terminal, confirming one's airline reservations is the last problem. The person is usually lucky to take care of this task if it can be done without standing in a crowded line or being confronted with petty airline errors. For example, sometimes after standing in line for an irritating thirty minutes, one might be informed about having too many pieces of carry-on luggage, or no more seats left in the non-smoking section, or no listing of the name on the reservation list. To be sure, there are a few aggravations the traveler must face before departing on a flight from many international airports.

Discovery Exercise

1. Identify the topic sentence
   a. the subject being discussed: ____________________
   b. the controlling idea: ____________________
2. Identify the three major subtopics: ____________________

   ____

   ____
3. Identify the logical order of the major subtopics:

   ______ time/chronological ______ alternating

   ______ climactic ______ general to particular
4. Identify the point of view: ______ person
5. Identify the verb tense: ____________________
6. Circle the transitional expressions.

7. Select **ten** words and phrases that illustrate the diction:

______________________	______________________
______________________	______________________
______________________	______________________
______________________	______________________
______________________	______________________

8. Choose terms from the diction chart that characterize the diction: ______________________
9. Choose terms from the tone chart that describe the tone:

____

10. After reviewing Chapter 16, bracket **ten** prepositional phrases, one type of grammatical structure used in this paragraph.

STUDENT SAMPLE—Expository Paragraph 3

Source of material: textbook on architecture

Every architectural design by Frank Lloyd Wright contains three essential qualities. First, the exquisite design of the building must correlate with the surrounding landscape. An example of such precise correlation is the "Falling Water House," whose plans use both horizontal and vertical building frames to simulate the leveling off of the hillside along the stream and sloping downward of the waterfall where the house is constructed. In order to accentuate the correlation, the house's building frame is constructed from a rough ashlar base and smooth concrete slabs in a manner related to the jaggered formation of the waterfall and the smooth level lands along the stream. A second quality is the harmonizing of the interior with the exterior design. For instance, in the "Hollyhock House" an abstract hollyhock motif was used as an exterior rim around the roof of the house, but inside, the motif was woven into the carpet and used on some of the pillars. It is also interesting to note that the "Imperial Hotel" not only has lava carvings of conventionalized peacocks on the exterior but also is embroidered with lava carvings and peacock paintings inside. Third, all of Wright's buildings have a multi-functional quality. To illustrate, even though the "Hollyhock House" was built as a home for Miss Barnsdall, he focused on her love for the theater by building areas where rehearsals could be held and performances could be given. Another is the "Jiyu Gakuen School" which functions as an elementary school, but because of the U-shaped design focusing directly on an elaborate auditorium of panelled glass and wood, it is also used by other schools and the community for social functions. Naturally, none of Wright's architectural designs is similar to any other, but everyone of them contains three essential qualities that are woven together to create an exquisite architectural design.

Discovery Exercise

1. Identify the topic sentence
   a. the subject being discussed: ______________________________
   b. the controlling idea: ______________________________
2. Identify the three major subtopics: ______________________________
   ____
   ____
3. Identify the logical order of the major supporting ideas:
   ______ time/chronological ______ alternating
   ______ climactic ______ general to particular
4. Identify the point of view: ____________ person
5. Identify the verb tense: ______________________________
6. Circle the transitional expressions.
7. Identify **ten** words and phrases that illustrate the diction:
   ______________________ ______________________
   ______________________ ______________________
   ______________________ ______________________
   ______________________ ______________________
   ______________________ ______________________
8. Choose terms from the diction chart that characterize the diction: ______________________
9. Choose terms from the tone chart that describe the tone:
   ____
10. After reviewing Chapter 16, bracket **three** infinitive verbal phrases, one type of grammatical structure used in this paragraph.

STUDENT SAMPLE—Expository Paragraph 4

Source of material: textbook on the elements of fiction

Notice that the following paragraph contains several variations from the 11-sentence form. There are three sentences of introduction before the topic sentence. Also there are three level 3's for the first two level 2's. The last level 2 is followed by only one level 3.

When fiction writers construct a short story or novel, they must choose a point of view for their narrative. Point of view refers to the position from which the events of the story are related. Writers may select from a range of viewpoints, such as first person, third-person omniscient, or third-person limited. The technique of first-person narrative point of view offers writers several important advantages. One advantage is the discipline and demands it imposes on writers to adhere totally to the protagonist's viewpoint. By using the simple tool of "I" instead of "he" or "she" for their hero or heroine, they can not unintentionally wander into another character's viewpoint. One strength of this choice is that authors are less likely to drift between characters and lose focus. For example, Mark Twain in The Adventures of Huckleberry Finn filters everything through the consciousness of his first-person point-of-view character, Huck. Another important advantage for writers using this method is that it forces them to carefully consider if their chief character has compelling qualities. For instance, authors must ask themselves if the protagonist abounds with strength, humor, and excitement, or if he or she is intriguing and entertaining enough to filter the story through his or her consciousness. For example, in Invisible Man by Ralph Ellison, the first-person protagonist functions effectively because he is intelligent, caring, and sensitive. With this technique authors can not camoflauge uninteresting characters by inserting their own observations or comments within the text. Finally, this method of single-person narrative provides the important advantage of allowing writers to penetrate and relate in depth their protagonist's character and personality. They know all the hero knows; they see all the hero sees, and they feel all the hero feels. In conclusion, this technique affords authors the important advantage of achieving their ultimate goal by leading the reader to identify completely with their character.

Suggested Ideas to Explain in a Paragraph

Select one of the following or similar ideas. Make sure that it is not too broad or too general to be treated in a single paragraph.

Politics or economics: Discuss three reasons why there should be a change in the existing state of affairs.

Architecture: Discuss three favorite architectural achievements, **or** three aspects of one particular architectural achievement, **or** three reasons for the success of one achievement.

Biology: Discuss three behavioral characteristics of some wild animal.

Communications: Discuss three types of television commercials.

Environmental Science: Discuss three wasteful comsumption habits that are evident in the United States (for example: unnecessary use of energy, packaging of throwaway products, overeating), **or** discuss three ways to conserve our resources.

Health science: Discuss three harmful effects of improper diet **or** three ways of coping with stress.

Business: Discuss three advantages or disadvantages of owning a franchise **or** three problems involved in owning a business.

Select some other academic course and develop a similar type of topic with information drawn from it.

Select a personal experience as the basis for a paragraph.

WORKSHEET FOR EXPOSITORY PARAGRAPH

1. Complete the top half of the worksheet, and get approval from your instructor.
2. Complete the remainder of the worksheet **before** writing the paragraph.
3. Attach the worksheet to the finished paragraph.
4. Attach the Paragraph Cover Sheet to the finished paragraph.

Source of material: ____________________

Subject to be discussed: ____________________

Controlling idea: ________ (number) + ________ (adjective) + ________ (noun)

Order of major subtopics: ____________________

List three subtopics: ____________________

____

____

Point of view: ____________________

Verb tense: ____________________

Tone: ____________________

Diction: ____________________

Level 1, topic sentence in sentence form: ____________________

____

____

____
(instructor approval)

Level 2, first major subtopic: ____________________

Level 3, support for subtopic: ____________________

Level 3 or 4: ____________________

Level 2, second major subtopic: ____________________

Level 3, Support for subtopic: ____________________

Level 3 or 4: ____________________

Level 2, third major subtopic: ____________________

Level 3, support for subtopic: ____________________

Level 3 or 4: ____________________

Level 1, concluding sentence: ____________________

Name: ______________________

Date: ______________ Class: __________

PARAGRAPH COVER SHEET		
Structure/Ideas		+ ________
Usage/Mechanics		− ________
	Total	________
Rewrite points		+ ________
	TOTAL	________

Structure and Ideas (50 points)	**Original**	**Rewrite**
Topic sentence with controlling idea (level 1)	5________	________
Three major subtopics (level 2)	10________	________
Sufficient development using concrete supporting details; two level 3's for each level 2	20________	________
Logical order with transitional expressions	10________	________
Concluding sentence	5________	________
Total	50________	+ ________

The points in this section reflect your score for structure and ideas. If you have received fewer than 50 points, you may rewrite your paper to earn them. Use the numbers as a guide to what areas need revision.

Usage and Mechanics (minus points). See Correction Symbol Chart.		
You **may** earn these points in revision:		
Usage: adj; adv; agr; awk; col; dm; frag; mm; ref; rep; shift; verb; ww; / /; ¶	−3 ea. ________	________
You **may not** earn these points in revision, but you must correct the errors:		
Mechanics: abbr; apos; cap; lc; p; ro; sp; ∧	−1 ea. ________	________
Total	− ________	+ ________

CHAPTER 5
Exposition—The Essay

Expanding the Paragraph to the Essay

You can see in the diagram below that the essay is an expansion of the paragraph. This chapter will focus on the essay by illustrating the nine writing steps of the writing process discussed in detail in Chapter 1.

Paragraph		Essay
topic sentence—the main idea of the paragraph (level 1)	→	thesis statement—the main idea of the essay (level 1)
three major subtopics (level 2)	→	topic sentences—the major subtopics of the essay given in paragraphs 2, 3, and 4 (level 2)
concluding sentence (level 1)	→	concluding paragraph (level 1)

An essay is a group of related paragraphs containing one main idea called the **thesis statement** (level 1), major subtopics (level 2), and supporting details (levels 3 and 4). In an expository essay, the thesis statement is usually presented in the introductory or first paragraph. All of the essays in this chapter contain a clearly worded thesis statement with a formal controlling idea. This outer structure helps develop a unified essay.

While the majority of essays in this text contain five paragraphs, the form of the essay is flexible. The number of paragraphs increases or decreases according to the number and complexity of the subtopics. The long comparison-contrast paper in Chapter 11, the book analysis in Chapter 14, and the term paper in Chapter 15 illustrate the longer essay. The usefulness of the essay form is that it can explain ideas and show their relationships to each other in greater detail than can the paragraph.

Elements of Essay Writing

- a title and thesis statement with a controlling idea
- sufficient and unified development by means of supporting details
- a semiformal level of language and an appropriate style
- a logical order of ideas
- a consistent point of view, verb tense, and tone

Expository Patterns of Development

An idea can be explained in a variety of ways. The following are the most widely used.

- **Illustration** (Chapter 6) conveys information by giving examples.
- **Classification** (Chapter 7) informs by sorting a group into types.
- **Analysis** (Chapters 8, 9, 10) explains an idea by identifying the parts of a structure (functional), by showing how a structure works (process), or by giving reasons or results (causal).
- **Comparison-Contrast** (Chapter 11) examines similarities and differences between two items.
- **Extended definition** (Chapter 12) develops the meaning or limits of an abstract word or concept.

Problems to Avoid

First, the subject you choose should not be too limited, too broad, or unfamiliar. A topic that is too limited for an essay is one that can usually be covered in just one paragraph, for example, a discussion of a pet's eating habits. This discussion could be expanded by explaining several habits that give the pet its personality. A topic that is too broad for an essay is one that cannot be developed adequately in five or so paragraphs, such as the problems caused by all the kinds of pollution. This topic could be limited by confining the discussion to a few major effects of one type of pollution. An unfamiliar topic is one removed from the writer's personal experience or knowledge, such as the customs of a primitive culture or the latest medical developments in treating cancer. If you wish to attempt this last type of topic, you must first research the subject. In general, the best advice is to select a subject drawn from personal experience.

Another problem you should avoid is using supporting details that are vague and general. By using the techniques of description, you can make ideas concrete and vivid. By using the techniques of narration, you can use anecdotes to illustrate general ideas. The patterns of exposition that are presented in Chapters 6 through 12 offer additional ways to make writing specific.

Finally, using ineffective diction such as slang, clichés, and jargon weakens the expository essay. Descriptions and examples of poor word choices are presented in the diction chart in Chapter 1.

The Essay Writing Process

An effective way to write an essay is to follow the nine step process which is usually divided into the stages of prewriting, writing, and rewriting. The first two stages are illustrated with the student sample "An Unexpected Bonus." The last stage is shown by a first draft and a much improved rewrite.

PREWRITING—THE INVENTING STAGE

The first stage in the writing process is primarily concerned with thinking about your subject and focusing on a specific area to develop in detail. Here is where note taking or questioning or freewriting becomes crucial. The effort you spend in thinking and planning will result in a better essay.

After you have narrowed your subject, you are ready to prepare a thesis statement and subtopics and then sketch an outline. Both a conventional outline and worksheet are included for the sample essay. You can refer to Chapter 1 for more details about the four steps of prewriting or inventing.

Step 1: Choose a Subject

Think of a subject to discuss, explain, or examine. Refer to Chapter 1 for sources for ideas.
Jot down interesting information about the subject.

```
Personal experience: carpooling
                     grocery shopping
                     PTA
                     sports--soccer (subject chosen)
                         girls, parents, aggravations, feelings, win-
                         ning and losing
```

Step 2: Focus the Subject

Limit the subject to what can be covered in five paragraphs.
Decide on the purpose, audience, tone, and diction.

Purpose: to explain some of the difficulties I experienced when coaching my daughter's soccer team

Audience: general college reader

Tone: humorous and ironic

Diction: figurative, connotative, concrete

Step 3: Frame the Thesis Statement and Subtopics

Select the controlling idea which will give the subject focus. Include a number (to identify how many major supports will be covered), an adjective (to indicate the primary attitude or approach to the subject), and a noun (to name the nature of the subtopics).

Subject: coaching a soccer team

Controlling idea:	several	valuable	experiences
	(number)	(adjective)	(noun)

Establish the point of view and verb tense.

Point of view: first person
Verb tense: past

Write a tentative thesis statement and three subtopics.

THESIS STATEMENT = SUBJECT + VERB + CONTROLLING IDEA

The thesis statement conveys the main idea the essay is going to develop. It has the same format as the topic sentence. However, the thesis is a larger idea than is suitable for one single paragraph and must be developed in greater detail.

THESIS STATEMENT—Analyzed for Structure

Thesis Statement (Level I): Coaching my daughter's soccer team (*Subject*) provided (*Verb*) me with several valuable experiences. (*Controlling Idea = Number + Adjective + Noun*)

Subtopic Sentence (3 subtopics): Three of these which gave me new insights were dealing with different types of girls, (1) parents, (2) and problems. (3)

Step 4: Sketch an Outline

Develop a sketch or blueprint for the essay. Both a conventional outline and a worksheet for this essay are included. Worksheet forms for each assignment are provided for you in this text. If, however, you or your instructor chooses to use the conventional outline format, you may simply disregard the worksheets. In any case, a good sketch of your ideas is important before you begin to write.

Instructions for completing the worksheets in the text:

1. Identify the source of your material as coming from personal experience or some objective writing, such as textbook, magazine article, or news item.
2. Enter in phrase form the subject to be discussed.

3. Fill in the appropriate number, adjective, and noun for the controlling idea.
4. From your freewriting or notetaking, determine the order of your subtopics and indicate that order on the appropriate line.
5. Write the point of view, verb tense, tone, and diction.
6. In one or two sentences give your thesis statement, and enumerate your three subtopics.
7. Write topic sentences with transitions for **each** subtopic.
   Topic sentence = transitional expression + brief reference to thesis statement + subtopic
8. Sketch the supporting details in sentences or phrases for each paragraph in the body of the essay.
9. Choose the tentative order of the supporting details in each paragraph to make sure they are arranged to convey ideas clearly.
10. Complete the material for the introduction by selecting and entering a title and a good beginning.
11. Complete the material for the conclusion by choosing and entering one of the good endings.

Conventional Outline of Five Paragraph Essay

Each heading includes at least two supporting items. For every I there is a II. For every A there is a B. For every 1 there is a 2.

Thesis statement:

Coaching my daughter's soccer team gave me several valuable experiences. Three of these were dealing with different types of girls, parents, and problems.

I. Different types of girls
  A. One girl wanting to be a goalie
  B. Girls behaving like juveniles
    1. Refusal to participate
    2. Giggling
  C. One girl suffering from star syndrome

II. Different types of parents
  A. Fathers too helpful
    1. Coaching from sidelines
    2. Yelling at referee
    3. Too demanding of daughters—female Pelé
  B. Fathers perplexed by woman coach
    1. Snide remarks
    2. Change in attitude when team won championship
  C. Parents who never attended games

III. Different types of problems
  A. Problem of overconfidence of players
    1. Not wanting to learn new skills
    2. Continually challenging referee
    3. Arriving late to games
  B. Lecture about after-game etiquette

SAMPLE WORKSHEET FOR FIVE-PARAGRAPH ESSAY

1. Select a subject to discuss and complete the top half of the worksheet.
2. Write your thesis statement and enumeration of subtopics and then get approval from your instructor.
3. Complete the worksheet **before** writing the essay.
4. Attach the worksheet to the finished essay.
5. Attach the Expository Essay Cover Sheet to the finished essay.

Source of material: personal experience

Subject to be discussed: coaching my daughter's soccer team

Controlling idea: several (number) valuable (adjective) experiences (noun)

Order of three major subtopics: general to particular

Point of view: first person - I Verb tense: past tense

Tone: ironic, humorous Diction: connotative, concrete

Thesis statement + enumeration of subtopics:

Coaching provided me with several valuable experiences. Three of these which gave me new insights were dealing with different types of girls, parents, and problems.

MS/RW
instructor approval

OUTLINE

Title: An Unexpected Bonus

Paragraph 1: Introduction (five sentences):

(level 1) Choose a good beginning from the list in Chapter 1. Give necessary background material.

Good beginning # 1 : Give a brief dramatic incident. My daughter persuaded me to be her soccer coach. I bought a guide to the game.

When you write your introduction, include the approved thesis statement and subtopics at the end of paragraph 1.

Paragraph 2: Transition + topic sentence: The first experience was handling fifteen unique personalities.

(level 2)

supporting details

(3) One girl wanted to be a goalie.
(4) how I dealt with her
(3) Others behaved like juveniles.
(4) refusal to participate
(4) giggling
(3) One girl suffered from star syndrome.
(4) difficulty in convincing her about team playing

Paragraph 3: Transition + topic sentence: another experience involved the team parents.

(level 2)

supporting details

(3) Some fathers were too helpful.
(4) coaching from the sidelines
(4) yelling at the referee
(4) too demanding of daughters—female Pelé's
(3) Other fathers were perplexed by a woman coaching.
(4) snide remarks
(4) change of attitude with championship team
(3) Some parents never attended the games.
(4) daughters indifferent and casual

Paragraph 4: Transition + topic sentence: Finally, my coaching caused some unforeseen dilemmas.

(level 2)

supporting details

(3) Problems of overconfidence developed among the girls.
(4) didn't want to learn new skills
(4) continually challenged referee
(4) arrived late to games
(3) Lecture about after-game etiquette was necessary.
(4) shaking opponents' hands

Paragraph 5: Conclusion (three sentences):

(level 1)

Choose one of the good endings from the list in Chapter 1.

Good ending # 7: Offer final evaluation of subject matter. Feeling of accomplishment in winning and teaching the game; willingness to coach again.

WRITING—THE CONSTRUCTING STAGE

During this stage you will develop your outline into paragraphs. A good place to begin is with the body of the essay because that is the substance of the paper. Even though you are working from an outline, you may make alterations by adding or deleting material. In any event, it is important to construct your ideas with details that are vivid and concrete.

The next step involves writing the introductory material. Although the title and introduction are read first, you write them after the body paragraphs. That way you are sure of the material you are presenting to the audience. The last step in the writing stage is the concluding paragraph.

Step 5: Develop the Body Paragraphs

Indent the beginning of each new paragraph.

Recopy the topic sentences from the worksheet, and then develop each body paragraph with concrete supporting material, anecdotes, examples, facts, and details.

Use transitional expressions to make the ideas move smoothly. Refer to the list of transitional expressions for words that are appropriate to the context of the paragraphs.

Note that the outline is only a framework and a plan which must be developed and enlarged and even changed as you write.

BODY PARAGRAPHS—Analyzed for Structure

Topic Sentence (Level 2)

Although I knew I would teach the technical skills of soccer, the first experience I confronted was handling fifteen unique personalities.

Transitional expression + Reference to Thesis Statement + Subtopic 1

Supporting details (Level 3, 4)

One little darling spent all her energy annoying everyone by wanting to be the goalie. Insisting on playing the sport by her own rules was the method she chose to gain my attention. I allotted extra time for her and soon discovered she came from a broken home. I eventually decided the best way to deal with the frustrated child was to be a friend rather than an antagonist. Other cherubs displayed behavior indicative of over-indulged juveniles. They vehemently refused to participate in any exercises they judged too difficult or unnecessary. While half of the team warmed up with dribbling exercises and jumping jacks, this group giggled and reclined on the ground. I toiled at gaining their respect and diligently stressed the necessity of working together as a unit. In my new avocation as amateur therapist, I quickly learned that no team was complete without at least one individual who suffered from the star syndrome. It was not an easy task convincing one egomaniac that she could not win the game all by herself. Instead, she had to learn what playing on a team meant. That confrontation took three weeks to settle. Finally, I had a team of fifteen skilled players.

Topic Sentence (Level 2)

Transitional expression + Reference to Thesis Statement + Subtopic 2

Another experience with coaching involved dealing with team parents. Some of the fathers were too helpful. Even though they did not know the difference between a left wing and a center fullback, they felt qualified to coach from the sidelines. Trying to deter their inclination to yell at the referee for a bad call was as impossible as threading a needle on roller skates. They were most demanding of their own daughters, perhaps secretly hoping for a female Pelé. This hostile concentration usually reduced the girls to sobs. Other dads found it perplexing that a woman could

Supporting details (Level 3,4)

penetrate the predominantly male world of coaching. I eventually became immune to the snide remarks filtering through from the sideline spectators. Only when it became apparent that I had the championship team did my abilities receive recognition. Suddenly, my male adversaries were enthusiastic and helpful. On the other hand, a few parents never found the time to attend any of the games. The disappointment their daughters felt was reflected in the indifferent and casual manner in which they played the game.

Topic Sentence [Level 2]

Finally, even though I took pride in winning, my coaching caused some unforeseen dilemmas. Once the girls realized that they had clinched the championship, overconfidence plagued every one of them. Learning the game and developing new skills were the values I continually stressed, but somehow the girls chose to relegate these ideals to secondary position. They considered their expertise in soccer to be unequalled by the end of the season, and they continually challenged the referees. This attitude also revealed itself in the way they would arrive only ten minutes before the starting kick. It was even necessary to lecture them about the aftergame etiquette. Eventually, they did shake their opponents' hands graciously after a game.

Transitional expression + Reference to Thesis Statement + Subtopic 3

Supporting details [Level 3,4]

Step 6: Write the Title and Introductory Paragraph

Title

The title is usually a fragment. It has two functions: to identify the subject and to capture the reader's attention and create interest.

Center the title on the paper. If it is comprised of your own words, do not underline or put it in quotes.

Capitalize the first letter of the first word and the first letter of all important words.

Skip three lines after the title before you begin your first paragraph.

Introduction

Develop at least five sentences, and be sure to indent the first sentence. Select a good beginning from the list in Chapter 1. Capture your reader's attention so that he or she will want to read further. Create an interest in your subject by stressing its interesting or pleasurable aspects. Provide at least three sentences of background information leading up to your thesis statement. The thesis statement and enumeration of subtopics are the most important part of the introduction. Although they may appear at any point, they usually come at the end of the introductory paragraph. Do not develop your ideas in this paragraph but only identify them for later development.

TITLE AND INTRODUCTORY PARAGRAPH—Analyzed for Parts

Title — An Unexpected Bonus

Good Beginning #1

Background Information

Thesis Statement + Subtopic Sentence

Last year my daughter prevailed upon me, her inexperienced mother, to coach her soccer team. Frantically I purchased a comprehensive guide that illustrated in elaborate detail the basic skills of the game. I did not realize I would be gaining so much more than just the basic knowledge of the sport.

Coaching provided me with several valuable experiences. Three of these which gave me new insights were dealing with different types of girls, parents, and problems.

Step 7: Write the Concluding Paragraph

Develop at least three sentences, and indent the first sentence. If you use a transitional expression to begin the paragraph (and this is optional), choose a transitional expression from the Conclusion/Result and Summary list of transitional expressions. Select a good ending from the list in Chapter 1. Leave the reader with an overview of the subject and its complexities. Stress the value, purpose, or importance of the subject. Do not introduce any new information.

CONCLUDING PARAGRAPH—Analyzed for Structure

Transitional Expression

Despite the fact that coaching soccer was more complex than I had originally anticipated, I finished the season with more than just a team picture and a trophy. The feeling of accomplishment not only in winning but also in teaching will last me for soccer seasons to come. Next time my daughter will not have to plead so much with me to coach.

Good Ending #7

At this point, the student essay "An Unexpected Bonus" has illustrated the stages of prewriting and writing. Because this essay has already been revised and corrected, the last stage of rewriting will be discussed in detail later in the chapter where a first draft and rewritten essay are included. If you are instructed to write an essay at the end of this chapter, you may refer to the "Suggested Ideas" for the paragraph assignment in Chapter 4.

Organizational Pattern for the Five Paragraph Essay

Study this blueprint so that you can see and better understand the elements necessary for the expository essay. Then use the pattern as a guide in assembling your own essay. Note that all the student samples in the chapter use this organizational pattern.

Title

Introduction—paragraph 1

At least five sentences

Use of one of the good beginnings

Establishment of order of subtopics
point of view
verb tense
tone and diction

Thesis statement = subject + verb + controlling idea

number + adjective + noun

may be 1 or 2 sentences

Subtopic sentence = enumeration of three major subtopics

Body—paragraphs 2, 3, and 4

Presentation of three major subtopics

Logical order of three major subtopics

____ general to particular

____ time/chronological

____ climactic

**Paragraph 2:* Topic sentence = transitional expression + reference to thesis statement + subtopic 1

Sufficient development of subject with supporting details such as specific examples, facts, illustrations, anecdotes

**Paragraph 3:* Topic sentence = transitional expression + reference to thesis statement + subtopic 2

Sufficient development of subject with supporting details such as specific examples, facts, illustrations, anecdotes

**Paragraph 4:* Topic sentence = transitional expression + reference to thesis statement + subtopic 3

Sufficient development of subject with supporting details such as specific examples, facts, illustrations, anecdotes

Transitional expressions: see especially

Addition
Emphasis/Intensification
Introduction of Illustration/Example
Cause
Purpose
Time/Chronology

Conclusion—paragraph 5

At least three sentences

Transitional expression (optional): see Conclusion/Result and Summary

Use of one of the good endings

*These elements may be rearranged within the sentence.

STUDENT SAMPLE—Five Paragraph Essay—Analyzed for Parts

Observe that elements of structure and content are labeled on the left while elements of style are identified on the right. This detailed analysis will help you plan your own essay.

Title

An Unexpected Bonus

Introduction ¶ 1 — Good beginning #1

Last year my daughter prevailed upon me, her inexperienced mother, to coach her soccer team. Frantically I purchased a comprehensive guide which illustrated in elaborate detail the basic skills of the game. I did not realize I would be gaining so much more than just the basic knowledge of the sport. Coaching provided me with several valuable experiences. Three of these which gave me new insights were dealing with different types of [1] girls, [2] parents, and [3] problems.

Point of view: first person

Verb tense: past

Thesis Statement — Coaching provided me with several valuable experiences.

Subtopic Sentence — Three of these which gave me new insights were dealing with different types of girls, parents, and problems.

Topic Sentence ¶ 2

Body ¶ 2, 3, 4

Although I knew I would teach the technical skills of soccer, the (first)* experience I confronted was handling fifteen unique personalities. One little darling spent all her energy annoying everyone by wanting to be the goalie. Insisting on playing the sport by her own rules was the method she chose to gain my attention. I allotted extra time for her and soon discovered she came from a broken home. I eventually decided the best way to deal with the frustrated child was to be a friend rather than an antagonist. Other cherubs

Diction: connotative — One little darling

Sentence structure: introductory verbal phrase — Insisting on playing the sport by her own rules

*Coherence: transitional expressions circled.

displayed behavior indicative of over-indulged juveniles. They vehemently refused to participate in any exercises they judged too difficult or unnecessary. While half of the team warmed up with dribbling exercises and jumping jacks, this group giggled and reclined on the ground. I toiled at gaining their respect and diligently stressed the necessity of working together as a unit. In my new avocation as amateur therapist, I quickly learned that no team was complete without at least one individual who suffered from the star syndrome. It was not an easy task convincing one egomaniac that she could not win the game all by herself. Instead, she had to learn what playing on a team meant. That confrontation took three weeks to settle. Finally, I had a team of fifteen skilled players.

Diction: concrete

Diction: slanted

Diction: figurative (metaphor)

Topic Sentence ¶ 3

Another experience with coaching involved dealing with the team parents. Some of the fathers were too helpful. Even though they did not know the difference between a left wing and a center fullback, they felt qualified to coach from the sidelines. Trying to deter their inclination to yell at the referee for a bad call was as impossible as threading a needle on roller skates. They were most demanding of their own daughters, perhaps secretly hoping

Sentence Structure: Introductory dependent clause

Diction: figurative (simile)

for a female Pelé. This hostile confrontation usually reduced the girls to sobs. Other dads found it perplexing that a woman could penetrate the predominantly male world of coaching. I eventually became immune to the snide remarks filtering through from the sideline spectators. Only when it became apparent that I had the championship team did my abilities receive recognition. Suddenly, my male adversaries were enthusiastic and helpful. On the other hand, a few parents never found the time to attend any of the games. The disappointment their daughters felt was reflected in the indifferent and casual manner in which they played the game.

Diction: figurative (allusion)

Diction: alliterative (s)

Sentence Structure: noun clause

Topic Sentence A4

Finally, even though I took pride in winning, my coaching caused some unforeseen dilemmas. Once the girls realized that they had clinched the championship, overconfidence plagued every one of them. Learning the game and developing new skills were the values I continually stressed, but somehow the girls chose to relegate these ideals to secondary position. They considered their expertise in soccer to be unequalled by the end of the season, and they continually challenged the referees. This attitude also revealed itself in the way they would arrive only ten minutes

Diction: concrete

before the starting kick. It was even necessary to lecture them about the after-game etiquette. Eventually, they did shake their opponents' hands graciously after a game.

Conclusion ¶ 5 *Good ending #7*

Despite the fact that coaching soccer was more complex than I had originally anticipated, I finished the season with more than just a team picture and a trophy. The feeling of accomplishment not only in winning but also in teaching will last me for soccer seasons to come. Next time my daughter will not have to plead so much with me to coach.

A Sentence Structure: parallelism

Note how this essay avoids excessive repetition by using synonyms for key terms. This technique increases the paper's coherence.

Coherence: repeated terms for

girls	**parents**
little darling	fathers
child	dads
cherubs	male adversaries
players	
egomaniac	

STUDENT SAMPLE—Five Paragraph Essay

Source of material: textbook on American history

Coming to America

Imagine sailing on a small, crude ship to an unknown destination, with only a compass made up of a magnetized needle floating in water to guide the ship. Perhaps there are aboard one or two hundred other passengers brave enough to venture forth into the unknown. All of the early immigrants to our country dealt with this plight. In spite of this situation, the Englishmen came to America in the 1600s for three main reasons. These reasons were to escape the economic strife, social problems, and religious persecution in England.

The first reason the immigrants were motivated to come to America was England's changing economy. The population of England grew steadily, but the food supply did not increase proportionately. Agricultural land was taken over by grazing sheep. This condition severely limited the food supply, thus driving the price of food up. Raising sheep and manufacturing wool for cloth were the primary types of employment. But with England's rising population there just were not enough jobs to go around. Beggars roamed the countryside looking for food or work. England, it seemed, contained either too many people or too many sheep.

Another reason Englishmen migrated to the new world was to escape from England's social class structure. This structure consisted of four classes. The first class, nobility, was just a step below the king. The nobles owned large estates and could sit in Parliament's House of Lords. The gentry, which was the next class, also owned large pieces of land and could become members of the House of Commons, thereby providing a check and balance system. Being landowners they could vote and hold office. Many of the gentry were justices of the peace or sheriffs; consequently, they possessed political power. The next two lower classes were the yeomanry and the peasantry. The yeomanry owned acres of land and small shops; although they could vote, they could not hold office. The peasants were very poor and did not own land or vote. The yeomen and peasants migrated to America for promised acreage and equal opportunity.

The most important reason for migration to America was to escape religious persecution. The official church of England, the Anglican Church, was influenced by the Catholic religion. Anglicans still honored saints' days, had a cross as a symbol of their beliefs, and knelt at the altar. All subjects were forbidden by law to be absent from Anglican services or to hold unauthorized religious meetings. The Puritans thus wanted to reform or purify the church by abolishing these practices, but they were persecuted by Queen Elizabeth. As a result, the Separatists wanted to establish their own church without any outside influences imposed on their religion. To accomplish these goals, nonconformists looked for refuge outside the kingdom.

These, then, were the main reasons the Englishmen came to America. In America the immigrants were free from the economic strife in England and established a new and steadily growing economy in their new country. They had also escaped the confinements of the social structure and religious persecution in England; the immigrants had found a new home in America.

Discovery Exercise

1. Identify the thesis statement

   a. the subject being discussed: ____________________

   b. the controlling idea: ____________________

2. Identify the three major subtopics: ____________________

   ____

   ____

3. Identify all orders of the subtopics:

    ____ general to particular ____ climactic

    ____ time/chronological

4. Identify the point of view: __________ person
5. Identify the verb tense: ____________________
6. Circle **ten** transitional expressions.
7. Select **ten** words and phrases that illustrate the diction:

    ______________________ ______________________

    ______________________ ______________________

    ______________________ ______________________

    ______________________ ______________________

    ______________________ ______________________

8. Choose terms from the diction chart that characterize the diction:

    ____

9. Choose terms from the tone chart that describe the tone: ____________________

    ____

10. After reviewing Chapter 16, bracket **five** compound verbs, one type of grammatical structure used in the essay.

STUDENT SAMPLE—Five Paragraph Essay

Source of material: personal experience

The Way the Leader Crumbles

With my daughter's seventh birthday came the culmination of a longstanding promise: I would become her Brownie troop leader. Only weeks into the troop year I discovered that it was cookie time. While visions of dozens of unsold thin mints filled my dreams, I attended cookie workshops on how to successfully fill out forms, recruit help, and juggle boxes. Armed with naive enthusiasm, I presented the cookie pep talk to my girls and proceeded to outline the three basic stages of the activity. First, I would need volunteers; second, I had to explain the financial aspects; and then, third, we could go out and sell.

The first order of business was filling all of the job positions with parent volunteers. Each scout took home a flyer with a job roster on it to be returned at the next meeting. Then I could coordinate the parents into an army of cookie salespeople. An hour after the girls went home, the first mommie called. "I would really like to help," she said, "but our dog is expecting puppies any minute, and I couldn't possibly leave her." Within two hours all the moms or dads had called with their regrets. They all remembered selling cookies as children and said it was such fun. But, of course, next year they would be glad to help. That evening the first wave of panic came over me as I counted out the colorful cookie brochures for each girl.

The second stage of the fund-raising activity was to discuss the business aspects. At our next meeting, I gave my Brownies a pep talk on money. I had to explain to the eager little entrepreneurs what percentage of the sale of the cookies belonged to the troop. At that point, Ingrid jumped up. "You mean we don't get to keep all the money ourselves?" she squeaked. Because each girl's visions of buying Christmas presents with her cookie money had crystalized in her head, I found it difficult to convince them that we would keep only 25 cents of each two dollars. As a selling incentive to the girls, we discussed what to do with the profits. After much consideration of the merits of Magic Mountain versus Farrell's, I suggested going to Catalina, something few of the girls might ever have a chance to do. Because I successfully swayed the vote, the trip to Catalina won out, and they were ready to sell.

Finally, cookie-selling day dawned cloudy and moist. My VW bus was filled with girls, card tables, jugs of punch, and cartons of cookies. Away we went to a prearranged market entrance. Getting set up became the worst part of the day. The girls who brought money were in the store buying snacks to get through the day. The girls without money tearfully asked to open the boxes of vanilla creams and chocolate chips so they wouldn't starve. Half the troop went to the bathroom every fifteen minutes. The most popular activity of the day was deciphering the graffiti on the bathroom walls. Customers who didn't want to buy were followed through the market until they produced the money whether they took the cookies or not.

I was gratified to find that I had actually lived through cookie-selling day but vowed never to work alone again. We all learned valuable lessons about free enterprise and working together as a team rather than as individuals out for themselves. Now, whenever I see Brownies selling cookies, I'm the first to buy a box.

Discovery Exercise

1. Identify the thesis statement

   a. the subject being discussed: ____________________

   b. the controlling idea: ____________________

2. Identify the three major subtopics: ____________________

   ____

   ____

3. Identify all orders of the subtopics:

   ____ general to particular　　____ climactic

   ____ time/chronological

4. Identify the point of view: __________ person

5. Identify the verb tense: __________

6. Circle **ten** transitional expressions.

7. Select **ten** words and phrases that illustrate the diction:

8. Choose terms from the diction chart that characterize the diction:

9. Choose terms from the tone chart that describe the tone:

10. After reviewing Chapter 16, bracket **five** dependent clauses, one type of grammatical structure used in the essay.

STUDENT SAMPLE—Five Paragraph Essay

Source of material: textbook on design and color

How Color Affects Our Lives

A struggling sixteen-year-old boy, high on the drug PCP, is escorted by four policemen into an 8 by 4 foot concrete room with walls of bright, eye-shocking pink. At first the drugged youngster pounds the walls violently, but six minutes later he is sitting calmly. In another nine minutes he is lying on the floor almost asleep. This wild teenager has been calmed by the color pink. We are discovering that certain colors have a profound influence on our thoughts and behavior. Indeed, color affects our lives in several different ways: to persuade, to arouse, and to calm us.

One way that color affects us is through the persuasion of advertisements. Businesses have spent millions of dollars on research to discover which colors and patterns will prompt people to buy their products. The consumer will only quickly glance at a package; in that time the item must arrest the eye and convey a positive feeling. Red and yellow have that effect; they also make the package appear larger than it really is. For example, many cigarettes and soft drink makers wrap their products in red; it conjures up images of power and vitality. Yellow is associated by most people with achievement and the future. It is no accident that so many boxes on the shelves in our supermarkets are red and yellow. Manufacturers and advertisers know that the product that is well "wrapped"--properly colored and designed--will, in a sense, sell itself.

Also, colors have the ability to arouse emotions in us. The right blend of colors and shapes can act as a key in unlocking automatic impulses in our minds. For example, we can be prompted to feel patriotic when we see the colors red, white, and blue. We associate black with feelings of sadness and loss, red with danger, green with envy. The widespread use of lipstick and blush by women since the time of the Pharaohs has probably served as a trigger to arouse emotions in men. In our homes we surround ourselves with those colors that make us feel most comfortable and happy.

Not only do colors persuade and arouse us, but they also calm us. As shown by the drugged boy in the pink cell, colors do induce direct biological changes in people. In numerous tests where violent prisoners were put in pink cells, the results proved that bright, eye-shocking pink can replace aggressive impulses with passivity. Even brief exposure to the color pink can cause weakening of the body's muscles that lasts for about thirty minutes. In addition, pink detention cells have the same tranquilizing effects on color-blind prisoners who are unable to "see" pink. One researcher says the pink rooms seem to induce long-term changes in those individuals exposed to them.

The facts seem to indicate that people can be influenced by exposure to colors. Most people, however, are not conscious of the relationship between color and behavior. Nevertheless, colors have a significant effect on our bodies and moods and can persuade, arouse, and calm us.

REWRITING—THE POLISHING STAGE

Rewriting refers to polishing an essay at two different times: before the paper is submitted for an initial grade and when and if the instructor permits a revision for a second evaluation. In either case, the checklists included for structure and ideas (step 8) and for mechanics and usage (step 9) will guide your revisions. Generally, the polishing of content precedes the correcting of mechanics.

The instructor may permit you to rewrite after the essay has been graded a first time. Then use the individual scores on the cover sheet as a guide to improving the content and presentation. To revise the mechanics and usage errors, check the correction symbol sheet and refer to Chapter 16 for specific information. Use a thesaurus to eliminate unnecessary repetition and a dictionary to correct spelling. One specific suggestion to find spelling errors is to read your paper backwards. In this way you will see words as words rather than as parts of a thought.

Step 8: Revise for Structure, Ideas, Logic, and Style

Introduction

—attention-getting title
—five sentences
—one of the good beginnings used
—thesis statement with controlling idea
—three subtopics enumerated

Body

—topic sentences with transition + reference to thesis + subtopics 1, 2, 3
—paragraphs developed

sufficient and complete	well-chosen	appropriate
specific details	concrete	precise

Conclusion

—three sentences
—one of the good endings used

Essay

—ideas in logical order
—reasoning correct
—style effective
diction appropriate
tone consistent
sentence structure varied
coherent transitional expressions

Step 9: Revise and Correct Mechanics and Usage

Usage

Check for fragments
modifier mistakes
faulty pronoun reference
faulty agreement
shifts
faulty parallelism
awkward phrasing
colloquialisms, clichés, slang

Mechanics

Check for errors in punctuation
capitalization
spelling

Name: ______
Date: ______ Class: ______

Type of Exposition: ______

Strength of 1st personal draft is concrete details. Rewrite to focus on specific experiences.

EXPOSITORY ESSAY COVER SHEET		
Structure/Ideas	+	76
Usage/Mechanics	−	23
Total		53
Rewrite points	+	41
TOTAL		94

Structure and Ideas (100 points)		Original		Rewrite
INTRODUCTION (at least five sentences):				
title; one of good beginnings leading to thesis	10	7		3
thesis statement + enumeration of subtopics	5	3		2
BODY (three supporting paragraphs):				
three topic sentences = transition + reference to thesis + subtopic	15	13		2
development of paragraphs: sufficient, concrete, appropriate, relevant	45	35		8
CONCLUSION (at least three sentences):				
one of good endings	5	4		1
ESSAY: (underdeveloped contrast)				
logical order of ideas and correct reasoning	5	4		1
effective style = tone + diction + sentence structure + coherence	15	10		3
Total	100	76	+	20

The points in this section reflect your score for structure and ideas. If you have received fewer than 100 points, you may rewrite your paper to earn them. Use the numbers as a guide to areas needing revision.

Usage and Mechanics (minus points). See Correction Symbol Chart.				
You **may** earn these points in revision:				
Usage: adj; adv; agr; awk; col; dm; frag; mm; ref; rep; shift; verb; ww; / /; ¶	−3 ea.	21		+ 21
You **may not** earn these points in revision, but you must correct the errors:				
Mechanics: abbr; apos; cap; lc; p; ro; sp; ∧	−1 ea.	2		
Total	−	23	+	21

STUDENT SAMPLE—Five Paragraph Essay

To help you in the revision process, a marked student essay and rewritten copy are preceded by a cover sheet that has been scored. By reading the first draft and noting the scores and comments in the first column of the cover sheet, you should observe the essay's strengths and weaknesses. Then turn to the rewritten copy and note how the student has revised the essay along the suggested lines.

First draft to be graded
Source of material: personal experience

A Trip Abroad

For three months in 1970, I lived 6,000 miles away from home. My mother migrated to the United States from Austria, a wee country situated in the heart of Bavaria. Wanderlust seized me when I acquainted myself with my maternal heritage, and I arrived at my grandmother's house in early spring, fresh and ready for exploration of another mode of living. Throughout my stay, I noted three major differences between United States and European culture. Relationships between adults and children, religious beliefs, and history of the country are the well-marked dissimilarities.

In Europe, there is a vast difference in role perception of young people in society. At this time, for example, I was aged twelve and had long since been doing as I pleased at home in Los Angeles. Not knowing the difference between my role here and mine at home, I made a mistake. One day, I strolled into a large Austrian department store and began handling merchandise freely. A harassed, red-faced saleswoman spyed my audacious actions, commenced a ferocious scolding in German, and rapped my impertinent hands. I acquired knowledge the difficult way. Another time, as I walked the crawling boulevards of Salzburg, a sour housewife administered an impatient jostling and the pointed tip of an umbrella to my person, for no apparent reason. Obviously youth did not command the respect and adoration of European adults, as it does in the United States. Tradition grips concretely, and the orientation towards youthfulness never acquired a foothold.

Religion is another obvious diversity. Catholicism, naturally, is the predominant belief in Western Europe. I found unaccustomed fascination in traditions which managed survival through hundreds of years. Rituals are constantly performed such as baptism, communion, mass, confession, and other ceremonies which occur less frequently. The United States also follows these traditions, but other religions are of equal importance. Here there is no prevalent belief. As many protestants as Catholics live here, and others such as the Jewish and Eastern religions are noteworthy. Also tremendous care is shown to religious facilities. Artists and sculptors arrived in droves to do ornamentation of cathedrals. During the Middle Ages, church ruled state. Control of lands and peoples belonged to the pope and his advisors, through methods of force and brutality, myths and fear of God. Appropriations of tax money and donations led to the intricately detailed construction of these cathedrals. By careful examination, I noted the complexity of the art work. Angels' wings, shaped into a creation of feathery lightness. The real-life droop of flowers on the walls. The precision cutting and tinting of stained glass windows, most dramatic with the last rays of sunshine spilling through. All of this history yields a strong bond connecting central Europeans to Catholicism.

Lastly, yet scarcely least, is the history of Austria. Almost all central European countries were being settled soon after Rome's fall. This dates over one thousand years of history. Museums, churches, palaces, government buildings, fortresses, prisons, all were built years ago. History, not written in pages of a book, but on downtown street corners, in crowded market platzes, on the unpaved backways to grandmother's farmhouse, and throughout the continent. For instance, it is possible to shop in an 800 year old market platz in Salzburg. It also is possible to tour a stone fortress, built when men rode the crusades. Homemakers purchase food supplies in a wide open market platz, which carries anything from eggs collected early that bleak, chillingly damp morning, to juicy, luscious, red-ripe strawberries picked yesterday in the warm rays of sprng sunshine, clear and bright. It will not happen here, because this is the land of vast supermarkets, reputed to service one speedily and conveniently. However, one suffers having less tasteful food.

When I arrived home in Los Angeles, I easily returned to my old way of life. However, I did not forget the loss of role status, the amazement at lavishly adorned cathedrals, or my grandmother's tenacity that I learn my heritage. They are branded on my brain and leave me with a sense of camaraderie and national unity through an understanding of one's heritage.

STUDENT SAMPLE—Five Paragraph Essay—Rewritten Copy

The Land of the Strauss Waltzes

Six thousand miles is a long way from home. My mother migrated this distance from her home, Austria, coming as a war bride to the United States. Wanderlust seized me at twelve years of age when I discovered my maternal heritage and arrived at my grandmother's Austrian farm in March 1970. While there, I had many new cultural experiences. Learning the role of children, seeing the lavish religious ornamentation, and realizing a sense of history were the three most memorable.

First, I discovered that the child in Austrian society plays an insignificant role and is not permitted much freedom. In Salzburg, I once strolled into a fair-sized department store and handled the brightly colored scarves freely. A bull-like, harassed saleswoman spied my bold actions and immediately began a ferocious scolding, all the while rapping my impertinent hands. I acquired knowledge during that frightening moment. Another time, while I was wandering the crawling city boulevards, a sour housewife administered an impatient jostling and the pointed tip of an umbrella to my person, for no apparent reason. I certainly realized that as a child I was not important.

Second, during my stay, I visited Austrian cathedrals and was impressed by their costly decorations. For instance, I saw a seventeenth-century Renaissance cathedral and was awestruck by the gold, silver, and brass statues, by the diamonds, rubies, emeralds, and amethysts inlaid in panel work and tapestries. The church itself was huge. Towering marble columns lined the entire structure. Polished cement walkways extended through massive arched doorways to a garden, a scaled-down version of Paradise. These doorways were surrounded by shimmering, colorful lights coming from thirty large stained glass windows. All this wealth and beauty amazed me.

My most memorable experience was developing a feeling for the past. Austria's history began after Rome's fall. Museums, churches, palaces, government buildings, fortresses, and prisons were all built during the Middle Ages. This was history, not written in books, but on downtown street corners, in crowded market *platzes*, and on the unpaved backways to grandmother's farmhouse. For instance, it was possible to shop in an 800-year-old market *platz*. It was possible to tour a stone fortress, built when men rode to the Crusades. Wherever I went, I saw markers on houses and buildings commemorating particular historical events. The birthplace of the famous composer Mozart was clearly identified. The trip gave me an opportunity to experience European history first-hand rather than from my school textbook.

When I arrived home, I easily returned to my old way of life. However, I did not forget the loss of role-status, the amazement at lavishly adorned cathedrals, or the chance to learn about my heritage. These experiences made me realize that my background was a much richer and larger one than I had known about before.

Discovery Exercise for Evaluating an Essay

Read the student essay "Who Am I?" on the pages following these directions to prepare for evaluating it objectively. Weigh each of the areas identified on the expository essay cover sheet. Then you will begin to understand how your paper is scored. You will also be able to recognize your weak and strong areas. You should have an easier time evaluating other types of writing, especially nonfiction prose.

After you have read the paper and marked the errors, respond to each of the following sections on structure and ideas by entering a score on the expository essay cover sheet in the appropriate category.

Introduction: worth 15 points

Deduct	3 points	if the title is missing.
	2	for each sentence fewer than 5.
	2	if the thesis statement lacks a controlling idea.
	1	for each subtopic that is not named.

Body: worth 60 points

Deduct	5 points	for each missing topic sentence.
	1	for each missing transition in the topic sentence.
	1	for each missing reference to the thesis in the topic sentence.
	3	for each missing subtopic in the topic sentence.

Each body paragraph is worth 15 points. Deduct up to that number for each paragraph that lacks sufficient, concrete, appropriate, relevant illustrations, details, and explanations.

Conclusion: worth 5 points

Deduct	2 points	for each sentence fewer than 3.
	2	if a new topic is introduced.

Essay: worth 20 points

Deduct	5 points	if the three subtopics are out of logical order.
	2	for each of the following errors in reasoning: straying from the topic; using irrelevant supporting material; oversimplifying material; stating the obvious; overgeneralizing.
	3	for lack of variety in scntence structure.
	3	for limited diction and unnecessary repetition of words.
	2	for change of tone: for example, injecting sarcasm into an objective essay.
	5	for failure to include transitional expressions between words, phrases, sentences.

After you have entered the score for each individual category under Structure and Ideas, add the points and transfer the score to the top line in the box on the top left-hand side of the cover sheet.

Now read the paper again, this time for usage and mechanics. Identify each usage error in the essay, using the symbols listed on the cover sheet. (For a fuller discussion of these, refer to Chapter 16.) Multiply the total number of usage errors by 3, and enter the minus score on the top line in the bottom box.

Identify each mechanical error, using the symbols listed on the cover sheet. Each error counts as −1 point. Enter the minus score on the next line in the bottom box.

Add the minus points and transfer the total to the second line in the box on the top left-hand side of the cover sheet.

Subtract the Usage/Mechanics points from the Structure/Ideas points. The total is the grade earned for the first draft.

Discovery Exercise Student Sample

Who Am I?

There are many qualities about myself which I have realized. It seems I have many multi-characteristics. Observing my daily routine life, there is a child, an adolescent, and an adult who resides within myself. Wanting to be a different person in different situations, I find myself acting out all of these different roles. I assume everyone could bring out the child-like and adult-like qualities about themselves.

One of the quality about myself is I could bring out the child in me. Sometimes I find myself wanting to express my child ambition. Just the other day it was raining like cats and dogs. Feeling weirdly, I wanted to go out side and be soaked by the rain. Putting on a over-coat, jumping frantically like an excited child I dashed outside to greet the rain. Having my shoes in the puddle, I giggled like a child who had no worries.

After being soaked, I started wondering if I was crazy being out there. But I realized it is just the child in me which made me behave so oddly.

There is another quality about myself which is being an irresponsible adolescent. Eventhough I am twenty-one years old, a legal adult, I find myself being irresponsible at certain times. To illustrate my irresponsibility, I must tell you this story. I was in an auto accident recently. I had to go and claim the accident. My mother had made an appointment for me to meet an insurance agent at a certain date. Although I knew I had to be at the insurance company that day, I bluntly decided to play golf with couple of friends of mine. After playing golf, I cam home to find out that my mother was furious. She could not comprehend my action, asked my why I acted this way. My reply was blank. I could not think of an answer. Even I started wondering about my irresponsiveness. Sometimes I wonder why I act like an adolescent but I guess I'm not a fully mature adult at times.

Finally, my best quality is revealed when I act according to a mature adult. Couple of days ago, my sister ran in to the house replying her car was stolen. I reacted calm and collectively. My parents were at work and I did not want to burden them, so I decided to take action by myself. First I told my sister to get a grip on her-self. She was in tears and shaking like a leaf. I quickly called the police station and found out that the car was not stolen but had to be towed away. I told her this fact and she glistened with joy. I gave her a ride to pick up her car and paid the fine. She thanked me with her life and was amazed with how I dealt this situation. It really made me feel as a capable adult.

In conclusion, my multi-characteristics are various and sometimes odd, but I enjoy finding out these qualities about myself. I think we all possess these certain personalities. We all should be able to apply these qualities fully to enjoy our lives.

Discovery Exercise Cover Sheet

EXPOSITORY ESSAY COVER SHEET		
Structure/Ideas		+ ______
Usage/Mechanics		− ______
	Total	______
Rewrite points		+ ______
	TOTAL	______

Structure and Ideas (100 points)		**Original**
INTRODUCTION (at least five sentences):		
title; one of good beginnings leading to thesis	10	______
thesis statement + enumeration of subtopics	5	______
BODY (three supporting paragraphs):		
three topic sentences = transition + reference to thesis + subtopic	15	______
development of paragraphs: sufficient, concrete, appropriate, relevant	45	______
CONCLUSION (at least three sentences):		
one of good endings	5	______
ESSAY:		
logical order of ideas and correct reasoning	5	______
effective style = tone + diction + sentence structure + coherence	15	______
Total	100	

The points in this section reflect your score for structure and ideas. If you have received fewer than 100 points, you may rewrite your paper to earn them. Use the numbers as a guide to areas needing revision.

Usage and Mechanics (minus points). See Correction Symbol Chart.		
You **may** earn these points in revision:		
Usage: adj; adv; agr; awk; col; dm; frag; mm; ref; rep; shift; verb; ww; / /; ¶	−3 ea.	______
You **may not** earn these points in revision, but you must correct the errors:		
Mechanics: abbr; apos; cap; lc; p; ro; sp; ∧	−1 ea.	______
Total	−	______

Peer Evaluation of Essays

Students read and comment on each other's papers before they are submitted to the instructor for a grade. This exercise makes you aware of the fact that you are writing for a real audience who must be able to follow the development of your ideas. In addition, you have the opportunity to receive comments about your writing from someone other than your instructor. A description of how the peer session is conducted is followed by a checklist of items to guide your critical comments.

One way of evaluating writing involves students helping each other in a classroom setting. Students break into small groups and distribute duplicated copies of their papers to all members of the group. The essay that is to be evaluated should be in as finished form as possible.

Students take turns reading their papers aloud while classmates correct their copies and make comments, both written and vocal. These comments are helpful only if they are impersonal and deal with the essay's strengths and weaknesses. Saying that a paper is "nice" or "interesting" is not helpful. Simply marking comma errors or misspelled words is also not useful. Honest comments should not hurt students' feelings but should aid in improving the writing.

A specific portion of time should be designated to the evaluation of each student's paper. In this way, all students will have an opportunity to have their papers read and evaluated.

During the evaluation, students should use the checklist that follows as a guide in reading and commenting on each other's papers. Another list of criteria that students can consult is the chart on Standards for English Essays in Chapter 1. At the end of the class, students return the marked copies of the essays to the original writers. After the peer evaluation, students rewrite their essays and incorporate the corrections, comments, and suggestions which they accept. The finished, edited essays are then submitted for grading.

Peer Evaluation Checklist

STRUCTURE AND IDEAS

Introduction

—attention-getting title
—five sentences
—one of the good beginnings
—thesis statement with controlling idea
—three subtopics enumerated

Body

—topic sentences with transition + reference to thesis + subtopics 1, 2, 3
—paragraphs developed

sufficient and complete	well-chosen	appropriate
specific details	concrete	precise

Conclusion

—three sentences
—one of the good endings

Essay

—ideas in logical order
—reasoning correct
—style effective
diction appropriate
tone consistent
sentence structure varied
coherent transitional expressions

USAGE AND MECHANICS (Mark these errors on your copy of the essay.)

—fragments, awkward phrasing
—clichés, slang
—shift in person, tense
—faulty agreement
—faulty reference of pronouns
—faulty parallelism
—dangling modifiers
—faulty punctuation and run-ons
—misspelled words
—faulty capitalization

Suggested Ideas to Explain in an Essay

Unless your instructor assigns a specific topic, refer to page 67 for ideas to develop.

WORKSHEET FOR FIVE-PARAGRAPH ESSAY

1. Select a subject to discuss and complete the top half of the worksheet.
2. Write your thesis statement and enumeration of subtopics and then get approval from your instructor.
3. Complete the worksheet **before** writing the essay.
4. Attach the worksheet to the finshed essay.
5. Attach the Expository Essay Cover Sheet to the finished essay.

Source of material: ______________________________

Subject to be discussed: ______________________________

Controlling idea: ____________ (number) + ____________ (adjective) + ____________ (noun)

Order of three major subtopics: ______________________________

Point of view: ____________ Verb tense: ____________

Tone: ____________ Diction: ____________

Thesis statement and enumeration of subtopics (may be 1 or 2 sentences):

____

____

____

____
(instructor approval)

OUTLINE

Title: ______________________________

¶1: Introduction (five sentences):

Choose a good beginning from list.
Give necessary background material.

Good beginning # ________ : ______________________________

____

____

____

____

____

When you write your introduction, include the approved thesis statement and subtopics at the end of paragraph 1.

Body (three paragraphs)

¶2: Transition + topic sentence: ______________________________

supporting details

¶3: Transition + topic sentence: ______________________________

supporting details

¶4: Transition + topic sentence: ______

supporting details

¶5: Conclusion (three sentences):
Choose one of the good endings from the list.

Good ending # ______

Name: ____________________

Date: ______________ **Class:** __________

EXPOSITORY ESSAY COVER SHEET		
Structure/Ideas	+	________
Usage/Mechanics	−	________
Total		________
Rewrite points	+	________
TOTAL		________

Structure and Ideas (100 points)		**Original**		**Rewrite**
INTRODUCTION (at least five sentences):				
title; one of good beginnings leading to thesis	10	________		________
thesis statement + enumeration of subtopics	5	________		________
BODY (three supporting paragraphs):				
three topic sentences = transition + reference to thesis + subtopic	15	________		________
development of paragraphs: sufficient, concrete, appropriate, relevant	45	________		________
CONCLUSION (at least three sentences):				
one of good endings	5	________		________
ESSAY:				
logical order of ideas and correct reasoning	5	________		________
effective style = tone + diction + sentence structure + coherence	15	________		________
Total	100	________	+	________

The points in this section reflect your score for structure and ideas. If you have received fewer than 100 points, you may rewrite your paper to earn them. Use the numbers as a guide to areas needing revision.

Usage and Mechanics (minus points). See Correction Symbol Chart.				
You **may** earn these points in revision:				
Usage: adj; adv; agr; awk; col; dm; frag; mm; ref; rep; shift; verb; ww; / /; ¶	−3 ea.	________		________
You **may not** earn these points in revision, but you must correct the errors:				
Mechanics: abbr; apos; cap; lc; p; ro; sp; ∧	−1 ea.	________		________
Total	−	________	+	________

CHAPTER 6
The First Pattern: Illustration

When you read an abstract work, you probably notice that it is difficult to understand the concepts being discussed unless they are accompanied by examples or illustrations. The examples maintain your interest and teach you. Using examples is an effective way to convey information; that is why most good writers are careful to incorporate concrete illustrations for their generalizations. Readers should not be expected to provide these details.

Because it is concrete, illustration is one of the most basic elements in writing. Most essays contain examples in order to convey information efficiently and to clarify an idea. Writers illustrate their generalizations either with short examples or with one long example. In addition, illustration can be the basis for an entire essay. More often, examples are used to develop other patterns of exposition.

Illustration in this chapter is used as the pattern of exposition that supports a general statement by citing specific examples. It is necessary to select vivid, particular instances to represent a broad category or class. A class may be an item, a condition, or an idea or generalization. Ideas are conveyed by means of the examples rather than by direct discussion. Often a specific example helps the reader to understand the class being represented or discussed. For example, the essay "The First and the Worst" has as its thesis that "the first case of homesickness is usually the worst." Instead of talking about why homesickness is so unpleasant, the writer selects three specific experiences in Paris, Marseilles, and Germany to convey the idea in concrete, vivid terms.

Requirements of Illustration

A successful illustration essay uses examples that stand for or represent the chief characteristics of the class. In addition, the examples must be interesting and concrete in themselves. That is, you must emphasize the individual, specific, detailed aspects of the examples. Consequently, the pattern of illustration may be developed in one of two ways. You may use one long example or several brief ones. If only one example is used, it must be more fully developed and more detailed than would be the case if several examples were used. It must include parts, elements, or qualities that the essay illustrates. For instance, the illustration paper entitled "Melting Confidence" gives one long example to illustrate its generalization. On the other hand, several examples give an idea of the range of possibilities in the class. For instance, in this chapter, the first student illustration paper, "More Value for Life," gives a series of three short examples.

Problems to Avoid

First, the idea being illustrated must speak for itself. That is, the example must show the idea rather than tell about it. Showing by example makes ideas easier to remember. Second, to avoid being vague, you must offer a sufficient number of vivid and concrete details to maintain reader interest and to aid comprehension.

As you prepare your illustration essay, you should select an idea or item that you know a great deal about through experience, research, or study. Then it will be easier to develop the specific details of the generalization. If you select an item or condition to illustrate, you will need to provide a thesis or generalization about that item. For example, if you choose the item *hobby* to illustrate, you might state as your thesis, "Nearly anyone can have a creative hobby." In addition, you will have to decide whether to illustrate with several shorter examples or with one lengthy example.

Organizational Patterns for Illustration

Study this blueprint so that you can see and better understand the elements necessary for illustration. Then use the pattern as a guide in assembling your own essay. Observe that the two forms for the body paragraphs are presented: three examples or one example. Note that all the student samples in the chapter use this organizational pattern.

Title

Introduction—¶ 1

At least five sentences

Use of one of the good beginnings

Establishment of order of subtopics
- point of view
- verb tense
- tone and diction

Item or idea to illustrate

Thesis statement =	subject + controlling idea	usually one sentence
Subtopic sentence =	enumeration of three specific examples or one specific example with three parts	

Body—¶ 2, 3, 4

-three examples-	OR	-one example-
Presentation of three specific examples		Presentation of three stages, qualities, parts
Logical order of three examples: climactic		Logical order of one example: chronological
**Paragraph 2:* Topic sentence = transition + reference to thesis statement + example 1		**Paragraph 2:* Topic sentence = transition + reference to thesis statement + stage 1
Supporting details using details/facts/anecdotes		Supporting details using details/facts/anecdotes
**Paragraph 3:* Topic sentence = transition + reference to thesis statement + example 2		**Paragraph 3:* Topic sentence = transition + reference to thesis statement + stage 2
Supporting details		Supporting details
**Paragraph 4:* Topic sentence = transition + reference to thesis statement + example 3 (most important example)		**Paragraph 4:* Topic sentence = transition + reference to thesis statement + stage 3
Supporting details		Supporting details

Transitional expressions: see especially

- Addition
- Emphasis/Intensification
- Introduction of Illustration/Example
- Time/Chronology

Conclusion—¶ 5

At least three sentences
Transitional expression (optional): see Conclusion/Result and Summary
Restatement of generalization
Use of one of the good endings

*These elements may be rearranged within the sentence.

STUDENT SAMPLE—Illustration Essay (Using Three Examples)—Analyzed for Parts

Observe that elements of structure and content are labeled on the left while elements of style are identified on the right. This detailed analysis will help you plan your own essay.

Source of material: personal experience

Tone: serious
Diction: concrete, literal
Order: climactic

Title

More Value for Life

Introduction ¶ 1
Good beginning #8

Most of the time, we go from one experience to another, treating them as separate, isolated moments in our lives. Rarely do we look more deeply into the overall significance of these events. Perhaps the daily pressures and responsibilities force us to overlook how really important life is. (However),* through each encounter we can value life more fully. During my volunteer work at a local hospital, I had three different experiences involving an elderly man, a teenage boy, and a middle-aged man which illustrate the truth of this idea to me.

Generalization to be illustrated

Thesis statement and subtopic sentence (3 specific examples)

Point of view: first person

verb tense: past

Topic Sentence ¶2

The (first) opportunity I had to value life more fully occurred as I watched an elderly man grow sicker daily. I can remember the first day I walked into his room. The old man had snow white hair, a stubby white beard, and wrinkled skin. Slouching in his bed, he mumbled indistinguishable words under his breath. To carry on an intelligent conversation with him was difficult since he abruptly changed the subject when his memory

Diction: concrete

Sentence Structure: 2 Verbal phrases

*Coherence: transitional expressions circled

Body
¶ 2,3,4

deserted him. However, we could walk around the circular corridor several times daily. He amazed me with his strong arms and his steady feet. For about six weeks his physical condition remained stable. Then he slowly began to worsen and changed into a different person. Because he yelled and screamed, flailing arms and legs uncontrollably, the nurses strapped his hands to the mattress with a Posey belt. His weight dropped noticeably, and he was no longer able to feed himself. From that point, he had to be treated and cared for like a child. That experience helped me to value my health and my youth more completely.

A Sentence Structure: compound object of preposition

Diction: concrete

Concluding Sentence

Topic Sentence ¶3

Another situation which helped me value life more fully was seeing scars being formed on a young boy's face. During my fourth week as a volunteer aide, I was working in the emergency room. One afternoon I recall the paramedics quickly wheeling in a fourteen-year-old boy who had had a motorcycle accident. As they transferred him from the stretcher to the operating table, he shouted and cried from the pain. Peering through the window of the swinging doors, I saw his dirty face slashed with deep cuts. The plastic surgeon began operating immediately. First, he injected

Diction: literal

Sentence Structure: 2 Verbal phrases

novacaine into the skin of the boy's face. After the medication took effect, the doctor began scraping off the epidermal layer of skin which was clogged with dirt and gravel. Then he took a needle and thread and started sewing the gashes together carefully. During the three hours the boy was on the table, he sobbed and screamed with pain, despite the novacaine. This incident was unforgettable and helped me value my body and good fortune more.

Diction: literal

Concluding Sentence

Finally, watching cancer take the life of a happy family man made me value my life most. When this man was admitted to the hospital, his face glowed with smiles. I remember visiting with him and his family. Laughing and telling jokes, we sat around his bed. But as the days passed, he slowly got thinner, his thick brown hair gradually fell out, and he lost all strength in his legs. Each day, the malignant tumor on the right side of his head grew bigger and bigger. His features drooped slowly to the right side and distorted his once-attractive face. Then he lost his memory. No longer could he recognize his wife or children. Eventually, he needed the help of a nurse to move his arms and legs in bed. I watched day by day until this fifty-two-year-

Topic Sentence A4

B Sentence Structure: Series of independent clauses

C Sentence Structure: compound verb

old smiling, laughing man finally died. After this tragic experience, I try to live each day as if it were my last.

Concluding Sentence

Sentence Structure: Coordinate Adjectives

The value of life is worth more than the most precious gem to me. These three experiences have changed my attitude about being alive. They have made me realize how valuable my life really is.

Conclusion ¶ 5

Good Ending #10

Diction: figurative (simile)

STUDENT SAMPLE—Illustration Essay (Using One Example)

Source of material: personal experience

Melting Confidence

A few months ago I realized that due to the soaring cost of textbooks and the recent raising of my rent I would have to abandon the life of a professional student and find some form of employment. Armed with a great deal of self-confidence and an equally vast lack of skills, I eagerly leapt into this search. I sat through countless interviews, filled out innumerable applications, and even lied about my personal background and employment record. Every night I stayed home, waiting patiently for the telephone to ring, but nothing happened. My confidence slowly eroding, the dreadful idea of being unemployable crept into my thoughts. Then, after weeks of silence, the telephone suddenly rang. The owner of Smith's Ice Cream Parlor informed me that there was an opening for a counterperson at his store. I was finally employed. What could be easier than scooping ice cream or more fun than making hot fudge sundaes? I soon discovered that the best lessons in life usually come from the worst experiences. In fact, while working at Smith's I had to endure the three frustrating difficulties of mastering the store's complicated machinery, coexisting with the other workers, and accepting the criticism of my employer.

Not being mechanically inclined, my first episodes of shame arrived as I made fruitless attempts to operate various machines in the shop. The cash register was my initial obstacle. It had so many numbers, codes, and symbols imprinted on its keys that it was an open invitation to disaster. My sweaty, trembling fingers slithered over the slippery keys, rarely striking the right ones. And when I hit the wrong ones, an ear-splitting shriek shot forth from that ugly gray box, letting the world know that I had made another error. All eyes were upon me. I wanted to sink down and crawl under the counter to conceal my embarrassment. After a few days, I had to learn how to make milkshakes. Putting milk and ice cream into the six-inch-high shake tin posed no problems. On the other hand, mixing the two together was a new lesson in humility. The thick lumps of ice cream at the bottom of the tin trapped the blender's beater. It rumbled angrily, made a few futile attempts to turn, and then gave up the fight. In my panic, I grabbed the tin and struggled to pull it off the blender. The beater, suddenly freed from the gluey globs of ice cream, whirled wildly and threw a white sheet of milk over me, the counter, and the walls. Even the whipped cream dispensers turned into dangerous weapons when they fell into my hands. These camouflaged grenades cackled and spattered creamy drops of shrapnel over a radius of five feet, covering anything in their path with a blanket of white foam. As my fear of machines continued to be justified, I tried to avoid their use as much as possible.

My difficulties with the other workers at Smith's proved to be equally humiliating. All of these children were at least ten years younger than I. I had not seen so many pairs of braces since high school, well over a decade ago. During my first night at work, five of these youngsters asked me my age. The charming adolescents could not believe that their boss would hire anyone so old. Every time I made a mistake I saw their eyes roll in disbelief and their angelic faces grimace in scorn. They made me so self-conscious that I was afraid to look in the mirror, certain that new wrinkles and gray hairs had suddenly appeared. To add to my shame, one teen-age girl, a self-appointed assistant supervisor, took great pleasure in barking out orders and scolding me whenever these tasks were not done immediately. I soon realized that the myth of the generation gap was more than just some psychologist's hypothesis; it was a fact.

Although the antics of those mechanical monsters and snide smiles of the snickering employees dealt heavy blows to my withering pride, the owner's constant and ridiculing criticism hit me with the final knock-out punch. This entrepreneur had chiseled an eleventh commandment onto the original tablet of ten: Thou shalt not overscoop. He considered this sin to be of overwhelming magnitude, especially since it endangered the sanctity of his profits. Strategically located next to the time clock, a typewritten manifesto, the sacred "Oath Against Overscooping," spelled out in a carefully calculated series of figures the exact amount that one malicious overscooper could cost the company--a stunning seventeen thousand six hundred and twenty-eight dollars a year. Filled with guilt, I signed the oath and staggered to the cone counter, aware of the heavy shame a miscalculated scoop would bring me. Unlike those smooth, unblemished spheres of frozen delight pictured in the Smith's Instruction Manual, my scoops were less than perfect. Jagged peaks and deep ravines marred the surface of these angular, overweight clumps. After a few hours, my employer had the courtesy to inform me that my scoops were the worst he had ever seen. Only whipped cream and hot fudge could shelter these odd-shaped orbs from further scrutiny. But even hot fudge sundaes offered only temporary salvation. Often I had too many sodas, sundaes, and shakes to make at one time. In my hurry, I made the sundaes first instead of last. The hot fudge, poured over vanilla ice cream, quickly thawed the frozen white mounds. Within thirty seconds they all had mixed together, forming a sticky, mud-colored gravy which spilled over the sides of the parfait glass. Only my confidence melted faster. After a quick glimpse of the owner's livid face, I prepared myself for his latest series of reprimands. But my pride, though punch-drunk from the endless jabs and hooks of others' criticism and my own lack of self-esteem, still had enough strength to strike a blow of its own. I tore off my apron, marched out of the store, and never returned.

Clearly, one can take the worst experiences and turn them into lessons of value. Even though my experiences at Smith's were not pleasant, I learned a great deal about the working conditions at a minimum-wage job. Most important of all, in spite of my lack of skills and numerous failures, I realized how important it is to possess good self-esteem.

Discovery Exercise

1. Identify the idea or generalization being illustrated.

   ____

2. Identify the thesis statement
   a. the subject being discussed: ______________________________

      ____

   b. the controlling idea: ______________________________

      ____

3. Identify the three major subtopics: ______________________________

   ____

   ____

4. Identify the order of the subtopics: ____ climactic ______ general to particular

   ____ chronological

5. Identify the point of view: __________ person
6. Identify the verb tense: ______________________________
7. Circle **five** transitional expressions.
8. Identify **ten** specific words or phrases that make this essay concrete:

   ____

   ____

   ____

   ____

9. Choose terms from the diction chart that characterize the diction: ____________________

10. Choose terms from the tone chart that describe the tone: ____________________

11. After reviewing Chapter 16, bracket **four** coordinate adjectives, one type of grammatical structure used in this essay.

STUDENT SAMPLE—Illustration Essay (Using Three Examples)

Source of material: personal experience

Facing Up to Failure

My mother had been an actress on the London stage before her marriage. After her separation from my father, she brought me to Hollywood in the hope that both she and her adolescent daughter would become film actresses. At first, we managed to get a few small parts, but it soon became clear that our road to success would be as steep as the fire escape that rusted outside our apartment. Indeed, learning to accept failure is an important part of maturing. It was only after the third of three vivid experiences I had with a stage audition, a film audition, and an unsuccessful actor that I understood the truth of that statement.

Accepting failure was far from my thoughts as I faced my first theatrical audition. My hands were icy cold, but my voice was calm as I read for the ingenue lead in the professional stage production of a new comedy. The rest of the company listened quietly, and after a short rustling of papers and a whispered conference between producer and director, I was told that the part was mine. Controlling a mad desire to jump over the theater seats, I left the theater sedately enough, clutched my precious script to the front of my blue crepe "interview" dress, and floated home down Hollywood Boulevard. I might have been walking down the aisle of a rose-windowed cathedral for all I saw of my surroundings. My mother's face was pink with pride as I told her my news, the news all actors love to give: "I got the part!" But I had the part in my hands for exactly one day. The rude awakening came as I tiptoed into the darkened theater next morning, script in hand. Whipping off my dark glasses and blinking into the footlights, I focused on a slim blonde girl in pink slacks. She was the sister of an already established star, and she was reading my lines. As I sank shakily into a seat, the grey-bearded director put down his script and laid a heavy arm around my shoulders. His words struck my ears in sharp, separate blows as he explained that the producer wanted her for my role. He was sure, he added, that with my looks and talent I would soon be playing on some other stage. Wordlessly, I groped for my glasses to hide a sudden gush of tears and struggled out into the blinding sunshine.

Though I felt that my career had collapsed, I still clung to the hope of success as I next auditioned for a film part. The thought of failure was neatly pushed aside as I prepared for the audition. I applied my make-up in the latest style--arched eyebrows, heavily lined eyes, and darkly painted lips. I wore my most sophisticated dress and assumed a cosmopolitan manner as I entered RKO Studios. Soon I found myself sitting under an artificial apple tree on a soundstage and playing a three-minute love scene with a handsome, famous leading man. I had the opening scene in the film. As we finished rehearsing our last kiss, the director, rubbing his chin, watched me. After a moment, he told me that he liked my work and that he would suggest putting me under long-term contract at RKO. I should hear about the matter in a few days. I heard about it quite soon. The studio heads decided that I looked a little too old and sophisticated for their training program, so they signed a younger-looking girl instead.

The experience that finally taught me to accept failure involved an unsuccessful actor. Pete Smith, a thirty-five-year-old who was sharing our home at the time, had been struggling to survive on occasional acting jobs. He seldom spoke, and his shoulders hung in a perpetual slump. Every night after going to bed, I would hear the fumble of his key in the lock and then his heavy tread as he thumped his way up the uncarpeted stairs to his room. I knew how he felt, and staring at the scraggly palm tree menacing the moon outside my window, I began to share his sorrow. Events came to a climax one morning when I asked him why he did not abandon acting. Drooping over a cup of coffee at the dining-room table, he lifted his sallow, dark-lined face and stared at me, tears trembling on the reddened rims of his eyes. Why, I wondered, after all these years of frustration, did he not try something else. His worn shoulders shrugged under his faded shirt, and he told me why he had to go on. Quite simply, he was not trained for anything else, and he was too old to change jobs. Perhaps it was too late for Pete, but not for me. At twenty-three, I could admit my failure and go on to something else.

While trying to become an actress, I had been writing show business interviews for out-of-town papers. The money from these articles was barely enough to support me. Finally having admitted my failure, I slipped into a business-like, navy-blue dress and hiked down the boulevard to Columbia Studios to beg an interview with the head of the publicity department. In his office, I pulled out the fistful of my film-gossip columns I had stuffed into my plastic bag. As I talked my way into my first regular job, I held the face of my friend firmly on the screen of my mind.

Discovery Exercise

1. Identify the idea or generalization being illustrated. ______________________________

   ____
2. Identify the thesis statement

   a. the subject being discussed: ______________________________

      ____

   b. the controlling idea: ______________________________

      ____
3. Identify the three major subtopics: ______________________________

   ____

   ____
4. Identify the order of the subtopics: ____ climactic

   ____ chronological
5. Identify the point of view: __________ person
6. Identify the verb tense: __________
7. Circle **five** transitional expressions.
8. Identify the images that illustrate the following emotions:

   a. apprehension: ______________________________

   b. happiness/joy: ______________________________

   c. disappointment: ______________________________

   d. confidence: ______________________________

   e. depression: ______________________________
9. Choose terms from the diction chart that characterize the diction: ______________
10. Choose terms from the tone chart that describe the tone:

    ____
11. After reviewing Chapter 16, bracket **five** verbal phrases, one type of grammatical structure used in this essay.

STUDENT SAMPLE—Illustration Essay (Using Three Examples)

Source of material: personal experience

The First and the Worst

All of the passengers seated near me on that ill-fated charter flight to Paris were chattering merrily as they compared brochures, maps, and guidebooks for survival in a foreign country. Being seasoned travelers, they had all spent a great deal of time and money preparing for their vacation. I, on the other hand, was on my first trip away from home and had succumbed to the enticements of an unplanned adventure--a do-it-yourself bicycle tour of Europe. It did not take long for my adventure's bright shining star to tarnish. Only a few hours after my arrival on foreign soil, home seemed light years away, and the eighty-three day round-trip ticket portended a long, lingering illness called homesickness. In fact, several events which occurred on this voyage proved to me that the first case of homesickness is usually the worst. Three personal experiences which involved getting lost in Paris, being manhandled in Marseilles, and spending a night in a German jail illustrate how painful this disease can be.

Getting lost my first night away from home brought on the initial chills of homesickness. Unlike the warm summer nights of Los Angeles, those of Paris were cold and damp. Unaccustomed to such cold and under the influence of a bona fide case of jet lag, I shivered and stumbled as I tried to find the Paris Youth Hostel, a cheap hotel for young travelers. The thin tires of my bicycle were no match for the infamous cobblestones; riding a ten-speed on the oily streets of Paris was like trying to ski uphill. After several hours of pushing bike and baggage through narrow, winding streets, I noticed that certain storefronts of bakeries and boutiques began to look curiously familiar. I had been walking in circles and at one o'clock in the morning was hopelessly turned around. When I finally found the hostel an hour later, the hard, lumpy bed and scratchy wool blanket gave no solace to my aching body. I cried myself to sleep that night, dreaming not of the wonders of Paris but the comforts of home.

After a few cold days in Paris, I headed my handlebars south towards the warm beaches of the Mediterranean, where a second experience renewed my suffering. The streets of Marseilles, lined with majestic palms, brought me a little closer to home. The men, however, served as a painful reminder that I was very far away. In the eyes of the North African immigrants of Marseilles, any female foolish enough to venture out unaccompanied was like a Thanksgiving turkey ready to be plucked. These apostles of male chauvinism hounded me constantly. I soon began to yearn for the freedom I had enjoyed at home, where I could walk down a street without being molested. As I returned to my hotel one evening, my temper overpowered my better judgment. An Algerian had been on my trail for over half an hour, and when he tried to grab me, I spit at him. My aim was perfect, for the strategically guided projectile of saliva hit the middle of his forehead. His face turned purple with rage, while mine paled considerably when he kicked me in the stomach. I lashed back at him; the crunching sound of broken enamel rivaled the pounding of my heart as my right fist and high school senior ring made contact with his teeth. Later that night, my stomach and fist still ached, but what really hurt was the recurring bout of homesickness, for which I had found no cure.

A third adventure, which ended in the confines of a German jail, revived the ever-present pangs of homesickness. Still traveling by bicycle, I had the bad luck to get three flat tires during one day in the middle of a German forest. Not being mechanically inclined, I spent hours repairing inner tubes only to have them go flat again after a few miles. By the time I had patched and pumped up my third puncture, night had fallen, and I was stranded thirty miles from the nearest youth hostel. To make matters worse, it started to rain. After a few hours, I reached a small town and found shelter under a covered bus stop. Images of my bathtub filled with hot, steaming water, and my warm, dry bed flashed across my mind as I tried to stop shivering. The flashing red lights of the green and white police car awoke me from my reverie, and I watched, paralyzed with terror, while the same car slowly rolled to a halt in front of the bus stop. Fully aware of the Germanic affection for law and order, I was certain that I would be arrested and sentenced to a long term in prison. But my fears were unwarranted, because the police were very understanding and even offered me a place to stay--the town jail. Although I was grateful for the free accommodations, my longing for home hit a high point that night as I tried to sleep behind the bars of cell number one. However, the fact that my nightmare journey was almost over helped to soothe my pain, for only a few days remained until my return flight home.

I never appreciated how much home meant to me until the first time I left it. These three memorable experiences made me realize how much I had been taking for granted at home: simple comforts and amenities such as a hot shower, warm meal, and soft mattress. By surviving that first painful case of homesickness, I also gained a great deal of self-confidence, and since then no country has seemed too far away.

PROFESSIONAL SAMPLE—Illustration

Read the following essay to see how a professional writer has used the technique of illustration. Then answer the discovery questions which focus on the major elements of illustrative writing.

Ilene Kantrov (1950–), a writer, teacher, and editor, taught freshman writing at Tufts University from which she received her doctorate. In addition to being a senior staff editor for *Notable American Women,* a Radcliffe College publication, she writes and consults for the Education Development Center.

Women's Business

1 The face of the kindly matron beamed from the pages of newspapers and magazines across the country. The advertising copy promised relief from "falling of the womb and all female weaknesses," touting the product as "the greatest remedy in the world." The year was 1879, and the product was an unproven home remedy called Lydia E. Pinkham's Vegetable Compound. Lydia Pinkham, the woman whose countenance graced the periodical pages, developed the advertising campaign that traded on her benign image.

2 Pinkham brought to her marketing effort the passionate social activism characteristic of many women of her era. Convinced that she offered more than a mere product, she used her advertising to champion women's rights, temperance, and fiscal reform. One of her cleverest marketing techniques was a Department of Advice. Encouraging women to bypass male physicians to seek guidance from another woman, she dispensed practical suggestions about diet, exercise, and hygiene, along with endorsements of her own medicine.

3 Yet Pinkham did not hesitate to exploit traditional feminine fears—and feminine stereotypes—to market her product. She printed testimonials from women reporting cures not only for a range of physical symptoms, but also for infertility, "nervousness," "hysteria," and even marital discord. According to one early newspaper ad, the murder of a Connecticut clergyman by his wife, whose insanity was "brought on by 16 years of suffering with Female Complaints," could have been prevented by timely administration of the Compound to the afflicted woman.

4 As a result of such bold marketing, the company that Pinkham had founded with her sons earned $200,000 in 1881. Lydia Pinkham herself became something of a folk heroine—the subject of popular songs, jokes, and bawdy verse.

5 Pinkham's introduction of feminine packaging to capitalist enterprise earned her a special place in the annals of American business as well as women's history. It also set a pattern for women entrepreneurs in the following century. The handful of women who emulated Pinkham's success likewise followed her in importing traditional feminine roles into the masculine world of commerce. When feminine ideals collided with the realities of the marketplace, however, the businesswoman often bested the lady.

6 Like Pinkham, her successors consciously exploited their images as women to promote their products. In some cases, the image was that of glamorous socialite: arch-rivals Helena Rubinstein and Elizabeth Arden competed not only in selling cosmetics but also in luring publicity by their marriages to European aristocrats. More often the image cultivated was that of mother or grandmother: following Pinkham in this mold, for example, were Margaret Rudkin, founder of Pepperidge Farm, Inc., and Jennie Grossinger, who ran a resort hotel in upstate New York renowned for its food and entertainment. Grossinger managed to remain the solicitous Jewish grandmother in the eyes of her customers long after she had hired a public relations man and Grossinger's Hotel began serving 150,000 guests a year.

7 Women's businesses tended to grow out of traditional women's skills and catered mainly to women. Lydia Pinkham had collected and administered folk remedies to her family for years before the collapse of her husband's real estate business led her to begin marketing herbal preparations for "female complaints." Margaret Rudkin, faced with a comparable need to supplement her husband's income, also looked close to home. She reportedly baked her first loaf of additive-free whole wheat bread as part of a special diet for an asthmatic son, and secured her first order from her neighborhood grocer in 1937.

8 To transform a home craft into a thriving business, these female capitalists joined a canny sense of women's tastes with the audacity of a gambler in creating and marketing innovations designed to shape those tastes. In 1909 Elizabeth Arden introduced her first line of makeup, not then widely considered respectable, as "facial treatments." As the beauty market began to expand in the 1920s she kept several steps ahead of demand: introducing, for example, such exotic and vaguely medicinal concoctions as Sensation salve, Arden gland cream, and the Vienna Youth Mask. Applications of the Youth Mask, constructed of papier-mâché and tinfoil, required the customer to be hooked up to a diathermy machine, which applied heat via electric current. Arden assured the women who submitted to the treatment—and paid dearly for the privilege—that they were restoring dead skin tissue.

9 In addition to skin care and cosmetics, Elizabeth Arden salons eventually added hairstyling, ready-made and custom clothes, and advice on nutrition and exercise. Arden herself practiced and advocated yoga, adapting the exercises for the women who frequented her salons and Maine health spa. Competing salon proprietor Helena Rubinstein published a book expounding the benefits of eating raw foods and sold her customers on the diet. In promoting the idea that a beauty salon could provide women with the means to "remake" themselves, inside and out, both women manifested the conviction of American businesswomen from Lydia Pinkham on that they were providing other women with something more than a product.

10 Few of them matched Pinkham in the degree to which she merged her marketing effort with a crusade for economic and social change. But other American women entrepreneurs combined an equally shrewd eye for profit with a passionate belief in their products' social or moral efficacy. Gertrude Muller, who invented the "toidey seat" in 1924 and parlayed it into an entire line of child care products, in 1930 began enclosing in the packages pamphlets she wrote about child raising. Her products, and the literature that accompanied them, embodied a progressive philosophy of child rearing, and one of her booklets was widely distributed by doctors and used by home economics instructors. Of course, none of this free publicity hurt business.

11 A black female capitalist, Annie Turnbo-Malone also cast herself in the role of social activist. Her business was founded at the turn of the century on a hairdressing preparation that, like Lydia Pinkham's Vegetable Compound, was of questionable efficacy. But, again like Pinkham, she developed an innovative marketing strategy—a network of franchised sales agents—and used it both to earn big money and to promote her causes. Turnbo-Malone established a school for training agents in her "poro" system of hairdressing, named it Poro College, and advertised it as a vehicle for the uplift of her race and a passport to economic independence for women. Her literature also branched out beyond hair care to advocate the benefits of good hygiene, thrift, and other homely virtues.

12 Turnbo-Malone and her sister capitalists genuinely believed in the beneficence of their products and services. If not all of them proclaimed themselves, as Lydia Pinkham did, "Saviour of her Sex," several of them acted the part. And a number turned their profits into good works: Turnbo-Malone, Helena Rubinstein, and Jennie Grossinger, for example, were noted philanthropists as well as executives. They contributed lavishly to hospitals, schools, and cultural organizations.

13 Though they aimed to serve as well as to sell, however, these businesswomen frequently put profit ahead of altruism. Their advertising claims were often extravagant, even misleading. And when regulatory agencies such as the FDA and FTC began to crack down on questionable business practices, female entrepreneurs were as likely to be cited as their male counterparts. Helena Rubinstein, for instance, was forced by the FDA to withdraw some of the medicinal claims she made for her products.

14 The latent conflict between the profit motive and the social service ethic of female entrepreneurs is perhaps best exemplified once again by Lydia Pinkham: a passionate temperance advocate who had no qualms about selling a product that contained sufficient alcohol to make it 40 proof. "Grandma," backed by the Women's Christian Temperance Union, was selling booze.

Discovery Questions

1. What is the idea or generalization being illustrated, and in which paragraph is it found?
2. How many examples does Kantrov use, and what are they?
3. a. How did the business women differ from their male counterparts?
   b. How did they resemble each other?

Suggested Items or Conditions to Illustrate:

Sclcct one of the following or similar items that you know about through experience or study. You will have to provide a thesis for the item you are illustrating.

the liberated woman	addiction
the ideal teacher	the typical sports fan
courage	the male chauvinist
the do-it-yourselfer	dreams
the ideal job	products that feature someone's name
a contemporary business executive	

Suggested Ideas or Generalizations to Illustrate:

Select one of the following or similar items that you know about through personal experience or study.

Life is something we do not always appreciate until we come close to death.

Being part of a large (or small) family can be a valuable experience.

The experiences of childhood can leave lasting impressions.

The first case of homesickness is usually the worst.

The well-meaning attempts of another person can hurt an individual.

Learning to cope with stress (or unhappiness or guilt or shame or discomfort) is part of growing up.

A new experience often creates mixed feelings.

Seeing another person's unhappiness (or misfortune) can help a person reexamine himself or herself.

Freedom means more than just license to do as one pleases.

Accepting new responsibilities (a job, a home, a spouse) can create mixed emotions.

Successful business people often use similar tactics regardless of whether they are male or female.

Each family has its distinctive lifestyle.

Books can change our lives.

WORKSHEET FOR ILLUSTRATION

1. Select a subject to discuss and complete the top half of the worksheet.
2. Write your thesis statement and subtopic sentence and then get approval from your instructor.
3. Complete the worksheet **before** writing the essay.
4. Attach the worksheet to the finished essay.
5. Attach the Expository Essay Cover Sheet to the finished essay.

Source of material: ______________________________

Item or idea to be illustrated: ______________________________

____

Controlling idea: ____ three specific examples

____ one specific example with three stages

Order of three major subtopics: ____ climactic

____ time/chronological

Point of view: ____________ Verb tense: ____________

Tone: ____________ Diction: ____________

Thesis statement and enumeration of subtopics (may be 1 or 2 sentences):

____

____

____

____

(instructor approval)

OUTLINE

Title: ______________________________

¶1: Introduction (five sentences):

Choose a good beginning from list.
Give necessary background material.

Good beginning # ________ : ______________________________

____

____

____

____

____

When you write your introduction, include the approved thesis statement and subtopics at the end of paragraph 1.

Body (three paragraphs)

¶2: Transition + topic sentence: ____________________

____

supporting details

____

¶3: Transition + topic sentence: ____________________

____

supporting details

____

¶4: Transition + topic sentence: __________

supporting details

¶5: Conclusion (three sentences):
Restatement of item or idea
Choose one of the good endings from the list.

Good ending # ____

Name: ____________________

Date: ____________ Class: ________

Type of Exposition: ____________________

EXPOSITORY ESSAY COVER SHEET		
Structure/Ideas	+	________
Usage/Mechanics	−	________
Total		________
Rewrite points	+	________
TOTAL		________

Structure and Ideas (100 points)	**Original**	**Rewrite**
INTRODUCTION (at least five sentences):		
title; one of good beginnings leading to thesis	10 ________	________
thesis statement + enumeration of subtopics	5 ________	________
BODY (three supporting paragraphs):		
three topic sentences = transition + reference to thesis + subtopic	15 ________	________
development of paragraphs: sufficient, concrete, appropriate, relevant	45 ________	________
CONCLUSION (at least three sentences):		
one of good endings	5 ________	________
ESSAY:		
logical order of ideas and correct reasoning	5 ________	________
effective style = tone + diction + sentence structure + coherence	15 ________	________
Total	100 ________	+ ________

The points in this section reflect your score for structure and ideas. If you have received fewer than 100 points, you may rewrite your paper to earn them. Use the numbers as a guide to areas needing revision.

Usage and Mechanics (minus points). See Correction Symbol Chart.		
You **may** earn these points in revision:		
Usage: adj; adv; agr; awk; col; dm; frag; mm; ref; rep; shift; verb; ww; //; ¶	−3 ea. ________	________
You **may not** earn these points in revision, but you must correct the errors:		
Mechanics: abbr; apos; cap; lc; p; ro; sp; ∧	−1 ea. ________	________
Total	− ________	+ ________

CHAPTER 7

The Second Pattern: Classification

The last time you went to a party of strangers and acquaintances, did you consciously or unconsciously separate them into groups? Listening to their topics of conversation, you might have recognized the sports fans, the political enthusiasts, the economic experts, and the travel buffs. The following diagram illustrates this grouping:

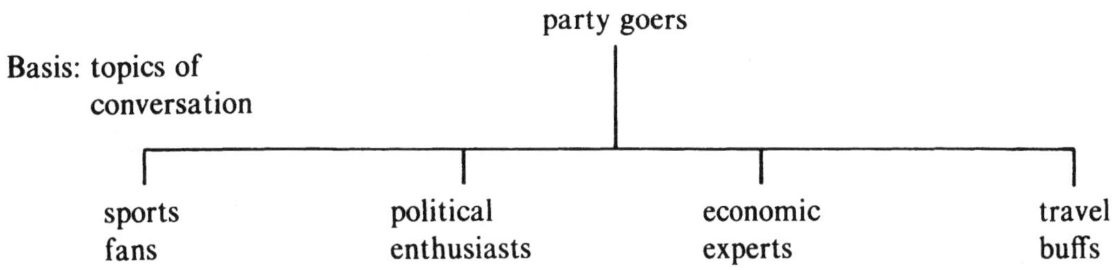

Or you could have grouped these same people according to a different basis—their manner of speaking. You might then have easily identified the bores, the conversation monopolizers, and the jokers. If you observed each bore carefully, you might have distinguished among kinds of bores such as the complainer, the repeater, and the authority. The diagram below illustrates that groups can be divided and subdivided:

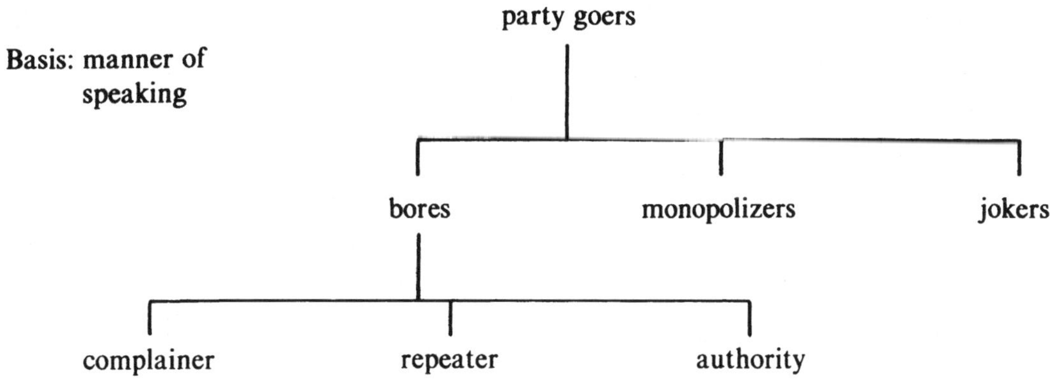

There are many other ways to arrange the party goers into groups: for example, according to their clothing, their choice or amount of beverage, or their dancing preferences.

More generally, the same group of people can be categorized in many different ways. Some of these ways are their religion, level of education, marital status, or occupation, depending on your need or interest. The process you used to group the party goers is classification. It is the mode of exposition that categorizes items in relationship to the other items of the same overall group.

However, no one of these classifications is ever enough to describe the essence or true nature of an item or a group. For example, at the end of this course your teacher has to give you a final grade—A, B, C, D, or F. Certainly the grade you are awarded does not describe "the real you," yet it is one of many bases for classifying you. If people put you in a class and assume that you share all of the characteristics with the members of the group, they are **stereotyping** you. Thus, some people may judge you irresponsible or lazy if you got a D in English while others may think you are brilliant just because you received an A. Both conclusions are faulty, however. An analysis of the classification just illustrated reveals the error in stereotyping—while all the A students in English share certain characteristics, they also have significant differences.

You can recognize, therefore, the fact that you naturally use the process of classification in your spontaneous reactions to people, places, events, or objects. Under these conditions, you are probably not concerned about the precision or accuracy of your divisions or subdivisions. As you prepare your formal classification, you will follow the same process; however, you will focus on four basic elements to achieve accuracy. Your objective is to clarify the distinctions that exist among the members of a group and that might otherwise be unrealized or ignored.

One important term you need to know is the word **class,** which means a group whose members share at least one significant characteristic or quality. What is significant depends on your intent. The same item may be classified in many ways according to the necessity of your situation. So, for example, the basis of your classification of party goers would change depending on whether you were primarily concerned about the topics of conversation or the mannerisms of the speakers or their availability for further relationships.

REQUIREMENTS OF CLASSIFICATION

Complexity

A simple subdivision would exhaust a class by arranging it into only two types of items: an X and a non-X. This grouping is too vague and tells little about the subject. An example is grouping gems into precious and semiprecious on the basis of value. However, a more informative classification comes from dividing a group into at least three types or kinds of items. When divided this way a classification has complexity. Such a division conveys a range of items. For example, on the basis of magical powers, precious gems can be classified into the diamond, ruby, and emerald. These relationships are illustrated in the following diagram.

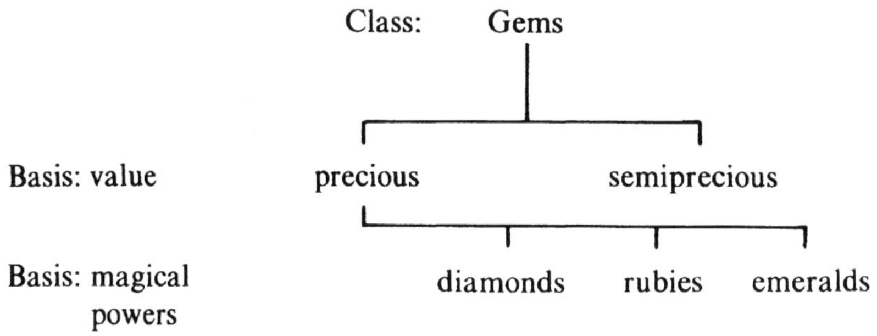

Consistency

A classification is consistent when the same basis is applied to all members of the group. This basis must not change during the classification. To illustrate, you can classify three types of grocery shoppers according to the foods they buy. If you were to identify two types of shoppers on the basis of food and one on the basis of personality, the classification would shift and, therefore, be inconsistent. When a new basis is applied, the classification must move to a new level as illustrated in the arrangement of the class *gems* above.

Exclusiveness

In classification the three or more types of items also must be mutually exclusive, not overlapping. That is, each type can belong to only one category at a time. For example, aggressive, shy, and affectionate types of dogs are overlapping because both aggressive and shy dogs can be affectionate. Using the same basis of temperament, you can classify dogs more consistently into aggressive, calm, and shy ones.

Coordination

In addition, the types in the classification must be at the same level of generality. For instance, classifying the five kinds of basic foods as meat, dairy products, grains, fruits, and green vegetables is making the error of having uncoordinate types. Green vegetables must be changed to vegetables. Another example is classifying college humanities courses, on the basis of subject matter, into English, sociology, anthropology, American history, and psychology. Since the category American history is a subdivision of history, the classification is not coordinate. Even though types or kinds are coordinate, they can be arranged in climactic order: for instance, from commonplace to fascinating, from oldest to newest.

Problems to Avoid

As you prepare your essay, you will have to select a clear basis for dividing the group. Then make sure that the types display these four qualities of complexity, consistency, exclusiveness, and coordination. If your group is too large, you may limit the classification to a manageable number of items by means of a controlling idea. For example, there are too many types of love to discuss all of them in a short essay. This class may be limited by focusing on three types of family love: parent, child, and sibling. Or you could focus on what you consider to be the three most important kinds of love. Finally, if it is appropriate, arrange your items in climactic order.

Discovery Exercise for Classification

I. The greatest difficulty in constructing a classification of items is choosing the correct types or kinds of members. These items may not be simple, may not be classified with a changing basis, may not be overlapping, or may not be uncoordinate.

DIRECTIONS: In the samples below, identify the errors in classification as being inconsistent, overlapping, or uncoordinate. Reconstruct the samples to make them effective and identify your basis.

1. cars: American
   foreign
   sports

2. teenage problems: no money for dates
   fighting over television
   doesn't understand algebra
   problems with family
   arguing with parents
   missed book report assignments
   problems with money

3. love: puppy love
   love of country
   motherly love

4. students: above average
   average
   disorganized

II. In order to have an effective classification, you must select a **basis** on which to classify the group. Then you must choose at least three types of items within the group which are complex, exclusive, equal, and consistent. The following classifications of art show the range of possibilities within a given group or class.

Class: Art

basis #1—**subject matter**

types: still life
landscape
portrait

basis #2—**medium**

types: water color
oil
acrylic

basis #3—**style**

types: impressionism
cubism
realism

DIRECTIONS: For each of the two groups that follow, select two bases for classifying, and list three types or kinds of members.

Class: Restaurants

basis #1— ____________________

types: 1 ____________________

2 ____________________

3 ____________________

basis #2— ____________________

types: 1 ____________________

2 ____________________

3 ____________________

Class: Parents

basis #1— ____________________

types: 1 ____________________

2 ____________________

3 ____________________

basis #2— ____________________

types: 1 ____________________

2 ____________________

3 ____________________

Organizational Pattern for Classification

Study this blueprint so that you can see and better understand the elements necessary for classification. Then use the pattern as a guide in assembling your own essay. Note that all the student samples in the chapter use this organizational pattern.

Title

Introduction—¶ 1

At least five sentences

Use of one of the good beginnings

Establishment of order of subtopics — verb tense, point of view, tone and diction

Thesis statement = subject (group to be classified) and basis of classification + controlling idea (number + adjective + types)

Subtopic sentence = enumeration of three types

(Thesis statement and subtopic sentence: may be 1 or 2 sentences)

Body—¶ 2, 3, 4

Presentation of three major types

Logical order of three major types

_____ general to particular

_____ time/chronological

_____ climactic

**Paragraph 2:* Topic sentence = transitional expression + reference to thesis statement + type 1

Sufficient development of subject using supporting details such as specific examples, facts, illustrations, anecdotes.

**Paragraph 3:* Topic sentence = transitional expression + reference to thesis statement + type 2

Sufficient development of subject using supporting details such as specific examples, facts, illustrations, anecdotes.

**Paragraph 4:* Topic sentence = transitional expression + reference to thesis statement + type 3

Sufficient development of subject using supporting details such as specific examples, facts, illustrations, anecdotes.

Transitional expressions: see especially

Addition
Emphasis/Intensification
Introduction of Illustration/Example
Time/Chronology

Conclusion—¶ 5

At least three sentences

Transitional expression (optional): see Conclusion/Result and Summary

Restatement of group classified

Use of one of the good endings

*These elements may be rearranged within the sentence.

STUDENT SAMPLE—Classification Essay—Analyzed for Parts

Observe that elements of structure and content are labeled on the left while elements of style are identified on the right. This detailed analysis will help you plan your own essay.

Source of material: personal experience

Tone: sarcastic, caustic, ironic
Diction: connotative, overstated, concrete
Order: general to particular

Title

The Personalities of Instructors

Introduction ¶ 1 — Good Beginning #3

Most teachers are sincere, dedicated individuals trying to share their knowledge with their students. A few are exceptionally talented, and an experience in their classroom is a memorable one. On the other hand,* unfortunately, throughout my years of attending school, I have found myself in the class of an instructor who was absolutely abhorrent to me. Three distinct types of instructors fall into this category on the basis of their personality. They are the Adolph Hitlers,[1] the Albert Einsteins,[2] and the Jack Bennys.[3]

- Verb Tense: present ("are")
- Point of view: first Person ("I")
- Thesis Statement (group to be classified and basis of classification): "Three distinct types of instructors fall into this category on the basis of their personality."
- Subtopic Sentence (3 types): "They are the Adolph Hitlers, the Albert Einsteins, and the Jack Bennys."
- Diction: allusion

Body ¶ 2, 3, 4

Topic Sentence ¶ 2

The first personality is the Adolph Hitler type. Professor Despot is immediately identified as he strides into class, marching to the martial beat of an unseen drum. Another interesting feature of this instructor is the ease with which he flies into paroxysms of rage when confronted by the unmitigated gall of a student who dares to interrupt a lecture to ask a question. This instructor's entire existence is centered around the oppression and misery of the class.

- Diction: concrete ("strides")
- Sentence Structure: verbal phrase ("marching to the martial beat of an unseen drum.")
- Diction: connotative ("paroxysms", "unmitigated gall")

*Coherence: transitional expressions circled (On the other hand; first; Another)

He enjoys assigning two term papers, five supplementary reading books, and many essay exams, in addition to the regular course requirements. Barely treating his students humanely or with the slightest respect, he usually experiences an extremely high drop rate, almost always within two hours after classes begin.

A Sentence Structure: items in a series

Diction: overstated

Topic Sentence ¶3

Another recognizable personality is the Albert Einstein type. Professor Egghead enters the class with intelligence radiating from every pore and orifice. He is undeniably brilliant, but that fact does not mean that the instructor knows anything about instruction of the course. His lectures are lengthy dissertations spoken with a vocabulary that very few of us understand. The class is not on the same intellectual level as the instructor, and in some cases, may not even be in the same universe. For example, he often refers to obscure original sources that no one has ever heard of. Although he may cover all material thoroughly, the student should have a dictionary available at all class meetings.

Diction: overstated

Diction: connotative

Diction: overstated

Topic Sentence ¶4

The third personality is the Jack Benny type. As he enters the class, one can almost hear the announcer's introduction: "And now--Heerrrre's Professor Performer." The instructor immediately begins his monologue. However, instead of a ten-minute spread of fast-paced humor, the class must suffer through fifty minutes of stale jokes and other ridiculous attempts at humor. He unsuccessfully attempts to mimic well-known individuals while attempting to teach the course material. To illustrate, if he has assigned "The Gettysburg Address," he delivers the entire speech as he thinks Lincoln might have. Instead of applause from the audience, this self-appointed comic reaps only a few snores. To make matters worse, the instructor attempts to provide his own applause by laughing hysterically at his own jokes.

Diction: connotative

Diction: concrete

Diction: Concrete

Sentence Structure: 2 verbal phrases

Conclusion
¶ 5
Good Ending #7

These three personality types are found at every school. The traits of any one of these instructors are enough to make me withdraw from the class in which they are instructing. I can only hope that some day these types will disappear from the classroom.

Sentence Structure: noun dependent clause

STUDENT SAMPLE—Classification Essay

Source of material: personal experience

Looking for Ms. Goodclerk

In this age of double-digit inflation, saving money has become a national pastime. However, there still exists a small number of consumers willing to sacrifice bargain-basement values for the luxurious atmosphere and exceptional service promised by expensive department stores. With plastic charge plates clutched in diamond-studded hands, these prestige-minded customers search for the bright, polite, and knowledgeable clerk who will help them find their heart's desire among the price tags and designer labels. Unfortunately, the enthusiastic and professional salesperson that the customer expects and the actual person standing behind the cash register are occasionally quite different. On the basis of their behavior three types of salespeople--the Barracuda, the Dreamer, and the Primadonna--found in most department stores often fall short of their customers' expectations.

The first type of salesclerk is the Barracuda. To the Barracuda, nabbing a customer and transacting a sale are her only two reasons for living. The other salespeople always find that when the highly competitive Barracuda is cheated out of a client she is not a gracious loser. The unfortunate novice who unwittingly infringes on the Barracuda's territory is likely to find herself locked in the back stockroom with a broken arm. To further insure first crack at the buying public, the Barracuda uses the latest in closed circuit video cameras and other high technology surveillance equipment, often knowing who her victims will be before they leave the parking lot. Once the unsuspecting customer is caught, the Barracuda begins to erode her victim's resistance with all the compassion of a Gestapo interrogator. Using threats, lies, and other persuasive tactics, the Barracuda pushes her customers into buying everything shown, whether or not it is what they needed. To the Barracuda, it doesn't matter if her customer has to take out a second mortgage to pay for the purchase, just as long as the customer buys.

The second type of salesclerk is the Dreamer. Living on a plane of higher consciousness, the Dreamer spends little time attending to mundane and tedious chores, such as waiting on customers. Contemplating important tasks like completing the perfect manicure, extending the ten-minute coffee break to three hours, and counting the number of angels that fit on the cover of Vogue occupies most of Dreamer's working hours. Naturally, she resents being distracted from these crucial issues by some unenlightened customer wishing to make a purchase. To avoid being disturbed, the Dreamer uses self-hypnosis to block out any irritating intruders. Long hours of practice and strict discipline allow the dedicated Dreamer to ignore even the most persistent shopper.

The Primadonna is the third type of salesperson. No longer a mere mortal salesclerk, the Primadonna will wait upon only those clients who meet her exacting standards. Any new customer wishing to be helped by this especially qualified consultant must supply her with a list of references, an income statement, a birth certificate, and a handwritten promise never to make a purchase under one thousand dollars. Once customers accept these terms of surrender, the Primadonna will give them all the benefits of her superior merchandise knowledge, providing of course they have made an appointment in advance. However, the Primadonna is not completely inflexible with her standards. Under special circumstances, customers wishing to make purchases greater than the national deficit, for example, will be assisted without the normal formalities. Nevertheless, all unworthy shoppers are directed to less gifted salesclerks.

Small wonder, then, that so many customers are offended by these salesclerks, especially because these women are being paid to serve the very customers they are being rude to. Perhaps one day these salesclerks will change their attitudes. After all, no matter what the inflation rate, a smile is still free.

Discovery Exercise

1. Identify the thesis statement
   a. the group being classified: ______________________
   b. basis of the classification: ______________________
2. Identify the three major types: ______________________
   ____
   ____
3. Identify the order of the types:
   ________ general to particular
   ________ climactic
   ________ time/chronological
4. Identify the point of view: ________ person
5. Identify the verb tense: ________
6. Circle **six** transitional expressions.
7. Identify **five** of the most concrete supporting details: ______________________
   ____
   ____
   ____
   ____
8. Choose terms from the diction chart that characterize the diction: ______________________
9. Choose terms from the tone chart that describe the tone:
   ____
10. After reviewing Chapter 16, bracket **five** examples of items in a series, one type of grammatical structure used in this essay.

STUDENT SAMPLE—Classification Essay

Source of material: textbook on logic

Logical Thinking

Thomas Jefferson, the third President of the United States, once said, "In a republican nation, whose citizens are to be led by reason and persuasion and not by force, the art of reasoning becomes of first importance." Jefferson was speaking of the same subject which has confused and bewildered many a college undergraduate: logic. Logical thinking heightens one's ability to express ideas clearly and concisely; it increases one's skill in defining one's terms. In addition, logic enhances one's ability to form arguments or propositions clearly and to analyze them critically. A place to begin the study of this vast field is with a classification of the three basic types of reasoning. On the basis of how one thinks, these forms can be identified as symbolic, inductive, and deductive logic.

Arguments presented in English, French, German, or any other natural language are often misleading and difficult to evaluate; therefore, one form of reasoning, symbolic logic, was established to avoid these problems. Using symbols to replace words avoids ambiguity and equivocation, and also, more importantly, removes the emotive significance of a word. For example, if one saw the argument

All politicians are crooks.
Abraham Lincoln was a politician.
Abraham Lincoln was a crook.

it would clearly evoke some type of response. The words *politicians*, *crooks*, and *Abraham Lincoln* are all very emotional words. They produce a specific feeling inside a person. Some people may react positively while, at the same time, others will react with anger. This emotional reaction has gotten in the way of one's purpose--to analyze the form, structure, and validity. In symbolic logic, the words from the previous argument would be changed from English to some given symbolic language. For example, keeping the form and structure intact, the same argument in a less emotive language would be

All M are P
S is M
Therefore, S is P.

The argument is still valid in this new language where it is easier to manipulate statements, draw inferences, and appraise arguments. However, although natural languages do cause difficulties, the majority of propositions are written in this form.

The second form of reasoning is inductive logic, the form commonly used in daily life. Reasoning by analogy involves using past experiences to arrive at conclusions about the future. The premises of such a proposition assert that the conclusion is probably true and is based on experience. To illustrate thinking by analogy, people may infer that they will enjoy a new book by a certain author because they really enjoyed the writer's last book. None of these inductive arguments is certain or demonstratively valid. None of the conclusions follows with logical necessity from the premises. It is logically possible that people may hate the new book of that certain author. But then, no argument by analogy is meant to be mathematically certain. Probability is all that is asserted.

Although every argument involves the claim that its premises provide some grounds for the truth of its conclusion, only a deductive argument, the third form of reasoning, involves the claim that its premises provide conclusive grounds. Such arguments can be evaluated in three different ways. First, the conclusion is rejected because the premises are false and the reasoning is false. In this case, the argument is false. An example is the deductive argument

> All people who attend church are religious.
> John is religious.
> Therefore, John attends church.

A second type of argument occurs when the premises are false but the reasoning is correct. In this case, the argument is valid but not true because the conclusion follows from the premises which are false. Therefore, the conclusion is rejected. An example is the argument

> All gentlemen prefer blondes.
> John is a gentleman.
> Therefore, John prefers blondes.

The last type of argument involves true premises and correct reasoning. In this case, the argument is both valid and true. So the conclusion is accepted. To illustrate this argument

> All humans are mortal.
> Socrates is human.
> Therefore, Socrates is mortal.

The task of deductive logic is to clarify the nature of the relation between premises and conclusion and, thus, to distinguish true from untrue arguments.

Logic assists the mind in making inferences, evaluating assertions, and checking for validity and truth. As Juliana Guana Pilon claimed, "Civilized life depends upon the success of reason in social intercourse, the prevalence of logic over violence in interpersonal conflict." These forms of reasoning are important in the development of arguments and in the understanding of ideas.

Discovery Exercise

1. Identify the thesis statement
   a. the group being classified: ______________________________
   b. basis of the classification: ______________________________
2. Identify the three major types: ______________________________
   ____
   ____
3. Identify the order of the types:
   __________ general to particular
   __________ climactic
   __________ time/chronological
4. Identify the point of view: __________ person
5. Identify the verb tense: __________
6. Circle **six** transitional expressions.
7. Select **five** examples that characterize the diction: ______________________________
   ____
   ____
   ____
   ____
   ____
8. Choose terms from the diction chart that describe the diction:
   ____
9. Choose terms from the tone chart that describe the tone: ______________________________
   ____
10. After reviewing Chapter 16, bracket **four** appositive phrases, one type of grammatical structure used in this essay.

STUDENT SAMPLE—Classification Essay

Source of material: personal experience

Ten for the Perfect Tan

On the warm sunny beaches of Southern California, people of all types join in an age-old custom called sunbathing. It is a sport without rules which anyone can play, the young and the old, the male and the female, the fat and the skinny and, of course, the rich and the poor. However, the participants in this event choose several techniques to attain their goal, the ultimate tan. The players can be identified on the basis of their enthusiasm for the sport and their ability to brown. Three of the most recognizable types are the "incognito paleface," the "typical tanner," and the "daystar devotee."

One type of tanner, the "incognito paleface," begins the season as white as a blank page and ends it as red as a fire engine. She hasn't seen daylight through the winter months but decides to make up for that lost time on her first day at the beach. Of course, she comes prepared, bringing gobs of sun-protectant lotions. After applying sunscreens #6 through #15 to various portions of her body and a slimy white substance on her nose, the sunbather dons sunglasses and a huge straw hat. At this point, she positions her beach chair under an umbrella, sits down, places a large towel over her legs, and pleasantly but defiantly awaits the "great race" of the sun. Inevitably, she takes a quick dip in the ocean to cool off, lies in the sun for "just a second" to dry off, and falls asleep only to be awakened by the excruciating pain of a second-degree sunburn. This sun worshipper has lost the game again.

Another type, the "typical tanner," is only a half-hearted competitor. He is more interested in the other games on the beach like girl watching, surf riding and frisbee throwing. The amount of sun he gets is directly proportional to the amount of time he spends at his other sports. He is not concerned with sun-blocking lotions or sun-protection paraphenalia, for he has been at these sports all year long and has already established a warm brown tan. He will not, however, be a close competitor for the world's greatest tan because his indoor sports are just as important to him. His tan is a bonus from his outdoor activities rather than a result of hours of lying prone in the sun. Therefore, his tan will never get past the stage of warm brown.

Now, "daystar devotees" are the most earnest of all game players. They take the sport most seriously; they would never think of using any kind of sun-blocking lotion. Instead, these tanners continually search for the gel or lotion that will assist the sun in giving them the deepest, darkest, most golden tan imaginable. They are quite easy to notice on the beach, for they are the ones with the oiled-down bodies surrounded by bottles and bottles of suntan lotion. Their bodies will be in a prone position facing sunward and will move periodically like the shadow on a sundial. They are on the beach from sunrise to sunset with other fellow contestants clad in "barely there" G-string bikinis. Their tan lines will range from deep dark bronze to cherry red, reflecting the progressively skimpier bathing suits they wear as the summer draws to an end. However, the true fanatic sunbather may not show any suntan lines since he or she has found a nude beach or sundeck on which to soak in the rays for an all-over tan. He or she, of course, will get extra points for this daring feat. The "daystar devotee" is usually the winner at summer's end when all the votes are counted.

Sun worshipping, as a tradition, has been linked with religion, taboos and philosophies. Only recently has this practice been associated with sportsmanship. No matter whether tanners follow any special rules or whether they earn a full ten points, sunbathers always have something to show for their efforts.

PROFESSIONAL SAMPLE—Classification

Read the following essay to see how a professional writer has used the technique of classification. Then answer the discovery questions which focus on the major elements of classification writing.

Lewis Thomas (1913–), a medical doctor, formerly was president of Memorial Sloan-Kettering Cancer Center in New York. He is a regular contributor to the *New England Journal of Medicine.* In 1975 he won the National Book Award for *The Lives of a Cell: Notes of a Biology Watcher,* a collection of those magazine essays. This essay, "The Technology of Medicine," is an excerpt from that book.

The Technology of Medicine

1 Technology assessment has become a routine exercise for the scientific enterprises on which the country is obliged to spend vast sums for its needs. Brainy committees are continually evaluating the effectiveness and cost of doing various things in space, defense, energy, transportation, and the like, to give advice about prudent investments for the future.

2 Somehow medicine, for all the $80-odd billion that it is said to cost the nation, has not yet come in for much of this analytical treatment. It seems taken for granted that the technology of medicine simply exists, take it or leave it, and the only major technologic problem which policymakers are interested in is how to deliver today's kind of health care, with equity, to all the people.

3 When, as is bound to happen sooner or later, the analysts get around to the technology of medicine itself, they will have to face the problem of measuring the relative cost and effectiveness of all the things that are done in the management of disease. They make their living at this kind of thing, and I wish them well, but I imagine they will have a bewildering time. For one thing, our methods of managing disease are constantly changing—partly under the influence of new bits of information brought in from all corners of biologic science. At the same time, a great many things are done that are not so closely related to science, some not related at all.

4 In fact, there are three quite different levels of technology in medicine, so unlike each other as to seem altogether different undertakings. Practitioners of medicine and the analysts will be in trouble if they are not kept separate.

5 1. First of all, there is a large body of what might be termed "nontechnology," impossible to measure in terms of its capacity to alter either the natural course of disease or its eventual outcome. A great deal of money is spent on this. It is valued highly by the professionals as well as the patients. It consists of what is sometimes called "supportive therapy." It tides patients over through diseases that are not, by and large, understood. It is what is meant by the phrases "caring for" and "standing by." It is indispensable. It is not, however, a technology in any real sense, since it does not involve measures directed at the underlying mechanism of disease.

6 It includes the large part of any good doctor's time that is taken up with simply providing reassurance, explaining to patients who fear that they have contracted one or another lethal disease that they are, in fact, quite healthy.

7 It is what physicians used to be engaged in at the bedside of patients with diphtheria, meningitis, poliomyelitis, lobar pneumonia, and all the rest of the infectious diseases that have since come under control.

8 It is what physicians must now do for patients with intractable cancer, severe rheumatoid arthritis, multiple sclerosis, stroke, and advanced cirrhosis. One can think of at least twenty major diseases that require this kind of supportive medical care because of the absence of an effective technology. I would include a large amount of what is called mental disease, and most varieties of cancer, in this category.

9 The cost of this nontechnology is very high, and getting higher all the time. It requires not only a great deal of time but also very hard effort and skill on the part of physicians; only the very best of doctors are good at coping with this kind of defeat. It also involves long periods of hospitalization, lots of nursing, lots of involvement of nonmedical professionals in and out of the hospital. It represents, in short, a substantial segment of today's expenditures for health.

10 2. At the next level up is a kind of technology best termed "half-way technology." This represents the kinds of things that must be done

after the fact, in efforts to compensate for the incapacitating effects of certain diseases whose course one is unable to do very much about. It is a technology designed to make up for disease, or to postpone death.

11 The outstanding examples in recent years are the transplantations of hearts, kidneys, livers, and other organs, and the equally spectacular inventions of artificial organs. In the public mind, this kind of technology has come to seem like the equivalent of the high technologies of the physical sciences. The media tend to present each new procedure as though it represented a breakthrough and therapeutic triumph, instead of the makeshift that it really is.

12 In fact, this level of technology is, by its nature, at the same time highly sophisticated and profoundly primitive. It is the kind of thing that one must continue to do until there is a genuine understanding of the mechanisms involved in disease. In chronic glomerulonephritis, for example, a much clearer insight will be needed into the events leading to the destruction of glomeruli by the immunologic reactants that now appear to govern this disease, before one will know how to intervene intelligently to prevent the process, or turn it around. But when this level of understanding has been reached, the technology of kidney replacement will not be much needed and should no longer pose the huge problems of logistics, cost, and ethics that it poses today.

13 An extremely complex and costly technology for the management of coronary heart disease has evolved—involving specialized ambulances and hospital units, all kinds of electronic gadgetry, and whole platoons of new professional personnel—to deal with the end results of coronary thrombosis. Almost everything offered today for the treatment of heart disease is at this level of technology, with the transplanted and artificial hearts as ultimate examples. When enough has been learned to know what really goes wrong in heart disease, one ought to be in a position to figure out ways to prevent or reverse the process, and when this happens the current elaborate technology will probably be set to one side.

14 Much of what is done in the treatment of cancer, by surgery, irradiation, and chemotherapy, represents halfway technology, in the sense that these measures are directed at the existence of already established cancer cells, but not at the mechanisms by which cells become neoplastic.

15 It is a characteristic of this kind of technology that it costs an enormous amount of money and requires a continuing expansion of hospital facilities. There is no end to the need for new, highly trained people to run the enterprise. And there is really no way out of this, at the present state of knowledge. If the installation of specialized coronary-care units can result in the extension of life for only a few patients with coronary disease (and there is no question that this technology is effective in a few cases), it seems to me an inevitable fact of life that as many of these as can be will be put together, and as much money as can be found will be spent. I do not see that anyone has much choice in this. The only thing that can move medicine away from this level of technology is new information, and the only imaginable source of this information is research.

16 3. The third type of technology is the kind that is so effective that it seems to attract the least public notice; it has come to be taken for granted. This is the genuinely decisive technology of modern medicine, exemplified best by modern methods for immunization against diphtheria, pertussis, and the childhood virus diseases, and the contemporary use of antibiotics and chemotherapy for bacterial infections. The capacity to deal effectively with syphilis and tuberculosis represents a milestone in human endeavor, even though full use of this potential has not yet been made. And there are, of course, other examples: the treatment of endocrinologic disorders with appropriate hormones, the prevention of hemolytic disease of the newborn, the treatment and prevention of various nutritional disorders, and perhaps just around the corner the management of Parkinsonism and sickle-cell anemia. There are other examples, and everyone will have his favorite candidates for the list, but the truth is that there are nothing like as many as the public has been led to believe.

17 The point to be made about this kind of technology—the real high technology of medicine—is that it comes as the result of a genuine understanding of disease mechanisms, and when it becomes available, it is relatively inexpensive, and relatively easy to deliver.

18 Offhand, I cannot think of any important human disease for which medicine possesses the outright capacity to prevent or cure where the cost of the technology is itself a major problem. The price is never as high as the cost of managing the same diseases during the earlier stages of no-technology or halfway technology. If a case of ty-

phoid fever had to be managed today by the best methods of 1935, it would run to a staggering expense. At, say, around fifty days of hospitalization, requiring the most demanding kind of nursing care, with the obsessive concern for details of diet that characterized the therapy of that time, with daily laboratory monitoring, and, on occasion, surgical intervention for abdominal catastrophe, I should think $10,000 would be a conservative estimate for the illness, as contrasted with today's cost of a bottle of chloramphenicol and a day or two of fever. The halfway technology that was evolving for poliomyelitis in the early 1950s, just before the emergence of the basic research that made the vaccine possible, provides another illustration of the point. Do you remember Sister Kenny, and the cost of those institutes for rehabilitation, with all those ceremonially applied hot fomentations, and the debates about whether the affected limbs should be totally immobilized or kept in passive motion as frequently as possible, and the masses of statistically tormented data mobilized to support one view or the other? It is the cost of that kind of technology, and its relative effectiveness, that must be compared with the cost and effectiveness of the vaccine.

19 Pulmonary tuberculosis had similar episodes in its history. There was a sudden enthusiasm for the surgical removal of infected lung tissue in the early 1950s, and elaborate plans were being made for new and expensive installations for major pulmonary surgery in tuberculosis hospitals, and then INH and streptomycin came along and the hospitals themselves were closed up.

20 It is when physicians are bogged down by their incomplete technologies, by the innumerable things they are obliged to do in medicine when they lack a clear understanding of disease mechanisms, that the deficiencies of the health-care system are most conspicuous. If I were a policy-maker, interested in saving money for health care over the long haul, I would regard it as an act of high prudence to give high priority to a lot more basic research in biologic science. This is the only way to get the full mileage that biology owes to the science of medicine, even though it seems, as used to be said in the days when the phrase still had some meaning, like asking for the moon.

Discovery Questions

1. What is the group being classified, and what is the basis of the classification?
2. What is Thomas's thesis, and where is it located?
3. What are the three types? Why does he use both words and numbers to distinguish them?
4. What is the order of his types? Why does he use that order?
5. Is Thomas's treatment of his types coordinate? What information does he present for all three?

Suggested Groups to Classify

Select one of the following or similar groups. Decide on a single basis of classification before you break your group into its types or kinds.

athletes
babies
bad habits
blind dates
cigarette smokers
comedians
dancers
dieters
drinkers

eaters
employers
exercisers
fellow employees
gems
grocery shoppers
inconsiderate people
kites
movie goers

neighbors
newspapers
salespeople
schools
skiers
sleeping patterns
sports fans
summer jobs
vacations

WORKSHEET FOR CLASSIFICATION

1. Select a group to classify and complete the top half of the worksheet.
2. Write your thesis statement and enumeration of subtopics and then get approval from your instructor.
3. Complete the worksheet **before** writing the essay.
4. Attach the worksheet to the finished essay.
5. Attach the Expository Essay Cover Sheet to the finished essay.

Source of material: ____________________

Group to be classified: ____________________

Basis of classification: ____________________

Controlling idea: ______ (number) + ______ (adjective) + types/kinds (noun)

Order of three major types:

______ general to particular ______ time/chronological

______ climactic

Point of view: ______ Verb tense: ______

Tone: ______ Diction: ______

Thesis statement + enumeration of types (may be 1 or 2 sentences):

____

____

____

____
(instructor approval)

OUTLINE

Title: ____________________

¶1: Introduction (five sentences):

Choose a good beginning from the list.
Give necessary background material.

Good beginning # ______ : ____________________

____

____

____

____

When you write your introduction, include the approved thesis statement and subtopics at the end of paragraph 1.

Body (three paragraphs)

¶2: Transition + topic sentence: ______________________________

supporting details

¶3: Transition + topic sentence: ______________________________

supporting details

¶4: Transition + topic sentence: ______

supporting details

¶5: Conclusion (three sentences):
Restatement of class.
Choose one of the good endings from the list.

Good ending # ______

Name: ____________________

Date: ____________ **Class:** ________

Type of Exposition: ____________________

EXPOSITORY ESSAY COVER SHEET		
Structure/Ideas	+	________
Usage/Mechanics	−	________
Total		________
Rewrite points	+	________
TOTAL		________

Structure and Ideas (100 points)		**Original**		**Rewrite**
INTRODUCTION (at least five sentences):				
title; one of good beginnings leading to thesis		10________		________
thesis statement + enumeration of subtopics		5________		________
BODY (three supporting paragraphs):				
three topic sentences = transition + reference to thesis + subtopic		15________		________
development of paragraphs: sufficient, concrete, appropriate, relevant		45________		________
CONCLUSION (at least three sentences):				
one of good endings		5________		________
ESSAY:				
logical order of ideas and correct reasoning		5________		________
effective style = tone + diction + sentence structure + coherence		15________		________
	Total	100________	+	________

The points in this section reflect your score for structure and ideas. If you have received fewer than 100 points, you may rewrite your paper to earn them. Use the numbers as a guide to areas needing revision.

Usage and Mechanics (minus points). See Correction Symbol Chart.				
You **may** earn these points in revision:				
Usage: adj; adv; agr; awk; col; dm; frag; mm; ref; rep; shift; verb; ww; / /; ¶	−3 ea.	________		________
You **may not** earn these points in revision, but you must correct the errors:				
Mechanics: abbr; apos; cap; lc; p; ro; sp; ∧	−1 ea.	________		________
Total	−	________	+	________

CHAPTER 8

The Third Pattern: Analysis Functional

The concept of analysis is one which you have met before now. Perhaps you have had to analyze a chemical compound in the chemistry lab or a piece of literature in an English class. These situations involve the concept of analysis, that is, breaking an item into the parts that comprise it in order to understand the nature of the item.

Unlike classification, which relates something to its larger class or group, analysis is the form that relates something to its own parts. Analysis conveys an understanding of a structure, something with components that have a mutually supporting function. Examples are an object like an advertisement, a process like riding a horse, or an event like a revolution in Latin America.

Depending on the structure and the writer's purpose, there are three types of analysis: functional (discussed below), process (Chapter 9), and causal (Chapter 10). Chapter 14 examines in detail the critical analysis of nonfiction prose in anthologies, newspapers, magazines, and books.

Functional analysis answers the question "What is the purpose of the structure?" by showing the workings of the parts in relation to a characteristic role or function of the whole structure. In this type of analysis you must identify the role or purpose the structure performs and then show what parts contribute to that function. The function of a structure may vary depending on the writer's perspective.

For example, the function of a tree varies depending on whether it is viewed by a botanist, an artist, or a builder. A botanist sees a tree as a living organism whose parts contribute to its growth and development. An artist looks at a tree as an object whose parts create design, texture, and visual beauty. A builder examines a tree for the parts that contribute to the quality of the wood for building furniture or a house. Analysis shows what the parts of a mechanism are in relation to each other and the whole. Mechanisms are structures like poems, advertisements, movies, political parties, as well as a car or tele vision.

Requirements

You must clearly identify the function of the structure and apply the same characteristic function throughout the analysis in selecting the individual elements. You should account for all of the significant parts or elements. Omitting a part alters the structure and thereby destroys its unity. For example, the student essay entitled "Fascinating, Fiery Flamenco" analyzes the art of flamenco. The purpose of this essay is to convey the idea that the flamenco is an ancient art that is still popular. The writer discusses those significant elements—the dance, the guitar, and the song—which contribute to that function. Omitting any one of the elements of dance, guitar, or song would weaken the reader's understanding of the popularity of this art.

In functional analysis you must also show the mutual interdependence of elements to each other and to the whole. You must not just enumerate or itemize the parts but must establish the relationships among them. For example, in the same student essay the writer shows how these elements work together to make the flamenco the popular art form that it is.

Functional analysis, then, requires you to identify what elements make a structure perform its purpose or function effectively. It focuses on **what** makes something work. You should consider what contributions each of the main elements makes to the total structure. For instance, if you are analyzing an advertisement, poem, short story, play, or movie, you should account for the impact that the structure has on the audience. You accomplish this objective by showing how the parts work together.

Organizational Pattern for Functional Analysis

Study this blueprint so that you can see and better understand the elements necessary for functional analysis. Then use the pattern as a guide in assembling your own essay. Note that all the student samples in the chapter use this organizational pattern.

Title

Introduction—¶1

At least five sentences

Use of one of the good beginnings

Establishment of order of subtopics — verb tense
point of view — tone and diction

Structure to be analyzed and its characteristic function or purpose

Thesis statement = subject + controlling idea (number + adjective + elements)
Subtopic sentence = enumeration of three elements
} may be 1 or 2 sentences

Body—¶2, 3, 4

Presentation of three major elements

Logical order of three major elements

____ general to particular ____ climactic

**Paragraph 2:* Topic sentence = transitional expression + reference to thesis statement + element 1

Sufficient development of subject using supporting details such as specific examples, facts, illustrations, anecdotes. Relate the contribution made by the element to the function of the whole structure.

**Paragraph 3:* Topic sentence = transitional expression + reference to thesis statement + element 2

Sufficient development of subject using supporting details such as specific examples, facts, illustrations, anecdotes. Relate the contribution made by the element to the function of the whole structure.

**Paragraph 4:* Topic sentence = transitional expression + reference to thesis statement + element 3

Sufficient development of subject using supporting details such as specific examples, facts, illustrations, anecdotes. Relate the contribution made by the element to the function of the whole structure.

Transitional expressions: see especially

Addition — Purpose
Introduction of Illustration/Example — Spatial/Direction

Conclusion—¶5

At least three sentences

Transitional expression (optional): see Conclusion/Result and Summary

Restatement of structure analyzed and its overall impact

Use of one of the good endings

*These elements may be rearranged within the sentence.

Reprinted by permission of Philip Morris Incorporated.

STUDENT SAMPLE—Functional Analysis Essay—Analyzed for Parts

Observe that elements of structure and content are labeled on the left while elements of style are identified on the right. This detailed analysis will help you plan your own essay.

Source of material: magazine advertisement

Tone: serious
Diction: concrete, technical
Order: General to particular

Title

A Long Way to Here

Introduction ¶ 1 — Good Beginning #14

Newsweek magazine is published weekly and is directed toward an audience desiring information on national and world events. An advertisement for Virginia Slims Lights cigarettes appeared in its February 2, 1985, issue. This ad appeals to the woman of today who wants to be liberated yet does not want to give up her sex appeal. Its primary function is to sell Virginia Slims cigarettes. The ad achieves its purpose by means of three important elements: [1] layout, [2] artwork, and [3] language.

Verb tense: present (appeals)

Function of the Structure

Thesis Statement (subject and controlling idea) and Subtopics (3 elements)

Point of view: third person (its)

Topic Sentence ¶2

The first* basic element of the advertisement is the layout.+ It consists of three main sections. The most dominant is the full-length picture of a beautiful, slim woman occupying the right third of the page. The next part, located in the top left corner, is a simulated photograph of a typical 1910 couple.

Diction: technical (layout)

Transitional expressions: spatial (right third; top left corner)

[Paragraph continues on the next page.]

* *Coherence: transitional expressions circled.*

\+ *The general physical position or arrangement of the different areas of the advertisement on the page: background, foreground, top, bottom, center, size of print.*

Under the photo, a two-line caption comments on the scene. The remaining two-thirds of the left-hand side shows in large letters the cigarette's logo and two packs, one opened and one closed. Beneath them is the famous Virginia Slims slogan. Completing the layout in the lower left-hand corner is the required surgeon general's warning and the tar and nicotine contents. All of these sections are presented against a light neutral background. The audience's attention is drawn to the figure of the woman smoking because she dominates the picture. Thus, the layout links the modern, beautiful woman with the cigarettes.

A second important part of the advertisement is the artwork.‡ The neutral background delineates all the parts sharply and crisply. The independence and self-confidence of the shapely young woman is conveyed by her pose. She stands sideways, casting an appealing half-smile over her shoulder. Her casual, windblown hair complements her soft falling, chocolate brown, geometrically bordered designer dress and shoes. One arm is crossed in front of her while the other

Diction: technical

Diction: technical

(Contribution of element to function of structure)

Concluding Sentence

Topic Sentence ¶3

Diction: technical

Diction: concrete

Body ¶ 2,3,4

‡ the specific details of the visual material of the advertisement: colors, kinds of letters, subject of photo

authoritatively holds up a long, slim cigarette. Her legs capture an easy, self-assured stride. This liberated female contrasts vividly with the 1910 woman in the simulated reproduction. She stands outside covered with the falling snow, and lugging logs for the lord of the house. He haughtily waits inside at the door, pipe in mouth, dressed in a geometrically printed bathrobe similar in design to the dress of the liberated woman. The message underlines the change in roles from 1910 to today. The various printing styles complement the advertisement's ideas. For instance, the caption under the 1910 photo uses old-fashioned lettering. In contrast, the cigarette's logo and its slogan use modern, trim print. Therefore, the artwork makes the audience identify with the liberated woman smoking the Virginia Slims.

A Sentence Structure: compound verbal phrase

Diction: alliterative (L)

Diction: concrete

Diction: technical

(Contribution of element to function of structure)

Diction technical

Concluding Sentence

Topic Sentence ¶4

The language is the ad's final significant element. The small, vertical printing in the right corner reads, "Fashion: Reiko" to emphasize the contemporary, high-fashioned clothes that this modern female wears. Such a reference is rare in advertisements. Further, the insert's caption reads, "Virginia Slims recalls how the woman of 1910 brought a little warmth into the house." This statement, in normal contexts, would be a metaphor for love, caring, concern, and all the other qualities a woman brings to a home. However, the advertisers have used this figurative statement literally, so that the woman carries the firewood that will warm the house. Thus, she is pictured as the servant and the inferior of her husband. In addition, the cigarette's name--Virginia Slims Lights--captures the qualities that every girl wants to have: slimness and lightness. The most important sentence, "You've come a long way, baby," underlines how far the modern female has progressed since 1910. She is clearly separated from her earlier counterpart; she stands alone by choice and seems to relish her new role. The advertiser wants the cigarette to be associated with all these positive feelings of independence, attractiveness, and progress, symbolized by the modern woman.

B Sentence Structure: items in a series

Diction: technical

Diction: technical

Sentence Structure: appositive phrase

Sentence Structure: noun dependent clause

(Contribution of element to function of structure)

Concluding Sentence

Conclusion ¶ 5

Good Endings #1 and 7

Consequently, the advertiser has effectively combined all the elements of a successful appeal: the layout, artwork, and language. It is clear that this product is designed solely for women, especially those who like to think of themselves as liberated yet still appealing. Thus, the subconscious message is that women who smoke this brand are somehow part of the universal advancement of their sex.

STUDENT SAMPLE—Functional Analysis Essay

Source of material: personal experience

If This Is Summer, It Must Be Tour Time

A packaged group tour has several advantages over sojourning alone. The friendly tour company makes all the bothersome arrangements for the globe trotters and usually saves them money in the process. Thus, when people take a vacation, they expect to leave their aggravations and worries with the housesitter. However, not all holiday tours are successful, although they all are memorable. A vacation can be disastrous if any one of its three main parts--location, fellow travelers, or activities--fizzles.

One basic element that can create a catastrophe is the location. Assuming that the local guide and the excited adventurers find each other, they trek off to the hotel, which is supposed to be on the beach, not on the highway. Or the hotel is so far out in the suburbs that there is much time and expense involved in getting to the center of activity. After endless time is consumed distributing the rooms and keys, the next hurdle to overcome is waiting for the luggage to appear. Invariably, someone's suitcase containing the party clothes is flying off to the plane's next destination. The accommodations are the next snag because family members are assigned to rooms on different floors or on opposite sides of the hotel. Insistence on three separate beds in one room predictably means two double beds. Waiting for the extra bed wastes some more valuable time. If the checking-in process might, by some slim chance, proceed smoothly, then the tourists can be assured that the weather will be either windy or rainy.

Fellow voyagers, another part of a vacation, can turn a tour into a travesty. There are always a few tipsy tourists who get their spirit from a flask that they are never without. Also, whenever the group is squeezed into a bus, a restaurant, or any other confined area, the cigar smokers light up and puff away. Their acrid, pungent smoke mingles with that of the occasional pipe and the numerous cigarette smokers. Then, the ubiquitous laughers, shouters, and complainers add noise to the background odors. If tour members successfully elude these annoying traveling companions, then the family fighters disturb the tranquility. The most frustrating type of tour taker is encountered during the sightseeing trips. The group waits and waits and waits for the stragglers to finish eating or drinking, photographing sites, and buying souvenirs before they reboard the bus. A two-week respite can quickly become a crash course in group interaction.

Tour passengers who miraculously survive these threats to sanity can have a holiday ruined by a third element--the activities. While sightseeing is often the prime purpose of excursionists, it often is the source of anxiety. It is an accepted universal truth that never enough time is set aside to see the sights properly. The time that is spent is often wasted with a tour guide who speaks English poorly or who can only replay the memorized speech like a tape recorder. Having planned to see the most famous sights, the explorers find that these are not included in the base price and, consequently, cost extra. Eating is the other favorite activity prone to calamity. Often on tours, because the food has been prepaid, the travelers have to eat what they are given. With no choice, many palates are disappointed. The other response is to overeat in order to get what has already been paid for. Even if the vacationers consume wisely, they risk indigestion and nausea from the change of climate or diet. Certainly, no one can enjoy a trip when suffering such physical discomforts.

All these elements can destroy the most anticipated and best planned holiday. The packaged group tour is even more likely to leave the travelers disappointed because they have had so little control over the arrangements. Consequently, the weary, bedraggled, nauseated wayfarers are happy to return to their familiar frustrations and annoyances.

Discovery Exercise

1. Identify the structure being analyzed and its characteristic function: ______________________
2. Identify the thesis statement
   a. the subject being discussed: ______________________
   b. the controlling idea: ______________________
3. Identify the three main elements: ______________________
   ____
   ____
4. Identify the order of the elements:
   ____ climactic
   ____ general to particular
5. Identify the point of view: __________ person
6. Identify the verb tense: __________
7. Select **three** examples of overstatement:
   ____
   ____
   ____
8. Chose terms from the diction chart that characterize the diction: ______________________
9. Choose terms from the tone chart that describe the tone: ______________________
10. List all the synonyms for the following terms:

trip	**travelers**
____________	____________
____________	____________
____________	____________
____________	____________
____________	____________
____________	____________
____________	____________
____________	____________

11. After reviewing Chapter 16, bracket **five** compound adjectives, one type of grammatical structure used in the essay.

Reprinted by permission of Carte Blanche Corp.

STUDENT SAMPLE—Functional Analysis Essay

Source of material: magazine advertisement

I'm Giving You "Carte Blanche"

Los Angeles magazine is directed to the affluent individual and contains articles of current social, political, and economic interest about the city. The November 1985 issue presented an advertisement for Carte Blanche, a major credit card honored around the world. The ad appeals to the middle-class person who desires to be sophisticated, modern, financially independent, well-dressed, and well-groomed and to be surrounded by the ultimate in luxury. Obviously the ad's prime purpose is to convince people to apply for and use the Carte Blanche card. It accomplishes its function by using several major elements: layout, artwork, and language.

The layout is the first important part of this ad. On the upper half of the page, a man and a woman stand at the opposite front doors of an automobile. Behind them is the facade of a building and shrubbery. In the upper left-hand corner are three small lines of print. The bottom half of the page contains nothing but two medium lines of words directly below the picture and two additional lines at the very bottom of the page with a Carte Blanche card centered directly above them. Because of the perspective of the car's front grill and hood ornament which gives the impression that the vehicle is driving out of the picture, one's eye is immediately drawn to the center of the photo. Thus, the focal point emphasizes the message printed under the automobile.

The ad's next significant element is the artwork. The top half is constructed to show extreme wealth. The Rolls Royce Silver Shadow dominates the photo. The well-dressed people are standing nonchalantly against the shiny, expensive car. The man, holding a newspaper while his leather attaché case rests on the auto's hood, wears an elegant tie, a long-sleeved, cuff-linked shirt, and a fashionable dark suit with a boutonniere. The lady wears an expensive wool tweed jacket, a silk ascot, leather gloves, and a sophisticated coiffure. Behind the couple is the side wall of what appears to be a mansion with a large, elaborate, twisted column. The building's lines as well as the shrubbery are slightly out of focus to complement rather than detract from the main scene. The bottom half of the page is black in order to convey attitudes of elegance, good taste, understatement, and sophistication. These attitudes would appeal to the potential consumer. The Carte Blanche credit card, because it is primarily white, stands out clearly. Thus, the key to the artwork is that the top half equals the bottom half; in other words, the equation translates into the idea that if people have a Carte Blanche credit card, they can think of themselves as wealthy and elite.

Finally, language is a fundamental part of this commercial message. The subdued printing in the upper half of the ad reads, "The Rolls Royce Silver Shadow. Available upon qualified reservation. Avis Rent a Car, Heathrow Airport, London." These words, first of all, identify the make of the car to anyone who might not be sure. Then, they suggest that, even though most people can not own one, such a vehicle can be rented. Third, the city named connotes upper-class status and refined dignity. At the bottom of the page is printed, "Carte Blanche, honored by major airlines, hotels, rent-a-car agencies and fine restaurants throughout the world. To apply for membership call. . . ." This language illustrates the idea that Carte Blanche is for the wealthy who stay in hotels, not the average people who stay in motels; for the wealthy who use major airlines, not the average ones who use regular airlines; for the wealthy who eat in fine restaurants, not the average individuals who eat in coffee shops. The main message is contained in two simple yet connotative sentences in the center of the page: "Some people travel with credit cards. Some people have carte blanche." On one level, it suggests that ordinary people use credit cards while the wealthy have an unlimited amount of financial resources, the figurative translation of the French phrase carte blanche. On a second level, the message suggests that, while Carte Blanche is a credit card, it is in a completely different category from other such cards. Knowledgeable, well-to-do individuals use this particular credit card, drive this particular car, wear these particular fashions, not just any. The appeal is clearly a snob appeal.

In conclusion, the elements of layout, artwork, and language function successfully in this advertisement. It inspires readers to apply for financial independence, affluence, and social status rather than just a credit card. Hence, when people receive Carte Blanche, they are receiving the ultimate symbol of luxurious living. This ad certainly illustrates Samuel Johnson's well-phrased and insightful statement, "Promise, large promise, is the soul of an advertisement."

Discovery Exercise

1. Identify the structure being analyzed and its characteristic function: ____________________
2. Identify the thesis statement
   a. the subject being discussed: ____________________
   b. the controlling idea: ____________________
3. Identify the three main elements: ____________________

   ____

   ____
4. Identify the order of the elements:

   ____ climactic

   ____ general to particular
5. Identify the point of view: __________ person
6. Identify the verb tense: __________

7. Identify the overall impact of the structure.

____

____

____

8. Choose terms from the diction chart that characterize the diction: ____________

9. Choose terms from the tone chart that describe the tone: ____________

10. After reviewing Chapter 16, bracket **five** compound adjectives, one type of grammatical structure used in this essay.

STUDENT SAMPLE—Functional Analysis Essay

Source of material: book on dance

Fascinating, Fiery Flamenco

Music is an art that includes many forms; one of the most expressive and beautiful of these forms is flamenco. It originated several hundred years ago from the souls of the oppressed, yet proud and change-resistant, gypsies of southern Spain. The full range of human emotions is touched by this sometimes haunting, sometimes fiery music. There are set flamenco rhythms that make up the repertoire of this art, yet flamenco encourages its performers to improvise within the set pattern, and thus, the music has remained vibrant throughout the years. The three main components of flamenco, which are the dance, the guitar, and the song, combine together to produce an overall effect that is spellbinding.

The dance or *baile* is flamenco's most popular segment because it captures the attention of the eye as well as the ear. The staccato rhythm produced by the heels of a lone male dancer on a wooden stage, often in counterrhythm to the guitarist, can mesmerize an audience. The masculine Farruca, a fast-paced flamenco dance, is best suited to the male dancer's talent. His back is held straight, as opposed to the female dancer who arches her back slightly when she dances. Often wearing a figure-hugging *bata de cola*, which is a colorful gown with a trail, she places less emphasis on her heelwork. The female dancer concentrates her efforts on the graceful movement of the arms, hands, and fingers. Her *duende* or true flamenco spirit can best be observed when she performs a Seguiriya, perhaps one of the most complicated and beautiful of all the flamenco rhythms. A flamenco dancer appears to stare straight ahead as the dance progresses, but an observer can feel the emotions that are contained behind those austere eyes.

The classical Spanish guitar is the second component of flamenco. Seated behind the moving dancer, on a staight-back chair, is the musician. He accompanies with rhythms produced by the flourish of fingers across the strings of the guitar. He does not attract the eye as the dancer does. However, without the sounds he produces on his instrument, the dance would be an empty act. His music can range from mournful to joyful depending on the particular flamenco number he is playing. His versatility is evidenced when he follows the chords of a melancholy Soleares with the lively strains of a carefree Buleria. His facial expressions, like the dancer's, do not betray his innermost feelings, but the strength and character of his music hide no emotions.

The third component, the *cante* or song, is the backbone of flamenco. The singer's rendition of a flamenco tale speaks of love, jealousy, hate, grief, or joy. The guitarist and dancer will respond to the story with their own emotions which are reflected in their performances. The singer, like the guitarist, sits on a straight-back chair, and from there he performs the art of the flamenco song. There are many female singers of *cante* flamenco, but commercially it is the male who most often is heard. When he performs a song, such as a grief-filled Taranto, he goes beyond singing. Unlike the dancer and guitarist, every emotion can be evidenced on his face, as well as through his voice which cries out in a rough, primitive manner that contacts the heart of the listener.

A perfect harmony of dance, guitar, and song is the essence of flamenco. Each component is a strong, yet pliable thread, but only when the threads are interwoven does the true design appear. The audience, also, becomes a part of this design because of the emotional interaction between observer and performer. Flamenco is an art that is ancient in years, but its soul is eternal.

PROFESSIONAL SAMPLE—Functional Analysis

Read the following essay to see how a professional writer has used the technique of analysis. Then answer the discovery questions which focus on the major elements of functional analysis.

Daniel Boorstin (1914–), a prominent American historian, is currently Librarian of Congress. He was a Rhodes scholar at Oxford, a barrister-at-law at the Inner Temple, London, and a professor of American history at the University of Chicago. He received a Pulitzer Prize for his three-volume reinterpretation of American history, *The Americans* (1958–1973). He has written many articles on numerous topics for professional and popular magazines. This excerpt comes from his book *Democracy and Its Discontents* (1974).

American Advertising

1 Here I wish to explore the significance of advertising, not as a force in the economy or in shaping an American standard of living, but rather as a touchstone of the ways in which we Americans have learned about all sorts of things.

2 The problems of advertising are of course not peculiar to advertising, for they are just one aspect of the problems of democracy. They reflect the rise of what I have called Consumption Communities and Statistical Communities, and many of the special problems of advertising have arisen from our continuously energetic effort to give everybody everything.

3 If we consider democracy not just as a political system, but as a set of institutions which do aim to make everything available to everybody, it would not be an overstatement to describe advertising as the characteristic rhetoric of democracy.

One of the tendencies of democracy, which Plato and other antidemocrats warned against a long time ago, was the danger that rhetoric would displace or at least overshadow epistemology, that is, *the temptation to allow the problem of persuasion to overshadow the problem of knowledge.* Democratic societies tend to become more concerned with what people believe than with what is true, to become more concerned with credibility than with truth. All these problems become accentuated in a large-scale democracy like ours, which possesses all the apparatus of modern industry. And the problems are accentuated still further by universal literacy, by instantaneous communication, and by the daily plague of words and images.

4 In the early days it was common for advertising men to define advertisements as a kind of news. The best admen, like the best journalists, were supposed to be those who were able to make their news the most interesting and readable. This was natural enough, since the verb to "advertise" originally meant, intransitively, to take note or to consider. For a person to "advertise" meant originally, in the fourteenth and fifteenth centuries, to reflect on something, to think about something. Then it came to mean, transitively, to call the attention of another to do something, to give him notice, to notify, admonish, warn or inform in a formal or impressive manner. And then, by the sixteenth century, it came to mean: to give notice of anything, to make generally known. It was not until the late eighteenth century that the word "advertising" in English came to have a specifically "advertising" connotation as we might say today, and not until the late nineteenth century that it began to have a specifically commercial connotation. By 1879 someone was saying, "Don't advertise unless you have something worth advertising." But even into the present century, newspapers continue to call themselves by the title "Advertiser"—for example, the Boston *Daily Advertiser,* which was a newspaper of long tradition and one of the most dignified papers in Boston until William Randolph Hearst took it over in 1917. Newspapers carried "Advertiser" on their mastheads, not because they sold advertisements but because they brought news.

5 Now, the main role of advertising in American civilization came increasingly to be that of persuading and appealing rather than that of educating and informing. By 1921, for instance, one of the more popular textbooks, Blanchard's *Essentials of Advertising,* began: "Anything employed to influence people favorably is advertising. The mission of advertising is to persuade men and women to act in a way that will be of advantage to the advertiser." This development—in a country where a shared, a rising, and a democratized standard of living was the national pride and the national hallmark—meant that advertising had become the rhetoric of democracy.

6 What, then, were some of the main features of modern American advertising—if we consider it as a form of rhetoric? First, and perhaps most obvious, is *repetition.* It is hard for us to realize that the use of repetition in advertising is not an ancient device but a modern one, which actually did not come into common use in American journalism until just past the middle of the nineteenth century.

7 The development of what came to be called "iteration copy" was the result of a struggle by a courageous man of letters and advertising pioneer, Robert Bonner, who brought the old New York *Merchant's Ledger* in 1851 and turned it into a popular journal. He then had the temerity to try to change the ways of James Gordon Bennett, who of course was one of the most successful of the American newspaper pioneers, and who was both a sensationalist and at the same time an extremely stuffy man when it came to things that he did not consider to be news. Bonner was determined to use advertisements in Bennett's wide-circulating New York *Herald* to sell his own literary product, but he found it difficult to persuade Bennett to allow him to use any but agate type in his advertising. (Agate was the smallest type used by newspapers in that day, only barely legible to the naked eye.) Bennett would not allow advertisers to use larger type, nor would he allow them to use illustrations except stock cuts, because he thought it was undignified. He said, too, that to allow a variation in the format of ads would be undemocratic. He insisted that all advertisers use the same size type so that no one would be allowed to prevail over another simply by presenting his message in a larger, more clever, or more attention-getting form.

8 Finally, Bonner managed to overcome Bennett's rigidity by leasing whole pages of the paper and using the tiny agate type to form larger letters across the top of the page. In this way he produced a message such as "Bring home the New York Ledger tonight." His were unimaginative messages, and when repeated all across the page they technically did not violate Bennett's agate rule. But they opened a new era and presaged a new freedom for advertisers in their use of the

newspaper page. Iteration copy—the practice of presenting prosaic content in ingenious, repetitive form—became common, and nowadays of course is commonplace.

9 A second characteristic of American advertising which is not unrelated to this is the development of *an advertising style*. We have histories of most other kinds of style—including the style of many unread writers who are remembered today only because they have been forgotten—but we have very few accounts of the history of advertising style, which of course is one of the most important forms of our language and one of the most widely influential.

10 The development of advertising style was the convergence of several very respectable American traditions. One of these was the tradition of the "plain style," which the Puritans made so much of and which accounts for so much of the strength of the Puritan literature. The "plain style" was of course much influenced by the Bible and found its way into the rhetoric of American writers and speakers of great power like Abraham Lincoln. When advertising began to be self-conscious in the early years of this century, the pioneers urged copywriters not to be too clever, and especially not to be fancy. One of the pioneers of the advertising copywriters, John Powers, said, for example, "The commonplace is the proper level for writing in business; where the first virtue is plainness, 'fine writing' is not only intellectual, it is offensive." George P. Rowell, another advertising pioneer, said, "You must write your advertisement to catch damned fools—not college professors." He was a very tactful person. And he added, "And you'll catch just as many college professors as you will of any other sort." In the 1920's, when advertising was beginning to come into its own, Claude Hopkins, whose name is known to all in the trade, said, "Brilliant writing has no place in advertising. A unique style takes attention from the subject. Any apparent effort to sell creates corresponding resistance. . . . One should be natural and simple. His language should not be conspicuous. In fishing for buyers, as in fishing for bass, one should not reveal the hook." So there developed a characteristic advertising style in which plainness, the phrase that anyone could understand, was a distinguishing mark.

11 At the same time, the American advertising style drew on another, and what might seem an antithetic, tradition—the tradition of hyperbole and tall talk, the language of Davy Crockett and Mike Fink. While advertising could think of itself as 99.44 percent pure, it used the language of "Toronado" and "Cutlass." As I listen to the radio in Washington, I hear a celebration of heroic qualities which would make the characteristics of Mike Fink and Davy Crockett pale, only to discover at the end of the paean that what I have been hearing is a description of the Ford dealers in the District of Columbia neighborhood. And along with the folk tradition of hyperbole and tall talk comes the rhythm of folk music. We hear that Pepsi-Cola hits the spot, that it's for the young generation—and we hear other products celebrated in music which we cannot forget and sometimes don't want to remember.

12 There grew somehow out of all these contradictory tendencies—combining the common-sense language of the "plain style," and the fantasy language of "tall talk"—an advertising style. This characteristic way of talking about things was especially designed to reach and catch the millions. It created a whole new world of myth. A myth, the dictionary tells us, is a notion based more on tradition or convenience than on facts; it is a received idea. Myth is not just fantasy and not just fact but exists in a limbo, in the world of the "Will to Believe," which William James has written about so eloquently and so perceptively. This is the world of the neither true nor false—of the statement that 60 percent of the physicians who expressed a choice said that our brand of aspirin would be more effective in curing a simple headache than any other leading brand.

13 That kind of statement exists in a penumbra. I would call this the "advertising penumbra." It is not untrue, and yet, in its connotation it is not exactly true.

14 Now, there is still another characteristic of advertising so obvious that we are inclined perhaps to overlook it. I call that *ubiquity*. Advertising abhors a vacuum and we discover new vacuums every day. The parable, of course, is the story of the man who thought of putting the advertisement on the other side of the cigarette package. Until then, that was wasted space and a society which aims at a democratic standard of living, at extending the benefits of consumption and all sorts of things and services to everybody, must miss no chances to reach people. The highway billboard and other outdoor advertising, bus and streetcar and subway advertising, and skywriting, radio and TV commercials—all these are of course obvious evidence that advertising abhors a vacuum.

15 We might reverse the old mousetrap slogan and say that anyone who can devise another place to put another mousetrap to catch a consumer will find people beating a path to his door. "Avoiding advertising will become a little harder next January," the *Wall Street Journal* reported on May 17, 1973, "when a Studio City, California, company launches a venture called Store Vision. Its product is a system of billboards that move on a track across supermarket ceilings. Some 650 supermarkets so far are set to have the system." All of which helps us understand the observation attributed to a French man of letters during his recent visit to Times Square. "What a beautiful place, if only one could not read!" Everywhere is a place to be filled, as we discover in a recent *Publishers Weekly* description of one advertising program: "The $1.95 paperback edition of Dr. Thomas A. Harris' million-copy best seller 'I'm O.K., You're O.K.' is in for full-scale promotion in July by its publisher, Avon Books. Plans range from bumper stickers to airplane streamers, from planes flying above Fire Island, the Hamptons and Malibu. In addition, the $100,000 promotion budget calls for 200,000 bookmarks, plus brochures, buttons, lipcards, floor and counter displays, and advertising in magazines and TV."

16 The ubiquity of advertising is of course just another effect of our uninhibited efforts to use all the media to get all sorts of information to everybody everywhere. Since the places to be filled are everywhere, the amount of advertising is not determined by the *needs* of advertising, but by the *opportunities* for advertising which become unlimited.

17 But the most effective advertising, in an energetic, novelty-ridden society like ours, tends to be "self-liquidating." To create a cliché you must offer something which everybody accepts. The most successful advertising therefore self-destructs because it becomes cliché. Examples of this are found in the tendency for copyrighted names of trademarks to enter the vernacular—for the proper names of products which have been made familiar by costly advertising to become common nouns, and so to apply to anybody's products. Kodak becomes a synonym for camera, Kleenex a synonym for facial tissue, when both begin with a small k, and Xerox (now, too, with a small x) is used to describe all processes of copying, and so on. These are prototypes of the problem. If you are successful enough, then you will defeat your purpose in the long run—by making the name and the message so familiar that people won't notice them, and then people will cease to distinguish your product from everybody else's.

18 In a sense, of course, as we will see, the whole of American civilization is an example. When this was a "new" world, if people succeeded in building a civilization here, the New World would survive and would reach the time—in our age—when it would cease to be new. And now we have the oldest written Constitution in use in the world. This is only a parable of which there are many more examples.

19 The advertising man who is successful in marketing any particular product, then—in our high-technology, well-to-do democratic society, which aims to get everything to everybody—is apt to be diluting the demand for his particular product in the very act of satisfying it. But luckily for him, he is at the very same time creating a fresh demand for his services as advertiser.

20 And as a consequence, there is yet another role which is assigned to American advertising. This is what I call "erasure." Insofar as advertising is competitive or innovation is widespread, erasure is required in order to persuade consumers that this year's model is superior to last year's. In fact, we consumers learn that we might be risking our lives if we go out on the highway with those very devices that were last year's lifesavers but without whatever special kinds of brakes or wipers or seat belts is on this year's model. This is what I mean by "erasure"—and we see it on our advertising pages or our television screen every day. We read in the *New York Times* (May 20, 1973), for example, that "For the price of something small and ugly, you can drive something small and beautiful"—an advertisement for the Fiat 250 Spider. Or another, perhaps more subtle example is the advertisement for shirts under a picture of Oliver Drab: "Oliver Drab. A name to remember in fine designer shirts? No kidding. . . . Because you pay extra money for Oliver Drab. And for all the other superstars of the fashion world. Golden Vee [the name of the brand that is advertised] does not have a designer's label. But we do have designers. . . . By keeping their names *off* our label and simply saying Golden Vee, we can afford to sell our $7 to $12 shirts for just $7 to $12, which should make Golden Vee a name to remember. Golden Vee, you only pay for the shirt." [Therefore, I have] . . . mentioned two special characteristics—the self-liquidating tendency and the need for erasure—which arise from the dynamism of the American economy. . . .

Discovery Questions

1. What particular "good beginning" (from Chapter 1) does Boorstin use to introduce his subject?
2. What is Boorstin's thesis, and in what paragraph is it located?
3. What are the elements of the structure being analyzed?
4. One of the elements is classified into different types. Which element is it, and what are the types?
5. What two special characteristics does Boorstin say that all advertising contains? What does he mean by those terms?

Suggested Structures to Analyze According to Function

Select one of the following or similar structures. Decide what basic elements enable this structure to fulfill its purpose.

a magazine advertisement
a poem
a supermarket
a telescope
a play or movie
a school
a business office
a political party
a hospital
a computer
a short story
a television program
an automobile
a calculator

WORKSHEET FOR FUNCTIONAL ANALYSIS

1. Select a structure to analyze and complete the top half of the worksheet.
2. Write your thesis statement and enumeration of subtopics and then get approval from your instructor.
3. Complete the worksheet **before** writing the essay.
4. Attach the worksheet to the finished essay.
5. Attach the Expository Essay Cover Sheet to the finished essay.

Source of material: ______________________________

Structure to be analyzed: ______________________________

Function of the structure: ______________________________

Controlling idea: __________ (number) + __________ (adjective) + elements (noun)

Order of three main parts:

____ climactic

____ general to particular

Point of view: ______________ Verb tense: ______________

Tone: ______________ Diction: ______________

Thesis statement + enumeration of elements (may be 1 or 2 sentences):

____

____

____

____

____
(instructor approval)

OUTLINE

Title: ______________________________

¶1: Introduction (five sentences):

Choose a good beginning from list.

Give necessary background material.

Good beginning # ________ : ______________________________

____

____

____

____

When you write your introduction, include the approved thesis and subtopics at the end of paragraph 1.

Body (three paragraphs)

¶2: Transition + topic sentence: ______________________________

supporting details

¶3: Transition + topic sentence: ______________________________

supporting details

¶4: Transition + topic sentence: ______________________________

____

supporting details

____

____

____

____

____

____

____

____

____

____

____

____

____

____

¶5: Conclusion (three sentences):

Restatement of structure to be analyzed and its overall impact.

Choose one of good endings from list.

Good ending # ______

____

____

____

____

____

____

Name: ______________________

Date: ______________ Class: ____________

Type of Exposition: ______________________

EXPOSITORY ESSAY COVER SHEET		
Structure/Ideas	+	________
Usage/Mechanics	−	________
Total		________
Rewrite points	+	________
TOTAL		________

Structure and Ideas (100 points)	Original	Rewrite
INTRODUCTION (at least five sentences):		
title; one of good beginnings leading to thesis	10______	______
thesis statement + enumeration of subtopics	5______	______
BODY (three supporting paragraphs):		
three topic sentences = transition + reference to thesis + subtopic	15______	______
development of paragraphs: sufficient, concrete, appropriate, relevant	45______	______
CONCLUSION (at least three sentences):		
one of good endings	5______	______
ESSAY:		
logical order of ideas and correct reasoning	5______	______
effective style = tone + diction + sentence structure + coherence	15______	______
Total	100______	+ ______

The points in this section reflect your score for structure and ideas. If you have received fewer than 100 points, you may rewrite your paper to earn them. Use the numbers as a guide to areas needing revision.

Usage and Mechanics (minus points). See Correction Symbol Chart.		
You **may** earn these points in revision:		
Usage: adj; adv; agr; awk; col; dm; frag; mm; ref; rep; shift; verb; ww; / /; ¶	−3 ea.______	______
You **may not** earn these points in revision, but you must correct the errors:		
Mechanics: abbr; apos; cap; lc; p; ro; sp; ∧	−1 ea.______	______
Total	− ______	+ ______

CHAPTER 9

The Third Pattern: Analysis Process

The concept of analysis is one which you have met before now. Perhaps you have wrestled with directions for assembling some complicated object, or you have recounted how some accident occurred. These situations involve the concept of analysis, that is, breaking an item into the parts that comprise it in order to understand the nature of the item.

Unlike classification, which relates something to its larger class or group, analysis is the form that relates something to its own parts. Analysis conveys an understanding of a structure, something with components that have a mutually supporting function. Examples are an object like an advertisement, a process like riding a horse, or an event like a revolution in Latin America.

Depending on the structure and the writer's purpose, there are three types of analysis: functional (Chapter 8), process (discussed below), and causal (Chapter 10). Chapter 14 examines in detail the critical analysis of nonfiction prose in anthologies, newspapers, magazines, and books.

Process analysis answers the question "How do the steps work together to produce the structure?" by showing their relationship in a time sequence. Because it analyzes a process or event (structure) in terms of time, it has a chronological framework. Thus, it relies on narration. There are two types of process analysis. **Mechanical** analysis identifies the stages by which a structure is put together or operates and gives how-to directions that can be repeated. For example, the student essay entitled "When in Need" outlines the steps in how to get money from your parents. **Historical** analysis describes the steps by which an event took place and identifies how something that cannot be repeated happened. For instance, the recounting of the development of the atomic bomb in the Manhattan Project in World War II identifies the steps by which the event occurred.

Requirements

You must clearly identify the process or event and enumerate all of the steps in the correct time order from beginning to end. If you omit a step, you alter the event. In addition, you must not confuse the sequence of steps because, otherwise, the relationship of the steps in the process will be altered and will change the event itself. For example, when making a pair of slacks, you must both follow the steps in proper sequence and complete all of the steps or there will be no wearable product. Furthermore, include any specialized information necessary in order to follow the process, such as tools, skills, knowledge, definitions of terms, and explanations. For instance, to take an artistic picture, the photographer must select the correct camera shutter speed, lens opening, and film speed and type. Since some of this information is technical, you should first clearly identify the audience in order to know how much explanation is necessary.

The process analysis should include cautions in order to prevent the reader from making mistakes or misinterpreting the process. For example, if the time lapse between or within steps is crucial to the outcome, this fact should be identified. Finally, in most cases you should try to avoid the use of the second-person pronoun "you" because of its monotonous and preaching tone. To tell readers, "Do not separate the egg yolks from the whites." or "Lift the car with a jack." is using the second person in an implied manner. The second-person pronoun can weaken an essay. However, its use in the student sample "When in Need" makes the essay more forceful and the steps more clear.

Process analysis requires you to explain how something works or how something happened. The analysis may be a specific one (how a particular football game was won) or a more general one (how to win football games). It focuses on **how** the steps work together in time to produce a process or event.

Organizational Pattern for Process Analysis

Study this blueprint so that you can see and better understand the elements necesary for process analysis. Then use the pattern as a guide for assembling your own essay. Note that all the student samples in the chapter use this organizational pattern.

Title

Introduction—¶1

At least five sentences, including any necessary materials, skills, qualities, and/or terms

Use of one of the good beginnings

Establishment of order of subtopics — verb tense
point of view — tone and diction

Thesis statement = subject (process to be analyzed) + controlling idea (number + adjective + steps or stages)

Subtopic sentence = enumeration of three steps

} may be 1 or 2 sentences

Body—¶2, 3, 4

Presentation of three major steps

Logical order of three major steps: time/chronological

**Paragraph 2:* Topic sentence = transitional expression + reference to thesis statement + step 1

Sufficient development of subject using supporting details such as specific examples, facts, illustrations, anecdotes. Cautions to avoid and special conditions and circumstances.

**Paragraph 3:* Topic sentence = transitional expression + reference to thesis statement + step 2

Sufficient development of subject using supporting details such as specific examples, facts, illustrations, anecdotes. Cautions to avoid and special conditions and circumstances.

**Paragraph 4:* Topic sentence = transitional expression + reference to thesis statement + step 3

Sufficient development of subject using supporting details such as specific examples, facts, illustrations, anecdotes. Cautions to avoid and special conditions and circumstances.

Transitional expressions: see especially

Addition
Introduction of Illustration/Example
Time/Chronology

Conclusion—¶5

At least three sentences

Transitional expression (optional): see Conclusion/Result and Summary

Restatement of process analyzed and establishment as a structure

Use of one of the good endings

*These elements may be rearranged within the sentence.

STUDENT SAMPLE—Process Analysis Essay—Analyzed for Parts

Observe that elements of structure and content are labeled on the left while elements of style are identified on the right. This detailed analysis will help you plan your own essay.

Source of material: personal experience

Tone: facetious, humorous
Diction: concrete, overstated
Order: chronological

Title

Saddle Sore

Introduction ¶ 1
Good Beginning #14

There is an old Irish superstition that a pure white horse ridden by its owner confers upon him the special gift of being able to cure all physical ailments. Since most people are prone to some form of physical ailment during their lifetimes, it would be prudent, as a precautionary measure, to have tucked away in some corner of the garden a noble white steed. However,* just having this equine creature nibbling peacefully at the alfalfa is not sufficient, for in order to avail oneself of the special gifts, it is imperative that the noble mount be ridden. There is more to riding a horse than jumping in the saddle, but most beginners think all they have to do is straddle the beast, shout, "Hi-ho, Silver," and away they gallop into the sunset. Occasionally, a panic-stricken neophyte realizes that he should have learned the three basic steps of horsemanship: getting[1] the beast to move, making it stop[2] on command, and dismounting[3] from it.

Diction: formal
Diction: concrete
Verb tense: present
Point of view: third person
Diction: allusion
Diction: connotative and formal

Thesis Statement (process to be analyzed) + Subtopics (3 basic steps)

* Coherence: transitional expressions circled

Topic Sentence ¶2

The first step, getting the horse to move, is not such a difficult task in itself. All it requires is a steady hand and a strong pair of legs. Horses are like sports cars; their engines are in their rear. Therefore, in order to move this marvel of strength, the rider must pick up his reins with both hands and kick with his legs towards the rear of the animal. This little piece of fancy footwork informs his four-legged friend that it is about to be taken somewhere. Once in a while, a stubborn beast has been known to ignore both of these strategies and continue to stand with all fours firmly planted on the ground. In this case, a back-up system of click-clicking noises made with the tongue or a rather loud "giddy-up" roared in its ear is usually effective in making it ambulatory. Another technique is a sharp whack on the flank to shake it out of its lethargy and send old equus flying over the fence. Almost everything man asks of the horse runs contrary to the creature's natural inclination; therefore, man has had to create, develop, and master numerous techniques to guarantee instant obedience from his equine friend.

Diction: figurative (metaphor)

Diction: alliterative (f)

Diction: concrete (sound)

Diction: formal

Diction: formal

A Sentence Structure: items in a series

Body
¶ 2,3,4

Topic Sentence ¶3

Trying to stop a twelve-hundred pound creature without a brake is the second step in horsemanship. A steed is not stopped by pulling on its mane with all one's might and shouting, "Stop," in a very loud voice. These gentle creatures do not like having their hair pulled any more than humans do, and they happen to have their own special language into which the word stop has been translated as "whoa." The correct way then to halt one's horse is to pull tightly back on the reins and shout one simple "whoa." A series of "ho-ho-ho's," as some people are prone to shout, has no effect whatsoever on the beast, except possibly to mislead it into thinking that Santa is on his way with a big bag of oats for it.

Diction: allusion

Topic Sentence ¶4

The last step in riding a horse is the dismount. When the rider has had enough of his four-legged friend and would like to be back on old terra firma again, there is a correct way to get down off a horse without sticking one's foot in its eye or strangling oneself with the stirrups. A horse is always dismounted from the left side. In order for the rider to dismount, the horse should be absolutely still. Being dragged twenty miles with one foot in the stirrup while the other one trails in the dust might look chic in western movies, but

Diction: overstated

Diction: overstated

in real life, it can be extremely painful. The left foot is the one which remains in the stirrup while the rider brings the right one behind him and plants it on the ground. The left foot is then brought down to complete the set. Having reached the ground with arms and legs intact, the rider can feel proud of his accomplishment.

Diction: understated

Sentence Structure: dependent clause with compound verb

Conclusion ¶ 5

Good Ending #10

All one needs for a successful life as an equestrian is the courage of a lion, the strength of an elephant, and the speed of a cheetah. The combination of these characteristics, coupled with good horse sense, is what makes a great rider. And if one rides a pure white horse, one receives the added advantage of being able to cure physical ailments.

Note how this essay avoids excessive repetition by using synonyms for the key term. This technique increases the paper's coherence.

Coherence: repeated terms for **horse**

noble white steed	equine creature
noble mount	beast
animal	four-legged friend
old equus	equine friend

STUDENT SAMPLE—Process Analysis Essay

Source of material: personal experience

The Pain of Getting Relief

Perhaps the most complicated device ever to be invented is the lid designed to keep children out of the aspirin bottle. Yet, because we live in a society dependent upon these analgesic tablets, the prying open of one of these inventions is a daily occurrence. Consequently, every adult eventually has to wrestle with removing the lid from a child-proof aspirin container. Though a highly exhausting task, it involves only three basic steps. These steps are buying the appropriate aspirin for the particular ailment, locating and unscrambling the manufacturer's instructions on lid removal, and, finally, opening the container despite these instructions.

The first step, deciding which type of aspirin to buy, is enough to give anyone a headache! After determining what kind of relief is needed, the adult must reserve an afternoon that can be dedicated to choosing one of the dozen or more different types of aspirin available at the pharmacy. Among the more popular types to choose from are those that give extra relief, those that give fast relief, and those that give extra fast relief. Some aspirins relieve pain from arthritis, hepatitis, and tonsilitis. Others relieve pain from masticating, ruminating, and eliminating. Some don't upset the stomach; none of them causes cancer, and most do nothing at all. There are even tablets that relieve just plain pain, anything from a major flea bite to a minor shark bite. More serious problems should be handled by an ambulance attendant. However, once the exact kind of relief needed has been determined, the coinciding type of aspirin may be purchased.

Step two, locating and unscrambling the manufacturer's instructions on how to open the lid, is not as simple as it sounds. To begin, locating the instructions requires ingenuity. Rarely are these directions located in an obvious place--on the outside of the box or on a sheet inserted in the box. More often they will be written on top of the lid that is to be removed. Sometimes they can be found on the bottom of the container. And in one reported incident, they were located on the underside of the lid. In any event, once the instructions have been spotted, one can continue with decoding them. For those people without X-ray vision, a magnifying glass is essential. If the instructions indicate to turn the lid to the left, it should be turned to the right. If the instructions indicate to push the lid down in the center, it should be lifted from the back. Directions are written this way to discourage any master brainchild who has learned to read before learning what "child-proof" means. Too, the manufacturer feels that most adults can't or don't read the instructions, so these don't matter anyway. Once the directions have been located and carefully "un"followed, it is time to begin the actual challenge.

The final step is to open the container despite the instructions. Desperate people have tried everything from tooth and nail to saw and drill to open these containers. But for guaranteed success, more extreme measures are available. For example, in some of the mining towns in West Virginia, a stick of dynamite has proven to be highly effective. In New York City, people have been launching these miniature strongboxes from the towering heights of the Empire State Building for years with good results. For the outdoor aspirin popper, a method that comes well recommended by residents of the Okefenokee Swamp area and other parts of the South is the "tempt a crocodile with a leg and thrust the container in its mouth just before it takes the bait" method. And for those who live in Los Angeles, one has only to walk the quarter mile to the nearest freeway during rush-hour traffic, fling the receptacle into the fast lane, and before one can say, "bumper to bumper," enough automobiles will have driven over the container to render removal of the lid quite easy. Unfortunately, not all of these methods are practical or accessible during moments of excruciating pain. In those instances, the adult must resort to the newest, easiest, and most foolproof method available: to grab the nearest child and ask for help in opening the container. I have been using this approach recently with the two- and three-year-old children next door and have yet to see it fail!

This, then, is the process by which adults should open a child-proof aspirin container. Having memorized these steps, they can relax and enjoy easy access to aspirin and wallow in this analgesic bliss for the rest of their lives. However, I would recommend that aspirin users reach for the pills when the pains are tolerable, because after removing the child-proof lid, the backache, heartache, or headache will be much worse.

Discovery Exercise

1. Identify the thesis statement, the process being analyzed: ______________________
2. Identify the three major steps or stages: ______________________

   ____

   ____
3. Identify the point of view: ____________ person
4. Identify the verb tense: ____________
5. Circle **five** transitional expressions.
6. Select **five** details that are funny:

   ____

   ____

   ____

   ____

   ____
7. Choose terms from the diction chart that characterize the diction: ______________________
8. Choose terms from the tone chart that describe the tone: ______________________

   ____
9. After reviewing Chapter 16, bracket **five** dependent clauses, one type of grammatical structure used in the essay.

STUDENT SAMPLE—Process Analysis Essay

Source of material: textbook on archeology

Digging Up the Past

Archeological research usually takes the form of survey, excavation, and laboratory analysis. Nothing else can substitute for the understanding of the past which comes from fieldwork and labwork. Such investigations can shed light on those people of the past for whom there are no written records. It can fill in the gaps in the written history of the world. Archeological research, however, cannot proceed without completing three important steps: laying a test trench, excavating the entire site, and securing the site.

The first step in archeological research is laying the test trench. A test trench allows the archeologist to check out what is beneath the surface of the ground. The excavator is then able to "read" the layers under the ground since the test trench provides a below-ground profile of the area in question. The archeologist can then decide on what method of excavation is best for the site. The scientist is looking for a possible feature, some type of artifact which cannot be removed, such as a wall or floor. For example, he or she may be attracted by a depression in the ground which may turn out to be only a hole after the test trench is completed. This trench also allows the archeologist to rank different sites according to their relative importance. Since research funds are limited, the test trenches enable the investigator to excavate only the most promising sections. All of the fill, the dirt and anything else mixed in which was removed from one trench is carefully screened for all possible artifacts. The sifting may even include flotation screening, a technique where the fill is immersed in a fluid and then separated. The dirt sinks and passes through the mesh, leaving only the larger items, rocks, worms, and artifacts. The dry-screened dirt is moved to a spoiled dirt pile out of the way. This step can involve many months of painstaking effort.

After the team lays the test trench, the next step is to excavate the entire site. The researcher will divide up the site into a grid system. The squares range in size from a meter square to ten or more meters square. If a feature is located, the archeologist will most likely decide to excavate the feature itself, forgetting the grid system temporarily. As with the test trench, the fill taken from the site is carefully examined for artifacts and then dumped in the spoiled dirt pile. While the excavation is in progress, the integrity of the below-ground layers is preserved as much as possible. The artifacts collected from the site are placed in plastic bags which are labeled with their provenience number, the artifact's "address" or source of origin. It will usually include the square number, the layer, and the date the item was found. Sometimes the position within the square or feature is also recorded. Finding an unusual or rare artifact is the reward for all the hard work and patience.

After completing the excavation of the site comes the third and final step, securing the site. In the simplest of terms, securing a site refers to trying to make sure that the site will still be there next year, next decade, or even next century in some cases. Depending on the financial resources of the expedition, different methods are used in securing the site. The easiest and least expensive is to cover the site with some type of plastic sheeting and then cover the plastic with sand. A similar method is to cover the site with plastic sheeting, cover the plastic with hay, and then cover the entire site with another layer of plastic. The advantage of this method is to facilitate uncovering the site in the near future and to protect it from the rain and cold. The third and most expensive method is to surround the site with a fence and then shelter the excavated area with a roof. This method facilitates public viewing of the site while protecting it. People travel great distances to see excavations like the Egyptian tombs, the fortress of Masada in Israel, and the La Brea tar pits in Los Angeles.

Archeology cannot simply be reduced to the techniques described above. Although excavation is the central and perhaps the essential key to such research, the science of archeology requires more than just well-followed instructions. It is the critical and intuitive abilities of archeologists which guide them in selecting sites that yield rich finds.

Discovery Exercise

1. Identify the thesis statement, the process being analyzed: ______________________________
2. Identify the three major steps or stages: ______________________________

   ____

   ____

3. Identify the point of view: ____________ person
4. Identify the verb tense: ____________
5. Circle **five** transitional expressions.
6. List all the synonyms for the word **archeologist.**

   ______________________ ______________________

   ______________________ ______________________

7. Choose terms from the diction chart that characterize the diction: ______________________
8. Choose terms from the tone chart that describe the tone: ______________________
9. After reviewing Chapter 16, bracket **three** appositive phrases, one type of grammatical structure used in the essay.

STUDENT SAMPLE—Process Analysis Essay

Source of material: personal experience

When in Need

There are certain times in your life when you need money. During these times, you must have a source of money to go to. For most people, this source is their parents. The difficult task of getting money from your parents involves three necessary steps. These steps are finding out what kind of mood your parents are in, being charming and helpful to them, and asking at the right moment for the money needed.

The first step you must observe before getting the money is to find out what kind of mood your parents are in. This stage requires that you must talk to the parents. During the conversation, you should note how they are talking. For example, are they telling jokes or grimacing? Do they look depressed or happy? You can also test the parents' mood by asking hypothetical questions, such as "What would you say if I told you . . . ?" This method will vary in its effectiveness depending on what information is put at the end of the hypothetical question. If after this test your parents seem angry or unamused, it is best just to forget about asking for money at this time and come back later. However, if the parents seem to be in a good mood--that is, they don't throw an object or raise their voices--it is time to press forward.

The second step in the procedure of getting money is to be charming and helpful to your parents. This step can involve many clever methods. First, you can compliment the parents with statements such as "Gee, you look nice." or "That was a brilliant suggestion." Questions like "Where did you get that outfit?" and "Have you lost some weight?" are also very effective. Second, you can improve the chances of getting money by willingly performing some hated chore. For instance, cleaning the house for your parents without their asking sways them because they feel that they have done a wonderful job of raising a child who is so well trained and thoughtful. Another method that helps soften the parents is making dinner for them. Once again, this approach reinforces the parents' delusions that they could author a book about child rearing. It is important to remember that the parents will especially love the dinner if it is gourmet. It is also a shrewd ploy to let them enjoy the meal alone. After following all of the above methods, you are ready for the last and most difficult step.

The final step is to ask at the right moment for the money needed. It is vital that you pick a time when the parents are most vulnerable. This is usually right after the special dinner that their darling child cooked for them. When posing the question for money, you should try to involve some guilt. It is imperative to point out how broke you are, how much you hate coming to your parents, and how much the money is needed. It is essential to make the parents feel as sorry as possible for their poor child. A tear or two, some minor groveling, and a few vague promises won't hurt your chances either.

In conclusion, when getting money from your parents, you must follow these steps. It is doubtful that the unsuspecting parents can resist their poor child's request for money. Young people with wads of money or numerous luxury items have probably already mastered this technique.

PROFESSIONAL SAMPLE—Process Analysis

Read the following essay to see how a professional writer has used the technique of analysis. Then answer the discovery questions which focus on the major elements of process analysis.

John von Rhein (1945–), music critic and writer, received his higher education in Los Angeles and has a Master of Arts degree in music. He has contributed articles to many publications and was the recipient of two Kennedy Center Music Association fellowships. He currently is music critic for the *Chicago Tribune*.

Listen, and Listen Good: How to Attend a Concert

1 The cards seem to be stacked against our enjoyment of great music. Sitting in a concert hall cheek to jowl with people we are convinced are having the time of their cultural lives, we are equally convinced we'll never understand the nuances of serious music.

2 And we may go home feeling that the concert *was* over our heads. Everything, that is, but "The Star-Spangled Banner," which we are proud to say we recognized almost immediately. It was all that noisy stuff that came afterward that gave us trouble.

3 To make matters worse, the learned program annotator intoned that all that noisy stuff consisted of great music. The man on the podium conducted it in a manner befitting great music. To judge by their jubilant applause, everyone else in the hall embraced it as great music. So how dare we doubt the general judgment?

4 Relax. This is a case of nothing more than a musical inferiority complex. It's a widespread malady, socially embarrassing but curable in most cases. The following handy hints, if diligently applied, should relieve those nagging doubts and make you a better listener.

5 You still might not be able to tell the difference between the "Hammerklavier" Sonata and the "Anvil Chorus," but now, while the orchestra is playing, you will be able to affect an expression of such knowing contentment that everyone seated in your vicinity will marvel at your obvious connoisseurship.

6 First of all, you must rid yourself of the "great music is too great for me" syndrome. So much of the orchestral music that forms the bulk of our listening diet comes salted with such a formidable reputation that it can only be swallowed with the greatest of awe. Many people who attend concerts regularly are convinced high art by its very nature must be forbidding, unapproachable except by those having special knowledge.

7 Who or what perpetuates such nonsense? The overly technical jargon that oozes from most orchestra program books certainly does its best to intimidate, puzzle or simply alienate the average listener. Others may be frightened off by lingering memories of a childhood spent trudging wearily through finger exercises on the violin or piano.

8 Before you can understand serious music, you must learn how to make the initial approach—directly and simply, without fear or reverence. And, yes, without special preparation. The only way to learn how to listen is by listening.

9 Unfortunately, true listening—an active rather than passive pursuit—is impossible if you regard music as aural bathwater, something warm and lulling in which you can float yourself away

from reality. "What most people relish is hardly music," wrote George Santayana. "It is rather a drowsy reverie interrupted by nervous thrills." Wandering attention is the great enemy of experiencing music to its fullest.

10 Come on, now, confess. You *are* a habitual wanderer, aren't you? The climaxes, the loud and fast passages—these things send nervous thrills up and down your vertebrae. But let the music turn soft and slow, and you start to float. You hear but you no longer listen. Before you know it, you have forgotten all about the music and the performance.

11 There is nothing inherently wrong, of course, with listening for the sheer pleasure of the musical sound itself. The danger, as noted above, comes when you regard music *only* as a sensuous experience, something you don't have to think about or bring any conscious effort to; then it becomes classical Muzak. Shoving symphonic music into the background may be all right when you are at home washing dishes to the Pachelbel Canon, but it insults those ninety hardworking musicians up there on stage—not to mention the composer.

12 Concentration is not really all that difficult to achieve. It comes with experience and repeated hearing. But if you're going to really flex your listening muscles, you must learn how to listen on more than one plane. The composer Aaron Copland has identified two of these: the expressive plane and the purely musical plane.

13 First, a caveat about the expressive plane. For the novice the danger lies in trying to read extramusical meaning into each and every opus. Most of us, when we first start out going to concerts of classical music, search for specific word pictures on which to hang our reactions to hearing a given work. When listening to the Fifth Symphony, for example, we like to fall back on the image of Fate knocking on Beethoven's door. Why? Because Beethoven himself suggested the metaphor. But also because it seems to give the music a tangible reality that is far more "real" to us than a purely musical analysis. In other words, we are only too anxious to hang onto any explanation that seems to bring us closer to the music's meaning.

14 Music expresses, at different moments, joy or sadness, triumph or tragedy, serenity or unrest. It may express each of these moods, and any number of others, in an infinite variety of shadings. Or, depending on your stance, it may express nothing but the notes themselves. Arnold Bennett once observed: "What makes music the greatest of all the arts is that it can express emotion without ideas. Literature can appeal to the soul only through the mind. Music goes direct."

15 Useful as it may sometimes be for the beginning listener to assign expressive associations to the scores you hear, you can greatly profit from approaching them purely and simply *as music*. Listen for the melody, which is perhaps the simplest element to follow. Try to follow its journey through the musical structure. It is the development of melodies as themes, whether in a symphony, concerto, overture or tone poem, that forms the basis of most symphonic works the average listener encounters. Think of a melodic theme as a river: Following its path may prevent you from losing your bearings.

16 Once a theme has stuck in your ears, its musical adventures become more interesting, as it is supported by different harmonies, chased into various keys and through various expressive modes, broken into pieces and put back together, tossed back and forth between various intruments and instrumental choirs.

17 As you proceed to search through symphonic music for more than melody, you will become aware of beauties of structure, of contrasts of tone color and musical texture, of dynamic and rhythmic influences, of the logic and cohesiveness of a score. The greater the music, the more pronounced those qualities.

18 You will soon begin to discern differences of style by the shape of a composer's melodies. A composer's grammar can be as individual as an author's prose. Just as we speak of a Dickensian figure or a Dostoevsky character, so can we identify a typical Verdi melody or Beethoven theme. It is part of each composer's musical fingerprints. Recognizing them gives you the satisfying feeling of "knowing" Verdi or Beethoven or Brahms, even if you may never plunge any deeper into their works.

19 To find out for yourself—rather than being told by a teacher or program annotator—how all these things work simultaneously to produce a work of art is one of the more delicious discoveries available to the neophyte music lover.

20 To explain symphonic form in any detail here would require twice as much time as it takes to listen to the entire "Jupiter" Symphony of Mozart. Any music appreciation text will give you the basic information. Suffice it to say that the classic symphony has four contrasting move-

ments, each with a different mood, pace. The form of each movement varies—sonata form, three part song form, minuet-and-trio, scherzo, theme and variations, etc.—according to the work's overall structural and expressive scheme. There is, however, a certain thematic unity that links one movement to the next. Often, particularly in much nineteenth-century Romantic music, the unity also may derive from key, tone color, style or programmatic content.

21 Do not expect every symphony you hear to conform to such a baby-simple schemata, however. Part of the excitement of experiencing the symphonic masterworks of the last 200 years lies in discovering how composers departed from the prescribed forms and content of the Viennese classical composers. If Mahler could write a symphony in six movements, Stravinsky a symphony in three parts, and Sibelius a symphony in a single movement, anything goes.

22 The pleasure you take from listening to a symphony performance will derive from many things. It will depend first of all on your ability to grasp and enjoy the melodic materials and the musical and sonorous quality with which they are combined. Out of this should grow naturally an understanding of musical design. This, of course, will not be the understanding of a professional musician. It need not be as broad or deep as that. Intricacies of structure and harmonic nuance can be sensed, you don't have to be armed with all sorts of technical knowledge to feel these things operating in the music. The powerful effect of the finale to Beethoven's Symphony No. 5 is unmistakable even if you do not know that, for the reappearance of the theme, Beethoven adds a bassoon under the strings.

23 Virgil Thomson, the composer and critic, once described the ideal listener as "a person who applauds vigorously." By that witticism he no doubt meant to imply that only a listener who really involves himself is of importance to music or the matters of music. Are you aware of the interpreter's part in the performance you are hearing? Music, after all, does not live in isolation. It must be created anew every time.

24 Hearing a lot of symphonic music over and over again by different conductors and orchestras will give you, among other things, a most useful frame of reference. You will eventually adopt for yourself a more or less ideal conception of the style that applies to a given composer. You will then be able to sense to what degree the conductor and orchestra are reproducing that style within the bounds of their musical personalities. This is no more or no less than what a music critic is paid to do professionally. You, however, will have the chance to practice the art in a less conspicuous fashion.

25 By now you must be pretty tired of being lectured on your responsibility as an informed and diligent listener. But it is true, as Copland pointed out, that "music can only be really alive when there are listeners who are really alive." That means listeners with taste and sensitivity, listeners who are willing to listen to music of all schools and periods with an open mind. The combined efforts of the composer and the performer have meaning only insofar as they find an intelligent audience.

Discovery Questions

1. What is Von Rhein's thesis, and in what paragraph is it located?
2. What are the steps in the process being analyzed?
3. Why does the author use unconventional grammar in the title?
4. Identify several characteristic examples of the diction. Using the diction chart in Chapter 1, describe the essay's diction.
5. What is the essay's tone?
6. Explain why this essay is effective despite the fact that the author uses diction and tone normally considered to be ineffective.

Suggested Subjects or Events to Analyze According to Process

Select one of the following or similar subjects or events. Decide what steps are necessary in order to produce the subject or event.

a frustrating situation: for example, how to buy stamps or mail objects at the post office, how to buy or exchange an item in a department store, how to adjust to the high cost of living, how to follow a diet, how to pass a difficult college course, how to teach a child to swim, how to eat an artichoke

correct behavior: for example, how to conduct yourself at a formal dinner or a football game, how to enlist people's confidence, how to enjoy an opera, how to behave on a first date

a technical subject for someone with no prior knowledge: for example, material drawn from other fields like business, psychology, science, sociology, astronomy

a mechanical subject: for example, how any machine works, how to decorate a Christmas tree, how to register for classes, how to collect some item (stamps, coins), how to raise a pet, how to bake bread, how to drive a car, how to catch fish, how to take a photograph, how to build (fly) kites

a past event: for example, how you failed a particular course, how any event in history occurred, how a particular personal event occurred, how you met a particular friend

WORKSHEET FOR PROCESS ANALYSIS

1. Select a process to analyze and complete top half of the worksheet.
2. Write your thesis statement and enumeration of subtopics and then get approval from your instructor.
3. Complete the worksheet **before** writing the essay.
4. Attach the worksheet to the finished essay.
5. Attach the Expository Essay Cover Sheet to the finished essay.

Souce of material: ____________________

Process to be analyzed: ____________________

Necessary materials, skills, qualities, and/or terms: ____________________

____

____

____

Controlling idea: ____________ (number) + ____________ (adjective) + steps/stages (noun)

Order of three major steps: time/chronological

Point of view: ____________ Verb tense: ____________

Tone: ____________ Diction: ____________

Thesis statement + enumeration of steps (may be 1 or 2 sentences):

____

____

____

____

____
(instructor approval)

OUTLINE

Title: ____________________

¶1: Introduction (five sentences):

Choose a good beginning from the list.

Give necessary background material, skills, qualities, and/or terms.

Good beginning # ______ : ____________________

____

____

____

____

When you write your introduction, include the approved thesis statement and subtopics at the end of paragraph 1.

Body (three paragraphs)

¶2: Transition + topic sentence: ______________________________

supporting details

¶3: Transition + topic sentence: ______________________________

supporting details

¶4: Transition + topic sentence: ______________________________

supporting details

¶5: Conclusion (three sentences):

Restatement of process analyzed.

Choose one of the good endings from the list.

Good ending # ______

Name: ______________________

Date: ______________ Class: __________

Type of Exposition: ______________________

EXPOSITORY ESSAY COVER SHEET		
Structure/Ideas	+	________
Usage/Mechanics	−	________
Total		________
Rewrite points	+	________
TOTAL		________

Structure and Ideas (100 points)	Original	Rewrite
INTRODUCTION (at least five sentences):		
title; one of good beginnings leading to thesis	10________	________
thesis statement + enumeration of subtopics	5________	________
BODY (three supporting paragraphs):		
three topic sentences = transition + reference to thesis + subtopic	15________	________
development of paragraphs: sufficient, concrete, appropriate, relevant	45________	________
CONCLUSION (at least three sentences):		
one of good endings	5________	________
ESSAY:		
logical order of ideas and correct reasoning	5________	________
effective style = tone + diction + sentence structure + coherence	15________	________
Total	100________	+ ________

The points in this section reflect your score for structure and ideas. If you have received fewer than 100 points, you may rewrite your paper to earn them. Use the numbers as a guide to areas needing revision.

Usage and Mechanics (minus points). See Correction Symbol Chart.		
You **may** earn these points in revision:		
Usage: adj; adv; agr; awk; col; dm; frag; mm; ref; rep; shift; verb; ww; / /; ¶	−3 ea. ________	________
You **may not** earn these points in revision, but you must correct the errors:		
Mechanics: abbr; apos; cap; lc; p; ro; sp; ∧	−1 ea. ________	________
Total	− ________	+ ________

CHAPTER 10

The Third Pattern: Analysis Causal

The concept of analysis is one which you have met before now. Possibly in your personal life you have spent time trying to understand the causes for or the effects of a traumatic event. This situation involves the concept of analysis, that is, breaking an item into the parts that comprise it in order to understand the nature of the item.

Unlike classification, which relates something to its larger class or group, analysis is the form that relates something to its own parts. Analysis conveys an understanding of a structure, something with components that have a mutually supporting function. Examples are an object like an advertisement, a process like riding a horse, or an event like a revolution in Latin America.

Depending on the structure and the writer's purpose, there are three types of analysis: functional (Chapter 8), process (Chapter 9), and causal (discussed below). Chapter 14 examines in detail the critical analysis of nonfiction prose in anthologies, newspapers, magazines, and books.

Causal analysis answers the question "Why do these causes produce that effect?" or "Why do these effects follow from this cause?" Thus, it shows why two or more events are related. It considers why certain events caused an effect. It also may explain why certain effects result from another event. Causes and effects may occur simultaneously, but they often begin and end at different times. Because events occur over a period of time, causal analysis has a chronological framework. However, it is not primarily narrative but focuses instead on the relationships within a series of events.

Events do not occur in isolation. Causal analysis establishes a cause or connection between two or more events. It shows why whenever A occurs, B will follow. For example, whenever the ignition is turned on, the car will start. It also may show why without A, B could not happen. For instance, the car will not start unless the ignition is turned on. Analysis must take into consideration any conditions that can alter the interpretation of the event. Analysis must also account for any factors that must be present for the event to occur. To illustrate, conditions for the car to start are a working battery, spark plugs, and gasoline.

Requirements

Causal analysis establishes the structure of an event. The sequence of individual events lead to or from the main one. You must identify an event as a cause or an effect before identifying all significant causes or effects. Individual events move in the following sequence: from remote causes to proximate causes to immediate causes to the event to immediate effects to proximate effects to remote effects. For example, if the event is receiving an A in a freshman college English course, the sequence of events might be the following: good elementary school English background → advanced writing classes in high school → effective material and instructor, regular attendance, assignments on schedule and well done → EVENT (the A grade) → good grade-point average, enrollment in an advanced English class → success in writing whenever required → ability to think clearly, organize ideas, and communicate well. This sequence could be altered if any of the important causes or effects were omitted.

Another possible causal relationship might include several simultaneous causes leading to an event. For example, if during childhood a person lived in many locations, had divorced parents, and attended inferior schools, then these simultaneous causes might lead to poor performance in high school. Also, several simultaneous effects could develop from one cause. To illustrate, the event of an automobile accident causes effects like bodily injury, wreckage to the car, and damage to the surroundings. These occur at roughly the same time. The connection between events must be relatively close in time, and you must consider all conditions or factors that might affect the interpretation. You must also establish the relationship of the events to each other and to the whole.

Causal analysis is the way to show why a series of events are related to one another and why adding or omitting conditions can alter the events. It shows that an event can have a number of causes or effects. Often the more complicated the event is, the more causes or effects are involved. Causal analysis focuses on **why** a series of causes work together to produce an event or **why** certain effects flow from an event. For example, the student essay "In the End, It Was Not Make Believe" gives three causes for the boys getting a whipping, while the student sample "Repent Your Cigarettes" identifies the three consequences of quitting smoking.

Problems to Avoid

Any one of several flaws in developing a relationship among events can weaken causal analysis. These flaws involve errors in reasoning which are discussed in Chapter 13. The **post hoc** error occurs when one event is said to be the cause of another simply because the one occurred before the other. An example is thinking that a broken leg suffered in the afternoon was caused by a black cat crossing one's path in the morning. A second error is **hasty generalization** which involves overlooking or ignoring most of the facts in a situation. For example, selecting a neighborhood to live in on the basis of a newspaper advertisement and a casual perusal of a few blocks in the area is generalizing too quickly.

Another error is **oversimplification** which occurs when one cause or effect is cited as the **only** explanation for the event. For example, saying that the only reason for a low grade in math was one missed test is oversimplifying. One way to avoid this problem is to offer **an** explanation which you admit is determined by your own point of view. Analyzing the same event from different perspectives can cause people to identify different causes or effects for that same event. For example, while the student thinks that one missed test is the cause of the poor grade, the teacher might identify poor attendance or weak skills, and the parents might cite too many responsibilities or too little time spent studying.

Organizational Patterns for Causal Analysis

Study this blueprint so that you can see and better understand the elements necessary for causal analysis. Then use the pattern as a guide in assembling your own essay. Observe that the two forms for the body paragraphs are presented: three causes or three effects. Note that all the student samples in the chapter use this organizational pattern.

Title

Introduction—¶1

At least five sentences, including the event as a cause or effect

Use of one of the good beginnings

Establishment of order of subtopics, point of view, verb tense, tone and diction

Thesis statement = subject (event to be analyzed) + controlling idea (number + adjective + causes or effects)

Subtopic sentence = enumeration of causes or effects

(Thesis statement and subtopic sentence: may be 1 or 2 sentences)

Body—¶2, 3, 4

—three causes—	OR	—three effects—
Presentation of three major causes		Presentation of three major effects
Logical order: chronological		Logical order: chronological
Paragraph 2:* Topic sentence = transitional expression + reference to thesis statement + **remote cause		**Paragraph 2:* Topic sentence = transitional expression + reference to thesis statement + **immediate** effect
Supporting details such as facts and anecdotes Concluding sentence		Supporting details such as facts and anecdotes Concluding sentence
Paragraph 3:* Topic sentence = transitional expression + reference to thesis statement + **proximate cause		**Paragraph 3:* Topic sentence = transitional expression + reference to thesis statement + **proximate** effect
Supporting details Concluding sentence		Supporting details Concluding sentence
Paragraph 4:* Topic sentence = transitional expression + reference to thesis statement + **immediate cause		**Paragraph 4:* Topic sentence = transitional expression + reference to thesis statement + **remote** effect
Supporting details Concluding sentence		Supporting details Concluding sentence

Development by emphasizing a **sequence** of events leading from one to another

Transitional expressions: see especially

- Addition
- Causal (for causes)
- Conclusion/Result (for effects)
- Time/Chronology
- Summary

*These statements may be rearranged within the sentence.

Conclusion—¶5

At least three sentences

Transitional expression (optional): see Conclusion/Result and Summary

Restatement of event analyzed and establishment as a structure

Use of one of the good endings

STUDENT SAMPLE—Causal Analysis Essay (Causes)—Analyzed for Parts

Observe that elements of structure and content are labeled on the left while elements of style are identified on the right. This detailed analysis will help you plan your own essay.

Source of material: personal experience

Tone: humorous, nostalgic
Diction: concrete, figurative
Order: chronological

Title

A Night in the Jungle

Introduction ¶ 1
Good Beginning #1

The rainstorm raged as the rusty Peugeot plunged into the blackness of an African evening. *(Diction: alliterative (r))* There were five of us, *(Point of view: first person)* all students from America, on our way to the village of Simbadi-Brassou to work for the summer. The thick mud squelched *(Diction: concrete)* around our tires as we drove off the highway onto the cowpath. A few feet later we sank down to the axle in the muddy water. Three unforeseen causes led *(verb tense: past)* my team and me to become stranded in the jungle that night. *(Thesis Statement (event to be analyzed + controlling idea))* [1] The old car we had been using for several weeks, [2] the summer monsoon, and [3] the cowpath to Simbadi-Brassou caused me to spend an adventurous night in the jungle. *(Subtopic Sentence (3 causes))*

Topic Sentence ¶2

The borrowed Peugeot was the (first)* cause of our predicament. Harvey, as we dubbed the little sedan, was a car that was not in the best condition. *(Diction: understated)* Our group had inherited the Peugeot several weeks before from an aging

*Coherence: transitional expressions circled.

French missionary who was returning to France. We later wondered if the missionary had received Harvey for his sixteenth birthday. The car at one time had been white, but years of driving in the damp, humid climate had rusted most of the paint off. One fender was missing, and we were even afraid to lean up against the body for fear it would dent. The rear windshield was recently deceased, so whoever sat in the back seat endured drenched shoulders when it rained. Having driven the car many miles as we worked our way to our base station, we had become familiar with the Peugeot's quirks. Harvey's top speed was not quite forty miles per hour. Going faster than that, the engine would go into convulsions. The little car also stalled whenever it was least convenient. Once stalled, Harvey had to be coaxed and begged to start again. Considered from any perspective, the cranky Peugeot was not suited for jungle driving.

Diction: overstated

Diction: figurative (personification)

Diction: Figurative (personification)

Diction: figurative (personification)

Body ¶ 2,3,4

Concluding Sentence

The unusual rainstorm that descended upon us that night was a second factor in stranding us in the jungle. Senegal, like other West African countries, has two seasons of extremes. The dry season lasts about nine months or until the drought is so severe that all the animals die and the tropical area becomes

Topic Sentence ¶3

barren. In contrast, the three-month rainy season floods the river: the rice paddies flourish, and the jungles become deep and entangled once again. The torrents come suddenly with a blackening sky that develops in minutes. The day we received our assignment to Simbadi was during the height of the rainy season. Rain had begun to fall steadily as we hurriedly climbed into the car for the drive to the village. The sky blackened, and the rain fell in torrents while we drove along Senegal's only paved highway. Passing by the various villages, we saw water swirl around the huts. It poured in our back window and soaked us in a matter of minutes. The weather continued to rage as we crawled along the highway towards our destination.

Diction: concrete

Sentence Structure: introductory verbal phrase

Concluding Sentence

Diction: figurative (personification)

One winding road was the final reason we were forced to spend the night in the jungle. Africa is not a fully modernized continent, and only lately have the different nations begun to pave their roads. Most thoroughfares are still the traditional cowpath. Animals, pedestrians, and jeeps are usually the only traffic that can navigate these roads. Simbadi was located at the end of the longest, bumpiest cowpath

Topic Sentence ¶ 4

Diction:

in Senegal. The path itself was carved out of the dense jungle and consisted of two deep parallel ruts with a tall mound of grass between them. Fairly navigable in good weather, the road could usually tolerate rain. This night, however, was the exception. Minutes before we arrived at the turn-off to the village, the storm reached its peak. Rain descended from the sky, as if someone had left the shower running full force, and we were forced to reduce our speed to a crawl. The deluge continued, and then a flash of lightning revealed, not a cowpath, but a huge lake of water created by the downpour. The water had washed away the road and almost everything around it. Too late to turn back, we, hoping the water wasn't too deep, drove onto the cowpath. Harvey stalled again, and with a gurgle, sank into the mud. Despite all our efforts, we were stuck for the night.

overstated

Diction: concrete

Sentence Structure: adjective out of normal order

Diction: figurative (simile)

[A] Sentence Structure: parallelism

Sentence Structure: verbal phrase

Diction: concrete

Concluding Sentence

Conclusion ¶ 5

Good Ending #8

Needless to say, my team and I, wet and tired, finally arrived in Simbadi-Brassou the next day. We spent the summer there in the village working with the people and accomplished what we intended. However, without that beat-up Peugeot, the rainy night, and the village's cowpath, five American students would have missed a unique adventure.

[B] Sentence Structure: items in a series

STUDENT SAMPLE—Causal Analysis Essay (Effects)

Source of material: personal experience

Necessities, Barely

Several years ago my husband and I moved from our comfortable two-bedroom home to a 96-square-foot, sixteen-foot-long travel trailer. We planted our new "home" on a three-acre olive orchard located in a rural area. There my optimistic spouse planned to construct a garage with electrical and plumbing facilities until our house could be built; however, because of strict zoning regulations, we spent nearly two years in our little trailer with neither electricity nor indoor plumbing. In attempting to survive during those grueling years, I experienced three startling consequences. These included temporary sensations of insanity, increased feelings of self-worth, and, finally, genuine appreciation for the pleasure life offers.

The immediate consequence I experienced as a result of life in a tiny trailer appeared as feelings of insanity. Acute depression set in as the lack of hot running water created difficulties in keeping ourselves clean. Even though my husband and I heated water on the four-burner propane stove, just trying to exercise the rules of basic hygiene was nearly impossible. During the winter, we shivered and sneezed while bathing. During the summer, cold sponge baths felt more comfortable but were sorely ineffective against the grimy sweat and dust. In addition, endless frustration beset me during the damp winter months when our ancient trailer failed to protect us from the moisture. A general feeling of dampness prevailed as, morning after morning, I donned my soggy uniform and escaped to the warmth of my car heater. Furthermore, I found it increasingly difficult to keep warm in winter and cool in summer. The uncomfortable temperatures kept me from sleeping adequately, further increasing the unhappiness I felt. Often I could only sit crying and screaming in overwhelming despair as I struggled to cope with life in the trailer. However, these negative reactions soon gave way to more positive effects.

As time progressed, the second result of trailer life appeared: I began to develop increased feelings of self-worth. As I learned to depend less and less on electrical appliances and similar luxuries, my self-reliance grew. After all, I managed to show up for my full-time nursing job day after day without the benefit of either curling iron or blow dryer. I also mixed chocolate chip cookies without an electric mixer and baked them in the midget-sized propane oven. In addition, I survived the trials of using a portable toilet and kept food cold with ten pounds of ice replenished daily in an icebox. Even more important, I felt proud that our monthly bills added up to a minimal two dollars for water and three dollars for propane. As I coped with each new challenge brought on by our odd life style, my self-esteem gradually increased.

Finally, as a result of living in our small trailer, I eventually developed a genuine appreciation for the natural pleasures life offers. For example, I turned on our dusty television set a total of two times in the last few months we lived in the trailer. I not only felt guilty about using precious electricity to watch my favorite show, but I also found that the fantasy world of Hollywood could not compare with the more pleasurable pastimes I enjoyed. For instance, I learned to love watching the ground squirrels gathering their olive seeds for winter, and the comic black crows provided endless entertainment as they waltzed around the yard. In addition, I found that one cannot hear the birds chirping when the stereo blares out the latest hit records, nor can one experience the blowing of a soft summer breeze with the air conditioner blasting. I attribute my genuine appreciation of these simple enjoyments to those years in the trailer.

Undoubtedly, the experience of living in such cramped quarters created three significant effects in my life. I appreciate what I have and realize this insight could not have occurred had I not felt the deep despair during those first few months. Looking back now seated on the comfortable couch in my spacious living room, I am thankful for those dark two years.

Discovery Exercise

1. Identify the thesis statement
   a. the event to be analyzed: ______________________________

   ____

   b. the controlling idea: ______________________________

   ____
2. Identify the three major subtopics: ______________________________

   ____

   ____
3. Identify the point of view: ____________ person
4. Identify the verb tense: ____________
5. Circle **five** transitional expressions.
6. Select **six** examples of concrete detail:

____

____

____

____

____

____

7. Choose terms from the diction chart that characterize the diction: ______________________________

____

8. Choose terms from the tone chart that describe the tone: ______________________________

____

9. After reviewing Chapter 16, bracket **five** consecutive adjectives, one type of grammatical structure used in the essay.

STUDENT SAMPLE—Causal Analysis Essay (Causes)

Source of material: personal experience

In The End, It Was Not Make Believe

Though I was only seven years old and my tall, lanky older brother nine, we shared in the work like men as each morning and afternoon we would pull on our dusty Lone Ranger leather-fringed gloves in preparation for the farm chores. Now, we were good responsible boys: twice a day we pitched hay to our black and white Holstein cows; fed a mixture of oyster shells, oats, and corn to our white chickens; slopped those "oinkie" dirty-reddish pigs; and curried, fed, and gave sugar cubes to our powerful, magnificent team of white work horses. That hot, sultry 1943 day in Montana began as any other with the morning chores, and later we climbed the vertical wood ladder to the hayloft for the afternoon chores. However, a series of three events caused us to receive the whipping of our lives. These were playing in the hayloft, experiencing a summer tornado, and neglecting our chores.

Playing in the hayloft was the first cause for the whipping of our lives. The long cold winters were difficult on a farm, and we had prepared by filling the loft with alfalfa. The bellowing of the cows was forgotten while we played hide and seek in the voids where the bales should have been. During the past summer, without approval we had constructed, in the stacks of bales, catacombs and tunnels like those of the pyramids. Another game was to pretend we were coal miners by carving out holes in the bales for pocket knives and special trinkets. Because of our boyish imaginations, we were engrossed in playing in the tunnels. Suddenly the loud swirling of the wind brought us to our senses, and we scurried down the ladder to the farmyard.

The second factor leading to our punishing was a Montana summer tornado. As we reached the farmyard, the sky had turned dark. The rain was falling like buckets of water. The wind was blowing against our bodies with tremendous force. We laughed as the wind blew us backwards. It was an imaginary game of running in place like a boxer in training. The wind had blown over oak trees, leaving mounds of tangled roots and dirt in the yard. As the wind increased, we proceeded to one of these tornado-made foxholes. Lying on the edge of the imagined foxhole, we peeked out as if we were combat soldiers. With our fingers pointed forward we simulated M-16's and fired round after round into the branches, boxes, and cans that were flying through the air. The chickens, cows, and horses had all been forgotten as we watched the blade assembly of our windmill break free and fly to the ground. We loved it! It was as if we had our very own "unidentified flying object." We fired burst upon burst of machine gun fire at the saucer. Instead of taking precautions against the storm, we were busy enjoying it.

Neglecting our chores was the final reason for the whipping of our lives. Unknown to us the wind had blown open the hen house, and the chickens, which had not been fed their share of oyster shells, oats, and corn, were blowing about like large white cotton balls. The tumbling chickens mixed with flying feathers made us laugh because neither of us was fond of gathering eggs. We should have run to close the double-hinged red barn doors. However, we only watched the wind swirl the golden straw through the barn to the pasture beyond. Our work horses in the pasture flew into the barn like two horses of the Apocalypse. They flew past the cows and out the open doorway. Finally, with lightning speed, the white work horses raced down the winding driveway. The farm was in shambles not only because of the storm but also because of our neglect.

The storm finally ended, and soon after my brother and I received the whipping of our lives. I still remember screaming, "It was the tornado's fault," but I also confessed to playing in the hayloft and neglecting the farm chores. Later, the white horses were found and sold, and we enjoyed cleaning our first shiny red tractor.

Discovery Exercise

1. Identify the thesis statement

   a. the event to be analyzed: ______________________________

   ____

   b. the controlling idea: ______________________________

   ____

2. Identify the three major subtopics: ______________________________

   ____

   ____

3. Identify the point of view: ____________ person

4. Identify the verb tense: ____________

5. Circle **five** transitional expressions.

6. Select **eight** examples of concrete detail:

7. Choose terms from the diction chart that characterize the diction:

8. Choose terms from the tone chart that describe the tone:

9. After reviewing Chapter 16, bracket **five** items in a series, one type of grammatical structure used in the essay.

STUDENT SAMPLE: Causal Analysis Essay (Effects)

Source of material: personal experience

Repent Your Cigarettes

Recently, I joined a program called Smokenders. Previously, I had smoked one pack of cigarettes a day for seven years. However, by using behavior modification techniques, I was able to stop smoking within five weeks. During the eight-week process, three unpleasant effects occurred: muddleheadedness, weight gain, and impatience. However, I managed to follow the rules of the program and finally abolished cigarettes from my life.

Muddleheadedness was the first effect to plague my body. During the third week, I had cut down on nicotine considerably. Ignorant about physiology, I paid little attention to the moderator as she warned of forgetfulness, drowsiness, and slurred speech. It was not until the fourth week, when I became fatigued and absent-minded, that I appreciated the warning. I was relieved to know that I was not having a nervous breakdown. Nevertheless, on the tennis court I experienced an unpleasant symptom, which alarmed me and rekindled a strong desire to smoke. The fuzzy chartreuse tennis balls started to blur, and the racket fell from my hand during the middle of the game. Unable to reorient myself with the aid of a cigarette, I continued playing while trying desperately to focus on the ball. Suddenly, I stood staring aimlessly like a child ready to burst into tears when he is lost in a shopping center during the Christmas season. Later that week, I encountered problems with my speech. Occasionally, I would drool, lose control of my lips, and utter unintelligible words. My mind vacillated between getting an instant cure from a cigarette and enduring these almost intolerable symptoms. Although my befuddlement seemed ludicrous, I felt confident that my body would restore itself.

The next result of my decision to stop smoking was weight gain. I was into the fifth or cut-off week when tapering off ended and smoking "zero" began. Cigarettes had always served as rewards for finishing menial tasks; however, now I was without those daily recompenses. Not long after my cut-off day, I invented several concoctions which served as new rewards. A few of these treats were hot-fudge sundaes with mounds of whipped cream and nuts, apple pies with freshly sliced pippin apples and homemade butter crust, and croissants from the French bakery down the street. Self-pity and self-denial were often the culprits behind my nightly excursions to the refrigerator. I soon found myself saddled with the double problem of being an overweight smoker. My body looked like an army tank, and yet I continued consuming at the rate of an elephant. I was quite aware of my compulsive eating and the motivation for it. However, merely being aware was not enough. I seriously considered taking up smoking again, but instead I decided to treat the problems separately.

A subsequent effect of not smoking was my low tolerance for unproductive situations and other people. By now I was in the seventh week of Smokenders and in my second week as a non-smoker. My relationships with close friends and acquaintances, which I thought I had understood, were now more clearly defined and circumscribed. Cigarettes were unhealthy pacifiers which had allowed me to tolerate inconclusive committee meetings and boring stories of my friends' self-obsessed sex-lives. Jane, a long-time friend, would often come by to converse because she found me attentive. She is very amusing at times and can carry on an intelligent conversation. Unfortunately, there are times when I would rather amuse myself than listen to her ramble about her social problems, conflict at work, and the incompetent individuals of the world. Playing the role of her "surrogate husband" is far from entertaining and totally unbearable without the diversion of cigarettes. On this occasion, I told her impatiently that I enjoyed the world, thought she should be happy to have a decent-paying job, and found most people not only able but delightful. Although my remarks were pure overstatement, I realized that I had usually placed cigarettes between other people and myself. Physically and mentally, cigarettes had removed me sufficiently from mundane conversations and boring or antagonistic people so that I was not upset by them. Although my newly developed abruptness and low tolerance with my friends have been unpleasant, these reactions have also been instrumental in helping me to evaluate the basis of my relationships.

Fortunately, these three unpleasant effects of quitting smoking were only temporary. Now, in my second month as a non-smoker, my body has restored itself naturally, and I have lost the fifteen pounds. Although a few of my friends remain distant, I have gained awareness about my behaviors. Thanks to Smokenders, I lost a bad habit and gained new insights.

PROFESSIONAL SAMPLE—Causal Analysis

Read the following essay to see how a professional writer has used the technique of analysis. Then answer the discovery questions which focus on the major elements of causal analysis.

Suzanne Gordon (1945–) earned an M.A. from Johns Hopkins University. She has been a substitute teacher in the public schools of Baltimore and an editor and translator for a French journalist. She has written articles, poems, and short stories for magazines and newspapers as well as books such as *Black Mesa: The Angel of Death* and *Lonely in America* (1975), from which this selection was taken.

The Geography of Loneliness

1 To be alone is to be different, to be different is to be alone, and to be in the interior of this fatal circle is to be lonely. To be lonely is to have failed. There is no excuse for that. It is clear to the teenager that he or she should have a date after school, and it is clear to the average man or woman that he or she should have a mate, family, a circle of friends. Or a consciousness-raising group—intimacy. There are maps to follow to get you there: grade school, high school, perhaps college, church, company, promotion. Or the People's Yellow Pages. We live in an era of openness and possibility. Never has there been so much talk of sharing, so many books and courses to facilitate smooth relating, explaining both how to begin and, in case of a mixup, how to end. The tight boundaries of rural, neighborhood, family-centered America have burst, breaking the bonds of exclusiveness and duty, freeing people for alternatives that seem to have no end, so much do they promise. And yet—the problem of loneliness. When it is mentioned, even the eyes of those who tend to deny its existence flicker inward for a moment.

2 Life in America has exploded, and loneliness is one main ingredient in the fallout. What was once a philosophical problem, spoken of mainly by poets and prophets, has now become an almost permanent condition for millions of Americans, not only for the old or divorced but also for the men and women filling singles bars and encounter groups, the adolescents running away from home or refusing to go to school, the corporate transients who move every two or three years, and the people calling suicide and crisis hotlines in search of someone to talk to. Knowing no limits of class, race, or age, loneliness is today a great leveler, a new American tradition.

3 To begin to understand the origins of the problem, one need only look at New York's high-rises, Los Angeles' pedestrianless streets, suburbia's front-porchless houses. The halls of large apartment buildings do not encourage conversation, nor do the aisles of supermarkets, the noise of factory assembly lines and factory-like offices, or the forbidding streets of the metropolitan areas that house 69 percent of the American population. Despite all the recently voiced desire for contact, there are few places where it can be made, spontaneously or otherwise. In the great rush for freedom we have lost the ability to be free together. And since personal identity seems to require the validation of another person's confirmation, many people feel faceless—empty, lonely.

4 In small towns or urban neighborhoods people had more than one strong relationship to affirm who they were. In their daily lives they reinforced and created networks of contacts. Doing daily chores, for instance, meant more than just purchasing the makings of the evening meal, cleaning the front stoop, or mailing a letter. These were more than just burdensome responsibilities, they were social events through which people gave each other mutual recognition. Today's American marvels at the "quaint" Europeans who still shop daily for groceries, visiting three or four small shops and taking as much time to buy food for a meal or two as an American in a supermarket might take to buy all the week's groceries. It's more than a question of pace; it's a question of people. It's pleasant to chat with your butcher or baker, to be handed a can rather than to take it off the rack in a store where efficiency has replaced humanity.

5 In rural settings people might, as the cliché goes, have known everybody else's business; but they were also there to help during a crisis, and one did not have to worry about calling for help in such a situation. Not so in contemporary America, as one California suburban resident vividly commented. When her husband had a stroke she hesitated before picking up the phone

to call a neighbor for help. It could have been an imposition. In small towns or extended families, not to have called would have been the insult. A woman rancher living alone in Montana explained that during the winter she calls her closest neighbors, who live miles away, to tell them when she leaves to feed her cows and when she returns. "If I don't call," she said, "my neighbors are furious. They'll have to come looking for me and take care of me if I should fall from my horse or have an accident. It saves them worry. They know something is really wrong if they don't hear the phone ring." Among the most rugged of America's rugged individualists such concern is second-sense. There is an aura of community that leaves the most physically isolated people with the feeling that they *belong.*

6 In the past, rural areas and urban neighborhoods also provided a center where people of all ages could meet. The old could maintain contact with the young, and youth had some familiarity with aging and death. Although generational conflict has always been present, old people and young were not as radically separated, with the old set aside and doomed to loneliness in euphemistically characterized "senior citizens' communities." Today age segregation has passed all sane limits. Not only are fifteen-year-olds isolated from seventy-year-olds but social groups divide those in high school from those in junior high, and those who are twenty from those who are twenty-five. There are middle-middle-age groups, late-middle-age groups, and old-age groups—as though people with five years between them could not possibly have anything in common. Like white light going through a prism, America divides into its component parts.

7 Mobility has a great deal to do with this erosion of American life. People move with such astounding frequency (40 million Americans change their residence once a year, and the average person will move fourteen times in his or her lifetime) that they lose family ties, friends, and themselves. There is a myth among the most highly mobile (corporate transients, academics, and those in the armed services) that those who have met in the past will, at one point or another, meet again. They will not entirely lose touch. There are also the mails, phone lines, and air routes. Just because we live three thousand miles apart doesn't mean it's over. You can call after six o'clock, visit regularly. Technology, however, is unable to completely vanquish distance. And distance undoes the ties formed by frequent contact—the thing that makes friends friends. People do indeed lose each other, and the pain of that loss, renewed every two or three years, makes people withdraw from further contact. "I sometimes feel that I don't ever want to make friends again," the wife of a university professor said. "You find people to get close to, and then they leave or you leave. At first it seems this will happen only every once in a while. But it happens over and over again. I sometimes wish I lived in a Chinese village where nothing changes and you know everyone from birth till they die."

8 Mobility does more than affect close friendships; it changes the whole tone of a neighborhood. When people lived in the same place for years, residents in a community knew one another. When someone moved onto the block you brought cake or candy. Today it is not unusual for people not to know their neighbors at all. Why should one make the effort of a welcome when the new arrivals will be leaving in a year? No sense wasting the energy. I knocked on the doors of a residence hall at the New York Hospital—Cornell Medical Center in Manhattan to ask the residents if they knew their neighbors or socialized with people living near them. All the residents in the building are doctors, nurses, or technicians; all are interested in the same things, presumably having strong interconnections. Yet very few even knew the names of the people living directly next door, and almost none met socially. Only the women with children met—and the children made much of the effort. It seems that even where we are the closest we can neither reach nor touch.

9 This communal apathy is also fertile soil for crime, since people have no idea which face goes with which front door. If someone walks out of the house with a TV set, a neighbor has no idea if it is the owner taking it to the repair shop or a burglar making off with an easy haul. And crime has never been noted for its healthy effect on human relationships. You are not likely to enter into a spontaneous conversation on the street if you think the person addressing you is a potential mugger, or open your door at night to help someone in trouble if you think that person might pull a knife. In a circular swing, more distrust and more loneliness. We feel like strangers on our streets. Where we should feel the safest, we rather feel that no one would help us if we were in trouble, that what happens to us, whether good or bad, makes no difference to the world around us—that *we* make no difference. And because we tolerate such antihuman life-styles, the encounters we have with others are more likely to be hostile

than pleasant. It is not only the muggers that are frightening but the faces of shoppers waiting on lines that are too long, and the ferociousness with which commuters honk their horns and curse in heavy traffic.

10 Another disturbing effect of the isolation from family, friends, and community is the added difficulty it imposes on the average marriage. Besides socially inherited communication problems and increasing dissatisfaction with our work, modern marriages have to cope with the added burdens of high mobility. In the past, husband and wife were to be "the one" for each other, the perfect companion. Now a woman or man must be not only confidant and lover, but family, community, friends—all things to one other man or woman.

11 In the past, relationships founded on large families and close communities gave people some options if things weren't going well at home. Today, when family bonds are weaker, more and more is being asked of the nuclear unit. It is as though one loaded a table with heavier and heavier weights while shrinking the circumference of the tabletop and chopping at its legs. The table will eventually collapse—just as the nuclear family is collapsing.

12 Change, mobility, freedom from burdensome commitments—all these can be exciting and enriching. Apologists for discontinuity in American life are fond of drawing upon an analogy between trees and people to support their positions. It is true, they admit, that some trees, in order to grow strong and healthy, need a great deal of time in one place so that they can send down solid, deep roots. Other varieties, however, can grow healthy despite frequent transplants and shallow roots. But the problem is that people are simply not trees. Trees, whether shallowly or deeply rooted, do not, as far as we know, need communication with other trees in order to flourish. Standing alone, they do not feel lonely.

13 What began as a great adventure may be turning into just another fetter. In retrospect, it is not clear from what exactly we have been running. Were small towns, for instance, suffocating or idyllic? Were ethnic, urban neighborhoods prisons or protectors? But whatever complicated reasons are behind the constant push for change and movement in urban and suburban America, people have a vision of where they are heading: toward technical and social progress—by definition a better state. What *will be* in America has generally been taken to be inherently superior to what *was*.

14 Our present, however, makes it abundantly clear that the price for such passionate optimism is the shattering of both personal and community life. It is a process that can only destroy much of the potential the future may hold and that is certainly demolishing any hope we may have in the present. We are paving the road forward with psychological wreckage, obstacles that make it impossible for many to make the journey and that provide a bumpy ride for those still able to travel.

15 Though there has been some attempt to treat the causes of the problem of "future shock," much of the emphasis has been toward disguising it—patching up the cuts, passing out the Valium, and hoping that the patient won't cause too much trouble in the future. For the most part, however, people are left alone to deal with the traumatic loneliness in modern life. And so for many Americans life becomes a bit like playing the stock market in a time of recession: one is less concerned with maximizing one's gain than with minimizing one's losses. To borrow from Karen Horney's description of the major preoccupation of neurotics, we are forced to seek safety rather than satisfaction, despite all our claims to the contrary.

16 It's obvious that loneliness is a human emotion common to all people in all eras. But at certain points in history, because of specific social changes, what were inevitable moments in life become, sometimes overnight, life-styles for millions of people. Mass loneliness is not just a problem that can be coped with by the particular individuals involved; it is an indication that things are drastically amiss on a societal level.

17 When the societal is distinguished from the psychological, as Jung has noted, an individual experience becomes a collective disturbance—a "social problem" in the sense in which Michel Philibert, the French gerontologist, uses the phrase. A social problem, says Philibert, is one that affects a category or group of people in a society, provided that the problem carries the following three qualifications.

18 1. It must be considered as deriving, at least in part, from the functioning of the structure of society itself.

19 2. It must be considered as affecting not only the category or group of people primarily involved but in some way having a pervasive influence on the rest of society, so that other people who do not face that specific difficulty are concerned about it; and it is seen as jeopardizing the

whole fabric of society and endangering the development of the health of the society, so that those not directly affected are made uneasy and think something should be done about this problem.

20 3. It must be considered as being susceptible to some sort of treatment through the action of society itself—that is, social action, and in the long run through political action.

21 People have always had to deal with hate and love, anxiety, aggression, violence, and loneliness. In certain epochs, however, these universals become the simultaneously held *preoccupation* of a major segment of the population. And the intensity of this concern is such that even those who do not feel it directly are disturbed.

22 To understand and begin to deal with loneliness as it exists today in America we must therefore consider more than the personal history of the particular lonely person and his or her emotional background. We cannot interpret the present problem exclusively in terms of childhood traumas: lack of affection from parents, for example, lack of openness, and thus loneliness. For present difficulties, while they encompass the problems of the past, are not simply mere reflections of it. The lonely person is not, as is commonly thought by many psychologists, lonely because he or she *needs to be lonely*, and is thus somehow enjoying it. People are lonely today because of both the psychological baggage they carry with them and the peculiar way American society alienates the potentially closest of friends, colleagues, lovers, and workmates.

Discovery Questions

1. What is the event being analyzed?
2. Identify some of the causes and effects of the event.
3. Identify several concrete details that illustrate her concepts.

Suggested Events to Analyze for Causes or Effects

Select one of the following or similar events. Decide whether you are going to analyze the causes leading up to that event or the effects following from that event.

a significant personal experience from your past: for example, losing a loved one, moving to a new neighborhood, getting or losing a job

an act of physical aggression: for example, hitting your sister or brother, punching a friend in the nose or vice versa

a social problem: for example, unemployment, inflation, discrimination, crime, scarcity of jobs for teenagers, rising college costs, the growing popularity of private schools, the pressure to conform to the standards of one's peers

a historical event: for example, the Industrial Revolution, World War II, the Renaissance, any invention

a political topic: for example, the absence of a peacetime draft, the installation of air bags in all new cars, the punishment for non-use of seat belts

WORKSHEET FOR CAUSAL ANALYSIS

1. Select an event to analyze and complete the top half of the worksheet.
2. Write your thesis statement and enumeration of subtopics and then get approval from your instructor.
3. Complete the worksheet **before** writing the essay.
4. Attach the worksheet to the finished essay.
5. Attach the Expository Essay Cover Sheet to the essay.

Source of material: ______________________________

Event to be analyzed: ______________________________

Controlling idea: ____________ (number) + ____________ (adjective) + causes or effects (noun)

Order of three main causes or effects: chronological

Point of view: ______________ Verb tense: ______________

Tone: ______________ Diction: ______________

Thesis statement + enumeration of causes or effects (may be 1 or 2 sentences):

____

____

____

____

____
(instructor approval)

OUTLINE

Title: ______________________________

¶1: Introduction (five sentences):

Choose a good beginning from the list.

Give necessary background material.

Good beginning # ______ : ______________________________

____

____

____

____

When you write your introduction, include the approved thesis statement and subtopics at the end of paragraph 1.

Body (three paragraphs)

¶2: Transition + topic sentence: ______

supporting details

¶3: Transition + topic sentence: ______

supporting details

¶4: Transition + topic sentence: ______________________________

____

supporting details
____
____
____
____
____
____
____
____
____
____
____
____
____
____

¶5: Conclusion (three sentences):

Restatement of event analyzed

Choose one of the good endings from the list.

Good ending # ______

____
____
____
____
____
____

Name: ____________________

Date: ____________________ **Class:** ____________

Type of Exposition: ____________________

EXPOSITORY ESSAY COVER SHEET		
Structure/Ideas	+	________
Usage/Mechanics	−	________
Total		________
Rewrite points	+	________
TOTAL		________

Structure and Ideas (100 points)	**Original**	**Rewrite**
INTRODUCTION (at least five sentences):		
title; one of good beginnings leading to thesis	10________	________
thesis statement + enumeration of subtopics	5________	________
BODY (three supporting paragraphs):		
three topic sentences = transition + reference to thesis + subtopic	15________	________
development of paragraphs: sufficient, concrete, appropriate, relevant	45________	________
CONCLUSION (at least three sentences):		
one of good endings	5________	________
ESSAY:		
logical order of ideas and correct reasoning	5________	________
effective style = tone + diction + sentence structure + coherence	15________	________
Total	100________	+ ________

The points in this section reflect your score for structure and ideas. If you have received fewer than 100 points, you may rewrite your paper to earn them. Use the numbers as a guide to areas needing revision.

Usage and Mechanics (minus points). See Correction Symbol Chart.		
You **may** earn these points in revision:		
Usage: adj; adv; agr; awk; col; dm; frag; mm; ref; rep; shift; verb; ww; //; ¶	−3 ea. ________	________
You **may not** earn these points in revision, but you must correct the errors:		
Mechanics: abbr; apos; cap; lc; p; ro; sp; ∧	−1 ea. ________	________
Total	− ________	+ ________

CHAPTER 11

The Fourth Pattern: Comparison-Contrast

If you spent part of last weekend watching several football games on television or going out to eat at two restaurants, most likely you discussed experiences in a casual manner and commented on which game or restaurant you liked better and why. These judgments are a form of comparison-contrast and a way of evaluating the relationship between two subjects, places, people, or events.

The expository pattern of comparison-contrast is based on this informal approach to related subjects. It systematically identifies the similarities or differences between two items in the same class. This method is more complex than the previous patterns of exposition because now you have two items to discuss and relate to each other.

Comparison-contrast is informative since it discusses a subject in one of two ways. Either it identifies likenesses between items commonly thought to be different, or it identifies differences between items commonly thought to be similar. For example, military and civilian life styles are usually thought to be different; therefore, an informative essay would compare them. Or two restaurants from the same ethnic background would appear to be similar; thus, an interesting essay would contrast them.

In addition, comparison-contrast clarifies a position and demonstrates relationships. It can draw attention to similarities and/or differences that exist between two items that might not ordinarily be thought of together. Examples are two paintings from different styles like eighteenth-century realism and twentieth-century cubism or two unrelated jobs like working in a band and teaching pre-school.

Comparison-contrast informs about an unknown item by comparing and contrasting it to a known one. One example is explaining the French system of government (President, Prime Minister, House of Deputies) by comparing it to the American system (President, House of Representatives, Senate). Thus, as a pattern of exposition, comparison-contrast gives you practice in handling more complex material because of the addition of a second item.

Methods of Organization

You may organize your comparison-contrast paper in either of two ways: subject-by-subject or point-by-point. In the **subject-by-subject** arrangement, you discuss the first subject or item along with all its supporting details in one section. Then you discuss the second subject and all its supporting details in another section. In the conclusion you present a brief overview summarizing the similarities or differences between the subjects. This arrangement is appropriate for chronological events, like two wars, or for subjects containing many small details, like the physical appearance of two individuals. An example of this method, illustrated below, is based on the student paper entitled "On Stage." The items being contrasted are high school and college theater arts departments.

Subject-by-Subject Arrangement

Class: Theater Arts departments

Subject (item) A: High school theater arts department

1. facilities
   a. gymnasium
   b. folding chairs
   c. fluorescent lighting
   d. poor acoustics
2. teachers--athletic coach
   a. whistle
   b. refereeing
   c. pep talk
3. students
   a. amateur attitude
   b. competition
   c. snobbishness

Subject (item) B: College theater arts department

1. facilities
   a. theater
   b. padded seats
   c. sophisticated lighting
   d. excellent acoustics
2. teachers--trained
   a. specialties
   b. professionalism
3. students
   a. dedicated attitude
   b. cooperation and support
   c. fairness

Subjects A and B: Overview summarizing the similarities or differences

The subject-by-subject method does not focus as sharply on similarities or differences as the second arrangement. In the **point-by-point** approach, you discuss one point at a time and deal with both items within each section. The same material from the student essay "On Stage" might be rearranged in the following manner.

Point-by-Point Arrangement

Class: Theater Arts departments

Point 1: Facilities

Item A High school
1. gymnasium
2. chairs
3. lighting
4. acoustics

Item B College
1. theater
2. seats
3. lighting
4. acoustics

Point 2: Teachers

Item A High school--coach

1. whistle
2. refereeing
3. pep talk

Item B College--trained teachers

1. specialties
2. professionalism

Point 3: Students

Item A High school

1. amateur attitude
2. competition
3. snobbishness

Item B College

1. dedicated attitude
2. cooperation and support
3. fairness

Requirements

You must clearly establish the class/basis of the comparison or contrast. In addition, you need to be sure that the items are in the same class and thus share a real kinship. For example, comparing a ballet dancer and a football player on the basis of physical skills and requirements is appropriate because the two items come from the same class, athletic activities. Then, you must identify important similarities or differences. The key to successful comparison-contrast is the systematic arrangement of points developed with concrete detail. Next, you should select one of the two methods of organization: subject-by-subject or point-by-point.

In the introductory paragraph you first identify the class and the two items to compare or contrast. It is more interesting to compare two items that most people think are different and to contrast two items thought to be similar. The introduction is a good place to enumerate the obvious likenesses and differences. Then you can move on to the more informative and less obvious similarities or differences that you have chosen for the body of the essay.

Each topic sentence should refer to both items and clearly state the point of similarity or difference. The body paragraphs present an evenly proportioned discussion of each item or subject. Transitional expressions are needed for coherence and ease of reading. When you discuss two separate subjects or items in the point-by-point arrangement, a concluding sentence for each body paragraph completes the thought. The concluding paragraph often contains a judgment about which item is preferable and why.

Problems to Avoid

One common mistake when writing comparison is to confuse it with **analogy.** If two items share a striking similarity but do not come from the same class, the comparison between them is not rhetorical. It is an analogy, an imaginative comparison between items that appear similar in some respects but belong to different classes and thus share no kinship. Writers frequently use this device to identify a striking resemblance between otherwise dissimilar objects. For example, comparing a poet to a diamond cutter, a writer to a builder, a river to an electric current, or a mirror to a lake reveals similarities that are not genuine but are effective. Analogy does not prove anything but instead offers a vivid illustration and thus makes an idea more clear.

Unless you are asked to both compare and contrast two items, the body of your essay should give only similarities or differences. Mixing the approaches is illogical and confuses your audience. Also, in a contrast essay when enumerating the points of difference, you must phrase your subtopics so that they refer to both items. For example, if you are contrasting military and civilian life, your subtopic should not be that "military life is restricting and lacking in freedom while civilian life offers many liberties." Instead, your subtopic should give the point of difference as "the degree or amount of freedom in military and civilian life."

Organizational Patterns for Comparison-Contrast

Study this blueprint so that you can see and better understand the elements necessary for comparison-contrast. Then use the pattern as a guide in assembling your own essay. Observe that this is the pattern for the point-by-point approach.

Title

Introduction—¶1

At least five sentences, including the relationship or class the items share

Use of one of the good beginnings

Establishment of order of subtopics — verb tense
point of view — tone and diction

Thesis statement = subject (two items to be compared or contrasted) + controlling idea (number + adjective + similarities or differences)
Subtopic sentence = enumeration of three points of similarity or difference
} may be 1 or 2 sentences

Body—¶2, 3, 4

Presentation of three major points of similarity or difference

Logical order of three major points of similarity or difference:

____ general to particular — ____ climactic

**Paragraph 2:* Topic sentence = transitional expression + reference to both items + point of similarity or difference 1

ITEM 1 (more familiar item first): concrete details, anecdotes, examples. Transitional expression +

ITEM 2: concrete details, anecdotes, examples.
Concluding sentence = reference to both items.

**Paragraph 3:* Topic sentence = transitional expression + reference to both items + point of similarity or difference 2

ITEM 1 (same order as paragraph 2): concrete details, anecdotes, examples. Transitional expression +
ITEM 2: concrete details, anecdotes, examples.
Concluding sentence = reference to both items.

**Paragraph 4:* Topic sentence = transitional expression + reference to both items + point of similarity or difference 3 (most important point last)

ITEM 1 (same order as paragraphs 2 and 3): concrete details, anecdotes, examples. Transitional expression +
ITEM 2: concrete details, anecdotes, examples.
Concluding sentence = reference to both items.

Transitional expressions: see especially
Addition — Emphasis/Intensification — Contrast
Comparison — Introduction of Illustration/Example

Conclusion—¶5

At least three sentences

Transitional expression (optional): see Conclusion/Result and Summary

Judgment about relationship: Is one preferable? Which one? Why?

Use of one of the good endings

*These elements may be rearranged within the sentence.

STUDENT SAMPLE—Comparison Essay—Analyzed for Parts

Observe that elements of structure and content are labeled on the left while elements of style are identified on the right. This detailed analysis will help you plan your own essay.

Source: book on art history

Tone: argumentative; serious
Diction: connotative; slanted; concrete
Order: general to particular

Title

Illustrations of War

Introduction ¶ 1

Good Beginning #12

basis of comparison

No doubt appreciating art is an individual pursuit because of the variations in subject and style. Certainly, traditional and modern paintings use strikingly different techniques. Despite these differences, two masterpieces can share the same theme. Francisco Goya's "Saturn Devouring One of his Children" and Pablo Picasso's "Guernica" are two such paintings which condemn war and oppression. They share three basic similarities: the occasion, the purpose, and the symbolism.

Thesis Statement (2 items to be compared)

Verb tense: present

Point of view: third person

Subtopic Sentence (Controlling Idea + 3 points of similarity)

Topic Sentence ¶ 2

One* similarity between Goya's powerful painting and Picasso's modernistic work is the occasion for the work. The historical event that inspired Goya's work occurred in Spain in the early nineteenth century. Under Napoleon Bonaparte I, Spain became the scapegoat for that tyrant's displaced hostility against Portugal. Goya used his artistic genius to capture forever the humiliation and turmoil that Spain suffered. Similarly, a historical event inspired Picasso's powerful painting. In 1937, the German military command randomly

Item 1

Diction: connotative, slanted

Coherence: Transitional expression to introduce Item 2

Item 2

*Coherence: transitional expressions circled.

chose the village of Guernica in Spain for military experimentation. While testing the capabilities of a new weapon, they destroyed this quiet town. "Guernica" is Picasso's memorial to that civil war. — *Diction: concrete, literal, denotative*

Concluding Sentence — Often, real events serve as the subject for art.

Topic Sentence ¶3 — A second similarity that the paintings share is their purpose. Goya's art committed this moment to canvas in order to reveal the despair of Spain. Under the tyrannical rule of Napoleon, civilians suffered and died. Goya conveyed that agony painfully and decisively. The staring eyes, the wild, unkempt hair, and the unclothed, uncivilized figure reveal the ferocious depths of human beings whose conscience is overcome and whose reason is lost. Certainly, the bizarre, grotesque figure of Saturn holding a bloody, headless corpse to his mouth suggests the madness and savagery of Napoleon. Goya was protesting inhuman violence and the liberation of destructive instincts. In the same way, Picasso used his art to make a social comment. He vented his anger at the outrage of a more modern war and recent oppression. His

Item 1 (Goya's art)

Sentence Structure: Introductory prepositional phrase (Under the tyrannical rule of Napoleon,)

Diction: concrete (The staring eyes, the wild, unkempt hair, and the unclothed,)

Diction: Connotative (bizarre, grotesque)

Diction: abstract, slanted (madness and savagery)

Coherence: Transitional expression to Introduce (In the same way,)

Item 2 (his art)

Body ¶ 2,3,4

painting speaks so loudly that we can hear the cries of the innocent men, women, and children as they witness and experience the destruction. His canvas reproduces feelings so sensitively that we can feel the people's pain and anguish. As social commentary, both paintings make dramatic statements.

Sentence Structure: two dependent clauses

Concluding Sentence

Finally, both artists use symbolism as a means of conveying the theme of war and oppression. In the traditional "Saturn Devouring One of his Children," Goya drew a comparison between the mythological Saturn and the ruthless emperor Napoleon. According to the legend, Saturn, fearing that a son would overthrow him, swallowed his sons one by one. In translating this analogy to canvas, Napoleon becomes the cannibalistic Saturn devouring, not his sons, but the flesh of Spain. In like manner, Picasso used symbolism in his modernistic "Guernica" to make a statement about war. In his painting, a horse represents the victims of war. Standing in the center of the work with his mouth contorted, he shrieks a futile protest while the victims gather around him. A mother clutching her dead child screams in anguish; a fallen warrior grasps a sword to represent the futility of war. Amid the turmoil, distant and dispassionate, stands the symbol of war--a bull, which Picasso uses

Topic Sentence A4

Item 1

Diction: connotative slanted

Sentence Structure: verbal phrase

A Sentence Structure: parallelism

Coherence: Transitional expression to introduce Item 2

Item 2

Sentence structure: Introductory Verbal phrase

Diction: concrete

Sentence structure: adjectives out of normal order

to express savage cruelty. Great art relies on symbolism to help convey its meaning.

Concluding Sentence

To summarize, even though two paintings may be separated by time or technique, great art has a message that transcends the moment. In this case, we can learn from the misery created by tyrants. The destruction and humiliation that ripped Spain apart are history; the children of Guernica are lost, locked into childhood forever that spring morning. But these two works of art help us stand against further such atrocities and demand that we not forget them.

Conclusion
¶ 5
Good Ending #5

Diction: connotative, concrete

STUDENT SAMPLE—Contrast Essay

Source of material: personal experience

On Stage

Many high school students rush headlong toward higher education in the hope of finding some drastic change from their boring academic routine. My dreams about college were certainly consistent with that attitude. The propaganda circulated via college pamphlets convinced me that I could look forward to broadening my interests and enjoying new experiences. When I finally did begin my higher education, I could not overlook three striking differences between high school and college, particularly in my major, theater arts. The facilities, teachers, and students contrast significantly.

To begin, the facilities in the two institutions differ. My small private high school found a way to make every piece of equipment or building do double duty. The gymnasium hosted school volleyball games on Saturday afternoons. By Saturday evening, the court was transformed into the theater by the removal of the poles and net and by the addition of noisy wooden folding chairs. While the chairs did not guarantee comfort, their major asset was the fact that they could be unstacked and set up in thirty-minutes' time. The lighting system of my alma mater consisted of two flourescent bulbs that blinked shakily because of faulty wiring.

While they flattered the volleyball players with the deep shadows they cast, they rarely complimented the actresses' make-up. Also, the acoustics in the gym were an engineer's nightmare. Night performances were haunted by the sounds of an afternoon volleyball game still reverberating off the brick proscenium arch. But the facilities in the college are clearly superior. Here is a large capacity theater whose sole function is to bring great dramas to life. Heavily padded seats envelope the audience in red velvet and make them temporarily forget their physical discomforts. A network of sophisticated lighting equipment can create daylight or evening with the flick of a switch. Colored filters can bathe a set in fiery red or cold blue instantaneously. Excellent acoustics allow a spectator in the last row to hear the rantings of a Lear or the whispers of a Hamlet equally well. Certainly, only hushed silence pervades the theater before the production begins. The college facilities are much more professional than those in my high school.

I have also found that the teachers in both schools are significantly unlike each other. In my high school, with the gymnasium posing as a theater, I suppose it follows logically that our athletic coach doubled as our drama instructor. Her shiny silver whistle was not decorative but was an extension of her body as it hung around her neck. She refereed rehearsals as though they were practice games. The actors would volley their lines back and forth. Dropping a line or forgetting some change of position was sure to be penalized. Before the opening night curtain, we could count on a fifteen-minute pep talk, complete with diagrams on the chalkboard and some last minute strategy. Indeed, there were times when the spectators cheered us instead of clapping sedately. However, in college my drama coaches are trained, competent teachers. Any sports that they enjoy are strictly leisure pursuits. An added feature is that each professor specializes in a different aspect of the theater--acting, set decoration, costumes, lighting. Since these areas include both the technical and creative sides of drama, I am learning my craft thoroughly. In this atmosphere of professionalism and mutual respect, I hope to develop my talent. If I have ability, the teachers in college will nourish it better than those in high school would.

A final difference between high school and college is the students themselves. One reason for the amateurish quality of our productions in high school was the general air of frivolity that pervaded the atmosphere. Since all of the roles were played by girls, making a love scene believable was impossible. Giggles and snickers inhibited even the most aspiring actress. Beyond that, one or two cliques dominated the influential positions and guaranteed their friends favors. Obviously, the captain of the cheerleading team also snatched the major role in each new production, even though she was tone deaf and could not inspire a serious emotion in any spectator. However, she was blonde and petite and could project her voice to the back of the gym. In college, however, we do not operate under such a handicap. The atmosphere here is conducive to learning and growth. The students are intense and dedicated individuals whose primary interest is drama and theater. Their height, coloring, and facial features are incidentals that only strengthen their performances on stage. Indeed, since they are devoted to perfecting their craft, cooperation and mutual support characterize their behavior. Tryouts for each part in a new production proceed in an objective, fair manner, and each actor knows he has earned the role he plays. In college no petty tyrants wield the undue power that some students in high school have.

After weighing the differences between both schools, I know my rush to graduate was vindicated. The facilities, teachers, and students have reenforced my attitude about the importance of a college education. At least my dream of seeing my name in lights is a step closer to reality.

Discovery Exercise

1. Identify the thesis statement
   a. the relationship or class the items share: ______
   b. the two items being contrasted: ______
   ______
2. Identify three points of difference: ______
   ______
   ______
3. Identify the order of the points of difference:
   ______ general to particular
   ______ climactic
4. Identify the point of view: ______ person
5. Identify the verb tense: ______
6. Circle **eight** transitional expressions.
7. Select **five** of the most concrete supporting details:
   ______
   ______
   ______
   ______
   ______
8. Choose terms from the diction chart that characterize the diction: ______
9. Choose terms from the tone chart that describe the tone: ______
   ______
10. After reviewing chapter 16, bracket **five** introductory prepositional phrases, one type of grammatical structure used in the essay.

STUDENT SAMPLE—Comparison Essay

Source of material: personal experience

Women: Both Sides of the Coin

Being a woman today can mean not only facing difficult problems but also making satisfying decisions. For the first time in history, a woman has options about the life style she will adopt. She can attempt to realize her own personal goals, pursue her own interests, and achieve her own success. Indeed, choosing between a liberated and a traditional role is a decision every woman can make. While these roles may seem polarized, these females share three inherent similarities: rigorous work, attitude about responsibilities, and insecurities about their social function.

The first way in which these women are alike is their work. A liberated woman may hold a job that is traditionally thought of as a man's job. For example, many women are now becoming phone linewomen, police officers, machinists, and truck drivers. Nor are these women necessarily masculine. Lady truckers do wear make-up and maintain shapely figures. Such women make a vital contribution to the culture by breaking the mold society has cast them into. In addition, they derive personal satisfaction in beginning to explore the limits of their own identity. In recent years, for instance, the fields of medicine, sports, politics, law, and science have admitted women in large numbers. Like the liberated woman, the traditional woman also works. Being a homemaker involves working long and hard hours at raising a family and running a home. She shops, gardens, cleans, cooks, car pools, and runs errands. In her spare time, she often volunteers to work for charity. Or a traditional woman may hold a job more commonly associated with the female gender, such as being a secretary, a nurse, an elementary school teacher, or a salesperson. Statistically, the majority of women now work outside of the home, whether or not they think of themselves as liberated or traditional.

Another parallel between the unfettered female and the customary one is their basic attitude about responsibilities. The liberated woman sees herself as equal to a man, entitled to the same opportunities available to men. A man should not be paid more for doing the same job as a woman. To the independent lady, pay should be based on ability, not sex. Such a woman feels comfortable being judged on her accomplishments and expects no empty courtesies from men like opening car doors or inheriting a seat on a crowded bus. Similarly, the tradition-bound woman with a family wants her husband to share equally in the household duties. His help should include such chores as changing diapers, washing dishes, and shopping for groceries. Rather than being underpaid, this housewife works from the moment her feet touch the carpet in the morning until she collapses into bed in the evening without receiving any paycheck. Her compensation is her family's appreciation. Inevitably, she is the last one on the list for a haircut or a new pair of shoes. But she expects no special favors, except perhaps breakfast in bed on Mother's Day. Regardless of whether the job is outside or inside the home, both women believe the responsibilities and obligations should be borne by male and female alike.

Third, both the emancipated and the time-honored woman have insecurities about their roles in society. The liberated lady may be a part of the working class, earning her own income. She may have money and be richer than the unsalaried female, but she is not necessarily happier. Some women who work feel guilty about not getting married and having a family. And to add to the confusion and guilt is the unclear message the career woman receives about her place in society. Many prejudiced people still feel a woman is not complete or fulfilled until she is married and is raising a family. Such attitudes add to the pressure she must already deal with. Likewise, there are many negative attitudes surrounding the female who chooses a customary life style. Although she is making a vital contribution to society by promoting family life, she is still viewed as "just a housewife." Society has forced her into a defensive position, and she responds by renaming herself a "homemaker." Suddenly, she feels trapped by the very role she was encouraged to embrace. To cast aside her responsibilities is self-indulgent, and to remain in her position is anticlimactic. Indeed, whichever role a female chooses, she will have to cope with fundamental conflicts.

In brief, the liberated and the traditional woman are alike in their work, attitudes of responsibility, and social insecurities. Women's roles are constantly changing, and more opportunities are available to them. The more liberated or the less traditional that women become, the easier it will be for them to adopt diversified life styles and experience satisfaction.

Discovery Exercise

1. Identify the thesis statement
   a. the relationship or class the items share: ______________________________
   b. the two items being compared: ______________________________
   ____
2. Identify the three points of similarity: ______________________________
   ____
   ____
3. Identify the order of the points of similarity:
   ________ general to particular
   ________ climactic
4. Identify the point of view: ____________ person
5. Identify the verb tense: ____________
6. Circle **ten** transitional expressions.

7. Select **five** of the most concrete supporting details:

8. List all the synonyms for the following words:

liberated	**traditional**	**woman**

9. Choose terms from the diction chart that characterize the diction: ____________

10. Choose terms from the tone chart that describe the tone: ____________

11. After reviewing Chapter 16, bracket **five** verbal phrases, one type of grammatical structure used in the essay. Select only those which function as the subjects of their sentences.

STUDENT SAMPLE—Contrast Essay

Source of material: personal experience

The Lady and the Libber

My two friends, Jane and Sally, are people who occupy a large space in my life. The only similarity they share is that they are both women. They have such diverse notions about what being a woman entails that it is sometimes hard to believe they are both members of the same sex. Three primary differences distinguish Jane, my traditional friend, from Sally, my liberated friend. These contrasts are defined in their attitudes toward women's liberation, toward men in general, and toward themselves.

One area in which they differ is their attitude toward women's liberation. Jane thinks E.R.A. is a laundry detergent and can't understand what all the equality fuss is about. The fact that women might someday be drafted into the army is enough to give her anxiety attacks. She hates those oversized khaki sweatshirts, and she thinks combat boots and rifles are "so unfeminine." There is no way Uncle Sam is going to get my friend Jane out on the battlefield unless she's allowed to wear her favorite designer jeans teamed with her pink western boots. Sally, on the other hand, has no time for such frivolities. She campaigns energetically for the E.R.A. and its ratification. She is prepared to do whatever is necessary in order to insure that women achieve equal status with men. Sally believes that women will never be free until they are prepared to stand side by side with their men at the front line. On the table next to her bed nestles Jane's make-up bag while Sally's gun stands at attention on her night table.

A second difference between the two women is their attitude toward men. Jane, like Will Rogers, never met a man she didn't like. She likes them all--all shapes and all sizes. Jane loves nothing better than to dress up for an evening out with a date. Her mother always told her to act cute and pretend she was dumb. Consequently, Jane never lost this habit, and it became part of her life style. In contrast, women who act flirtatious and silly, according to Sally, should be strung up by their heels and flogged. She says this type of behavior is exactly what has kept women oppressed for all these years. Sally does not like dressing up for a date with a man. The only satisfaction she gets from an evening out is watching the expression on her date's face when she picks up the check. While Jane giggles and coos at men, Sally converses with them as equals.

Finally, the two women differ in their attitude toward themselves. Jane lives in the ephemeral world of "the beautiful people." She is constantly trying to attain the current "in-look" but is never satisfied with the results. She feels she will never be good enough to compete in a man's world and has given up the whole idea as a hopeless cause. All she wants to do is dress in a sensual bikini and lie in her garden with her feet upon little velvet cushions. Her fantasy is to have a coterie of male servants dancing attendance on her and hourly feeding her champagne and caviar. She intends to live out the rest of her days as a lady of leisure. Meanwhile, Sally is planning the first all-female executive board with an all-male typing pool. Sally believes that women have the potential not just to be equal to men but to be superior. She has no qualms about entering the working world because she feels capable and confident enough to do so. For Sally, the moment of equality will have been achieved when she can lean over and pinch her attractive blond male secretary right on the rump. As Jane passively eats chocolates and watches television, Sally is actively organizing fund-raisers and marching on city hall.

Both Jane, the traditional woman, and Sally, the liberated female, are good friends of mine and are very special individuals in my life. Their opposing ideas make my life a lot more exciting. I look forward to the day when each achieves the level to which she aspires.

The previous sample student essays in this chapter have been either comparison or contrast. However, longer essays often require both a comparison and contrast of the same two items. If you are given such an assignment, organize it in the following manner.

Your introductory paragraph should mention that the essay will give both differences and similarities. But you should not mix together the contrasts and comparisons. Instead you need to decide which part of your discussion is stronger and present that section in the second half of the essay. If you contrast first, enumerate only the contrasting subtopics in the first paragraph. When you have completed the systematic discussion of points of difference, then a short transitional paragraph is useful to move the essay to the points of comparison. In this transitional paragraph, enumerate the points of similarity in the order that they will be developed. The conclusion must combine the first half and the last half of the discussion.

The sample essay which follows both compares and contrasts two famous dramas. In order to help you understand the ideas, plot summaries of the two dramas are included.

Plot Summaries

Oedipus Rex, by Sophocles, set in Greece in the third century B.C., dramatizes the legend of the Theban dynasty. Laius, king of Thebes, learning from an oracle that he would be killed by his own son, leaves the baby on a mountain to die. But the baby Oedipus is rescued by a shepherd and raised by the king and queen of Corinth as their own son. When Oedipus becomes an adult, the Delphic oracle warns him that he will kill his father and marry his mother. Horrified, he avoids returning to Corinth and, on the road to Thebes, meets and in anger kills Laius, unaware of his identity. Oedipus arrives at Thebes which is suffering from a plague brought on by the Sphinx. He answers her riddle, liberates the city, and as a reward, becomes king of Thebes and husband of Jocasta, the widowed queen of Laius. Together they have two sons and two daughters. Much later famine strikes Thebes, and the Delphic oracle advises Creon, Jocasta's brother, to find the slayer of Laius in order to free the city. Oedipus, to satisfy the gods further, decrees that the guilty person be found and expelled. The blind prophet Tiresias and the old shepherd eventually reveal that Oedipus has killed Laius, his father, and married Jocasta, his mother. Jocasta commits suicide, and Oedipus blinds himself and leaves the city to become a wandering outcast.

Death of a Salesman, by Arthur Miller, set in New York in the 1940's, tells the story of Willy Loman, an emotionally unstable and unsuccessful traveling salesman in his mid-sixties who has just been fired from his job. His two sons, Biff and Happy, returning home for a visit, witness his deterioration as he loses touch with reality. Their compassionate mother, Linda, realizes that Willy's peculiar behavior comes from the gulf between his expectations and his actual circumstances. Willy's dream, to be successful and well liked, makes him into a braggart and liar and eventually destroys him. Accepting society's false values, he cannot cope with his failure or the failure of Biff who had been a high school football star but is now jobless. At a dinner to celebrate his supposed new job, Biff reveals yet another failure which effectively destroys the last of Willy's unrealistic expectations. In a flashback Willy relives the moment when he devastated a younger Biff with his infidelity to Linda. Later, at home Willy fights with Biff and is reconciled to him when he realizes his son loves him. In a final gesture Willy commits suicide to provide Biff with insurance money to start a business. His funeral is poorly attended, a final irony to a man who wanted to be successful and well-liked.

STUDENT SAMPLE—Comparison and Contrast Essay

Source of material: two dramas

The Timelessness of Human Experience

The cultures of ancient Greece and modern America are very dissimilar. The art, music, education, and philosophy have marked external differences. Because of technological advances, the living, clothing, housing, and transportation have changed drastically from the past. However, there is a common thread joining these two civilizations--people themselves who still today think, feel, love, and worry as they did in ancient times. An example of this generalization is two tragic dramas, Sophocles' Oedipus Rex and Arthur Miller's Death of a Salesman, which exhibit striking differences as well as similarities. Three major differences involve the natures of the central characters, the circumstances of their conflicts, and the expository techniques used by the playwrights.

The central figures, Oedipus and Willy Loman, reveal important differences in their characters. Oedipus is an honorable, ethical protagonist who commits himself to saving Thebes, his city, by finding the truth about the identity of the killer of Lauis. Despite warnings to the contrary from Tiresias and the old shepherd and his wife, Oedipus relentlessly pursues his objective. Confronting the truth about himself, he carries out the decree of his own banishment from the kingdom. In contrast, Willy is a liar, a philanderer, and a braggart who evades and denies the truth whenever possible. He refuses to admit that he has just lost his job, that his sons are shiftless, unsuccessful adults, and that his whole life has been a lie. His ultimate rejection of the truth is illustrated in his committing suicide. Clearly, these men are motivated by different values.

A second significant difference between these protagonists is the circumstances surrounding their conflicts. Oedipus' predicament is unavoidable. Before his birth, the gods decreed that he would unknowingly kill his father and marry his mother. Despite his being left as a baby to die on a mountain, raised by foster parents, and warned by the Delphic oracle, he still fulfills the prophecy. On the other hand, there are no gods which predetermine Willy's fate; thus he has alternatives. He makes the choice to be unfaithful to Linda, to encourage his sons to deceive themselves and others, and to refuse a lower paying job offer from a friend. Throughout his life, he denies his talent of working with his hands because society considers that such jobs lack prestige. The fact that Oedipus had no alternatives while Willy had emphasizes their differences.

A third point of contrast between the two dramas is the expository techniques used by the playwrights. Sophocles' imparting of information is in the classical form. He employs the Delphic oracle, the Sphinx, the old shepherd, the blind prophet, and the chorus for plot development. They tell the audience about what has happened in the past, what is occurring offstage in the present, and what will transpire in the future. For instance, the old shepherd reveals to Oedipus that the king and queen of Corinth are not his real parents and that he was abandoned on a mountain, saved by this shepherd, and brought to Corinth. However, Arthur Miller is more experimental in his treatment of exposition. Instead of a typical flashback to realistically convey the past, he shows Willy hallucinating about it and confusing it with the present. The actual events of Willy's past are literally dramatized on stage. For example, the audience witnesses Willy's crucial confrontation with Biff in a Boston hotel room, an incident that Willy relives in a restaurant. Certainly, dramatic techniques differentiate these two plays.

Just as there are differences between these two dramas, there are several important similarities to be noted. These similarities include the protagonists' common flaw, the effect on the audience, and the underlying theme.

The first similarity between these two tragedies is that the protagonists share a common flaw--pride. When Tiresias accuses Oedipus of killing Laius, Oedipus responds with fury and anger. He exalts his own wisdom while degrading the blind prophet. Further, he accuses Tiresias of Laius' death and of conspiracy with Creon. Oedipus' prideful commitment to finding Laius' killer is the basis for his downfall. These actions reveal Oedipus' tragic arrogance. Likewise, Willy Loman can be accused of the same flaw. His pride is evident from the drama's first scene. He lies to Linda about his commissions and brags to his sons about how much more everyone liked him than other salesmen and how he was the one who opened up the East for his company. Also, his pride would not allow him to accept a lower paying, less significant job after he was fired. The excessive sense of self-importance ultimately results in Willy's suicide. Thus, both men have the tragic flaw of pride.

Oedipus Rex and *Death of a Salesman* share another similarity--the emotion of sympathy they elicit from the audience. Sophocles paints Oedipus as a man who, although he tries untiringly to avert the plague on Thebes, must suffer. After all his efforts to help his people, his reward is to find that he himself is guilty of murder and incest. But the most tragic scene of the play is that in which Oedipus, in his sorrow and remorse, blinds himself. Homeless, broken, without country or honor, and forced by his own decree to wander the land, Oedipus is pitiable in the true tragic sense. Similarly, Miller shows that Willy Loman is like so many people today who live out their lives and have so little to show for their efforts. Even though Willy's ambition was to achieve material success, it is ironic that his only legacy is a broken-down, fully paid for refrigerator and a $2,000 insurance policy. The audiences of these dramas sympathize greatly with both of the protagonists.

The most important likeness shared by these plays is their theme--people must accept responsibility for their actions and act on their beliefs. When Oedipus finally discovers the horrible truth about his identity, he responds with moral outrage and indignation. His blinding of himself is a symbolic act that expresses his realization that wisdom and understanding require inner sight, not external vision. He then accepts the responsibility for his horrendous deeds by fulfilling the curse he proclaimed unknowingly and ironically against himself. The audience admires and respects a hero who finally redeems himself and emerges a wiser person. In comparison, Willy refuses to accept his status in life passively. Although society has forced him into an inherently frustrating situation, Willy wages his own battle against the strong forces of his environment. Despite these odds, he holds onto his dream, even though this delusion leads to his ultimate defeat. The audience can admire such a commitment in the face of overwhelming obstacles since the easier course would be simply to yield to the external pressures to conform. These plays underscore the indestructible will of human beings to persist in their dreams and desires, no matter what the consequences.

The two-thousand-year gap between Greek and American cultures can probably account for most of the differences between these two outstanding works. While the protagonists have different personalities, they share the common tragic flaw of pride. While the circumstances surrounding their separate conflicts vary, audiences respond with sympathy to both. While the dramatic techniques contrast sharply, the same themes emerge from both. Sophocles' *Oedipus Rex* and Arthur Miller's *Death of a Salesman* are dramas that will endure because they question whether or not people are the masters of their destiny.

PROFESSIONAL SAMPLE—Comparison-Contrast

Read the following essay to see how a professional writer has used the technique of comparison-contrast. Then answer the discovery questions which focus on the major elements of comparison-contrast.

William Ouchi (1943–) earned an M.B.A. from Stanford University and a doctorate in business administration from the University of Chicago. A professor in the Graduate School of Management at U.C.L.A. and a prominent business consultant, he is the author of *Theory Z: How American Business Can Meet the Japanese Challenge* (1981), from which this section was taken.

Japanese and American Workers

Collective Values

1 Perhaps the most difficult aspect of the Japanese for Westerners to comprehend is the strong orientation to collective values, particularly a collective sense of responsibility. Let me illustrate with an anecdote about a visit to a new factory in Japan owned and operated by an American electronics company. The American company, a particularly creative firm, frequently attracts attention within the business community for its novel approaches to planning, organizational design, and management systems. As a consequence of this corporate style, the parent company determined to make a thorough study of Japanese workers and to design a plant that would combine the best of East and West. In their study they discovered that Japanese firms almost never make use of individual work incentives, such as piecework or even individual performance appraisal tied to salary increases. They concluded that rewarding individual achievement and individual ability is always a good thing.

2 In the final assembly area of their new plant long lines of young Japanese women wired together electronic products on a piece-rate system: the more you wired, the more you got paid. About two months after opening, the head foreladies approached the plant manager. "Honorable plant manager," they said humbly as they bowed, "we are embarrassed to be so forward, but we must speak to you because all of the girls have threatened to quit work this Friday." (To have this happen, of course, would be a great disaster for all concerned.) "Why," they wanted to know, "can't our plant have the same compensation system as other Japanese companies? When you hire a new girl, her starting wage should be fixed by her age. An eighteen-year-old should be paid more than a sixteen-year-old. Every year on her birthday, she should receive an automatic increase in pay. The idea that any one of us can be more productive than another must be wrong, because none of us in final assembly could make a thing unless all of the other people in the plant had done their jobs right first. To single one person out as being more productive is wrong and is also personally humiliating to us." The company changed its compensation system to the Japanese model.

3 Another American company in Japan had installed a suggestion system much as we have in the United States. Individual workers were encouraged to place suggestions to improve productivity into special boxes. For an accepted idea the individual received a bonus amounting to some fraction of the productivity savings realized from his or her suggestion. After a period of six months, not a single suggestion had been submitted. The American managers were puzzled. They had heard many stories of the inventiveness, the commitment, and the loyalty of Japanese workers, yet not one suggestion to improve productivity had appeared.

4 The managers approached some of the workers and asked why the suggestion system had not been used. The answer: "No one can come up with a work improvement idea alone. We work together, and any ideas that one of us may have are actually developed by watching others and talking to others. If one of us was singled out for being responsible for such an idea, it would embarrass all of us." The company changed to a group suggestion system, in which workers collectively submitted suggestions. Bonuses were paid to groups which would save bonus money until the end of the year for a party at a restaurant or, if there was enough money, for family vacations together. The suggestions and productivity improvements rained down on the plant.

5 One can interpret these examples in two quite different ways. Perhaps the Japanese commitment to collective values is an anachronism that does not fit with modern industrialism but brings economic success despite that collectivism. Collectivism seems to be inimical to the kind of maverick creativity exemplified in Benjamin Franklin, Thomas Edison, and John D. Rockefeller. Collectivism does not seem to provide the individual incentive to excel which has made a great success of American enterprise. Entirely apart from its economic effects, collectivism implies a loss of individuality, a loss of the freedom to be different, to hold fundamentally different values from others.

6 The second interpretation of the examples is that the Japanese collectivism is economically efficient. It causes people to work well together and to encourage one another to better efforts. Industrial life requires interdependence of one person on another. But a less obvious but far-reaching implication of the Japanese collectivism for economic performance has to do with accountability.

7 In the Japanese mind, collectivism is neither a corporate or individual goal to strive for nor a slogan to pursue. Rather, the nature of things operates so that nothing of consequence occurs as a result of individual effort. Everything important in life happens as a result of teamwork or collective effort. Therefore, to attempt to assign individual credit or blame to results is unfounded. A Japanese professor of accounting, a brilliant scholar trained at Carnegie-Mellon University who teaches now in Tokyo, remarked that the status of accounting systems in Japanese industry is primitive compared to those in the United States. Profit centers, transfer prices, and computerized information systems are barely known even in the largest Japanese companies, whereas they are a commonplace in even small United States organizations. Though not at all surprised at the difference in accounting systems, I was not at all sure that the Japanese were primitive. In fact, I thought their system a good deal more efficient than ours.

8 Most American companies have basically two accounting systems. One system summarizes the overall financial state to inform stockholders, bankers, and other outsiders. That system is not of interest here. The other system, called the managerial or cost accounting system, exists for an entirely different reason. It measures in detail all of the particulars of transactions between departments, divisions, and key individuals in the organization, for the purpose of untangling the interdependencies between people. When, for example, two departments share one truck for deliveries, the cost accounting system charges each department for part of the cost of maintaining the truck and driver, so that at the end of the year, the performance of each department can be individually assessed, and the better department's manager can receive a larger raise. Of course, all of this information processing costs money, and furthermore may lead to arguments between the departments over whether the costs charged to each are fair.

9 In a Japanese company a short-run assessment of individual performance is not wanted, so the company can save the considerable expense of collecting and processing all of that information. Companies still keep track of which department uses a truck how often and for what purposes, but like-minded people can interpret some simple numbers for themselves and adjust their behavior accordingly. Those insisting upon clear and precise measurement for the purpose of advancing individual interests must have an elaborate infor-

mation system. Industrial life, however, is essentially integrated and interdependent. No one builds an automobile alone, no one carries through a banking transaction alone. In a sense the Japanese value of collectivism fits naturally into an industrial setting, whereas the Western individualism provides constant conflicts. The image that comes to mind is of Chaplin's silent film "Modern Times" in which the apparently insignificant hero played by Chaplin successfully fights against the unfeeling machinery of industry. Modern industrial life can be aggravating, even hostile, or natural: all depends on the fit between our culture and our technology.

A Difference of Tradition

10 The *shinkansen* or "bullet train" speeds across the rural areas of Japan giving a quick view of cluster after cluster of farmhouses surrounded by rice paddies. This particular pattern did not develop purely by chance, but as a consequence of the technology peculiar to the growing of rice, the staple of the Japanese diet. The growing of rice requires the construction and maintenance of an irrigation system, something that takes many hands to build. More importantly, the planting and the harvesting of rice can only be done efficiently with the cooperation of twenty or more people. The "bottom line" is that a single family working alone cannot produce enough rice to survive, but a dozen families working together can produce a surplus. Thus the Japanese have had to develop the capacity to work together in harmony, no matter what the forces of disagreement or social disintegration, in order to survive.

11 Japan is a nation built entirely on the tips of giant, sub-oceanic volcanoes. Little of the land is flat and suitable for agriculture. Terraced hillsides make use of every available square foot of arable land. Small homes built very close together further conserve the land. Japan also suffers from natural disasters such as earthquakes and hurricanes. Traditionally homes are made of light construction materials, so a house falling down during a disaster will not crush its occupants and also can be quickly and inexpensively rebuilt. During the feudal period until the Meiji restoration of 1868, each feudal lord sought to restrain his subjects from moving from one village to the next for fear that a neighboring lord might amass enough peasants with which to produce a large agricultural surplus, hire an army and pose a threat. Apparently bridges were not commonly built across rivers and streams until the late nineteenth century, since bridges increased mobility between villages.

12 Taken all together, this characteristic style of living paints the picture of a nation of people who are homogeneous with respect to race, history, language, religion, and culture. For centuries and generations these people have lived in the same village next door to the same neighbors. Living in close proximity and in dwellings which gave very little privacy, the Japanese survived through their capacity to work together in harmony. In this situation, it was inevitable that the one most central social value which emerged, the one value without which the society could not continue, was that an individual does not matter.

13 To the Western soul this is a chilling picture of society. Subordinating individual tastes to the harmony of the group and knowing that individual needs can never take precedence over the interests of all is repellent to the Western citizen. But a frequent theme of Western philosophers and sociologists is that individual freedom exists only when people willingly subordinate their self-interests to the social interest. A society composed entirely of self-interested individuals is a society in which each person is at war with the other, a society which has no freedom. This issue, constantly at the heart of understanding society, comes up in every century, and in every society, whether the writer be Plato, Hobbes, or B. F. Skinner. The question of understanding which contemporary institutions lie at the heart of the conflict between automatism and totalitarianism remains. In some ages, the kinship group, the central social institution, mediated between these opposing forces to preserve the balance in which freedom was realized; in other times the church or the government was most critical. Perhaps our present age puts the work organization as the central institution.

14 In order to complete the comparison of Japanese and American living situations, consider flight over the United States. Looking out of the window high over the state of Kansas, we see a pattern of a single farmhouse surrounded by fields, followed by another single homestead surrounded by fields. In the early 1800s in the state of Kansas there were no automobiles. Your nearest neighbor was perhaps two miles distant; the winters were long, and the snow was deep. Inevitably, the central social values were self-reliance and independence. Those were the realities of that place and age that children had to learn to value.

15 The key to the industrial revolution was discovering that non-human forms of energy substituted for human forms could increase the wealth of a nation beyond anyone's wildest dreams. But there was a catch. To realize this great wealth, non-human energy needed huge complexes called factories with hundreds, even thousands of workers collected into one factory. Moreover, several factories in one central place made the generation of energy more efficient. Almost overnight, the Western world was transformed from a rural and agricultural country to an urban and industrial state. Our technological advance seems to no longer fit our social structure: in a sense, the Japanese can better cope with modern industrialism. While Americans still busily protect our rather extreme form of individualism, the Japanese hold their individualism in check and emphasize cooperation.

Discovery Questions

1. What is the thesis of the essay?
2. How and where does Ouchi use the methods of narration, description, illustration, and classification?
3. What are the points of contrast between Japanese and American workers?
4. Briefly describe the essay's diction and tone. Are they appropriate to the subject?
5. For what audience is this essay intended? Refer to Chapter 14 for information about the audience.

Suggested Items to Compare or Contrast

Select one of the following or similar sets of items from the same class. Decide whether you are going to develop either important similarities or differences.

two instructional teaching techniques

two important people you admire or dislike

two ways of learning a specific subject

two different cultures

two jobs you have had

two forms of entertainment

two places you have visited

two restaurants

two musical instruments

two musical groups

two types of love

two actors

two athletes

two types of parents

two attitudes toward life

two approaches to a task (finding a job, assembling a wardrobe, picking a spouse)

two types of travel

two leisure activities

two historical figures

two characters from a movie(s)

two historical events

two pieces of literature

expectation versus reality of one specific event or situation

WORKSHEET FOR COMPARISON-CONTRAST

1. Select two items to compare or contrast and complete the top half of the worksheet.
2. Write your thesis statement and enumeration of subtopics and then get approval from your instructor.
3. Complete the worksheet **before** writing the essay.
4. Attach the worksheet to the finished essay.
5. Attach the Expository Essay Cover Sheet to the finished essay.

Source of material: ______________________________

Two items to be compared or contrasted: 1 ______________ 2 ______________

Relationship or class the items share: ______________________________

Controlling idea: ______________ + ______________ + similarities/differences
(number) + (adjective) + (noun)

Order of three points of similarity or difference:

____ general to particular

____ climactic

Point of view: ______________ Verb tense: ______________

Tone: ______________ Diction: ______________

Thesis statement + enumeration of points of similarity or difference (may be 1 or 2 sentences):

____

____

____

____
(instructor approval)

OUTLINE

Title: ______________________________

¶1: Introduction (five sentences):

Choose a good beginning from the list.

Give necessary background material.

Good beginning # ________ : ______________________________

____

____

____

____

When you write your introduction, include the approved thesis statement and subtopics at the end of paragraph 1.

Body (three paragraphs)

¶2: Transition + topic sentence: ______________________________

____

Item 1: ______________________________

____

____

____

____

____

supporting details

Transitional expression + Item 2: ______________________________

____

____

____

____

____

Concluding sentence: ______________________________

____

¶3: Transition + topic sentence: ______________________________

____

Item 1: ______________________________

____

____

____

____

____

supporting details

Transitional expression + Item 2: ______________________________

____

____

____

____

____

Concluding sentence: ______________________________

____

¶4: Transition + topic sentence: ______________________________

____

Item 1: ______________________________________

supporting details

Transitional expression + Item 2: ______________________

Concluding sentence: ______________________________

¶5: Conclusion (three sentences):

Choose a good ending from list.

Make judgment about relationship of items.

Good ending # ______ : ______________________________

Name: ______________________
Date: ______________ Class: __________
Type of Exposition: ______________________

EXPOSITORY ESSAY COVER SHEET		
Structure/Ideas	+	________
Usage/Mechanics	−	________
Total		________
Rewrite points	+	________
TOTAL		________

Structure and Ideas (100 points)	Original	Rewrite
INTRODUCTION (at least five sentences):		
title; one of good beginnings leading to thesis	10________	________
thesis statement + enumeration of subtopics	5________	________
BODY (three supporting paragraphs):		
three topic sentences = transition + reference to thesis + subtopic	15________	________
development of paragraphs: sufficient, concrete, appropriate, relevant	45________	________
CONCLUSION (at least three sentences):		
one of good endings	5________	________
ESSAY:		
logical order of ideas and correct reasoning	5________	________
effective style = tone + diction + sentence structure + coherence	15________	________
Total	100________	+ ________

The points in this section reflect your score for structure and ideas. If you have received fewer than 100 points, you may rewrite your paper to earn them. Use the numbers as a guide to areas needing revision.

Usage and Mechanics (minus points). See Correction Symbol Chart.		
You **may** earn these points in revision:		
Usage: adj; adv; agr; awk; col; dm; frag; mm; ref; rep; shift; verb; ww; //; ¶	−3 ea. ________	________
You **may not** earn these points in revision, but you must correct the errors:		
Mechanics: abbr; apos; cap; lc; p; ro; sp; ∧	−1 ea. ________	________
Total	− ________	+ ________

CHAPTER 12

The Fifth Pattern: Extended Definition

How many times have you been in the middle of a serious discussion with someone only to discover that the two of you were using the same abstract word but were giving it different meanings? For example, you have to register for classes next semester, and you ask several acquaintances to recommend an "interesting" teacher. One friend recommends Teacher A because the lectures are fast paced and humorous. Another student considers Teacher B interesting because the presentations are thorough and detailed. A third individual recommends Teacher C because audio-visual material and exhibits are used often. Obviously, each person has a different definition of an "interesting" teacher.

Definition, therefore, is the pattern of exposition by which a general or abstract term is given limits. It assigns a specific meaning to the term. Concrete words like *car, horse,* and *table* present few problems because their meanings can be easily resolved with a dictionary. It describes and sets the limits of a word as currently used by the majority of educated speakers. However, abstract terms like *justice, happiness,* and *faith* mean different things to different people. Therefore, when dealing with such terms, you must give an extended definition that includes (1) the term itself, (2) the class or group to which the term belongs, and (3) the characteristics or qualities you assign to the term that distinguish it from all others in the class. Thus, you convey what you mean by the term, although the reader need not agree with that personal definition. Communication is achieved if the reader can understand the personal definition and can see the possible differences between his or her meaning and your meaning of the term.

Requirements of Extended Definition

Definition clarifies your thoughts by requiring precise thinking and representative examples. Good definitions prevent serious misunderstandings and encourage further communication by making argumentation more meaningful. Although dictionary definitions of concrete words frequently set limits, the dictionary defines an abstract term inadequately. The meaning of abstract terms is derived from individual experience, which varies from person to person. Consequently, defining abstract terms is difficult so you must rely on your personal experiences. These are the basis for your understanding of what the term means and for the concrete examples you use to illustrate your definition.

As you prepare your extended definition essay, you should realize that you are writing your personal definition of a term which the reader must understand but need not necessarily agree with. It is impossible in a short essay to cover all the possible meanings of an abstract word. Because you will be dealing with concepts and ideas, it will be crucial to include examples that are concrete and specific. You will also have to choose a way to develop your definition. One possibility is to enumerate several characteristics of terms you are defining, presenting each element in a separate paragraph. The other approach is to select a combination of several methods, devoting a paragraph to each form. These methods are described below with brief examples using the word *love.*

Methods for Extended Definition

Description pictures a physical object or the expression of an emotion or attitude in physical terms.
[Describe the meaning of love by showing how a person in love looks or feels.]

Narration relates a sequence of events in time.
[Narrate the meaning of love by telling the story of when you fell in love.]

Exposition explains the meaning of an idea in any one of the following ways:

- **Illustration** gives a representative and unique example.
  [Give a specific, concrete example that illustrates one quality of love, such as admiration, selflessness, or honesty.]
- **Classification** breaks down a group into the members which compose it.
  [Classify love into at least three types: parental, sibling, married.]
- **Analysis** breaks down a structure into the elements that comprise it, using one of the three approaches:

  Functional [Analyze love according to what elements or characteristics it contains: respect, honesty, unselfishness.] This method belongs in a separate essay of at least five paragraphs because a single paragraph cannot adequately define a concept in concrete terms. This method should not be used in one paragraph.

  Process [Analyze the stages of love according to how one falls in love: meeting, learning about each other, and making a commitment.]

  Causal [Analyze love according to the causes or the reasons why the relationship occurred. Analyze love according to the effects or the consequences that the relationship created.]
- **Comparison** shows points of similarity between terms thought to be different.
  [Compare love to hate.]

  Contrast shows points of difference between terms thought to be similar.
  [Contrast love with romance.]

  Analogy shows points of similarity between terms which belong to different classes.
  [Draw an analogy between being in love and riding a roller coaster.]
- **Definition** limits the meaning of a word by identifying the qualities that differentiate it from other terms in the same class. The process includes the following approaches:

  Etymology explains the derivation, background and history of the term (found in a dictionary). [Discuss love's origin from the Old English word *lufian* and the French word *lufu* meaning "to hold dear." It also comes from OE *lofian* which derives from the German *loben* meaning "to praise."]

  Exclusion explains what the term does not mean. It should be the first method after the introduction when you use a combination of methods to extend your term. Do not give obvious contrasts, such as "Love is not hate." Instead, give meanings that are often confused with the term but which you would not include in your definition.
  [Explain that the term *love* does not mean infatuation, romance, passion, or seduction.]

  Enumeration of characteristics identifies the qualities that the term possesses. This method is the same as Functional Analysis and should be developed in at least a five-paragraph essay.
  [Discuss the elements of love: respect, honesty, and unselfishness.]

Problems to Avoid

A common problem with this pattern is writing definitions that are too broad, too narrow, or circular. For example, the definition "an artist is a man, woman, or child" may be true, but it is too broad because many men, women, and children are **not** artists. The definition "an artist is a person who paints with watercolors" is also true, but it is too narrow because there are many other kinds of artists. The definition "an artist is a person who is artistic" is circular because the term *artist* is defined by a form of the same word *artistic* and so no meaning is developed. The definition "an artist is a person who is skilled in or makes a profession of painting, sculpture, or music" is sound because it places the term being defined in a class that includes other members and then identifies the characteristics that distinguish it from other members in that class.

Another difficulty occurs when you assume that a reader knows what you mean when you generalize. A definition must be as concrete and specific as possible. In order to make a term as understandable as it can be, you must convey your ideas by means of concrete, specific details along with a combination of methods of development.

When you refer to your term as a word and precede the term you are defining with the word *word* or *term,* then you underline your term. One example is, "The word *love* has been defined using several methods of development." Another illustration is, "The term *law and order* is difficult to define."

A further problem could occur when you select a term like *culture* that has numerous separate meanings. You must tell the reader what aspect of the definition you are going to develop. For example, culture refers to the cultivation of plants and animals or to the development of taste or to a specific period in the development of a civilization or to a biological medium for the growth of microorganisms, among other definitions. No extended definition should attempt to deal with all these aspects. In the introduction you would limit the area that you cover by saying, for instance, "The definition of culture refers only to the training, development, and refinement of artistic taste."

One other consideration is that your definition of the term might be applicable in a particular time or place but not for all times. For example, the word *patriotism* means one thing when a country is actually fighting for its survival and another when it is at peace. In your introduction you might say, "This definition of patriotism applies only when a country is fighting for its survival."

Discovery Exercises for Definition

A. **Evaluating a definition**

Study the sentences below to determine whether they are sound and logical definitions. If they are not, indicate whether they are too broad (the definition includes more than the term encompasses), too narrow (the definition covers less than the term encompasses), or circular (the definition gives the same meaning in different words).

	Sound	Broad	Narrow	Circular
1. A coal mine is a dirty, noisy place.	______	______	______	______
2. A teacher is a person who instructs.	______	______	______	______
3. A shelf is a piece of wood on which to put books.	______	______	______	______
4. The French word for dog is *chien.*	______	______	______	______
5. A Siamese is a short-haired cat.	______	______	______	______
6. A garage is a building in which vehicles are serviced or stored.	______	______	______	______
7. A coat is a piece of clothing to wear when it rains.	______	______	______	______
8. Love is a pleasant emotion.	______	______	______	______
9. A hat is a covering for the head, usually with a crown and brim.	______	______	______	______
10. A mountain is a hill to ski on.	______	______	______	______

B. **Constructing a definition**

Frame sound definitions by placing each term into its class and then enumerating the characteristics which differentiate it from the other members of the class.

TERM	= CLASS	+ DISTINGUISHING CHARACTERISTICS
telephone	= communication device	+ transports sound over a wire or other channel; uses electrical impulses

TERM	= CLASS	+ DISTINGUISHING CHARACTERISTICS
1. adjective	= ______________	+ ______________________________
2. book	= ______________	+ ______________________________
3. lake	= ______________	+ ______________________________
4. football	= ______________	+ ______________________________
5. dolphin	= ______________	+ ______________________________

C. **Defining from contexts**

Write a short definition based on the information in the following sets of sentences. Synonyms are not appropriate. Put the term into a class and then list its distinguishing characteristics.

1. Define "narfgiggle."
   a. No matter what you say, I think a "narfgiggle" is expensive.
   b. The new man is very fast with the "narfgiggle."
   c. My mother just received as a gift a blue portable electric "narfgiggle."
   d. The space bar on my "narfgiggle" is stuck.
   e. "Narfgiggle" ribbons are available in assorted colors.
   f. I can change some keys on my "narfgiggle."
   g. My uncle gave me his old "narfgiggle" because it still works well.

Class: ______________________________

Characteristics: ______________________________

____

____

2. Define "bliffy."
   a. "Bliff" up your day by singing a song.
   b. The "bliffy" young woman skipped down the street.
   c. He's so "bliffy" that he thinks he can get an A on his paper without doing a rough draft.
   d. You are a pleasure to be with because you are so very "bliffy."
   e. The flowers in the garden looked "bliffy" in the early morning light.
   f. When she enters a room, she "bliffs" it up.
   g. The child's "bliffy" smile lit up the dark room.

Class: ______________________________

Characteristics: ______________________________

____

____

Organizational Pattern for Extended Definition

Study this blueprint so that you can see and better understand the elements necessary for extended definition. Then use the pattern as a guide in assembling your own essay. Observe that the two forms for the body paragraphs are presented: three characteristics or three methods. Note that all the student samples in the chapter use this organizational pattern.

Title

Introduction—¶1

At least five sentences, including the following:
- the reason for defining the term
- the limits of the area to be covered (if necessary)
- the etymology of the word (if pertinent)
- the particular time/place (if relevant)

Use of one of the good beginnings
Establishment of order of subtopics — point of view — verb tense — tone and diction

Thesis statement = subject (term to be defined) + controlling idea (number + adjective + characteristics or methods)
Subtopic sentence = enumeration of three characteristics or methods
(may be 1 or 2 sentences)

Body—¶2, 3, 4

—three characteristics—

Presentation of three major characteristics.

Logical order:
_____ climactic
_____ general to particular

**Paragraph 2:* Topic sentence = transitional expression + reference to thesis statement + characteristic 1

Supporting details such as facts or anecdotes.
References to well-known experts or events.
Concluding sentence.

**Paragraph 3:* Topic sentence = transitional expression + reference to thesis statement + characteristic 2

Supporting details and references.
Concluding sentence.

**Paragraph 4:* Topic sentence = transitional expression + reference to thesis statement + characteristic 3

Supporting details and references.
Concluding sentence.

OR

—three methods—

Presentation of three major methods

Logical order: general to particular

Use of **three** of the following:

Exclusion	Etymology
Illustration	Causal Analysis
Classification	Comparison or Analogy
Process Analysis	Contrast

**Paragraph 2:* Topic sentence = transitional expression + reference to thesis statement + method 1

Supporting details and references.
Concluding sentence.

**Paragraph 3:* Topic sentence = transitional expression + reference to thesis statement + method 2

Supporting details and references.
Concluding sentence.

**Paragraph 4:* Topic sentence = transitional expression + reference to thesis statement + method 3

Supporting details and references.
Concluding sentence.

Transitional expressions appropriate to the characteristics or methods chosen.

*These elements may be arranged within the sentence.

Conclusion—¶5

At least three sentences

Transitional expression (optional): see Conclusion/Result and Summary

Restatement of term defined and completed definition

Use of one of the good endings

STUDENT SAMPLE—Extended Definition (Combination of Methods)—Analyzed for Parts

Observe that elements of structure and content are labeled on the left while elements of style are identified on the right. This detailed analysis will help you plan your own essay.

Source of material: personal experience

Title

"Wisdom, More Precious than Rubies"
—Proverbs

Tone: serious
Diction: abstract, concrete, denotative, subjective
Order: general to particular

reason to redefine
Introduction ¶ 1
Good Beginning #10

Most people hope that one day they will be thought of as wise. They think that to possess wisdom means showing sound judgment and deep understanding. That is, wise people see clearly what is right and then act according to the decision made. (However,)* wisdom is defined not only by the judgments made but also by the certain qualities and opportunities possessed.

Verb tense: present
Point of view: third person

Thesis Statement (term to be defined) + Subtopics (3 different methods)

(Thus,) the word wisdom needs fuller discussion using the three separate methods of [1] exclusion, [2] classification, and [3] illustration.

Topic Sentence ¶2

(One) method for defining wisdom is to tell what it is not. Wisdom is not letting emotions of love or hate cloud one's judgments. It is not selling or buying in the marketplace. It is not the acquisition of wealth or the possession of holiness. Wisdom

Sentence Structure: parallelism "Wisdom (it) is not . . ."

** Coherence: transitional expressions circled.*

is not knowing the information written in books, papers, or magazines. It is not a wise person sitting cross-legged on a mountain top thinking about the world. Wisdom is not making sudden, thoughtless decisions like quitting a job after a foolish argument. It is not expediency like dissolving a marriage and family for petty reasons. To conclude, wisdom is not just having knowledge but is using knowledge effectively.

Sentence Structure: parallelism "Wisdom (it) is not…"

Sentence structure: verbal phrase

Sentence structure: parallelism

Concluding Sentence

To classify some of the types of wisdom is to explain more fully what it means. One kind is sound sense displayed in practical affairs. The wise student, for example, registers for no more than 12 hours of classes if he also must work 30 hours a week. This balance will allow him to complete both responsibilities successfully. A second type of wisdom is soundness in the choice of means and ends. Thus, a wise person chooses not only a realistic career goal but also the proper schools or opportunities to achieve it. Another type of wisdom, the one most commonly thought to be the word's meaning, is formal knowledge, learning, and scholarship. An individual with encyclopedic information in a specialized area is often thought to be wise. The most abstract form of wisdom is correct judgment in matters concerning life and conduct. Accepting the death of an elderly parent,

Topic Sentence ¶3

Body
¶ 2, 3, 4

Diction: concrete

Diction: concrete

Sentence structure: items in a series

Diction: abstract

for example, without becoming emotionally distraught and irrational, reveals that the bereaved person possesses wisdom. This classification suggests that wisdom is a complex quality.

Concluding Sentence

Topic Sentence ¶4

The third way to define wisdom is to give an illustration of the concept. An example from history is one of the more gifted American politicians, Abraham Lincoln, our sixteenth president. An event which showed his wisdom in political matters was the Fort Sumter incident. Early in his presidency, South Carolina, where the fort was located, was on the verge of secession. The fort was occupied by Union troops in Southern territory. The citizens of South Carolina wanted the soldiers out of the state, so a blockade was organized. The commander at Sumter sent word to Lincoln of the situation and asked for supplies. Upon hearing the news, Lincoln knew that if he sent a ship to supply the fort, it would be attacked and war would break out. In an early campaign speech, Lincoln had promised that he would not lead the Union into war. Keeping this promise in mind, Lincoln sent a letter to the governor of South Carolina informing him that a ship was arriving with food but no ammunition. Neglecting Lincoln's letter,

Sentence Structure: appositive

Diction: concrete, denotative

Diction: concrete, denotative

Sentence structure: dependent clause

Diction: concrete, denotative

A Sentence structure: compound verb

Diction: concrete, denotative, objective

the citizens of the state fired upon the ship as it came sailing into the harbor four days later. One might not think that Lincoln's action was wise, but it was, since Lincoln's strongest support came from the northern citizens, many of whom wanted to keep the fort. Thus, he prudently accomplished two goals: to keep the fort in Union hands and to have the blame for starting the Civil War shifted to the South. Thus, Lincoln wisely protected his name and gained stronger national support.

[Margin notes: "wise" — Diction: subjective; "prudently" — Diction: subjective; Sentence structure: Independent clause with enumeration; "blame" / "starting the Civil War" — Diction: subjective; Concluding Sentence]

Conclusion ¶ 5
Good Ending #2

In summary, wisdom is using knowledge effectively. People who have wisdom are content and at peace with themselves and their surroundings. Centuries ago Sophocles aptly said, "There is no happiness where there is no wisdom."

STUDENT SAMPLE—Extended Definition Essay (Combination of Methods)

Source of material: personal experience

The Most Important Virtue

Courage is a word that is often misused in writing and speech. Journalists and newscasters constantly extol the virtues of men and women who have performed physical acts of courage. The main reason for the word's misuse is that courage is a term whose roots lie embedded in the turbulent whirlpool of human emotions and actions. The Shorter Oxford English Dictionary* traces the etymology of the word. In Middle English and Old French the word was corage which came from the Latin word cor meaning "heart," the organ once believed to be the seat of human thought. In the 1600's the word meant "spirit, mind, disposition, and nature." It also

**The Shorter Oxford English Dictionary*, 3rd ed. rev., 1962. Reprinted by permission of Oxford University Press, Walton Street, Oxford, OX2 6DP, England.

referred to "what was in one's mind or thoughts; purpose; inclination. "Later in the 1700's the term broadened to include "spirit, lustiness, and vigour." Even the modern-day definition of courage as "that quality of mind which shows itself in facing danger without fear" does not leave the reader with a clear understanding of the word. Thus, the word *courage* needs fuller discussion using the three separate methods of exclusion, process analysis, and illustration.

One method of defining courage is to tell what it is not. Courage is not the performance of death-defying feats like Evel Knieval's motorcycle flights across the Grand Canyon. It is not wearing a soldier's uniform, earning a Purple Heart, or returning home in a flag-draped coffin. Courage is not a loyal German shepherd's instinct to rush into a burning house in order to save its master. It is not a slender quarterback braving the onrush of 250 pound, muscle-bound linemen in order to throw a touchdown pass. Courage is not a midnight stroll through a crime-ridden section of town just to save cab fare. And courage is not a teenager committing an act of cruelty or violence to pass initiation and wear the leather jacket of the youth's chosen street gang. To conclude, courage is not just risking physical injury or death to gain fame, glory, and the admiration of other people.

To analyze the steps involved in becoming courageous is another way to clarify the concept of courage. For courage is based not on people's ability to react physically but on their ability to risk uncertain consequences in making or taking a chance. In the first step, an individual must be able to recognize and admit to a feeling of discomfort or discontent with the *status quo* and then feel a need to change the situation that brought about this dissatisfaction. For example, a housewife, after 20 years of marriage and several children, feels unhappy with her life and senses a need to change her present situation. The next step is that the person must examine the reason for the discontent, decide what changes should be made, and evaluate the consequences of these alterations. To illustrate, the unhappy housewife realizes that she feels useless now that her children are grown, and she decides to go to college to improve her situation. However, she is also aware that her decision may bring about a personal sense of failure should she not succeed in her classes. She also could incur the disapproval of her husband and children and become a joke to friends and neighbors. The final step towards gaining courage occurs when the individual follows his or her beliefs and makes the decision or takes the chance to change, regardless of the consequences. For example, the housewife, fully cognizant of both the positive and negative effects her choice may cause, follows through in her belief that she must change her life and enrolls in college. Although the housewife's decisions and actions will not make headlines in the local newspaper nor a good story for the six o'clock evening news, she has realized and has demonstrated an act of courage. Thus, taking the necessary steps to make a change, regardless of the uncertain consequences, shows courage.

A third way to define courage is to give an illustration of the concept. An example from medical history is the development and testing of the rabies vaccine by Louis Pasteur, a great French chemist and scientist of the nineteenth century. Although Pasteur had previously developed effective vaccines for the diseases of anthrax, chicken cholera, and swine fever, the French scientist remained troubled by the existence of rabies. Childhood memories of seeing a rabid dog foaming at the mouth and watching the painful cauterization treatment destroy the tissue damaged by a rabid animal's bite plagued Pasteur throughout his life. The terror of the disease and the suffering of its victims proved to Pasteur the need to find a remedy for rabies. After four years of experimentation, Pasteur was able to attenuate the rabies virus and inject the weakened strain into live animals. The innoculated dogs, whether exposed to the bite of a rabid animal before or after receiving the injections, were found to be immune to rabies. Pasteur thought that his anti-rabies vaccine would also protect humans, but he was aware that, if his attempt to vaccinate humans in order to save their lives failed, he would be forever discredited at the French Academy of Medicine. Finally, despite the risk of failure, Pasteur was compelled by an inner logic and firm belief in his theory to use the vaccine on a human subject, Joseph Meister, a young boy who had been bitten 12 times by a rabid dog. During the 14-day innoculation period, Pasteur suffered from anguish and anxiety equal to the physical pain endured by the young boy. Pasteur showed great courage when he risked public scorn and scandal in an attempt to change traditional medical theories against vaccination. His courageous action not only saved many lives but also inspired other scientists to develop new, non-traditional theories to benefit mankind. Indeed, Louis Pasteur's behavior is an excellent example of the meaning of the word courage.

In summary, courage is not the denial of fear but the ability to accept and conquer fear. Courage is more than a show of physical bravery; courage is the mental capability to make decisions and attempt changes even though the outcome of these efforts is uncertain. Or, as Robert Frost aptly said, "Courage is the human virtue that counts most--courage to act on limited knowledge and insufficient evidence. That's all any of us have."

Discovery Exercise

1. Identify the thesis statement
   a. the term being defined: ______________________
   b. the reason for defining the term: ______________________
   ____
   c. the controlling idea: ______________________
   ____
2. Identify the three main subtopics: ______________________
   ____
   ____
3. Identify the order of the subtopics:
   ____ climactic
   ____ general to particular
4. Identify the point of view: __________ person
5. Identify the verb tense: __________
6. Identify the **concrete examples** in the body paragraphs:
   ¶2: ______________________
   ____
   ¶3: ______________________
   ¶4: ______________________
7. Circle **six** transitional expressions.
8. Choose terms from the diction chart that characterize the diction: ______________________
9. Choose terms from the tone chart that describe the tone: ______________________
   ____
10. After reviewing Chapter 16, bracket **five** dependent adjective clauses, one type of grammatical structure used in the essay.

STUDENT SAMPLE—Extended Definition Essay (Combination of Methods)

Source of material: personal experience

How to Succeed by Really Trying

Success, today, is one of the primary motivating factors of human society. Perhaps it is even a basic biological need. Even though everyone has different concepts about what constitutes being successful, almost all individuals experience the constant pressure to succeed. While most people would still consider an important position or great wealth as a sign of success, others are realizing that the term embraces many more elements. My interpretation of the word success can be conveyed through the three different methods of illustration, comparison, and process analysis.

A marathon race in which I participated illustrates one aspect of my meaning of success. When the starting gun sounded, thousands of runners, closely packed together, began the inevitable struggle for position. The first few miles passed as slowly as a snail over a window. Sweat began shooting off my body like bullets. The throbbing pain in my legs produced a novocaine-like numbness. The miles stretched forever in front of me. The faceless bodies that passed me soon turned into dots on the horizon. Hours later, the last miles finally drew nearer, like the end of a college semester. I went beyond the point of feeling the physical pain that swept through my body. Tears filled my eyes as I sighted a huge white flag with the letters FINISH. While I counted the remaining steps, my legs shook from exhaustion. I tried to focus on the blurred ground at my feet. Finally, as I stumbled across the finish line like a tired hippo, I collapsed in relief. Although I finished well back in the pack and might have been considered a failure by some, I still felt successful. A tremendous sense of accomplishment is, to me, an essential element of success.

Another way to define the concept is by comparison with failure. The most significant similarity that they share is the element of fear. Since failure is unwanted and brings on feelings of depression and lack of self-worth, people naturally fear it. They will rarely attempt anything at which they feel they will not succeed. For example, average students in English will take only the required courses. Even though they might benefit from a literature class, their fear of failure will prevent them from registering for such a class. Similarly, success breeds fear even though most people would not connect the two. Constant pressure is exerted on successful people to succeed again and again. For instance, in the entertainment field, a person is only as successful as the profits on the last film, play, or record. Thus, show business people repeat the successful formula rather than branch out in a new direction. Indeed, success can be just as crippling as failure when it prevents anyone from experimenting in a different area. Therefore, while fear is an ingredient of both failure and success, successful people are measured by their ability to overcome fear and accept risks in attempting something worthwhile.

The process of becoming successful is the third way to clarify my definition. The first step toward success is establishing a realistic goal, something one wants and is capable of achieving. For example, a salesperson in a department store decides to become a manager. The next stage after setting the goal is to begin to conquer it. In order to reach most goals, one must be highly motivated because one can meet frustrations which must be overcome. For instance, the salesperson must conscientiously show tact in dealing with customers, honesty in handling merchandise, cooperation in working with managers and co-workers, and patience in waiting for a promotion. The next step in success is the growth that one achieves in conquering a goal. That is, the salesperson becomes a manager. The final stage is to set more goals, a situation that makes success a never-ending process.

In review, success is more than mere position or wealth. To me, success means the achievement of one's goals. It includes a feeling of accomplishment, a willingness to overcome fear in attempting something new, and a sense of self-improvement in reaching the goal.

Discovery Exercise

1. Identify the thesis statement
   a. the term being defined: ______
   b. the reason for defining the term: ______
   c. the controlling idea: ______
2. Identify the three main subtopics: ______
3. Identify the point of view: ______ person
4. Identify the verb tense: ______
5. Identify **six** similes and metaphors: ______
6. Identify the **concrete examples** in each of the body paragraphs:
   ¶2: ______
   ¶3: ______
   ¶4: ______
7. Circle **six** transitional expressions.
8. Choose terms from the diction chart that characterize the diction: ______
9. Choose terms from the tone chart that describe the tone: ______
10. Bracket **two** examples of a particular grammatical construction used in the essay and name the construction.

STUDENT SAMPLE—Extended Definition Essay (Functional Analysis—Characteristics)

Source of material: textbook on philosophy

Lovers of Reason

Most people scurry about their daily routines, giving little thought to the meaning of their existence. However, there is an exclusive group to which the majority of society is oblivious. The members of this company, known somewhat disdainfully, and yet somehow reverently, as philosophers, study the difficult concept of existence. Defining the word philosophers might best be done by identifying their three major characteristics. Philosophers are people who contemplate existence, who search for a certitude, and who display tolerance.

The fundamental trait of philosophers is that they think about the meaning of human life. They do not only turn their attention to external existence, but they also look within themselves; that is, they think about thinking. Being able to think involves knowledge, the ability to retain ideas. One aspect of knowledge is memory, the retention of past ideas and experiences in a fixed order. Another aspect of knowledge is imagination, putting those same ideas in a different order. Philosophers have a highly refined imagination which allows them to envision change and contemplate reality. In addition to thinking about thinking, reasoners question the existence of a deity. Starting from a neutral viewpoint, they arrive at different conclusions. Some, like Saint Augustine, Martin Buber, and Paul Tillich, came to the judgment that God is the source of the cosmos. Others, like John Locke, David Hume, and Bertrand Russell, reached an atheistic conclusion. Thus, philosophers contemplate thought and the existence of a supreme being.

As a second characteristic, philosophers move from the contemplation of thinking to the search for a certitude. They accept nothing at face value and take nothing for granted. Instead, applying logic, they focus on accuracy in speech and thought. This idea is illustrated in the following example: If 1 is greater than 2, and 2 is greater than 3, then 1 is greater than 3. The preceding syllogism is valid; that is, the conclusion is arrived at through logical thinking. The fact that it is not true is not the main issue, at this point, to the thinkers. Thus, their concern, in logical analysis, is with the form of a statement, the machinery of inference, rather than with facts or truth. So, philosophers, because of their concern with validity, attempt to find one absolute certitude that they can use to form a criterion by which the truth of other statements can be measured. For example, Rene Descartes, a seventeenth-century French philosopher, found his absolute certitude in the statement, "I think; therefore, I am." He measured the validity of all other ideas with this criterion as other reasoners use their own certitudes to measure truth.

The final attribute that defines philosophers is their display of tolerance. They realize that most people do not spend their time thinking about thinking. They also understand that most people's values and beliefs have not been arrived at logically. Therefore, since they know that educating people and making them question their ideas might cause difficulties for them, philosophers do not propagandize, sermonize, or insult. Instead, they educate by questioning because it does point one in a definite direction even though it leaves uncertainty. For example, Meno asked Socrates if virtue could not be taught to people. Socrates then asked Meno if virtue was a science, thereby implying that people can only learn through the scientific method. Thus, philosophers are tolerant, because the only absolute certainty is uncertainty.

Some people contemplate reality; some search for certainty; some show tolerance. However, true philosophers possess all three qualities simultaneously. While the Greek origin of the word means "lovers of wisdom," in fact, philosophers are lovers of reason.

PROFESSIONAL SAMPLES—Extended Definition

Read these essays to see how professional writers have used the technique of definition. Then answer the discovery questions which focus on the elements of extended definition.

William Hazlitt (1778–1830), English journalist, lecturer, painter, and essayist, knew Coleridge, Wordsworth, and Lamb. Although he was quarrelsome and unfriendly, he was brilliant and was one of the greatest essayists of the nineteenth century. While he wrote on art, drama, and traveling, his best essays are in literary criticism, such as *Characters of Shakespeare's Plays, Lectures on the English Poets,* and *English Comic Writers.*

On Gusto

1 Gusto in art is power or passion defining any object.—It is not so difficult to explain this term in what relates to expression (of which it may be said to be the highest degree) as in what relates to things without expression, to the natural appearances of objects, as mere colour or form. In one sense, however, there is hardly any object entirely devoid of expression, without some character of power belonging to it, some precise association with pleasure or pain: and it is in giving this truth of character from the truth of feeling, whether in the highest or the lowest degree, but always in the highest degree of which the subject is capable, that gusto consists.

2 There is a gusto in the colouring of Titian. Not only do his heads seem to think—his bodies seem to feel. This is what the Italians mean by the *morbidezza* of his flesh-colour. It seems sensitive and alive all over; not merely to have the look and texture of flesh, but the feeling in itself. For example, the limbs of his female figures have a luxurious softness and delicacy, which appears conscious of the pleasure of the beholder. As the objects themselves in nature would produce an impression on the sense, distinct from every other object, and having something divine in it, which the heart owns and the imagination consecrates, the objects in the picture preserve the same impression, absolute, unimpaired, stamped with all the truth of passion, the pride of the eye, and the charm of beauty. Rubens makes his flesh-colour like flowers; Albano's is like ivory; Titian's is like flesh, and like nothing else. It is as different from that of other painters, as the skin is from a piece of white or red drapery thrown over it. The blood circulates here and there, the blue veins just appear, the rest is distinguished throughout only by that sort of tingling sensation to the eye, which the body feels within itself. This is gusto.—Vandyke's flesh-colour, though it has great truth and purity, wants gusto. It has not the internal character, the living principle in it. It is a smooth sur-

face, not a warm, moving mass. It is painted without passion, with indifference. The hand only has been concerned. The impression slides off from the eye, and does not, like the tones of Titian's pencil, leave a sting behind it in the mind of the spectator. The eye does not acquire a taste or appetite for what it sees. In a word, gusto in painting is where the impression made on one sense excites by affinity those of another.

3 Michael Angelo's forms are full of gusto. They every where obtrude the sense of power upon the eye. His limbs convey an idea of muscular strength, of moral grandeur, and even of intellectual dignity: they are firm, commanding, broad, and massy, capable of executing with ease the determined purposes of the will. His faces have no other expression than his figures, conscious power and capacity. They appear only to think what they shall do, and to know that they can do it. This is what is meant by saying that his style is hard and masculine. It is the reverse of Correggio's, which is effeminate. That is, the gusto of Michael Angelo consists in expressing energy of will. In Correggio's faces as well as figures we see neither bones nor muscles, but then what a soul is there, full of sweetness and of grace—pure, playful, soft, angelical! There is sentiment enough in a hand painted by Correggio to set up a school of history painters. Whenever we look at the hands of Correggio's women or of Raphael's, we always wish to touch them.

4 Again, Titian's landscapes have a prodigious gusto, both in the colouring and forms. We shall never forget one that we saw many years ago in the Orleans Gallery of Acteon hunting. It had a brown, mellow, autumnal look. The sky was of the colour of stone. The winds seemed to sing through the rustling branches of the trees, and already you might hear the twanging of bows resound through the tangled mazes of the wood. Mr. West, we understand, has this landscape. He will know if this description of it is just. The landscape background of the St. Peter Martyr is another well-known instance of the power of this great painter to give a romantic interest and an appropriate character to the objects of his pencil, where every circumstance adds to the effect of the scene,—the bold trunks of the tall forest trees, the trailing ground plants, with that cold convent spire rising in the distance, admidst the blue sapphire mountains and the golden sky.

5 Rubens has a great deal of gusto in his Fauns and Satyrs, and in all that expresses motion, but in nothing else. Rembrandt has it in everything; everything in his pictures has a tangible character. If he puts a diamond in the ear of a Burgomaster's wife, it is of the first water; and his furs and stuffs are proof against a Russian winter. Raphael's gusto was only in expression; he had no idea of the character of anything but the human form. The dryness and poverty of his style in other respects is a phenomenon in the art. His trees are like sprigs of grass stuck in a book of botanical specimens. Was it that Raphael never had time to go beyond the walls of Rome? That he was always in the streets, at church, or in the bath? He was not one of the Society of Arcadians.[1]

6 Claude's landscapes, perfect as they are, want gusto. This is not easy to explain. They are perfect abstractions of the visible images of things; they speak the visible language of nature truly. They resemble a mirror or microscope. To the eye only they are more perfect than any other landscapes that ever were or will be painted; they give more of nature, as cognizable by one sense alone; but they lay an equal stress on all visible impressions; they do not interpret one sense by another; they do not distinguish the character of different objects as we are taught, and can only be taught, to distinguish them by their effect on the different senses. That is, his eye wanted imagination: it did not strongly sympathize with his other faculties. He saw the atmosphere, but he did not feel it. He painted the trunk of a tree or a rock in the foreground as smooth—with as complete an abstraction of the gross, tangible impression, as any other part of the picture; his trees are perfectly beautiful, but quite immoveable; they have a look of enchantment. In short, his landscapes are unequalled imitations of nature, released from its subjection to the elements,—as if all objects were become a delightful fairy vision, and the eye had rarefied and refined away the other senses.

7 The gusto in the Greek statues is of a very singular kind. The sense of perfect form nearly occupies the whole mind, and hardly suffers it to dwell on any other feeling. It seems enough for them *to be*, without acting or suffering. Their forms are ideal, spiritual. Their beauty is power. By their beauty they are raised above the frailties of pain or passion; by their beauty they are deified.

[1]Raphael not only could not paint a landscape; he could not paint people in a landscape. He could not have painted the heads or the figures, or even the dresses of the St. Peter Martyr. His figures have always an *in-door* look, that is, a set, determined, voluntary, dramatic character, arising from their own passions, or a watchfulness of those of others, and want that wild uncertainty of expression, which is connected with the accidents of nature and the changes of the elements. He has nothing *romantic* about him.

8 The infinite quantity of dramatic invention in Shakespeare takes from his gusto. The power he delights to shew is not intense, but discursive. He never insists on any thing as much as he might, except a quibble. Milton has great gusto. He repeats his blow twice; grapples with and exhausts his subject. His imagination has a double relish of its objects, an inveterate attachment to the things he describes, and to the words describing them.

—"Or where Chineses drive
With sails and wind their *cany* waggons *light*."

"Wild above rule or art, *enormous* bliss."

There is a gusto in Pope's compliments, in Dryden's satires, and Prior's tales; and among prose-writers, Boccaccio and Rabelais had the most of it. We will only mention one other work which appears to us to be full of gusto, and that is the *Beggar's Opera*. If it is not, we are altogether mistaken in our notions on this delicate subject.

Discovery Questions

1. What is Hazlitt's definition of gusto? To what area does he limit his term?
2. What methods of exposition does Hazlitt use to extend his definition, and in what paragraphs are they found?
3. Identify several characteristic examples of the diction. Using the diction chart in Chapter 1, describe the essay's diction.
4. What is the essay's tone?

Marie Winn, born in Czechoslovakia, came to the United States with her family and was graduated from Radcliffe College. She has written eleven books, all of them about children, and has contributed to the *New York Times* and other newspapers and magazines. "Television Addiction" is the title of a chapter in her book *The Plug-In Drug* (1977), and this selection is an excerpt from that chapter.

Television Addiction

1 The word "addiction" is often used loosely and wryly in conversation. People will refer to themselves as "mystery book addicts" or "cookie addicts." E. B. White writes of his annual surge of interest in gardening: "We are hooked and are making an attempt to kick the habit." Yet nobody really believes that reading mysteries or ordering seeds by catalogue is serious enough to be compared with addictions to heroin or alcohol. The word "addiction" is here used jokingly to denote a tendency to overindulge in some pleasurable activity.

2 People often refer to being "hooked on TV." Does this, too, fall into the lighthearted category of cookie eating and other pleasures that people pursue with unusual intensity, or is there a kind of television viewing that falls into the more serious category of destructive addiction?

3 When we think about addiction to drugs or alcohol, we frequently focus on negative aspects, ignoring the pleasures that accompany drinking or drug-taking. And yet the essence of any serious addiction is a pursuit of pleasure, a search for a "high" that normal life does not supply. It is only the inability to function without the addictive substance that is dismaying, the dependence of the organism upon a certain experience and an increasing inability to function normally without it. Thus a person will take two or three drinks at the end of the day not merely for the pleasure drinking provides, but also because he "doesn't feel normal" without them.

4 An addict does not merely pursue a pleasurable experience and need to experience it in order to function normally. He needs to *repeat* it again and again. Something about that particular experience makes life without it less than complete. Other potentially pleasurable experiences are no longer possible, for under the spell of the addictive experience, his life is peculiarly distorted. The addict craves an experience and yet he is never really satisfied. The organism may be temporarily sated, but soon it begins to crave again.

5 Finally a serious addiction is distinguished from a harmless pursuit of pleasure by its distinctly destructive elements. A heroin addict, for

instance, leads a damaged life: his increasing need for heroin in increasing doses prevents him from working, from maintaining relationships, from developing in human ways. Similarly an alcoholic's life is narrowed and dehumanized by his dependence on alcohol.

6 Let us consider television viewing in the light of the conditions that define serious addictions.

7 Not unlike drugs or alcohol, the television experience allows the participant to blot out the real world and enter into a pleasurable and passive mental state. The worries and anxieties of reality are as effectively deferred by becoming absorbed in a television program as by going on a "trip" induced by drugs or alcohol. And just as alcoholics are only inchoately aware of their addiction, feeling that they control their drinking more than they really do ("I can cut it out any time I want—I just like to have three or four drinks before dinner"), people similarly overestimate their control over television watching. Even as they put off other activities to spend hour after hour watching television, they feel they could easily resume living in a different, less passive style. But somehow or other while the television set is present in their homes, the click doesn't sound. With television pleasures available, those other experiences seem less attractive, more difficult somehow.

8 A heavy viewer (a college English instructor) observes:

"I find television almost irresistible. When the set is on, I cannot ignore it. I can't turn it off. I feel sapped, will-less, enervated. As I reach out to turn off the set, the strength goes out of my arms. So I sit there for hours and hours."

9 The self-confessed television addict often feels he "ought" to do other things—but the fact that he doesn't read and doesn't plant his garden or sew or crochet or play games or have conversations means that those activities are no longer as desirable as television viewing. In a way a heavy viewer's life is as imbalanced by his television "habit" as a drug addict's or an alcoholic's. He is living in a holding pattern, as it were, passing up the activities that lead to growth or development or a sense of accomplishment. This is one reason people talk about their television viewing so ruefully, so apologetically. They are aware that it is an unproductive experience, that almost any other endeavor is more worthwhile by any human measure.

10 Finally it is the adverse effect of television viewing on the lives of so many people that defines it as a serious addiction. The television habit distorts the sense of time. It renders other experiences vague and curiously unreal while taking on a greater reality for itself. It weakens relationships by reducing and sometimes eliminating normal opportunities for talking, fo communicating.

11 And yet television does not satisfy, else why would the viewer continue to watch hour after hour, day after day? "The measure of health," writes Lawrence Kubie, "is flexibility . . . and especially the freedom to cease when sated."[1] But the television viewer can never be sated with his television experiences—they do not provide the true nourishment that satiation requires—and thus he finds that he cannot stop watching.

Discovery Questions

1. What is Winn's reason for defining "addiction"?
2. What methods of exposition does Winn use to extend her definition?
3. Identify examples of the diction. Using the diction chart in Chapter 1, describe the essay's diction.
4. What is the essay's tone?

[1]Lawrence Kubie, *Neurotic Distortion and the Creative Process* (Lawrence: University of Kansas Press, 1958).

Suggested Terms to Define

Select one of the following or similar terms to define. Include your reason for defining this term and how you will limit the term if it is too broad for a short essay.

alienation	genius	pleasure
altruist	happiness	politician
beauty	honesty	pornography
civility	ignorance	prejudice
conservative	law and order	progress
courage	leisure	scholar
culture	liberal	sin
dictator	loyalty	social justice
education	obscenity	sportsmanship
equality	peace	superstar
failure	personality	truth
freedom	philanthropist	violence

WORKSHEET FOR DEFINITION

1. Select a term to define and complete the top half of the worksheet.
2. Write your thesis statement and enumeration of subtopics and get approval from your instructor.
3. Complete the worksheet **before** writing the essay.
4. Attach the worksheet to the finished essay.
5. Attach the Expository Essay Cover Sheet to the finished essay.

Source of material: ____________________

Term to be defined: ____________________

Etymology of term (if appropriate); cite source: ____________________

____

____

Reason for defining term: ____________________

____

Controlling idea: ____________ (number) + ____________ (adjective) + characteristics or methods (noun)

Point of view: ____________ Verb tense: ____________

Tone: ____________ Diction: ____________

Thesis statement + enumeration of characteristics or methods (may be 1 or 2 sentences):

____

____

____

____
(instructor approval)

OUTLINE

Title: ____________________

¶1: Introduction (five sentences):

Choose a good beginning from list.

Give necessary background material.

Good beginning # ______ : ____________________

____

____

____

When you write your introduction, include the approved thesis statement and subtopics at the end of paragraph 1.

Body (three paragraphs)

¶2: Transition + topic sentence: ______

supporting details

¶3: Transition + topic sentence: ______

supporting details

¶4: Transition + topic sentence: ____

____

supporting details

____

____

____

____

____

____

____

____

____

____

____

____

____

____

¶5: Conclusion (three sentences):

Restatement of term to be defined; complete definition.

Choose one of good endings from list.

Good ending # ________

____

____

____

____

____

____

Name: ____________________
Date: ____________ **Class:** ____________

Type of Exposition: ____________________

EXPOSITORY ESSAY COVER SHEET	
Structure/Ideas	+ ________
Usage/Mechanics	− ________
Total	________
Rewrite points	+ ________
TOTAL	________

Structure and Ideas (100 points)	**Original**	**Rewrite**
INTRODUCTION (at least five sentences):		
title; one of good beginnings leading to thesis	10 ________	________
thesis statement + enumeration of subtopics	5 ________	________
BODY (three supporting paragraphs):		
three topic sentences = transition + reference to thesis + subtopic	15 ________	________
development of paragraphs: sufficient, concrete, appropriate, relevant	45 ________	________
CONCLUSION (at least three sentences):		
one of good endings	5 ________	________
ESSAY:		
logical order of ideas and correct reasoning	5 ________	________
effective style = tone + diction + sentence structure + coherence	15 ________	________
Total	100 ________	+ ________

The points in this section reflect your score for structure and ideas. If you have received fewer than 100 points, you may rewrite your paper to earn them. Use the numbers as a guide to areas needing revision.

Usage and Mechanics (minus points). See Correction Symbol Chart.		
You **may** earn these points in revision:		
Usage: adj; adv; agr; awk; col; dm; frag; mm; ref; rep; shift; verb; ww; / /; ¶	−3 ea. ________	________
You **may not** earn these points in revision, but you must correct the errors:		
Mechanics: abbr; apos; cap; lc; p; ro; sp; ∧	−1 ea. ________	________
Total	− ________	+ ________

CHAPTER 13
Argumentation

If you want people to listen to you and be influenced by your opinions, you will need to know the techniques of argumentation. Otherwise, you may find that your ideas are discounted or rejected for lack of credibility. Similarly, knowing these principles of argumentation will help you to evaluate the opinions and judgments that are presented to you in personal relationships, the media, and politics, to name a few. You should carefully review all sides of an issue before you formulate your opinion.

The purpose of argumentation is to convince the audience, a sometimes hostile one, that your opinion is logical and preferable to any other opinions. In order to change someone's mind, you must be careful to support your opinion with evidence.

Unity is achieved in argumentation by presenting one opinion, called a **proposition,** that you want to have accepted. This proposition must have rational appeal. You must be careful to avoid faulty reasoning, emotional appeals, and statistical manipulation, which are detailed later in this chapter.

Order is achieved in argumentation by means of the pattern used to present the **proofs** of the proposition. These are the major supporting ideas of the argument. This sequence of proofs, based on carefully gathered evidence, must be arranged in a logical manner. One approach is **induction,** reasoning from the particular to the general. The other is **deduction,** reasoning from the general to the particular. Both types of order are outlined later in this chapter.

An argument, then, is not simply a quarrel; it is a form of logical discourse that aims through the presentation of evidence to gain acceptance of a proposition. Its appeal is fundamentally to reason, and, as noted, its purpose is to convince.

Parts of an Argument

The proposition, the first part, is the negative or affirmative opinion or judgment (based on facts) which the argument is about. This opinion is generally found in the introduction; however, with a potentially hostile audience, it is often saved for the conclusion. The proposition should be kept specific, detailed, and accurate and should raise the questions "Why?" and "Can it be supported?" A proposition is acceptable when the evidence is sound and the reasoning is logical. Because it cannot be absolutely proved or disproved, a proposition can only be judged acceptable (reasonable) or unacceptable.

The proposition must be supported by the second part of the argument, the major proofs. For example, the student essay entitled "A Vote for the Electoral College" presents the proposition that the electoral college system is worth preserving. The proofs are that this present system gives urban areas fair representation, eliminates uncertainty about alternatives, and serves American democracy well. The essay supports the proposition and develops these proofs by means of evidence.

Evidence is logical data used to support the proofs of the proposition. Evidence can consist of **facts:** events that occur, things that exist, deeds that are done, reports that can be verified or disproved. For example, "This book of 459 pages took one year to write. Its subject is the American Revolution." In addition, evidence can consist of **inferences:** conclusions or statements about matters not directly known made on the basis of observation and facts that are known. For instance, "The discussion of the American Revolution is very detailed and thorough." Evidence can also consist of **judgments**: expressions of approval or disapproval. That is, "The book on the American Revolution is excellent." However, the acceptability of this type of evidence depends heavily on who is making the judgment. For example, if a college professor of history or a Pulitzer prize historian expressed that judgment, one would accept it more readily than if it were made by a history student or a politician. Thus, the qualifications of the person making the judgment are significant. The same holds true for inferences. Acceptable judgments and inferences are based on experience, success, expertise, and knowledge.

In presenting evidence, you should cite all facts and significant ideas that oppose the proposition and acknowledge all sides to a question in anticipation of possible reader resistance. Refuting opposing positions is done throughout the argument. It includes pointing out inconsistencies and contradictions, offering counter evidence, and identifying instances of false reasoning. Finally, you should present your evidence in order of increasing importance and never invent facts or information to support the proposition.

METHODS OF LOGICAL REASONING

Reasoning is the process of examining evidence to determine whether it supports a proposition. As mentioned earlier, there are two types of logical reasoning: induction and deduction.

Induction is the method of reasoning that moves from the examination of evidence—individual instances, data, details, and particulars—to a generalization. To be acceptable, the particulars must include a representative and large enough sampling. This movement from "some" to "all," the inductive leap, must be supported by the evidence. It can only yield degrees of probability, never absolute certainty. For example, by polling enough representative precincts, researchers can often, but not always, successfully predict election results.

Deduction is the method of reasoning that applies an accepted assumption to a particular instance; it moves from a generalization to a particular conclusion. To be acceptable, the assumption must be generally believed and clearly and precisely stated. In addition, the movement from the generalization to the particular conclusion must be logical. If these conditions are met, the conclusion arrives at certainty. For example, since in the United States all citizens eighteen years old and older can vote in national elections and since John Smith and Sally Jones are nineteen-year-old citizens, they can vote in national elections.

Writing argumentation increases your ability to discriminate among facts, inferences, and judgments and encourages more critical awareness of the reasoning of other people. Moreover, it promotes fairness, intellectual honesty, and logical reasoning. On the other hand, bias and misrepresentation render an argument unacceptable. Therefore, you must avoid the following problems: faulty reasoning, emotional appeals, and statistical manipulation.

Types of Faulty Reasoning

Faulty reasoning can weaken or destroy your argument. It occurs when a conclusion is reached without the proper logical sequence. Thus, basing an argument on insufficient evidence or faulty assumptions leads to unacceptable conclusions. Because their appeal is to the intellect and they seem reasonable, these errors in thinking are often difficult to detect. There are several types of faulty reasoning that occur frequently. These common errors are called logical fallacies.

Non sequitur ("it does not follow") is arriving at a conclusion based on false assumptions or arriving at a conclusion not supported by the assumptions. Almost any kind of fallacious reasoning is a *non sequitur.*

—William Brown does not drink or smoke; he will make a good husband.
—Since both the Supreme Court and all communists oppose loyalty oaths, the Supreme Court must be communistic.

Hasty generalization results when not enough examples or untypical instances are used to reach a conclusion. It is also called an unqualified generalization or an overgeneralization.

—Everybody watches television.
—Women are terrible drivers.

Oversimplification reduces to a single cause or effect a complex event that has several causes or effects.

—Because I failed English, I can't get a good job.
—The result of World War II was inflation.

Post hoc ergo propter hoc ("after this, therefore because of this" often shortened to *post hoc*) occurs when two past events are cited, and because one occurred first, it is assumed to be the cause of the other. All superstitions are examples of this fallacy.

—Janice got a typewriter for her birthday, so now she receives A's in everything.

False analogy compares two items that are fundamentally unlike to prove or support a point.

—What if I did receive a poor transcript this semester? Thomas Edison's teachers thought he was stupid.

Circular reasoning assumes what is necessary to prove and builds an argument on that unproven assumption. Or it offers a restatement of the argument as a reason for accepting it. This type of fallacy is also called begging the question.

—Smoking is injurious because it harms the body.
—I only failed calculus because I couldn't do the problems.

Shift in terms means that there is a change in the meaning of a word and, therefore, the relationship between the words in the argument changes.

—You're not the only one whose mother works (job). My mother works (labor) hard all day. You should see her!

Faulty dilemma presents two equally unpleasant alternatives while hiding a third possibility. The dilemma is phrased as a leading question or an either-or situation.

—When did you stop passing counterfeit bills?

Attacking the person diverts attention from the issue by discrediting the individual rather than discussing the argument.

—You should not read Byron's poetry because his private life was immoral.

Types of Emotional Appeals

Another way to weaken the effectiveness of your position is to appeal to your audience's emotions. These techniques are often used by propagandists to influence your behavior for a desired purpose or predictable outcome. Although these appeals usually have only short-term effects and might be a way to arouse your reader's interest, you may not base an argument on them.

Name calling appeals to feelings of hate, dislike, or bigotry by using negatively connotative words to make the audience reject something. Prejudice is one example of this kind of appeal.

—The trouble is that this candidate is a crackpot radical.

Glittering generalities appeals to feelings of love and brotherhood by using positively connotative words to make the audience accept something.

—That sweet white-haired little old grandmother couldn't have committed the crime.

Plain folks appeals to the security that individuals feel when they are with people who are similar to themselves by implying an identification with the audience.

—Jane Doe, the girl next door who suffers from headaches, says that Remedy X relieves her pain.

Bandwagon appeals to the desire for group identity and security by assuming that people want to be like everyone else.

—Everybody who is anybody is eating at the Gourmand Restaurant.

Appeal to fear manipulates the audience's desire to avoid something negative happening.

—If you don't buy your children an encyclopedia, they will do poorly in school.

Appeal to pity manipulates the audience's sympathy and compassion to have them accept or reject something.

—This man deserves the job because his wife is ill, he has no money, and his five children are hungry.

Appeal to irrelevant authority manipulates the audience's respect or admiration for a person or institution that is an authority in one area by transferring it to an area in which the person or institution lacks authority.

—Reverend William Brown says that Candidate X is God's choice for president.

—George Washington loved Mrs. Gletch's cherry pies.

Types of Statistical Manipulation

Since people are usually impressed by numbers, percentages, graphs, and charts, a third way to render your argument unacceptable is to manipulate statistics. Numbers and studies can lead to divergent conclusions depending on the interpretation they are given. Accurate statistics are a good form of evidence in argument, but you should attempt to use them honestly.

Manipulating Averages

1. Impressive averages often distort an argument because the word *average* has three different meanings: the **mean** (the sum total of items divided by the number of items), the **median** (the middle number in the list), the **mode** (the number that appears most frequently).

   —Question asked of 30 housewives: "How many hours a day do you watch television?"

   Answers:

   10 9 9 8 8 8 8 8 7 7 7 7 6 6 6 6 5 5 4 4 3 3 2 2 2 2 1 1 1 0

   Mean is 5+
   Median is 6
   Mode is 8

   The average used is the one that best suits the purpose of the user.

2. Data derived from memory, guesswork, and exaggeration can produce impressively exact averages. These figures, because of their exactness and precision, are very deceptive.

   —From interviewing American adults, a psychologist reported that children from the ages of five through ten had 3.7 nightmares a month.

3. The averages based on a very small sampling can be used to make important decisions.

   —After interviewing 1,000 people, the results are published as the nationwide opinion on a television program.

Using irrelevant totals occurs when impressive numbers are cited as support in an argument, but these figures are totally pointless and meaningless.

—Cigarette companies responding to evidence that smoking causes cancer count filter traps even though filters do not protect the smoker.

Slanting figures occurs when statistics are chosen and interpreted according to a predetermined result. Only a partial picture is presented.

—In the 1960 Presidential campaign Vice-President Nixon boasted that more Americans were holding jobs than ever before; Senator Kennedy charged that more Americans were unemployed than ever before. Neither cared to relate his figures to population growth and admit that there were simply more Americans in the labor market.

Fabricating figures occurs when numbers are given about events too numerous to be counted or impossible to measure. These difficulties are compounded by the fact that the numbers cannot be verified.

—A magazine noted that as of February 1963 Judy Garland had sung her favorite song 10,122 times.

—A newspaper reported that there were 9 million rats in New York City.

Discovery Exercise for Argumentation

Determine the type of faulty reasoning, emotional appeal, or statistical manipulation in each of the following sentences.

1. Everyone should have plenty of exercise.

____

2. You will like the food at the Red Barn restaurant because it will taste good to you.

____

3. Oscar Wilde was a homosexual, so his poetry can not be very good.

____

4. If you do not insure now, you may die tomorrow and leave your family destitute.

____

5. Has Sam stopped cheating on his examinations?

____

6. O'Hara will make a good dean; he was an excellent professor.

____

7. If we let students evaluate teachers, pretty soon they'll be trying to decide on instructor's salaries.

____

8. Everyone should be required to serve in the United States Armed Forces.

____

9. Horses can be tamed by brute force. Consequently, parents should spank their children if they want them to behave.

____

10. Every time I wash my car it rains. If we plan a picnic, I won't wash my car.

____

11. Since the advent of television, the life expectancy has increased five years in the United States. Television must be healthful.

____

12. Everyone knows tension causes headaches.

13. Telegrams bring bad luck.

14. After a black cat crossed my path, I broke my leg.

15. The atomic bomb won World War II.

16. Swift's ideas must be discounted; he died insane.

17. Egbert died of a heart attack on that trip to Mexico. If he had stayed home, he would be alive today.

18. The surgeon general supports legislation favoring gun control.

19. I can't learn to spell. English has always been my worst subject.

20. This fluoridation referendum is a choice between either tooth decay or poison.

21. The top-seeded professional tennis player eats Go-Go nuts three times a day.

22. Since athletes are poor students and Joe Brown is an athlete, he must be a poor student.

23. "That copper kettle isn't worth anything because it can't even boil water."
"It is too worth something; it's an antique."

24. Since Jack Jones prefers blondes and all gentlemen prefer blondes, Jack Jones is a gentleman.

25. Playing soccer builds character.

26. If you wouldn't sweep dust under the rug, you shouldn't put clean food in a dirty oven. Buy Oven Cleaner X.

27. Since the cats and my wife chase mice, my wife is a cat.

28. I wouldn't believe anything he said; he cheats at cards.

29. Senator Smith's campaign song was heard 20,221 times during the 1980 election contest.

____

30. The in-people vacation on Floribunda Island.

____

31. This is the only hour I can take this course, and this is the last course I need to graduate. If I don't graduate, I won't be able to get a good job.

____

32. When did you stop peddling drugs?

____

33. If you love me, you'll call in sick to work and take me to the beach.

____

34. The leading mothball company warns that moths destroy $500 million worth of goods each year.

____

35. One phone is not enough in the modern home because modern homes have plenty of phones.

____

36. If you only knew how much time I spent on this essay, you would give me a better grade.

____

37. Buy a membership in our private campground now. The price of membership has risen 30% per year for the last six years.

____

38. He must be a hippie; he's wearing sandals, raggedy clothes, and a beard.

____

39. Since all housepets are lovable and my pet is a cat, my cat must be lovable.

____

40. All people born in the United States can become American citizens. John Doe is an American citizen. Therefore, he was born in the United States.

____

Organizational Pattern for Argumentative Essay

Study this blueprint so that you can see and better understand the elements necessary for argumentative writing. Then use the pattern as a guide in assembling your own essay. Note that all the student samples in the chapter use this organizational pattern.

Title

Introduction—¶ 1

At least five sentences

Use of one of the good beginnings

Establishment of authority and experience (if appropriate)
order of proofs
point of view
verb tense
tone and diction

Proposition	= subject (proposition to be argued) + controlling idea (number + adjective + proofs)	1 sentence
Subtopic sentence	= enumeration of three proofs	

Body—¶ 2, 3, 4

Presentation of three major proofs

Logical order of three major proofs: climactic

**Paragraph 2:* Topic sentence = transitional expression + reference to proposition + proof 1

Specific data and evidence (facts, inferences, and judgments to support the proof using logical reasoning).

**Paragraph 3:* Topic sentence = transitional expression + reference to proposition + proof 2

Specific data and evidence (facts, inferences, and judgments to support the proof using logical reasoning).

**Paragraph 4:* Topic sentence = transitional expression + reference to proposition + proof 3

Specific data and evidence (facts, inferences, and judgments to support the proof using logical reasoning).

Transitional expressions: see especially

Addition	Condition
Causal	Emphasis/Intensification
Concession	Introduction of Illustration/Example

Conclusion—¶ 5

At least three sentences

Transitional expression (optional): see Conclusion/Result and Summary

Summary of main ideas for and against

Strengths of evidence leading to opinion

*These elements may be rearranged within the sentence.

SAMPLE WORKSHEET FOR ARGUMENTATIVE ESSAY—"Should Pass-Fail Pass?"

SPECIFIC INSTRUCTIONS:

1. Select a proposition to argue.
2. Write your proposition, enumerate your proofs, and then get approval from your instructor.
3. Complete the worksheet **before** writing the essay.
4. Attach the worksheet to the finished essay.
5. Attach the Argumentative Essay Cover Sheet to the finished essay.

Source of material: personal experience

Proposition to be argued: the system of pass-fail grades should not be adopted in college.

Three proofs: 1 less work incentive

2 no criteria for transfer or graduate school

3 harmful effects on society

Order of three major proofs: climactic

Point of view: 3rd person

Verb tense: present

Tone: disinterested, serious

Diction: concrete, denotative, objective, technical

Proposition + enumeration of proofs:

This system (pass-fail) should not be adopted in college. Three main points support this opinion: less work incentive, no criteria for transfer or graduate school, and harmful effects on society.

MS/KW

(Instructor approval)

OUTLINE

Title: Should Pass-Fail Pass?

¶1: Introduction (five sentences):

Choose a good beginning from list.

Give necessary background material.

Good beginning # 2 & 12 :

explain the pass-fail system

When you write your introduction, include the approved proposition and enumeration of proofs at the end of paragraph 1.

Body (three paragraphs)

¶2: Transition + topic sentence: One argument against p-f grading system is that there will be less incentive for students.

supporting data & evidence

(3) students will only do C work
  (4) example - no revising essays
(3) students won't develop full potential
  (4) example - biology, 1 hour instead of 5 for test
(3) need rewards like letter grades
  (4) A gives sense of satisfaction
(2) Pass-fail encourages mediocrity, not mastery

¶3: Transition + topic sentence: Another reason to reject p-f policy is that there will be no criteria for employers/graduate schools

supporting data & evidence

(3) competition for jobs
  (4) employers need information
  (4) graduate at disadvantage
    (5) example - journalism, teaching, law
(3) application to graduate school
  (4) grades better than pass-fail
(2) Employers/graduate schools need precise standard

¶4: Transition + topic sentence: The last reason is that this policy is damaging to society as a whole.

supporting data & evidence

(3) discourage students
  (4) maximum learning necessary
(3) students don't develop their abilities
  (4) citizens need to be best
(2) Pass-fail students are less well prepared

¶5: Conclusion (at least three sentences):
Summary of main ideas for and against.
Strengths of evidence leading to opinion.

Good ending #7

Cons: Some exceptions don't need grade incentive
One course a semester pass-fail is good.
Pros: discouraging effort, eliminating useful criteria, eventually harming society.

STUDENT SAMPLE—Argumentative Essay—Analyzed for Parts

Observe that elements of structure and content are labeled on the left while elements of style are identified on the right. This detailed analysis will help you plan your own essay.

Title

Should Pass-Fail Pass?

Introduction ¶ 1 — *Good Beginnings #2 + 12*

Should colleges adopt a system of pass-fail grades instead of letter grades? The pass-fail grading policy is a system whereby students receive either a "pass" or a "fail" in every subject taken. If they receive a "pass," they obtain credit toward graduation or transfer.

Proposition (proposal to be argued) — This system should not be adopted in colleges.

Subtopic Sentence (Controlling idea + 3 proofs) — Three main points support this opinion: [1] less work incentive, [2] no criteria for transfer or graduate school, and [3] harmful effects on society.

Verb tense: present
Point of view: third person

Topic Sentence ¶ 2 — (One)* argument against a pass-fail grading system is that there will be less incentive for the students to work to the limits of their ability. If a "pass" covers grades A through C and sometimes even D, then why should any student do more than C work? Most people will not work any harder than they have to in order to achieve a goal. (For example,) even though revising an average essay would be beneficial, there is little reason for a student to spend time rewriting when the grade would not be raised. A (further) consequence of

Diction: concise, technical, concrete, objective

Diction: concrete

** Coherence: transitional expressions circled*

using pass-fail is that, without a challenge to their mental capacities, students will not develop their full potential or learn as much as they otherwise might. For instance, a student would most likely not spend five hours studying for a biology exam to receive a "pass" when one hour of quick review would earn the same grade. Under these circumstances, it is almost impossible to master the subject. It seems that most people need rewards in order to perform their best. Letter grades fulfill this function and, therefore, are a necessary part of higher education. The student experiences a tremendous sense of satisfaction when a difficult assignment receives an A. Consequently, with a pass-fail policy, standards and expectations are often lowered when the only measure of competence is pass. Such a system discourages mastery while it encourages mediocrity.

[A] Sentence Structure: Compound verb

Diction: concrete

Body
¶ 2,3,4

Sentence structure: dependent clause

Another reason to reject a pass-fail policy is that there will be no criteria for employers or graduate schools to use when judging students. The competition for jobs today is keen, so employers can discriminate carefully among potential workers and, therefore, need all the information possible

Topic Sentence
¶3

[B] Sentence structure: compound sentence

[C] Sentence structure: compound verb

about a future employee. When recent college graduates compete with experienced people, the graduates have only their academic records to indicate their abilities. If those records show pass-fail rather than grades, the employer has a weak basis for judgment so that the recent graduate is at a disadvantage. For example, since getting a position in journalism, teaching, or law is especially difficult today, the lack of a distinguishable academic record lessens one's opportunities. A similar problem exists when students apply to graduate school. While not the only criterion, grades are the most important in accepting applicants. To be rejected simply because transcripts contain only pass-fail grades seems unfair. Thus, it is important for employers and graduate schools to have a precise standard by which to evaluate candidates.

Diction: denotative, objective

Diction: technical

Topic Sentence ¶4

While the first two arguments against the pass-fail system suggest it is harmful to the students, the last reason is that this policy is damaging to society as a whole. Initially, not rewarding effort with letter grades discourages students from learning as much as they could. Since society benefits most when its members possess all the specialized knowledge possible about particular subjects, the correct environment for maximum learning is necessary. The pass-fail system does not provide this atmosphere. In addition, this system does not force students to develop their abilities to the fullest. Yet, the effective functioning of society is proportional to how many of its citizens participate to the best of their capacities. Society wants people to be the best secretaries, plumbers, teachers, artists, electricians, lawyers, carpenters, or musicians they can possibly be. However, under the pass-fail system of grading, students are less well prepared to become those vital, contributing members of society.

Sentence Structure: introductory dependent clause

Sentence structure: items in a series

Diction: concrete

Sentence structure: coordinate adjectives

Conclusion ¶5

Summary of Cons Good Ending #7

While these arguments support the retention of a letter-grade system, two related issues must be addressed. First, even though the majority of people will not work harder than necessary to receive a passing grade, there are always a few exceptions who do not need the incentive of grades to excel. Thus, this small group would not be harmed by a pass-fail system. Second, while the letter-grade system discourages students from investigating new subject areas because of lack of time or fear of failure, a modified use of pass-fail, such as one course a semester, would have value. However, because of discouraging effort, eliminating useful criteria, and eventually harming society, the pass-fail system should not be adopted as the grading policy in college.

Summary of Pros

F Sentence structure: verbals in a series

STUDENT SAMPLE—Argumentative Essay

Source of material: nonfiction book

The Clerks' Quirks

Will American citizens understand the workings of the United States Supreme Court better if they learn that Justice William Brennan referred to Chief Justice Warren Burger as "a bastard" in what Brennan thought was the privacy of his own chambers? No, this information is only destructive. In The Brethren by Bob Woodward and Scott Armstrong, a book published in 1980, this anecdote can be found. The entire book is a recounting of the behind-the-scenes conferences, struggles, interactions, and personalities of the nine U. S. Supreme Court justices. All the book's material is anonymous, and it is believed that the information was given to the authors by the clerks of the various justices. It is a reasonable contention that these clerks should not have revealed these matters. There are several major arguments to support this position: the tradition of confidentiality, the diminished effectiveness of the Court, and the characteristics of the clerks themselves.

The first reason the clerks should not have gossiped is that traditionally the deliberations and discussions of the justices in chambers have been kept secret from the media. Admittedly, the papers and correspondence of retired justices have been collected and published but have not revealed in great detail these private conversations. And so far as anybody knows, no previous sources have ever published the verbatim discussions among the justices at weekly case conferences or even pretended to convey this material. With the publication of The Brethren, for the first time we can read the private comments by one justice about another justice while both of them were serving on the Court. In addition, this tradition of confidentiality in the Court mirrors the relationship between lawyers and their clients. In other words, the lawyer is free to discuss clients and cases with partners, assistants, and clerical people in order to assist in preparing the best possible case. But all of these people are bound not to reveal these confidences to anyone outside their office. The Supreme Court is supposed to function similarly. Therefore, the clerks broke this important tradition that has been part of the legal profession in all its aspects.

A second argument in support of the opinion that the clerks should not have blabbed to the press involves the Court's diminished effectiveness. Over the last two hundred years in the United States government, the main role of the Supreme Court has become that of deciding on the constitutionality of legislation, and it is also the final arbiter of all legal cases. Therefore, it needs an aura of infallibility since its decisions must be accepted by everybody. For example, the Supreme Court outlawed prayer in public schools, a decision which disagreed with many people's beliefs but is observed as a law of the land. In addition, while it is important to understand thought processes and legal precedents used by justices to reach decisions, it is not enlightening to know about their personal foibles. Such trivial information clouds the legal issues involved. For example, an anecdote that quotes Justice Blackmun calling Chief Justice Burger "an uncontrollable, blustery braggart" is something to be found in Hollywood gossip columns about movie stars but should not be public information about Supreme Court justices. At a time when the legislative and executive branches of the government have lost much of the people's respect and admiration, they are presented with these judicial revelations. The judicial branch has been the last holder of this respect but has now, in fact, been compromised. Therefore, the result is a serious weakening of the Court's effectiveness.

The most persuasive argument against these revelations is the characteristics of the clerks themselves. First, these clerks are young, usually in their twenties, and are sophisticated about how to manipulate influential people. Second, they are exceptionally bright and well educated, having gone to the best colleges and law schools in the country. They are spoiled and have not had to work at a job or support themselves. Third, they are insular and narrow-minded, having been told what to read and what to think. They do not deal with facts themselves but rather with drawing inferences from facts. Therefore, they habitually leap to conclusions. Fourth, clerks are frequently liberally oriented because they resemble their law-school professors who realize how privileged they both are. The clerks see the system has helped them while discriminating against the have-nots; they want to help these less fortunate people and feel that is one of the lawyers' and Court's functions. Fifth, while they are clerks, they experience nothing that would make them question what they already believe. While they are academically bright, they have led sheltered lives and, therefore, are ignorant about the matters which the Court most commonly hears. Because of this bias, the clerks are unreliable sources.

In conclusion, while the Constitution of the United States protects freedom of speech and press, it is necessary to be responsible in reporting, writing, and publishing such material. The clerks of the Supreme Court have violated the lawyers' ethical code by revealing all of this personal information to the authors of *The Brethren*. The results have not enlightened the readers but have rather titillated the love of gossip that certainly sells books. Therefore, by leaking these revelations, these immature, biased clerks have betrayed the tradition of confidentiality and thus have diminished the effectiveness of the United States Supreme Court.

Discovery Exercise

1. Identify the proposition, the main point being argued: ______________________

   ____

2. Identify the three proofs: 1 ______________________

   2 ______________________

   3 ______________________

3. Identify the point of view: ______________ person
4. Identify the verb tense: ______________
5. Select **five** examples of concrete supporting details:

   ____

   ____

   ____

   ____

   ____

6. Select **ten** words or phrases that show the author's bias against the clerks:

   ______________ ______________

   ______________ ______________

   ______________ ______________

   ______________ ______________

   ______________ ______________

7. Choose terms from the diction chart that characterize the diction:

   ____

8. Choose terms from tone chart that describe the tone: ______________________

   ____

9. After reviewing Chapter 16, bracket **five** compound verbs, one type of grammatical structure used in this essay.

STUDENT SAMPLE—Argumentative Essay

Source of material: textbook on political science

A Vote for the Electoral College

The United States Constitution provides for the election of the President and Vice-President. Each political party nominates its candidate at a national convention held during the summer of the election year. Shortly after, in every state, the respective party selects a slate of electors pledged to that party's candidate for national office. On the first Tuesday of that November, voters go to the polls and vote for their party and candidates. The party that receives the majority of popular votes for its electors captures all the electoral votes of that state. The electors assemble at their state capitals, cast their votes, and send them to Washington, D.C., for counting. The candidates who receive an absolute majority, which is 270 electoral votes, become the President and Vice-President. Should the present system of electing the President and Vice-President of the United States be retained? Yes, the electoral college system is worth preserving. There are three main arguments to support this belief: it gives urban areas fair representation; it eliminates uncertainty about alternatives; and it serves American democracy well.

First, the electoral system should not be eliminated because it gives urban areas fair representation and is sensitive to urban interests which have been neglected elsewhere. This method of election gives urban areas some power. In those states where the political influence of large metropolitan centers is reduced in state legislatures, those same votes are important under the winner-take-all electoral college system. Further, urban states which are heavily populated by minority groups are permanently underrepresented on a per capita basis in the Senate, and election of Presidents by popular vote would take away the little power that urban states now have in the electoral college method. Indeed, the only way that important minorities can influence the political process is as the deciding factor about which major candidate wins a state's electoral votes. Consequently, urban interests, blacks, Latinos, other minorities, the handicapped and the elderly, the young, the poor, the rich, and the middle-aged all can vie for some attention and share of public policy. If the electoral college were abolished, there would be no need for the candidates to take the desires and wishes of the minorities into consideration, and all of America's minorities would suffer.

The second argument to support the retaining of the electoral college is that the weaknesses and uncertainties inherent in the alternative systems are eliminated. Two main alternative methods have been proposed. The first plan involves keeping the electoral vote system but eliminating its winner-take-all features. One suggestion is that electors should be chosen on a congressional district basis with only two electors per state chosen statewide. A second change would eliminate electors, as people, and the electoral votes of a state would be assigned to candidates on the basis of the popular vote they received. While these changes might make the popular vote less distorted, the people are still not electing the President directly. Neither of these plans eliminates the possibility of the popular-vote loser winning the electoral vote majority. Thus, nothing would be gained by changing the current system. The second major alternative that has been proposed is a constitutional amendment to eliminate the electoral college system and provide for the direct election of the President and Vice-President. The reason for making this change would be to elect the most popular candidate. However, direct voting does not insure that the most popular candidate will win except in elections with only two candidates. If there are five candidates in an election, one could win with as little as 21 percent of the vote. It could most likely be that any one of the defeated candidates could beat the winning candidate in a contest between the two. If a majority of the votes cast would be required for election, then the Presidential election might require costly runoffs and undue delays in time. It is clear, then, that these alternatives are by no means a great improvement on the present system.

The most convincing reason to preserve the current method of electing the President and Vice-President is that it serves American democracy well. This system thwarts the rise of multiple parties because these parties are unlikely to receive pluralities in many states and, consequently, are eliminated from decisive electoral vote competition. A direct election would encourage the rise of such splinter parties because they would hope to prevent any candidate from receiving a national majority or even a large plurality of popular votes. If a runoff between the two leaders is necessary in a direct election system, it would be an advantage to minor parties who would try to force a second vote so they could sell their support. In addition, the present system insures the dominance and the continued existence of two major political parties. The two-party system supports a politics of coalition, accommodation, and compromise rather than one of ideological fragmentation. Thus, governments are moderate and stable under this system. The direct election plan might result in the election of a President who is a demagogue or a self-nominated individualistic leader of transient groups or a charismatic leader using a single issue. The electoral system, on the other hand, elects Presidents who were nominated because of their moderation, experience, records of success in past elections, and service to permanent party organizations. Therefore, the present electoral plan preserves the prestige, power, and potential for leadership of the Office of the President. By appealing to broad geographical and ideological interests and thus promoting unity, this system serves American democracy well.

In conclusion, despite some imperfections, the present electoral college system works. As evidence, this country has not had a popular-vote loser elected in ninety years. President John F.

Kennedy defended the electoral college by arguing that changing its structure or abolishing it involves more than just technical details but a change in the whole "solar system" of interrelated subtle institutions, principles, and customs, perhaps even leading to the dismantling of the present federal system. The current electoral method produces a definite, accepted winner and has proven itself in time and practice; therefore, it should be retained.

PROFESSIONAL SAMPLE—Argumentative Writing

Read this essay to see how a professional writer has used the technique of argumentation. Then answer the discovery questions which focus on the elements of argumentation.

Jonathan Swift (1667–1745), writer, politician, and clergyman, grew up in Ireland although his parents were English. He spent time in London writing in support of the Tory political party. He became Dean of St. Patrick's (Anglican) Cathedral in Dublin where he defended the Irish against the English government. His chief works include the satires *The Battle of the Books, A Tale of a Tub,* and *Gulliver's Travels.*

A Modest Proposal

For Preventing the Children of Poor People in Ireland from Being a Burden to Their Parents or Country, and for Making Them Beneficial to the Public

1 It is a melancholy object to those who walk through this great town[1] or travel in the country, when they see the streets, the roads, and cabin doors, crowded with beggars of the female sex, followed by three, four, or six children, all in rags and importuning every passenger for an alms. These mothers, instead of being able to work for their honest livelihood, are forced to employ all their time in strolling to beg sustenance for their helpless infants, who, as they grow up, either turn thieves for want of work, or leave their dear native country to fight for the Pretender in Spain, or sell themselves to the Barbados.[2]

2 I think it is agreed by all parties that this prodigious number of children in the arms, or on the backs, or at the heels of their mothers, and frequently of their fathers, is in the present deplorable state of the kingdom a very great additional grievance; and therefore whoever could find out a fair, cheap, and easy method of making these children sound, useful members of the commonwealth would deserve so well of the public as to have his statue set up for a preserver of the nation.

[1] Dublin.

[2] The Pretender was James Stuart, exiled in Spain; in 1718 many Irishmen had joind an army seeking to restore him to the English throne. Others wishing to emigrate had signed papers as indentured servants, agreeing to work for a number of years in the Barbados or other British colonies in exchange for their ocean passage.

3 But my intention is very far from being confined to provide only for the children of professed beggars; it is of a much greater extent, and shall take in the whole number of infants at a certain age who are born of parents in effect as little able to support them as those who demand our charity in the streets.

4 As to my own part, having turned my thoughts for many years upon this important subject, and maturely weighed the several schemes of other projectors,[3] I have always found them grossly mistaken in their computation. It is true, a child just dropped from its dam may be supported by her milk for a solar year, with little other nourishment; at most not above the value of two shillings, which the mother may certainly get, or the value in scraps, by her lawful occupation of begging; and it is exactly at one year that I propose to provide for them in such a manner as instead of being a charge upon their parents or the parish, or wanting food and raiment for the rest of their lives, they shall on the contrary contribute to the feeding, and partly to the clothing, of many thousands.

5 There is likewise another great advantage in my scheme, that it will prevent those voluntary abortions, and that horrid practice of women murdering their bastard children, alas, too fre-

[3] Planners.

quent among us, sacrificing the poor innocent lambs, I doubt, more to avoid the expense than the shame, which would move tears and pity in the most savage and inhuman breast.

6 The number of souls in this kingdom being usually reckoned one million and a half, of these I calculate there may be about two hundred thousand couples whose wives are breeders; from which number I subtract thirty thousand couples who are able to maintain their own children, although I apprehend there cannot be so many under the present distress of the kingdom; but this being granted, there will remain an hundred and seventy thousand breeders. I again subtract fifty thousand for those women who miscarry, or whose children die by accident or disease within the year. There only remain an hundred and twenty thousand children of poor parents annually born. The question therefore is, how this number shall be reared and provided for, which, as I have already said, under the present situation of affairs, is utterly impossible by all the methods hitherto proposed. For we can neither employ them in handicraft or agriculture; we neither build houses (I mean in the country) nor cultivate land. They can very seldom pick up a livelihood by stealing till they arrive at six years old, except where they are of towardly parts;[4] although I confess they learn the rudiments much earlier, during which time they can however be looked upon only as probationers, as I have been informed by a principal gentleman in the country of Cavan, who protested to me that he never knew above one or two instances under the age of six, even in a part of the kingdom so renowned for the quickest proficiency in that art.

7 I am assured by our merchants that a boy or a girl before twelve years old is no salable commodity; and even when they come to this age they will not yield above three pounds, or three pounds and half a crown at most on the Exchange; which cannot turn to account either to the parents or the kingdom, the charge of nutriment and rags having been at least four times that value.

8 I shall now therefore humbly propose my own thoughts, which I hope will not be liable to the least objection.

9 I have been assured by a very knowing American of my acquaintance in London, that a young healthy child well nursed is at a year old a most delicious, nourishing, and wholesome food, whether stewed, roasted, baked, or boiled; and I make no doubt that it will equally serve in a fricassee or a ragout.[5]

10 I do therefore humbly offer it to public consideration that of the hundred and twenty thousand children, already computed, twenty thousand may be reserved for breed, whereof only one fourth part to be males, which is more than we allow to sheep, black cattle, or swine; and my reason is that these children are seldom the fruits of marriage, a circumstance not much regarded by our savages, therefore one male will be sufficient to serve four females. That the remaining hundred thousand may at a year old be offered in sale to the persons of quality and fortune through the kingdom, always advising the mother to let them suck plentifully in the last month, so as to render them plump and fat for a good table. A child will make two dishes at an entertainment for friends; and when the family dines alone, the fore or hind quarter will make a reasonable dish, and seasoned with a little pepper or salt will be very good boiled on the fourth day, especially in winter.

11 I have reckoned upon a medium that a child just born will weigh twelve pounds, and in a solar year if tolerably nursed increaseth to twenty-eight pounds.

12 I grant this food will be somewhat dear, and therefore very proper for landlords, who, as they have already devoured most of the parents, seem to have the best title to the children.

13 Infant's flesh will be in season throughout the year, but more plentiful in March, and a little before and after. For we are told by a grave author, an eminent French physician,[6] that fish being a prolific diet, there are more children born in Roman Catholic countries about nine months after Lent than at any other season; therefore, reckoning a year after Lent, the markets will be more glutted than usual, because the number of popish infants is at least three to one in this kingdom; and therefore it will have one other collateral advantage, by lessening the number of Papists among us.

14 I have already computed the charge of nursing a beggar's child (in which list I reckon all cottagers, laborers, and four-fifths of the farmers) to be about two shillings per annum, rags included; and I believe no gentleman would repine to give ten shillings for the carcass of a good fat child, which, as I have said, will make four dishes of excellent nutritive meat, when he hath only

[4] Teachable wits, innate abilities.

[5] Stew.

[6] Swift's favorite French writer, François Rabelais, sixteenth-century author not "grave" at all, but a broad humorist.

some particular friend or his own family to dine with him. Thus the squire will learn to be a good landlord, and grow popular among the tenants; the mother will have eight shillings net profit, and be fit for work till she produces another child.

15 Those who are more thrifty (as I must confess the times require) may flay the carcass; the skin of which artificially[7] dressed will make admirable gloves for ladies, and summer boots for fine gentlemen.

16 As to our city of Dublin, shambles[8] may be appointed for this purpose in the most convenient parts of it, and butchers we may be assured will not be wanting; although I rather recommend buying the children alive, and dressing them hot from the knife as we do roasting pigs.

17 A very worthy person, a true lover of his country, and whose virtues I highly esteem, was lately pleased in discoursing on this matter to offer a refinement upon my scheme. He said that many gentlemen of his kingdom, having of late destroyed their deer, he conceived that the want of venison might be well supplied by the bodies of young lads and maidens, not exceeding fourteen years of age nor under twelve, so great a number of both sexes in every county being now ready to starve for want of work and service; and these to be disposed of by their parents, if alive, or otherwise by their nearest relations. But with due deference to so excellent a friend and so deserving a patriot, I cannot be altogether in his sentiments; for as to the males, my American acquaintance assured me from frequent experience that their flesh was generally tough and lean, like that of our schoolboys, by continual exercise, and their taste disagreeable; and to fatten them would not answer the charge. Then as to the females, it would, I think with humble submission, be a loss to the public, because they soon would become breeders themselves; and besides, it is not improbable that some scrupulous people might be apt to censure such a practice (although indeed very unjustly) as a little bordering upon cruelty; which, I confess, hath always been with me the strongest objection against any project, how well soever intended.

18 But in order to justify my friend, he confessed that this expedient was put into his head by the famous Psalmanazar,[9] a native of the island Formosa, who came from thence to London above twenty years ago, and in conversation told my friend that in his country when any young person happened to be put to death, the executioner sold the carcass to persons of quality as a prime dainty; and that in his time the body of a plump girl of fifteen, who was crucified for an attempt to poison the emperor, was sold to his Imperial Majesty's prime minister of state, and other great mandarins of the court, in joints from the gibbet, at four hundred crowns. Neither indeed can I deny that if the same use were made of several plump young girls in this town, who without one single groat to their fortunes cannot stir abroad without a chair, and appear at the playhouse and assemblies in foreign fineries which they never will pay for, the kingdom would not be the worse.

[7]With art or craft.

[8]Butcher shops or slaughterhouses.

[9]Georges Psalmanazar, a Frenchman who pretended to be Japanese, author of a completely imaginary *Description of the Isle Formosa* (1705), had become a well-known figure in gullible London society.

19 Some persons of a desponding spirit are in great concern about that vast number of poor people who are aged, diseased, or maimed, and I have been desired to employ my thoughts what course may be taken to ease the nation of so grievous an encumbrance. But I am not in the least pain upon that matter, because it is very well known that they are every day dying and rotting by cold and famine, and filth and vermin, as fast as can be reasonably expected. And as to the younger laborers, they are now in almost as hopeful a condition. They cannot get work, and consequently pine away for want of nourishment to a degree that if any time they are accidentally hired to common labor, they have not strength to perform it; and thus the country and themselves are happily delivered from the evils to come.

20 I have too long digressed, and therefore shall return to my subject. I think the advantages by the proposal which I have made are obvious and many, as well as of the highest importance.

21 For first, as I have already observed, it would greatly lessen the number of Papists, with whom we are yearly overrun, being the principal breeders of the nation as well as our most dangerous enemies; and who stay at home on purpose to deliver the kingdom to the Pretender, hoping to take their advantage by the absence of so many good Protestants, who have chosen rather to leave their country than to stay at home and pay tithes against their conscience to an Episcopal curate.

22 Secondly, the poorer tenants will have something valuable of their own, which by law may be made liable to distress,[10] and help to pay their landlord's rent, their corn and cattle being already seized and money a thing unknown.

[10]Subject to seizure by creditors.

23 Thirdly, whereas the maintenance of an hundred thousand children, from two years old and upwards, cannot be computed at less than ten shillings a piece per annum, the nation's stock will be thereby increased fifty thousand pounds per annum, besides the profit of a new dish introduced to the tables of all gentlemen of fortune in the kingdom who have any refinement in taste. And the money will circulate among ourselves, the goods being entirely of our own growth and manufacture.

24 Fourthly, the constant breeders, besides the gain of eight shillings sterling per annum by the sale of their children, will be rid of the charge of maintaining them after the first year.

25 Fifthly, this food would likewise bring great custom to taverns, where the vintners will certainly be so prudent as to procure the best receipts for dressing it to perfection, and consequently have their houses frequented by all the fine gentlemen, who justly value themselves upon their knowledge in good eating; and a skillful cook, who understands how to oblige his guests, will contrive to make it as expensive as they please.

26 Sixthly, this would be a great inducement to marriage, which all wise nations have either encouraged by rewards or enforced by laws and penalties. It would increase the care and tenderness of mothers toward their children, when they were sure of a settlement for life to the poor babes, provided in some sort by the public, to their annual profit instead of expense. We should see an honest emulation among the married women, which of them could bring the fattest child to the market. Men would become as fond of their wives during the time of their pregnancy as they are now of their mares in foal, their cows in calf, or sows when they are ready to farrow; nor offer to beat or kick them (as is too frequent a practice) for fear of a miscarriage.

27 Many other advantages might be enumerated. For instance, the addition of some thousand carcasses in our exportation of barreled beef, the propagation of swine's flesh, and improvements in the art of making good bacon, so much wanted among us by the great destruction of pigs, too frequent at our tables, which are no way comparable in taste or magnificence to a well-grown, fat, yearling child, which roasted whole will make a considerable figure at a lord mayor's feast or any other public entertainment. But this and many others I omit, being studious of brevity.

28 Supposing that one thousand families in this city would be constant customers for infants' flesh, besides others who might have it at merry meetings, particularly weddings and christenings, I compute that Dublin would take off annually about twenty thousand carcasses, and the rest of the kingdom (where probably they will be sold somewhat cheaper) the remaining eighty thousand.

29 I can think of no one objection that will possibly be raised against this proposal, unless it should be urgent that the number of people will be thereby much lessened in the kingdom. This I freely own, and it was indeed one principal design in offering it to the world. I desire the reader will observe, that I calculate my remedy for this one individual kingdom of Ireland and for no other that ever was, is, or I think ever can be upon earth. Therefore let no man talk to me of other expedients: of taxing our absentees at five shillings a pound: of using neither clothes nor household furniture except what is of our own growth and manufacture: of utterly rejecting the materials and instruments that promote foreign luxury: or curing the expensiveness of pride, vanity, idleness, and gaming in our women: of introducing a vein of parsimony, prudence, and temperance: of learning to love our country, in the want of which we differ even from Laplanders and the inhabitants of Topinamboo:[11] of quitting our animosities and factions, nor acting any longer like the Jews, who were murdering one another at the very moment their city was taken:[12] of being a little cautious not to sell our country and conscience for nothing: of teaching landlords to have at least one degree of mercy toward their tenants: lastly, of putting a spirit of honesty, industry, and skill into our shopkeepers; who, if a resolution could now be taken to buy only our native goods, would immediately unite to cheat and exact upon us in the price, the measure, and the goodness, nor could ever yet be brought to make one fair proposal of just dealing, though often and earnestly invited to it.

30 Therefore I repeat, let no man talk to me of these and the like expedients, till he hath at least some glimpse of hope that there will ever be some hearty and sincere attempt to put them in practice.

31 But as to myself, having been wearied out for many years with offering vain, idle, visionary thoughts, and at length utterly despairing of success, I fortunately fell upon this proposal, which,

[11]District of Brazil inhabited by primitive tribes.

[12]During the Roman seige of Jerusalem (70 A.D.), prominent Jews were executed on the charge of being in league with the enemy.

as it is wholly new, so it hath something solid and real, of no expense and little trouble, full in our own power, and whereby we can incur no danger in disobliging England. For this kind of commodity will not bear exportation, the flesh being of too tender a consistence to admit a long continuance in salt, although perhaps I could name a country which would be glad to eat up our whole nation without it.

32 After all, I am not so violently bent upon my own opinion as to reject any offer proposed by wise men, which shall be found equally innocent, cheap, easy, and effectual. But before something of that kind shall be advanced in contradiction to my scheme, and offering a better, I desire the author or authors will be pleased maturely to consider two points. First, as things now stand, how they will be able to find food and raiment for an hundred thousand useless mouths and backs. And secondly, there being a round million of creatures in human figure throughout this kingdom, whose sole subsistence put into a common stock would leave them in debt two millions of pounds sterling, adding those who are beggars by profession to the bulk of farmers, cottagers, and laborers, with their wives and children who are beggars in effect; I desire those politicians who dislike my overture, and may perhaps be so bold to attempt an answer, that they will first ask the parents of these mortals whether they would not at this day think it a great happiness to have been sold for food at a year old in this manner I prescribe, and thereby have avoided such a perpetual scene of misfortunes as they have since gone through by the oppression of landlords, the impossibility of paying rent without money or trade, the want of common sustenance, with neither house nor clothes to cover them from the inclemencies of the weather, and the most inevitable prospect of entailing the like or greater miseries upon their breed forever.

33 I profess, in the sincerity of my heart, that I have not the least personal interest in endeavoring to promote this necessary work, having no other motive than the public good of my country, by advancing our trade, providing for infants, relieving the poor, and giving some pleasure to the rich. I have no children by which I can propose to get a single penny; the youngest being nine years old, and my wife past childbearing.

Discovery Questions

1. What is the problem that Swift identifies?
2. What is the proposition that he presents and argues for?
3. What proofs does Swift use to support his proposition?
4. What evidence does he use to develop **one** of his proofs?
5. Select one example to illustrate each type of evidence: fact, inference, and judgment.
6. Identify examples of the diction. Using the diction chart in Chapter 1, describe the essay's diction.
7. What is the essay's tone?
8. What real solutions does Swift give to the problem that he has identified?

Suggested Propositions to Argue

Do some research on a controversial topic that interests you. It is helpful if you have strong feelings about it. After you have studied all sides of the issue, decide which position you are going to argue for and formally state that opinion as the argument's proposition. Select one of the following or similar propositions to argue:

a current political controversy: for example, electing members of the Supreme Court or the United Nations

a solution to a social problem: for example, abolishing prisons or parental responsibility for a child's criminal acts

pending legislation: for example, draft registration or gun laws

a proposal for the economic situation: for example, tax credits for private school or tax incentives

an opinion about a military situation: for example, increasing the defense budget or drafting women

a current educational controversy: for example, forced busing or requirements for high school graduation

a problem created by scientific or technological developments: for example, genetic experimentation or safe disposal of wastes

an opinion about a facet of arts, theater, music, film, literature: for example, art as therapy or a particular work

WORKSHEET FOR ARGUMENTATIVE ESSAY

1. Select a proposition to argue.
2. Write your proposition, enumerate your proofs, and then get approval from your instructor.
3. Complete the worksheet **before** writing the essay.
4. Attach the worksheet to the finished essay.
5. Attach the Argumentative Essay Cover Sheet to the finished essay.

Source of material: ______________________________

Proposition to be argued: ______________________________

____

Three proofs: 1 ______________________________

2 ______________________________

3 ______________________________

Order of three major proofs: climactic

Point of view: ______________ Verb tense: ______________

Tone: ______________ Diction: ______________

Proposition + enumeration of proofs:

____

____

____

____

(instructor approval)

OUTLINE

Title: ______________________________

¶1: Introduction (five sentences):

Choose a good beginning from list.

Give necessary background material.

Good beginning # ________ : ______________________________

____

____

____

____

____

____

When you write your introduction, include the approved proposition and enumeration of proofs at the end of paragraph 1.

Body (three paragraphs)

¶2: Transition + topic sentence: ______

supporting data & evidence

¶3: Transition + topic sentence: ______

supporting data & evidence

¶4: Transition + topic sentence: ____________________

supporting data & evidence

¶5: Conclusion (at least three sentences):
Summary of main ideas for and against.
Strengths of evidence leading to opinion.
Good ending # ______

Name: ____________________

Date: ____________ Class: ________

ARGUMENTATIVE ESSAY COVER SHEET		
Structure/Ideas	+	______
Usage/Mechanics	−	______
Total		______
Rewrite points	+	______
TOTAL		______

Structure and Ideas (**100 points**)	**Original**	**Rewrite**
INTRODUCTION (at least five sentences):		
title; one of good beginnings leading to proposition	10______	______
proposition + enumeration of proofs	5______	______
BODY (three supporting paragraphs):		
three topic sentences = transition + reference to thesis + proof	15______	______
sufficient development of paragraphs using evidence	45______	______
CONCLUSION (at least three sentences):		
summary of main pros and cons; strengths of evidence leading to opinion	5______	______
ESSAY:		
logical order of ideas and correct reasoning	10______	______
effective style = tone + diction + sentence structure + coherence	10______	______
Total	100______	+ ______

The points in this section reflect your score for structure and ideas. If you have received fewer than 100 points, you may rewrite your paper to earn them. Use the numbers as a guide to what areas need revision.

Usage and Mechanics (**minus points**). **See Correction Symbol Chart.**			
You **may** earn these points in revision:			
Usage: adj; adv; agr; awk; col; dm; frag; mm; ref; rep; shift; verb; ww; / /; ¶	−3 ea.	______	______
You **may not** earn these points in revision, but you must correct the errors:			
Mechanics: abbr; apos; cap; lc; p; ro; sp; ∧	−1 ea.	______	______
Total	−	______	+ ______

CHAPTER 14
Nonfiction Prose Analysis

Nonfiction prose includes essays found in anthologies, newspapers, and magazines, as well as some complete books. The purpose of nonfiction prose is to discuss, explain, and analyze information and ideas that are actual rather than imaginary. (Imaginative writing is known as fiction and includes poetry, short stories, dramas, and novels.)

An important part of your learning to write effective prose is being able to analyze and evaluate the writing styles of professionals. You can also gain a broader awareness and knowledge of enduring ideas from the past and new ideas from current events by analyzing nonfiction prose.

There are several different forms that nonfiction prose analysis can take, depending on the length and complexity of your assignment. The most common forms are the summary, the outline report, and the essay. The summary paragraph is the simplest and shortest type of analysis. The outline report prepares for the full-length analysis in outline form. The analytical essay is the longest and most complex form. By completing several of these assignments, you should develop skill in reading and evaluating nonfiction prose.

Reading Process

The basis of thoughtful analysis is careful reading that involves several important steps. Before you begin to read, note the author, title of the work, publisher, place of publication, and date. Then skim the work quickly to get an overview of the main ideas. Read the work more carefully and slowly a second time, making notes on important points. Consult a dictionary for the meaning of unfamiliar words. Your notes should include information about the subject matter: the specific issue, idea, problem, or topic the author discusses. Next, determine the author's purpose or the reason(s) why the work was written. For example, purposes are to amuse, to inform or explain, to change an attitude, or to solve a problem.

Audience

As a result of these observations, you should be able to characterize the audience, the readers to whom the author appeals. The audience for nonfiction prose varies, according to subject matter, from special interest groups to the general reading public. The group is identified by the following three elements:

- the level of language: formal, semiformal, informal, technical, slanted
- the nature of the subject matter: philosophical, scientific, practical, artistic, economic, political
- the amount of background knowledge the reader is expected to have

In addition, the group is classified according to one or more of the following categories:

1. educational level: high school, college, graduate school
2. financial position: upper, middle, lower income
3. age: juvenile, adolescent, young adult, middle age, senior
4. sex
5. special interest: health, hobbies, religion, sports, general information
6. profession

Evaluation Process

After noting these points, you are ready to begin your analysis and evaluation of the selection. Evaluating nonfiction prose involves more than just a summary or understanding of the main ideas. It also includes judgments about logic, prose style, and significance of the ideas. These judgments must be supported by evidence, like quotations from the selection or critical reviews. The evaluation process involves three basic elements: theme, style, and value.

Theme is **WHAT** the author says.

1. Identify the thesis or main idea of the work.
2. Analyze the major supporting ideas. Select quotations and explanations from the work that illustrate these ideas.
3. Discuss the nature of the examples used in the work to develop the major supporting ideas. Determine whether these examples are clear, representative, relevant, and recent.
4. Present the conclusions of the work. Indicate whether they are a summary of the major supporting ideas or solutions to the problems raised or suggestions for action or for a new approach.

Style is **HOW** the author conveys the ideas.

1. Analyze the work's apparatus and specialized items: photographs, table of contents, preface, illustrations, advertisements, cartoons, maps, charts, glossary, index.
2. Indicate and evaluate with examples the author's diction or choice of vocabulary. See the diction chart in Chapter 1.
3. Indicate and evaluate with examples the author's tone or attitude toward the subject matter and the audience. See the tone chart in Chapter 1.
4. Identify with quotations the variations in sentence structure. See Chapter 16 for examples of sentence variety.

Value is **WHY** the work was effective and worth reading.

1. Analyze and evaluate **personal reactions** and offer evidence in considering the following:
    a. introduction to new ideas and information
    b. reassessment of attitudes, values, and opinions
    c. practicality and personal usefulness of the ideas
2. Analyze and evaluate **objective judgments** and offer evidence in considering the following:
    a. relevance of the ideas to people in general
    b. relevance of the ideas to the current situation
    c. practicality of the solutions given; for example, appropriate, feasible, effective
    d. durability of the ideas (ability to continue to generate interest and concern)

Problems to Avoid

To compose a competent and objective analysis, you must avoid a few basic problems. Unless the assignment is a summary, you must not just summarize the major ideas but evaluate and criticize them as well. You should also avoid selecting a work beyond your ability or interest. If it is necessary to consult a review from another source, the material should be properly credited. Refer to Chapter 15 for a full discussion of correct documentation. Finally, in your analysis do not offer statements or generalizations without evidence, such as quotations, illustrations, and explanations, to support each statement or generalization.

The four types of nonfiction material usually read and evaluated in expository writing classes are essays in anthologies, newspapers, and magazines, as well as some complete books. The following reference chart identifies five areas of comparison and contrast for each of the prose types.

NONFICTION PROSE ANALYSIS CHART

	Anthology	Newspaper	Magazine	Book
Function	to provide information, not necessarily currently relevant, on a wide variety of subjects drawn from many sources (chapters of books, lectures, speeches, magazines)	to provide the most complete information about happenings within the last 24 hours and on a wide variety of subjects, particularly those of current interest; written in an objective fashion; opinion usually limited to editorials and signed essays	to provide more current information than a book but less than a newspaper on some subjects of recent and continuing interest; may specialize in one subject field (sports, real estate)	to provide as complete information as possible about one subject; often includes secondary source material; information is less current than that in newspapers and magazines
Time lapse before printing	from approximately one year to centuries because of differing original dates of composition of the many essays	as short as a few hours	as short as a few weeks	usually at least one year
Style	generally polished and well developed	not a major feature because timeliness of content is essential; ease of readability important	more polished and developed than a newspaper but less than a book	fully developed, well polished, and carefully edited
Apparatus	table of contents, preface, glossary, index **no** illustrations, cartoons, maps, charts, advertisements	brief table of contents, illustrations, cartoons, advertisements, charts, photographs **no** preface, glossary, index	table of contents, illustrations, cartoons, maps, photographs, charts, advertisements **no** preface, glossary, index	table of contents, preface, illustrations, maps, charts, glossary, index **no** advertisements
Bibliographical information (placed at end of your analysis)	Author (Last Name, First Name). "Title of Essay." Title of Book. Ed. (Name of Editor). 3rd ed. City of Publication: Publishing Company, date of publication. Inclusive page numbers.	Author. "Title of Essay." Title of Newspaper date, section: page numbers.	Author. "Title of Essay." Title of Magazine date: page numbers.	Author. Title of Book. City of Publication: Publishing Company, date.

THE SUMMARY PARAGRAPH

A summary, also called a précis or an abstract, is a brief condensation of the most important ideas of a passage. The abbreviated version preserves the pattern of organization, the order of the ideas, the viewpoint of the author, and the proportions and emphasis of the original work. A summary is not a paraphrase or a close restatement of the original in other words. It is not the topic sentences of paragraphs or quotations made up of a few selected sentences. It is not a group of running or topical notes.

Much is lost in the condensation or summary of a work. The style, details, and implications (unstated ideas) are all lost when you put the main ideas into your own words. However, a summary is a good learning tool to help you understand the original work.

Writing summaries encourages you to read and think analytically. It helps you to separately identify the work's main idea, major supporting ideas, their development, and the conclusions. Putting others' ideas into condensed form will improve these writing skills:

- formulating your own topic sentence, supporting it with substantiating points in logical order, and presenting them coherently;
- using your knowledge of grammar to select more condensed grammatical structures (for example, substituting prepositional and verbal phrases for clauses);
- widening your vocabulary to find correct and shorter synonyms for longer ideas.

Steps in Preparing the Summary Paragraph

1. Read the passage to be summarized. Focus on getting the author's exact meaning.
2. Make sure to know the meaning of all words and allusions. Underline all important ideas.
3. Read the work a second time. Determine the author's subject matter, purpose, audience, and style. The summary should not discuss these items but should reflect them.
4. Identify the original work's main idea, major supporting ideas, and the conclusions, and include these in the summary.
5. Begin the summary with the name of the author and the title of the passage.
6. Write the summary in complete, well-constructed sentences, never in phrases or fragments. The sentences should be coherently grouped, and the summary should read smoothly and be easily understood. Be consistent in point of view and verb tense.
7. End the summary with a conclusion which is both true to the work being summarized and a good ending for the summary itself.
8. Do not include any unimportant information. Omit most examples, anecdotes, and illustrations. Do not refer to the original author or use the author's exact words.
9. Do not include critical or editorial comments unless the person requesting the summary specifically wants them; then be sure to indicate when they are not the author's ideas.
10. Compare the summary with the original by rereading the original a third time to make sure the summary includes the essential meaning and all important ideas.
11. Put the complete bibliographical information at the bottom of the last page of the summary.

STUDENT SAMPLE—Summary Paragraph

(See Chapter 10 for the Original Essay.)

"The Geography of Loneliness" by Suzanne Gordon explains that, although people today have more alternatives in their lives than they ever did before, loneliness is the main consequence of this new freedom. One major explanation of this isolation is the geographical layout of our lives. This situation is illustrated in the physical design and surroundings of our cities which discourage contact between people. While small towns, urban neighborhoods, and rural settings escape that problem, they share with the cities another reason for loneliness which is age segregation. Mobility, the frequency with which people move, is another part of the geographical explanation for loneliness. Mobility leads to communal apathy which, in turn, encourages crime. Another consequence of loneliness is an increased burden on marriage which leads to a higher divorce rate. People, in pursuing new freedoms, have high expectations for a better life. What has happened in reality is that many people are living emotionally and psychologically worse lives. People are left alone to deal with their loneliness and so turn to tranquilizers and other methods of relieving the pain. Since loneliness is a problem common to millions of people, it is an indication that there is a weakness in our society. Loneliness influences even those who are not lonely because the functioning of society itself is adversely affected. The only cure for this problem of loneliness is correct social and political action.

Gordon, Suzanne. "The Geography of Loneliness." Lonely in America. New York: Simon, 1976. 15-22.

Name: ____________________
Date: ____________ Class: ________

SUMMARY PARAGRAPH COVER SHEET		
Structure/Ideas	+	______
Usage/Mechanics	−	______
Total		______
Rewrite points	+	______
TOTAL		______

Structure and Ideas (100 points)	**Original**	**Rewrite**
Topic sentence, including author, title, and main idea of original	20______	______
Major supporting ideas	60______	______
Effective style = tone + diction + sentence structure + coherence	10______	______
Concluding sentence	5______	______
Bibliographical information	5______	______
Total	100______	+ ______

The points in this section reflect your score for structure and ideas. If you have received fewer than 100 points, you may rewrite your paper to earn them. Use the numbers as a guide to what areas need revision.

Usage and Mechanics (minus points). See Correction Symbol Chart.		
You **may** earn these points in revision:		
Usage: adj; adv; agr; awk; col; dm; frag; mm; ref; rep; shift; verb; ww; / /	−3 ea. ______	______
You **may not** earn these points in revision, but you must correct the errors:		
Mechanics: abbr; apos; cap; lc; p; ro; sp; ∧	−1 ea. ______	______
Total −	______	+ ______

THE OUTLINE REPORT

An outline report is a brief analysis of an essay usually found in an anthology, a newspaper, or a magazine or an analysis of a complete book. The report identifies the separate elements of theme, style, and value with summary and evaluation.

The report's purpose is to encourage experience in the process of reading critically. It also develops an awareness of the need to give evidence to support critical opinions.

Steps in Preparing the Outline Report

1. Read the work to be analyzed. Focus on getting the author's exact meaning.
2. Make sure to know the meaning of all words and allusions. Underline all important ideas.
3. On the report form, fill in the author, the title of the work, the expository type, the subject matter, the audience, and the purpose of the work. Put the complete bibliographical information at the bottom of the last page.
4. Analyze the **theme:**

   State in sentence form the main idea of the work and at least five major supporting ideas.
5. Analyze and evaluate the **style:**

   Select and write five quotations that best illustrate the work's language. These quotations may be brief excerpts or complete sentences. Using the diction chart and these quotations, list at least three terms that describe the work's diction. These terms must be based on the excerpts you have quoted.

   Using the tone chart and the conclusion about diction, list at least two terms that describe the work's tone.

   Select and quote three sentences that illustrate different grammatical structures. Label in the margin the types of grammatical structures used. Underline the corresponding structures in the sentences.
6. Analyze and evaluate the **value:**

   Formulate and write personal reactions to the work, referring to new information, reassessment of attitudes, and practical ideas.

   Formulate and write objective judgments of the work, referring to the relevance of the ideas, the practicality of the solutions, and the durability of the ideas.

Student Sample Outline Report (See Chapter 10 for the original essay.)

Name: Student X

Score: 100

Author: Suzanne Gordon

Title: "The Geography of Loneliness"

Expository type: causal analysis

Subject matter: the geographical aspects of loneliness

Audience: educated, middle-class people of all ages interested in or worried about loneliness 5/5

Purpose: to analyze why and how the explosion in American life has occurred and the loneliness it has led to 5/5

THEME

Main idea (a complete sentence): Life in America has exploded, freeing people for alternatives, and loneliness is one main ingredient of the outcome. 10/10

Major supporting ideas (at least five sentences):

Mobility has a great deal to do with the erosion of American life. People are lonely today because of the psychological load they carry. The strange way that American society alienates the closest of friends is a main factor in loneliness. Another important effect of isolation is the pressure it places on the institution of marriage by forcing husband and wife to satisfy all of each other's needs. Finally, in the great rush for freedom and possibilities, Americans have lost the ability to be free together. 30/30

STYLE

Diction: Five quotations: "America divides into its component parts like white light going through a prism." "anti-human life-styles" "traumatic loneliness" "This communal apathy is also fertile soil for crime. . . ." "Life becomes a bit like playing the stock market in a time of recession. . . ." "psychological baggage"

Diction: General conclusions (see diction chart): figurative, connotative, abstract 15/15

Tone (see tone chart): aggressive, argumentative, satiric 5/5

Sentence structure (three sentences **labeled** and underlined twice for grammatical patterns; see Sentence Structures section in Handbook):

noun clause as subject	1. "*What began as a great adventure* may be turning into just another fetter."
adjective verbal phrase	2. "*Standing alone,* they do not feel lonely."
items in a series and appositive phrase	3. "Knowing no limits of *class, race, or age,* loneliness is today a great leveler, *a new American tradition.*"

15/15

VALUE (at least 4 sentences):

1. Personal: The essay is informative because it made me aware of how much loneliness affects everybody, not just the unsuccessful or the elderly. I also enjoyed the author's figurative style which included very apt similes, metaphors, and analogies.

2. Objective: Gordon's thesis is relevant because loneliness is felt by almost everyone and because the functioning of society itself is adversely affected by it. Her suggestions for dealing with this problem are not specific; she only indicates that the answer lies in social and political action. 15/15

Gordon, Suzanne. "The Geography of Loneliness." Lonely in America. New York: Simon, 1976. 15-22.

OUTLINE REPORT

Name: ____ Score: __________

Author: ____

Title: ____

Expository type: ____

Subject matter: ____

Audience: ____ $\overline{5}$

Purpose: ____

____ $\overline{5}$

THEME

Main idea (a complete sentence): ____

____

____

____ $\overline{10}$

Major supporting ideas (at least five sentences):

____

____

____

____

____

____

____

____

____

____

____ $\overline{30}$

STYLE

Diction: Fivc quotations: ____

____

____

____

____

____

Diction: General conclusions (see diction chart): ______________________________ /15

____

Tone (see tone chart): ______________________________ /5

Sentence structure (three sentences **labeled** and underlined for different grammatical patterns; see Sentence Structures section in Chapter 16):

Type

[ ] 1. ______________________________

____

____

[ ] 2. ______________________________

____

____

[ ] 3. ______________________________

____

____

______________________________ /15

VALUE (at least four sentences):

Personal: ______________________________

____

____

____

____

____

Objective: ______________________________

____

____

____

____

______________________________ /15

____

Bibliographical information

OUTLINE REPORT

Name: ______________________________ Score: __________

Author: ______________________________

Title: ______________________________

Expository type: ______________________________

Subject matter: ______________________________

Audience: ______________________________ 5

Purpose: ______________________________

______________________________ 5

THEME

Main idea (a complete sentence): ______________________________

____

____

______________________________ 10

Major supporting ideas (at least five sentences):

____

____

____

____

____

____

____

____

____

____

______________________________ 30

STYLE

Diction: Five quotations: ______________________________

____

____

____

____

Diction: General conclusions (see diction chart): ______ 15

______

Tone (see tone chart): ______ 5

Sentence structure (three sentences **labeled** and underlined for different grammatical patterns; see Sentence Structures section in Chapter 16):

Type

1. ______

2. ______

3. ______ 15

VALUE (at least four sentences):

Personal: ______

Objective: ______ 15

______

Bibliographical information

THE ANALYTICAL ESSAY

An analytical essay criticizes and evaluates any work of fiction or nonfiction. In a nonfiction analysis, the separate elements of theme, style, and value are discussed. The length of the analytical essay can vary from 500 to 1,000 words, depending on the length of the original work and the wishes of the instructor. The expository form used is the functional analysis. (See the organizational pattern for functional analysis in Chapter 8.)

The analytical essay requires skill in the critical reading process and the formulating of conclusions about the work. It also requires you to support those conclusions with evidence, such as quotations, illustrations, and explanations, drawn from the original work. You must properly cite all direct quotations from the work. (Refer to Chapter 15 for a full discussion of correct documentation.)

Steps in Writing the Analytical Essay

1. Read the work carefully and attentively to get a clear idea of the author's purpose.
2. Make sure to know the meaning of all words and allusions. Take notes on the book's theme, style, and value.
3. Complete the worksheet for the analytical essay.

   Fill in the complete bibliographical information in proper form, which is given in the nonfiction prose chart.

   Write an imaginative title. Do not use just the title of the work being analyzed.

   Complete the introductory information, which includes subject matter, purpose, and a brief summary of contents. Note that the thesis statement and subtopic sentence have already been entered on the worksheet.

   Analyze the **theme:**

      Note that the topic sentence has been entered.

      State the main idea of the work and five to eight major supporting ideas **with examples, illustrations, and quotations.**

      Identify the nature of the examples and the conclusion of the work, **with supporting evidence.**

   Analyze and evaluate the **style:**

      Note that the topic sentence has been entered on the worksheet.

      Identify the apparatus or lack of it in the work.

      Select five to eight quotations that best illustrate the work's language. Using the diction chart and these quotations, state a general conclusion about the work's diction.

      Using the tone chart and the conclusion about diction, state a general conclusion about the work's tone.

      Refer to the Sentence Structures section in Chapter 16, and select a few examples to show the variation in sentence structure.

   Analyze and evaluate the **value:**

      Note that the topic sentence has been entered on the worksheet.

      Formulate and write personal reactions to the work, referring to new information, reassessment of attitudes, and practical ideas.

      Formulate and write objective judgments of the work, referring to the relevance of the ideas, the practicality of the solutions, and the durability of the ideas.

   Complete the concluding information:

      Write a well-phrased summary of the work's main idea.

      Recommend the work to a particular audience.

Make a general conclusion about whether or not the work fulfills its purpose.

Where appropriate, include a statement designed to make the reader think about or act upon the problem suggested by the work.

4. Using the worksheet, write a coherent essay. At the bottom of the last page of the essay, give the complete bibliographical information. Quotations need smooth, artful lead-ins so do not merely string together short statements for the sections outlined above. For complete information on how to include quotations in an essay, see the quotation section of the term paper chapter.

STUDENT SAMPLE—Analytical Essay (Book)

Study this sample essay so that you can better understand the elements included in a book analysis. Then use the essay as a guide in writing your own analysis. Note how to include both short and long quotations with page notations, how to break the long discussion of each subtopic (theme, style, and value) into a few paragraphs, and how to cite the bibliographical information.

Believing in _The True Believer_

The True Believer, a book in social philosophy, presents Eric Hoffer's theories about mass movements. Hoffer concentrates on the characteristics common to all such fanatical groups. In addition, the book deals with the psychological aspects of the people who devote their faith and energy to various mass movements. Hoffer's purpose is to inform readers about his personal theory of group actions and subtly to change public attitudes about them. To develop his theories, he uses anecdotes of mass movements and their supporters from early Christianity to modern Communism. He also identifies the range of movements and cites their common peculiarities. Hoffer includes religious, social, and nationalistic organizations in his theories. An analysis of this book includes three major elements: theme, style, and value.

To begin, the book's theme is effectively developed. The author's thesis is expressed clearly in his Preface: "All movements however different in doctrine and aspiration draw their early adherents from the same types of humanity; they all appeal to the same types of mind." Hoffer first describes and explains the appeal of mass movements. The elements of this appeal are twofold: people's desire for change because of frustration and discontent and a leader's ability to instill hope, arouse enthusiasm, and manipulate power. Next, Hoffer identifies the people who join such causes.

> Though the disaffected are found in all walks of life, they are most frequent in the following categories: the poor, misfits, outcasts, minorities, adolescent youth, the ambitious (whether facing insurmountable obstacles or unlimited opportunities), those in the grip of some vice or obsession, the impotent (in body or mind), the inordinately selfish, the bored, and the sinners. (30)

He then discusses each group in detail. For example, the permanent misfits are "those who because of a lack of talent or some irreparable defect in body or mind cannot do the one thing for which their whole being craves" (50).

After he discusses the people who participate in causes, Hoffer tells why these individuals are willing to sacrifice themselves. Their reasons include sacrificing individual identity to become part of a group, participating in make-believe in order to be able to kill or die when necessary, and giving up the past and present for the sake of a different future. Then Hoffer considers all the "unifying agents" which make the individual become completely a part of the mass movement. "Hatred is the most accessible and comprehensive of all unifying agents. It pulls and whirls the individual away from his own self. . . . He becomes an anonymous particle quivering with a craving to fuse and coalesce with his like into one flaming mass" (86). Other agents are obedience and uniformity and persuasion and coercion. Thus, "the chief preoccupation [of mass movements] is to foster, perfect, and perpetuate a facility for united action and self-sacrifice" (57).

Hoffer next points out that mass movements do not usually begin until those people presently in power have been discredited. This work is done by "men of words with a grievance" (119) who undermine the existing institutions and give the masses the idea of change. Then the fanatics capitalize on the unhappiness caused by "the men of words," move them and their theories aside, and begin the action of the movement. At this point, chaos and violence erupt, and the old order disintegrates. Finally, Hoffer shows that since the fanatics breed dissension, it is necessary to put them aside so that the practical men can save the movement. To sum up, "A movement is pioneered by men of words, materialized by fanatics, and consolidated by men of action" (134). Hoffer draws his examples from all kinds of causes including Christianity, Islam, Nazism, Zionism, and Communism and uses anecdotes from events in history, like the American Civil War. Through the book he seems negative about the nature of mass movements but concludes that fanaticism is necessary in order to change and improve society. Therefore, while some of these movements have been destructive, others in fact have been good. Hoffer has successfully presented his theme about the appeal of mass movements by analyzing in great detail their inner workings.

The style, another element of The True Believer, is appropriate. The book's apparatus includes a useful table of contents, a preface which gives the book's scope and limitations, and a listing of reference notes at the end of the book. Hoffer's diction is abstract because of the philosophical nature of the subject. However, he uses connotative and figurative language to visualize many of these ideas. The following passage is an example. "We have seen that the acrid secretion of the frustrated mind . . . acts yet as a marvelous slime to cement the embittered and disaffected into one compact whole" (114). His metaphor for events is effective: "The game of history is usually played by the best and the worst over the heads of the majority in the middle" (29). He describes actions figuratively; for example, "When the moment is ripe, only the fanatic can hatch a genuine mass movement" (130). Another aspect of the book's diction is its use of technical terms and jargon along with definitions to make the theories more understandable. For example, he uses such expressions as "religiofication" (151), "prevailing dispensation" (150), "byzantism, barbarism and ignorance of a Bolshevik bureaucracy" (105), and "xenophobia" (90).

As a result of this diction, Hoffer's tone is argumentative and serious. His sentence structure is varied, medium in length, and complex: "It is doubtful whether any gesture of good will or any concession from our side will reduce the volume and vemon of vilification against us emanating from the Kremlin" (86). This one sentence illustrates alliteration, a verbal phrase, a dependent clause, and compound objects. Thus, Hoffer's style is especially figurative and polished, making this difficult subject more readable.

In addition, The True Believer has value. First, I gathered a great deal of new information about the relationship of mass movements to events in history, past and present. More valuable was reassessing my negative attitudes about fanatics by becoming aware that these people can bring about worthwhile actions. Viewing this information from a new perspective, I even realized that I am unwittingly a member of a mass movement.

More generally, this book is valuable because its theories can be applied to actual situations, now and in the future. After reading this book it is easier to understand, for instance, how revolutions come about. It should be noted, however, that Hoffer did not intend to pass judgments or express preferences. His explanations "are in the nature of suggestions and arguments" (Preface) rather than concrete advice. No specific solutions are provided in the book; however, there are implications worth considering. For example, Hoffer's assumption is that "The less justified a man is in claiming excellence for his own self, the more ready is he to claim all excellence for his nation, his religion, his race or his holy cause" (23). Such an idea suggests that if they place less emphasis on these attitudes, people can concentrate more fully on their own self-esteem and self-confidence. Since there will always be dissatisfied people, some of whom succeed in creating tremendous change, this book will always offer valuable insights.

In conclusion, Hoffer's main idea is that mass movements are an essential part of human life and should be understood by all. This book would appeal to sophisticated, intelligent students of human nature who wish a deeper insight into influences that motivate people and into reasons for the current popularity of cults. Certainly, Hoffer succeeds in educating readers about his subject. It is amazing, unsettling, and worthwhile when people are encouraged to stop and think about themselves and others to determine whether or not they can be labeled fanatical. It is clear that almost everyone belongs to one of these groups, but not everyone is a fanatic.

Hoffer, Eric. The True Believer. New York: Harper, 1951.

WORKSHEET FOR SHORT ANALYTICAL ESSAY

1. Select an essay from an anthology, a newspaper, or a magazine or select a nonfiction book and complete preliminary plans.
2. Note the completed thesis statement and subtopics plus the topic sentences for the body paragraphs.
3. Complete the worksheet **before** writing the essay.
4. Attach the worksheet to the finished essay.
5. Attach the short Analytical Essay Cover Sheet to the finished essay.

Bibliographical information in proper form: ______________________________

____

TITLE: ______________________________

¶1: Introduction (five sentences)

Author and title of work: ______________________________

Subject matter: ______________________________

Purpose: ______________________________

____

Summary of contents (brief): ______________________________

____

____

____

____

Thesis statement and subtopics:

An analysis of this work includes three major elements: theme, style, and value.

Body (three paragraphs)

¶2: Theme (topic sentence): To begin, the book's theme is/is not effectively developed.

Main idea of work: ______________________________

____

____

At least five major supporting ideas with examples, illustrations, quotations:

____

____

____

____

Nature of examples:

Book's conclusions:

General conclusion about theme:

¶3: Style (topic sentence): `The style, another element of Title of Book, is/is not appropriate.`

Apparatus:

Diction: Examples

General conclusions (see diction chart) ______

Tone (see tone chart): ______

Sentence structure variation with examples (see Sentence Structures section in Chapter 16):

General conclusion about style: ______

¶4: Value (topic sentence): `In addition, the work has/lacks value.`

Personal reaction: ______

Objective judgment: ______

General conclusion about value: ______

¶5: Conclusion (three sentences)

Summary of work's main idea: ______

Recommendation-audience: ______

Fulfillment of work's purpose: ______

Name: ______________________

Date: ______________ Class: ______________

Type of Nonfiction Prose: ______________________

SHORT ANALYTICAL ESSAY COVER SHEET		
Structure/Ideas	+	______
Usage/Mechanics	−	______
Total		______
Rewrite points	+	______
TOTAL		______

Structure and Ideas (100 points)	**Original**	**Rewrite**
INTRODUCTION: five sentences		
essay title, author, title of work, subject matter, purpose, summary	10______	______
thesis statement + subtopics (copied from worksheet)	XXXX	XXXX
BODY: three paragraphs		
Theme topic sentence (copied from worksheet); main idea and five major supporting ideas; examples, conclusions, all with evidence from work	30______	______
Style topic sentence (copied from worksheet); apparatus, diction, tone, sentence structure, all with evidence from work	20______	______
Value topic sentence (copied from worksheet); personal reaction; objective judgment	10______	______
CONCLUSION: three sentences		
summary of work's main idea; general conclusion about work; recommendation-audience	5______	______
ESSAY:		
logical order of ideas and correct reasoning	5______	______
effective style = tone + diction + sentence structure + coherence	10______	______
evidence: six quotations	10______	______
TOTAL	100______	+ ______

Usage and Mechanics (minus points). See Correction Symbol Chart.

You **may** earn these points in revision:		
Usage: adj; adv; agr; awk; col; dm; frag; mm; ref; rep; shift; verb; ww; / /; ¶	−3 ea. ______	______
You **may not** earn these points in revision, but you must correct the errors:		
Mechanics: abbr; apos; cap; lc; p; ro; sp; ∧; bibliographic form	−1 ea. ______	______
Total	− ______	+ ______

WORKSHEET FOR LONG ANALYTICAL ESSAY

1. Select an essay from an anthology, a newspaper, or a magazine or select a nonfiction book and complete preliminary plans.
2. Note the completed thesis statement and subtopics plus the topic sentences for the body paragraphs.
3. Complete the worksheet **before** writing the essay.
4. Attach the worksheet to the finished essay.
5. Attach the long Analytical Essay Cover Sheet to the finished essay.

Bibliographical information in proper form:

TITLE:

¶: Introduction (eight sentences)

Author and title of work:

Subject matter:

Purpose:

Summary of contents (brief):

Thesis statement and subtopics:

An analysis of this work includes three major elements: theme, style, and value.

Body (three major sections—multiple paragraphs)

¶: Theme (topic sentence): To begin, the book's theme is/is not effectively developed.

Main idea of work:

At least eight major supporting ideas with examples, illustrations, quotations:

Nature of examples:

Book's conclusions:

General conclusion about theme:

¶: Style (topic sentence): The style, another element of Title of Book, is/is not appropriate.

Apparatus:

Diction: Examples

General conclusions (see diction chart) ______

Tone (see tone chart): ______

Sentence structure variation with examples (see Sentence Structures section in Chapter 16):

General conclusion about style: ______

¶: Value (topic sentence): `In addition, the work has/lacks value.`

Personal reaction: ______

Objective judgment: ______

General conclusion about value: ______

¶: Conclusion (five sentences)

Summary of work's main idea: ______

Recommendation-audience: ______

Fulfillment of work's purpose: ______

Name: ____________________

Date: ____________ Class: ____________

Type of Nonfiction Prose: ____________

LONG ANALYTICAL ESSAY COVER SHEET		
Structure/Ideas	+	______
Usage/Mechanics	−	______
Total		______
Rewrite points	+	______
TOTAL		______

Structure and Ideas (200 points)	Original	Rewrite
INTRODUCTION: eight sentences		
essay title, author, title of work, subject matter, purpose, summary	25______	______
thesis statement + subtopics (copied from worksheet)	XXXX	XXXX
BODY: three major sections—multiple paragraphs		
Theme topic sentence (copied from worksheet); main idea and eight major supporting ideas; examples, conclusions, all with evidence from work	60______	______
Style topic sentence (copied from worksheet); apparatus, diction, tone, sentence structure, all with evidence from work	40______	______
Value topic sentence (copied from worksheet); personal reaction; objective judgment	20______	______
CONCLUSION: five sentences		
Summary of work's main idea; general conclusion about work; recommendation-audience	10______	______
ESSAY:		
logical order of ideas and correct reasoning	10______	______
effective style = tone + diction + sentence structure + coherence	15______	______
evidence: ten quotations	20______	______
Total	200______	+ ______

Usage and Mechanics (minus points). See Correction Symbol Chart.		
You **may** earn these points in revision:		
Usage: adj; adv; agr; awk; col; dm; frag; mm; ref; rep; shift; verb; ww; / /; ¶	−3 ea. ______	______
You **may not** earn these points in revision, but you must correct the errors:		
Mechanics: abbr; apos; cap; lc; p; ro; sp; ∧; bibliographic form	−1 ea. ______	______
Total	− ______	+ ______

CHAPTER 15

The Term Paper

A term paper (also called a research or library paper) is a formal, well-documented composition of at least 1,500 words, exclusive of quotations, that is based heavily on outside readings. There are two types of term papers. In one type the writer summarizes and organizes information from a particular perspective or point of interest, in which case the paper contains a **statement of purpose.** For example, "The purpose of this paper is to trace the evolution of the stage and play house from antiquity to the modern age." In the other type the writer answers a question or formulates an attitude or opinion that the paper presents and supports, in which case it contains a **thesis statement.** For example, "Changing the presidential term of office from two four-year periods to one six-year term would be advantageous to the country."

The term paper includes the following parts:

Title page
Outline
Text with parenthetical citations
Works cited (includes bibliography)

In addition to prompting you to acquire new information on a subject of interest, writing a term paper gives you a chance to develop skills that you can use later in preparing reports, memoranda, speeches, articles, and other practical writing tasks. These skills include using the library to gather information, taking effective notes, developing critical judgment in evaluating the reliability and appropriateness of material to a main idea, organizing ideas, writing a long composition, and using correct manuscript style to document sources.

Time Schedule Chart for Term Paper

By following this schedule, you will be able to arrange your research and writing activities over a five-week period.

Week 1 Search	Select subject; prepare preliminary list of works cited; do general reading; form working statement of purpose or thesis statement; fill in prospectus.
Weeks 2–3 Research	Read books, periodicals, and other sources of information; start note taking; determine subtopics; begin working outline; complete note taking.
Week 4 Writing	Write final statement of purpose or thesis statement; complete outline; strengthen or eliminate weak sections; write first draft; mark quotations and parenthetical citations.
Week 5 Rewriting	Verify all facts, quotations, and sources; revise for structure, ideas, logic, and style; revise and correct mechanics and usage.

Search

Begin by selecting a subject, possibly from the list included in this chapter, that has aroused your curiosity and interest but is unfamiliar to you. As a result, you will have the opportunity to acquire new knowledge. Then check the card catalogue, magazine indexes, and reference books in the library, and prepare a preliminary list of sources with bibliographical data on index cards of between 12 and 15 sources on the subject selected. The purpose of this step is to make sure that there is enough material available on the subject in accessible libraries. Place each entry on a separate card for later ease in handling citations and sources. Include all necessary information: author(s), title, and publication data. (Refer to the Works Cited section for complete details.) Only some of these sources will be suitable for the writing of the paper.

Reference Materials

To help you search for information on your subject, consult this list of readily available indexes and guides.

Biographical Dictionaries

Biography Index, 1946–present
Dictionary of American Biography, 1944–present
Who's Who in America 1899–present

Booklists

Books in Print, 1948–present. Author and title.
Paperbound Books in Print, 1955––present.
Subject Guide to Books in Print. Subjects.

Indexes

Book Review Digest, 1905–present. Summarizes reviews of books.
New York Times Index, 1851–present. Subject index alphabetically.
Reader's Guide to Periodical Literature, 1900–present. Author and subject index for general interest articles.

Pamphlets and Government Publications

The U.S. government, other government agencies, private corporations, and nonprofit institutions publish information on many subjects.

Quotations

Familiar Quotations, John Bartlett, 15th ed., 1980
Dictionary of Quotations, Bergen Evans, 1968
The Home Book of Quotations, Classical and Modern, 10th ed., 1967

Other Sources of Information

atlases, yearbooks, and almanacs
dictionaries (see Chapter 1 for more information)
abstracts
bibliographies
encyclopedias (general and specialized)
MLA (Modern Language Association) Handbook for Writers of Research Papers, 2nd ed., 1984

Next, do some general reading in the library in order to limit the subject to a manageable size for the length of your assignment. Remember that the narrowing process may come at any stage of the research and even during the writing of the rough draft. If you can, check out your sources. The books, periodicals, pamphlets, magazines, and newspapers that cannot be checked out must be used in the library.

When you consult a book, start with the table of contents, and see if there is anything pertinent to your subject. Turn only to those chapters where you are likely to find material. Also check in the preface, introduction, conclusion and index to see which way the author is heading. When you have found the part of the book where there is good potential, start skimming (reading first sentences of paragraphs and looking for key words) until you find something worthwhile.

When you need a newspaper or magazine, note that the main ideas are usually presented in the beginning paragraphs. If you find large sections in any sources which you wish to take home, photocopy the pages. After you have done some preliminary reading, you will be able to form a working statement of purpose or thesis statement. You will modify and refine this statement as your research continues. Last, fill in the prospectus sheet at the end of the chapter and get instructor approval **before** continuing. This form is a preliminary statement of the main idea and a listing of possible sources. The prospectus provides for eight sources narrowed down from your tentative list of 12 to 15 items.

Research

Read the books, periodicals, pamphlets, and newspapers that are listed on your prospectus sheet as well as any new sources that are appropriate. Primary sources are original works, documents, and first-hand information on the subject. Secondary sources are reports or analyses of original documents and are more readily available than primary sources.

Another source of information is the **interview** of a person with expert knowledge of your subject. Three stages are involved in a successful interview.

Stage 1: **Preparation**

Read about the subject matter. Outline questions to ask. Select the person to be interviewed and telephone for an appointment. Never appear without an appointment. Familiarize yourself with the person's background in your subject. Such information may include the person's position, education, success, areas of expertise, published material.

Stage 2: **Interview**

Arrive shortly before the appointment and review your questions. Politely ask permission to take notes or use a tape recorder. Remember, however, that extensive note taking during an interview is usually distracting. Ask for permission to quote the interviewee. Begin by asking direct questions that relate to the subject. If the conversation begins to shift to other matters, bring it back to the subject by asking specific, relevant questions. Once the interview is progressing smoothly, do not monopolize the discussion. Instead, listen patiently, attentively, and courteously. Note important or significant items—dates, facts, figures, places, names. Ask for any available printed material pertaining to your subject. Save the most difficult questions for last. Do not go over your alloted time. Limit the interview to avoid overstaying your welcome.

Stage 3: **Post-Interview**

As soon as you are alone, make extensive notes. These will form the basis for what you will later include in your paper. Send a short note to the interviewee, thanking him or her for assistance. If you need to check the accuracy of facts, figures, or quotations, telephone the interviewee for verification. Document in your citations and list of works cited any of the material from the interview that you include in your paper.

As you continue your research, take notes on the readings. Because you cannot discuss your subject in its entirety, select several different aspects to develop. Refer to the "Questioning" techniques in Chapter 1 for different approaches to your topic. Do **not** limit your paper to only one aspect. Such possibilities include the following: problems, causes, effects, solutions, types, and benefits. Refer to the Controlling Idea Chart in Chapter 4 for more aspects. For ease of handling and arranging, use index cards. Limit the information to one idea, subdivision, or quotation per card. Be sure each card contains the aspect, a specific heading, the source, the page number, and the idea or quotation. Copying machines are useful but do not take the place of index cards which identify the references to the copied material.

If you copy three or more consecutive words from a source, put them in quotation marks; otherwise, you are plagiarizing, that is, committing literary theft. Another kind of plagiarism is paraphrasing someone else's original ideas or distinctive conclusions and presenting them without citations. A **paraphrase** is a rewording of information giving the meaning in another form but in about the same number of words. When this material is available from several different sources, it is not cited because it is considered general knowledge.

Card with direct quotation from text:

> TYPE
>
> Tudor stage— Whiting, p. 35
>
> "The Tudor Period combined the best features of the Middle Ages (its scope, imagination, homely realism, and hearty laughter) and the Renaissance (its classic form, sense of order, skillful plots, brilliant word play, and deft solution)."

Card with general idea taken from text:

> EVENT
>
> Campaign for re-election - Bowles, p. 12, lines 3-13
>
> As soon as elected first time, starts to campaign again. (Cites 5 specific examples of earlier presidents.)

During the research process, modify and refine the paper's main idea and determine your subtopics. When you think you have completed your note taking, sort your index cards by aspects. Then re-sort each aspect by specific headings. Put each set of cards into a logical sequence. From this sequence develop a preliminary outline. This outline is a guide for further note taking because it shows where more information may be needed or where there are logical gaps. If so, continue your research and complete the note taking.

Writing

Now that your research is concluded, write the final statement of purpose or thesis statement. This statement reflects your general conclusion from the completed research. Finish the outline, using the sorted index cards and the preliminary outline. The more detailed the outline, the easier it will be to write the paper and the better the paper will be. During this stage, strengthen or eliminate weak sections in the outline. Make sure that there are sufficient supporting details for each subtopic. Each category must contain at least two smaller items. Check for inconsistencies and overlapping of ideas. The outline may need minor changes during the writing of the paper. In its finished form the outline is usually submitted as part of the term paper. It reflects the final version of the paper.

Now write the first draft quickly, using the outline and the index cards. If you have trouble writing the introduction, skip over it at this point to focus on the larger ideas and how they relate to each other logically. Do not worry yet about mechanics or specific vocabulary choices. Quote whatever supporting material is appropriate by copying the information directly from the index cards and using quotation marks. Write the introduction and conclusion. The introduction should catch the reader's interest, clearly state the purpose or thesis of the paper, and indicate the direction the discussion will take. The conclusion should show the implications and significance of the purpose or thesis.

On the first draft informally in parentheses at the end of each quote, identify the author, the source cited, and the page or pages quoted. During the writing of the final draft, delete any repetitious information from the parentheses.

Rewriting

As you revise your rough draft, verify all facts, quotations, and sources. Lead into quotations smoothly. One way is to include the name of the author and some indication of his or her authority or profession. Use only quotations that contain necessary information or are effectively phrased. Do not string together long quotations or an excessive number of quotations. Check that the parenthetical citations are complete and accurate. (Refer to Documentation Guidelines later in the chapter for the proper forms.)

Then revise for structure, ideas, logic, and style. Look for logical progression, logical errors, ambiguities, too broad assumptions, and smoothness of transition. Now revise and correct mechanics and usage. (Refer to Chapter 16 for correction of mechanics and usage mistakes; check a dictionary and thesaurus for spelling and vocabulary.) Compile the list of the works cited. (Refer to the Documentation Guidelines section for the proper forms.)

Type the final draft of the paper, including a title page. (Refer to the Documentation Guidelines section for technical details.) Make a copy of the entire finished paper for your personal record. Reread the paper 24 hours after you type it to catch any previously overlooked errors or flaws.

SUGGESTED TOPICS FOR TERM PAPER

Select one of the following or similar topics that arouse your curiosity and interest and that you would like to know more about. Refer to "Questioning" in Chapter 1 for aspects.

adopted children's rights
affirmative action
aging population
air traffic control
airline safety
airplane hijackers
alcoholism
alternative sources of energy
animal shelters
anti-Semitism
apartheid
Arab oil
artificial sweeteners
aspirin
atomic bomb testing
automobile insurance rates
automobile safety devices
automobile theft

beauty contests
bilingual education
biofeedback training
biological warfare
biorhythms

cable television
capital punishment
child abuse
child care for working mothers
child custody for fathers
cholesterol and heart disease
civil disobedience
cloning
college sports corruption
computer crime
condominium conversion
consumer protection
contact lenses
corporal punishment
cosmetic surgery
cures for the common cold

DMSO (for arthritis)
dangers of radiation
defense budget
deregulation of the airlines
dieting
disarmament

divorce laws
draft
drugs in the Armed Forces
drunk drivers

earthquakes
effect of computers on society
electrical power shortages
endangered species
energy crisis
energy vs. environment
equal rights amendment
euthanasia

55-mile speed limit
film rating system
flexible working hours
fluoridation of water
food additives
fuel costs
funerals

gasoline controls (or rationing)
genetic engineering
grade inflation
guaranteed income
gun control

hair transplants
health foods
health insurance
holistic medicine
hospices for the dying

income tax structure
inflation
invasion of privacy
IQ tests

job safety
jogging
joint custody of children

Laetrile
legalization of drinking at 18
lottery

mammograms
mandatory retirement laws
mass transportation
megavitamin therapy
methadone treatment for heroin
midwifery
migrant workers
minimum wage for teenagers

national identity cards
national initiative
natural childbirth
Nazism in the U.S.
no-fault insurance
noise pollution
nonsmokers' rights
nuclear power plants
nuclear waste

ocean pollution
offshore drilling
oil spills
Olympic games
OPEC
organ transplants

pay TV
pesticides
prisons
processed foods
public financing of elections

recycling of waste
refugee problem
relevance of the college curriculum
right to die
rights of animals
rights of children
rights of handicapped
rights of students

single parent adoptions
Social Security system
solar energy
space exploration
strip coal mining
sugar in the American diet
suicide
supersonic airplanes
synthetic fuels

teenage drinking
television and children
television news
terrorism
tranquilizers
transcendental meditation

vegetarianism
violence in sports
violence in the schools
violence on TV
vitamins
volunteer army

voucher system for schools
wiretapping
women athletes on men's teams
year-round school sessions

DOCUMENTATION GUIDELINES

These guidelines are generally accepted ways of preparing researched material for course submission. They refer primarily to the correct forms for quotations, typing, works cited, and parenthetical citations. Examples are given of all important forms. These are the technical elements of the term paper which should be mastered. Careful attention to detail is necessary. However, your instructor may require minor variations which you should follow. The specific rules outlined in this section follow the guidelines described in the *MLA Handbook for Writers of Research Papers, 2nd ed., 1984.*

Quotations

Be sure to copy the excerpt accurately. Make a note of the material copied from any source. Avoid plagiarism by putting into quotations three or more consecutive words copied from a source. However, limit the number and length of quotations to those that are especially appropriate and well-phrased. Usually a quote should illustrate or support a point that you make in your own words. Too many quotations strung together are tiresome. They suggest your lack of understanding of the material. Include in the body of the paragraph and enclose within double quotation marks all quotes shorter than four typewritten lines. Indent 10 spaces only from the left margin and double space, without quotation marks, all quotes longer than four lines. End with a parenthetical citation.

Use three ellipsis periods for words omitted from a quoted passage, but do not begin a quotation with an ellipsis. Instead, use an introductory phrase before the ellipsis. Use four periods if the omission occurs at the end of a sentence. (The fourth dot is actually a period.) Use single quotation marks for quotations within quotations. Use these quotes within quotes sparingly. Instead, give the name of the person making the original statement, and include in the documentation that this information is being quoted indirectly from a secondary source. Enclose in square brackets [], not parentheses, your own comments, explanations, or additions for grammatical correctness. Insert these brackets by hand.

Include a parenthetical citation for every direct quotation and for important facts and opinions that you draw from the work of others and paraphrase even though they are not directly quoted. Otherwise, you are plagiarizing unless this material is available from several sources and is considered general knowledge.

Typing Format

Using black ribbon, type on 8½″ × 11″ medium-weight paper. Double-space the entire paper and fasten securely together in the top left-hand corner the following items in this sequence:

Term Paper Cover Sheet from this textbook
Title page
Outline
Text with parenthetical citations
Works Cited
Prospectus from this textbook

Title page

Center the title of the paper 3 inches from the top of the page.
Follow the rules for capitalization. (See Chapter 16.)
Underline or set off in quotation marks only those words in the title drawn from another source.
Center your name 5 inches from the top directly under the word *by*.
Center the name of your teacher and class and the date on separate lines, with the date line 3 inches from the bottom of the page.

Outline

Center the word *Outline* 2 inches from the top of the page.

Drop down 4 spaces and type your statement of purpose or thesis statement.

Using Roman numbers, capital letters, and regular numbers, double space the outline. Each category must include at least two items.

Numbering pages of the outline is not necessary.

If your instructor does not require a formal outline to be included with your research paper, then the separate title page may also be omitted. In that case, the first page of the paper contains the same information given on the title page in the following format:

Drop down 1 inch from the top of the page. Indent 5 spaces from the left side of this page and type your name.

Double-space the name of your teacher, the class, and the date on separate lines.

Text

Center the title of the paper 2 inches from the top of the page, if an outline is required.

Drop down 4 spaces and begin the text, indenting the first paragraph and all succeeding paragraphs 5 spaces.

If a folder is required, leave a 1½ inch margin on the left side of each page. Otherwise, use a 1 inch margin on the left, right, and bottom of each page. On all pages except the first, also leave a 1 inch margin at the top.

Number every page of the text throughout the paper in the upper right-hand corner, ½ inch from the top. Do not place any marks around the page number. Beginning with page 1, type your last name before the page number in order to avoid missing or incorrectly ordered pages. Follow this procedure beginning with page 2 if you do not have a title page.

Insert diagrams, tables, charts, graphs, illustrations, pictures, maps, or other visual materials as close as possible to the section of the text being illustrated.

Document all quoted and certain paraphrased material.

Works Cited

You have probably been used to the traditional method of giving credit to your sources of information. This format included a bibliography which refers only to printed materials. Since many sources today are drawn from other media, such as films, television programs, recordings, and personal interviews, this term is no longer appropriate and has been replaced by the more inclusive label **Works Cited.** All sources quoted or otherwise used in the research paper must appear in this section as the last page(s) of the paper.

Directions for Works Cited

Continue the page numbers of the text for this list. Drop down ½ inch from the top right-hand corner of the page, including your last name and the page number (e.g. Smith 13).

Center the words *Works Cited* 1 inch from the top of the page. Double space the entire list of works between and within each entry.

Begin each entry at the left-hand margin and indent all succeeding lines in the same entry 5 spaces. Do not number entries.

Arrange entries in alphabetical order, according to the author's last name. Alphabetize according to the first important word of the title if the author's name is not given.

Entry Format

Entries in the list of *Works Cited* may be either **printed material** or **nonprint media.** If you use photographically reproduced material (microfilm) drawn from books or periodicals, cite the source as if you read it in its original form. The guidelines that follow cover most of the situations you will meet in documenting your sources. However, certain disciplines have established their own conventions.

I. **Printed Material**

A printed source contains the following three basic items—author, title, and publication information. Sometimes other data are also necessary. A period and 2 spaces separate each item in an entry. Included as printed material are books, encyclopedias, and pamphlets and also magazines, periodicals, and newspapers. Since reviews present additional requirements, they are discussed at the end of this section. The conventions for each category are presented separately.

A. **Books, encyclopedias, and pamphlets**

Include in the following order every item of information that applies to each particular source. Observe and follow carefully the samples that illustrate these general rules.

1. **Author's name** in reverse order, separated by a comma and followed by a period and two spaces. Use the author's name exactly as it appears on the title page. With multiple authors, reverse only the name of the first author given, and separate each author's name with commas. When listing multiple works by the same author, cite the name in the first entry only. For subsequent entries, type three hyphens and a period, skip two spaces, and give the title. The author's works are listed alphabetically by title.
2. **Title of part of the book,** such as the title of an encyclopedia article or anthology selection, usually enclosed in quotation marks and punctuated with a period inside the end quotation mark. For a complete listing of work titles placed in quotes, refer to Chapter 16 under **quotation marks.** Capitalize the first letter of the first word and the first letters of the major words of the title.
3. **Title of the book,** including any subtitle, continuously underlined (in handwritten or typewritten papers) or italicized (in printed works). For a complete listing of work titles to be underlined, refer to Chapter 16 under **underlining.** End the unit with a period (not underlined) and two spaces.
4. **Name of the editor** must be cited if it appears on the source's title page. Precede the name with the capitalized abbreviation *Ed.* and follow with a period.
5. **Edition used** is identified on the title page by a number (e.g. 2nd ed., 3rd ed.) followed by a period.
6. **Numbers of volumes** includes the complete number in a set and is followed by the abbreviation **vols.**
7. **Place of publication, name of publisher, and date of publication** appear on the title and copyright pages. Use a colon and space after the city of publication, a comma after a shortened form of the publisher's name, and a period after the latest publishing date if it is a new or revised edition or after the original publication date if it is only a reprinting. If several cities are listed, name only the first one. If the city is generally unfamiliar, include the state or country.
8. **Page numbers** are given only for shorter pieces that appear within longer works. Then cite, without using the word or abbreviation for *page(s),* the page numbers of the entire piece, not just of the material used. End the entry with a period.

Sample Entries for Books, Encyclopedias, Pamphlets in *Works Cited*

One author

Flammonde, Paris. The Mystic Healers. New York: Stein, 1974.

Multiple authors

Butler, Robert N., and Myrna I. Lewis. Gerontological Psychology. 2nd ed. Springfield, IL: Thomas, 1972.

Work in an anthology

Hayakawa, S. I. "Our Son Mark." Outlooks and Insights. Ed. Paul Escholz and Alfred Rosa. 2nd ed. New York: St. Martin's, 1983. 115-22.

Work with an editor

Bradley, Sculley, et al., eds. The American Tradition in Literature. 4th ed. 2 vols. New York: Norton, 1974.

Work in more than one volume

Sandburg, Carl. Abraham Lincoln: The War Years. 4 vols. New York: Harcourt, 1939. Vol. 3.

Encyclopedia

"Lincoln, Abraham." World Book Encyclopedia. 1966 ed.

Pamphlets and bulletins

Stock Guide. New York: Standard and Poors, 1984.

B. **Magazines, periodicals, and newspapers**

Include in the following order every item of information that applies to each particular source. Observe and follow carefully the samples that illustrate these general rules.

1. **Author's name** as given on the first or last page of the article. Refer to the directions for listing names of authors of books.
2. **Title of the article** given completely and enclosed in quotation marks. Unless the title contains a question mark or exclamation mark, put a period inside the closing quotation marks, and skip 2 spaces. Follow the capitalization directions given under book titles.
3. **Name of the work,** excluding any introductory words like *the, a, an,* underlined, capitalized, and followed by a space.
4. **Date of publication** for daily, weekly, or monthly periodicals. Give the complete date—day, month (abbreviated except for May, June, and July), and year—followed by a colon and a space. For journals appearing less than six times a year, give the volume number followed by the year of publication in parentheses, a colon, and a space. For daily newspapers give the complete date (day, month, and year) followed by a comma. Then identify the edition if given on the masthead followed by a colon and a space.
5. **Page numbers** for the complete article, with a hyphen between the first and last pages. These page numbers appear after the colon without using the word or abbreviation for *page(s)* and conclude with a period. If the article skips pages rather than running continuously, give only the first page number followed by a plus sign and a period.

Sample Entries for Magazines, Periodicals, and Newspapers in *Works Cited*

Signed magazine article

Sklar, Dusty. "Grandparents of Divorce." Modern Maturity Apr.-May 1983: 81-82.

Unsigned weekly magazine article

"The Computer as Doctor." Newsweek 27 Dec. 1971: 52.

Newspaper article

Stumbo, Bella. "Cold Killer or Loving Grandma?" Los Angeles Times 19 Sept. 1984, late ed., part 1: 1+.

C. **Reviews**

Include in the list of *Works Cited* the reviewer's name and the title of the review (if given). Without underlining or quotation marks, write *Rev. of* followed by the title of the works reviewed, a comma, the word *by,* and the author's name. The review of a live performance needs additional information which includes the place and city of the production. Complete the entry with the name of the periodical and the rest of the publication data. A titled but unsigned review is alphabetized by the title of the review. The entry of an unsigned and untitled review begins with *Rev. of* but is alphabetized under the title of the work being reviewed.

Sample Entries for Reviews in *Works Cited*

Signed and titled

Sullivan, Dan. "Middle Ages is Nothing to Laugh At." Rev. of The Middle Ages, by A. R. Gurney Jr. Westwood Playhouse, Los Angeles. Los Angeles Times 19 Sept. 1984, late ed., part 6: 4+.

Unsigned and untitled

Rev. of Anthology of Sumerian Literature, ed. F. Jenkins and P. Mansen. Archeological Digest 8 July 1981: 185-86.

II. **Nonprint Media**

Entries for nonprint media generally begin with the author and title of the work (if given). Beyond that, each medium involves the reporting of specialized information. Consult the *MLA Handbook,* 1984 edition, for specific requirements for media such as computer software or service, an information service, performances, musical compositions, works of art, letters, cartoons, maps and charts, manuscripts and typescripts, and legal references. The examples included below are from media used more commonly by students.

Radio and television programs

"Deadly South American Snakes." Wild, Wild World of Animals PBS. KCET, Los Angeles. 5 Sept. 1984.

Begin with the title of the episode in quotation marks followed by the title of the program underlined; the title of the series if necessary but not underlined or enclosed in quotation marks; the network; the local station and its city; the date of broadcast. Use commas between the station and the city, and separate all other items with periods. You may also include other significant material, such as the names of director, narrator, producer, and writer.

Recordings

Yes. "The Solid Time of Change." Close to the Edge. Atlantic, SD 19133, 1972.

Begin with the name of the composer, conductor, or performer (depending on the focus); include the title(s), the artist(s), the manufacturer, the catalog number, and the year of issue if known. Separate the manufacturer and number with a comma; use a period to separate other items.

Maps and charts, tables and illustrations

```
Leading Economic Indicators of 1985. Chart. Washington D.C.: US
    Printing Office, 1986.
```

Treat maps and charts like anonymous books, but add the appropriate descriptive label (such as Map, Chart).

Motion pictures

```
Teachers. Dir. Arthur Hiller. United Artists. 1984.
```

Give the title of the movie underlined, followed by the director, the distributor, and the year separated by periods. Include other information like the writer(s), performers, and producer(s) after the title, if relevant.

Interviews

```
Oates, John Harrison. Personal interview. 25 Nov. 1981.
```

In a personal interview begin with the name of the person interviewed, the kind of interview (personal or telephone), and the date separated by periods.

Lectures and speeches

```
Hirshman, Carol A. "Anesthesia for Laser Surgery." Anesthesia
    Practice 1984. Anesthesiology Educational Foundation.
    Monterey, CA, 28 Sept. 1984.
```

Give the speaker's name, the title of the lecture (if known) in quotation marks, the names of the conference and sponsoring organization, the location, and the date. Separate the items by periods except for the comma between location and date. If the lecture has no title, use a descriptive name like Lecture or Keynote speech with no quotes or underlining.

Discovery Exercise for Works Cited

Put the following references into correct form and alphabetical order for a list of *Works Cited*. Use the blank spaces provided for your answers.

1. An essay entitled Some Thoughts on Dramatic Structure by Thomas Wilde found in an anthology called The Delights of the Theater edited by Jonathan Jones and published by Princeton University Press in Princeton in 1980. The essay appears on pages 69 to 79.
2. A review written by critic Samuel Twist of the play Vengeance by Night by playwright Eliza Johnson. The review is titled Some Relevance in Vengeance by Night, which appeared in the Los Angeles Times on December 7, 1984, in part 4 on pages 1 and 7.
3. A pamphlet called How to Write a Successful Mystery for the Stage published by Crown Publishers in 1979 in Chicago.
4. An unsigned untitled review of the play Vengeance by Night by playwright Eliza Johnson in Newsweek magazine of February 2, 1985, on page 48.
5. A 1½ hour telecast of the play Vengeance by Night by playwright Eliza Johnson on the program Playhouse 90 presented by Columbia Broadcasting System network and seen on KCBS in Los Angeles on October 8, 1984.
6. A book called Mystery Writing for Our Time edited by Rita Greene and Penelope Snodgrass published by Holt, Rinehart and Winston in New York in 1978.
7. The second volume of a series in five volumes called Crises and Conflicts by George Pruitt which was published by Harcourt Brace Jovanovich in New York in 1977.

8. A personal interview conducted on November 2, 1984, with Alfred Wilson, author of the book A Play and Its Audience.
9. Another review by critic Samuel Twist, called Vengeance by Night Stirring Up Its Audience, of the play Vengeance by Night by playwright Eliza Johnson found in the Los Angeles Times in the Calendar section on January 7, 1985, on page 36.
10. An unsigned magazine article called Writing Mysteries for Profit printed in Writers' Digest in August 1983 on pages 30 to 35 and 94.
11. The keynote speech by Frank W. Saddler, presented in Santa Barbara, California, on July 30, 1984, sponsored by the Playwrighters Association at the Beginning Playwrighters Workshop.
12. An article on Eliza Johnson in Encyclopedia Pacifica published in 1979.
13. The second edition of the book Mysteries for Modern Times by Alexander Smith and Paige Benton and Mary Thomas published in Boston by Little, Brown in 1980.
14. The play Vengeance by Night by playwright Eliza Johnson published by Evergreen Books in New York in 1979.

Exercise for Works Cited

Parenthetical Citations

All sources quoted and all original or distinctive ideas paraphrased must be acknowledged in the text of your research paper. However, if the material is common knowledge or available from several sources, documentation is unnecessary. In the past, this information was presented in numbered footnotes at the bottom of the appropriate pages or in endnotes at the end of the text. In 1984 the MLA simplified these conventions, and numbered notes contain only additional explanatory information. (Refer to the discussion on supplementary notes at the end of this section.) Now the newer style uses parenthetical citations which contain information necessary to direct the reader to the correct entry in the list of *Works Cited*. Any source that appears in a citation must also appear in this list.

Directions for Parenthetical Citations

Never abruptly introduce quotations into your discussion without smooth lead-ins. You may lead into a quotation by giving the author's name and/or title of the work.

Place the citation in parentheses immediately after the quotation or paraphrase. Skip one space after the end quotation marks or last word of the paraphrase, give the parenthetical note, and end with a period outside the parentheses. If the quotation ends in the middle of your sentence, the citation appears immediately after the end quotation marks. However, since this form interrupts the flow of the discussion, it is generally better to place quotations where they will coincide with the end of a sentence.

Generally speaking, a citation should not repeat information that is included outside the quotation. Include from the following list only those items that are necessary: the author's last name, key identifying words from the title, and the page number(s). Citations usually contain only two of these items because either you have already given some of this information in your text or you are using only one work of a particular author. The most important point is that the citation is keyed to the list of works cited. For example, the citation must include the name of the author unless the name is referred to in the text. If there is no author, a shortened title must be given either in the text or the citation.

Separate with a single space the two items within the citation. Cite the page number(s) without using the word or abbreviation for page(s). Use a hyphen to identify inclusive pages and a comma to cite noncontinuous pages.

Conclude lengthy indented quotations (more than 4 typewritten lines) with a period, and skip 2 spaces before the parenthetical citation. No period follows the citation.

Sample Parenthetical Citations

Study the following examples to see the correct form for presenting your quoted sources. Note that the complete bibliographical information about these citations is presented on page 350 titled *Works Cited* at the end of this section. You will need to refer to that list in order to understand the sample citations.

One author

```
Fessenden was one of the most influential senators in
preventing the conviction of Andrew Johnson. "As one of the
leading and most highly respected members of the Senate, he
would by his example be bound to influence the course of
others" (Jellison 230).
```

Because no reference to the author of the selection is included outside the parentheses, the citation identifies the author by last name. Because the author has only one work listed in the *Works Cited*, it is not necessary to give the title. Only one space and no punctuation separate the author and page reference. The period comes at the end of the citation.

Another way to lead into this quotation is to refer to the author in the text. Then only the page reference is necessary in the citation. Do not repeat any information within the parentheses that is given in the text.

According to Jellison, "As one of the leading and most highly respected members of the Senate, he would by his example be bound to influence the course of others" (230).

One author with multiple works

Although Trumbull denounced the vetoes, he refrained from personal attacks on the President: "He never personally indulged in remarks against the Executive or was found guilty of personal attacks against Johnson" (Krug, Trumbull 260).

Because Krug has two entries in the list of *Works Cited,* the parenthetical citation must identify which source is being quoted. A shortened form of the title is used. When the citation contains three elements, the author is separated from the title by a comma.

If the text outside the quotation marks refers to the author or title by name, then those items are omitted from the citation which simply identifies the page number.

In his biography Lyman Trumbull, Krug emphasizes that although Trumbull denounced the vetoes he refrained from personal attacks on the President: "He never personally indulged in remarks against the Executive or was found guilty of personal attacks against Johnson" (260).

Multiple authors

Fessenden the lawyer judged the case before him as impartially as possible. "A man of the strictest integrity, Fessenden's concept of public duty would not allow him to disregard his trial oath" (Milton and Baker 552).

Both authors are included in the parenthetical citation. If there are three authors, all three are named and separated by commas. If the three authors are Smith, Jones, and Brown, the citation would be (Smith, Jones, and Brown 125). If a source has more than three authors, the first author's name is given followed by *et al.*, the Latin abbreviation for "and others." If the four authors of a book are Smith, Jones, Brown, and Doe, the citation would be (Smith et al. 125).

No author

Just as Andrew Johnson's "career as president was of the essence of tragedy" ("Johnson"), so these three senators who voted for acquittal suffered greatly.

When there is no author given for the material quoted, the identifying information is the shortened title of the article (as alphabetized in the list of *Works Cited*) and the page number. Do not cite the title of the work since the reader would not find the reference presented that way in the list of *Works Cited.* Since this quotation is taken from an encyclopedia, no volume or page number is needed because entries are alphabetically arranged.

The quotation is generally placed at the end of a sentence to avoid unnecessarily interrupting the reader. However, if the quotation ends within the sentence, then the citation must appear immediately after the quotation marks.

Multivolume works

As Trumbull declared when Johnson vetoed his civil rights bill, "I regret it [the veto] on my own account because the just expectations raised when this bill was presented to the President before its introduction into the Senate have been disappointed" (qtd. in "Debate" 10: 18).

In a multivolume work, after the name of the author or after the title of the work (if no author is given), place the volume number in arabic numbers followed by a colon, a space, and the page number. If you give the author or title or volume number in the text, then these items may be omitted in the citation.

Multiple pages/Lengthy quotes

The character of the man Fessenden is of vital importance in considering his motive for voting against conviction.

> Dignified in bearing, cautious in judgment, experienced in public affairs, familiar with the finances. . . . A strict party man, ready to go great lengths with his party associations; yet, he had repeatedly shown, there were limits he would not transgress. He would not knowingly put by the restraints of the Constitution no matter how obstructive they were to the success of some favourite party project. (DeWitt 176-7)

A quote of more than four lines is set off from the text. Indent 10 spaces from the left margin. Do not indent the right margin. Double space the quotation without quotation marks. End the quotation with a period, and skip two spaces before giving the parenthetical information.

If the quotation continues beyond one page in the original source, use a hyphen to indicate continuous pages and a comma to indicate the quotation is found on two separate pages.

Indirect source

As Edmund Ross said to Senator Sprague of Rhode Island (who was incidentally the son-in-law of Chief Justice Chase), "So far as I am concerned, though a Republican and opposed to Mr. Johnson and his policy, he shall have as fair a trial as any accused man ever had on the earth" (qtd. in Kennedy 118).

Sometimes one of your sources may contain material quoted by others (for example, one writer's account of another person's words or ideas). Then include in the parenthetical citation the abbreviation *qtd. in* ("quoted in") before the indirect source.

Or you can indicate in the text that you are quoting indirectly by naming the author. In such a case, only the page number is needed in the citation.

Kennedy quotes Ross as having said to Senator Sprague of Rhode Island, "So far as I am concerned, though a Republican and opposed to Mr. Johnson and his policy, he shall have as fair a trial as any accused man ever had on the earth" (118).

Maps and charts, tables and illustrations

Label the visual item with the appropriate word, such as *Fig.* (figure), Chart, Graph, Table, and so on. Number with an arabic numeral, punctuate with a period, follow with a descriptive title, and end with a period.

Map 1. United States in 1865.

Chart 3. Leading Economic Indicators of 1985.

Supplementary notes

Occasionally it is necessary to give the reader supplementary information or explanation that would distract from the text. This material can be included in a footnote at the bottom of the appropriate page or an endnote at the end of the text. The note is double spaced. It begins with a raised arabic number and a space. The first line is indented five spaces from the left-hand margin, and all succeeding lines begin at the left-hand margin. Put a raised arabic number at the proper place in the text to correspond to the note. If more than one note is needed, number consecutively throughout the paper.

[1]Since the events discussed in this paper occurred in 1868, the original sources are not readily accessible. Therefore, mainly secondary sources which quote the individuals involved are used.

This sample page contains complete bibliographical information for the parenthetical citations discussed in the previous section. You must refer to this list in order to understand the sample citations.

WORKS CITED

Chicago Tribune 7 May 1868: 1.

"Debate on Civil States Rights." *The Annals of America*. 18 vols. Chicago: Encyclopaedia Britannica, 1968. Vol. 10. 11-21.

DeWitt, David Miller. *The Impeachment and Trial of Andrew Johnson*. New York: Russel, 1903.

Jellison, Charles A. *Fessenden of Maine, Civil War Senator*. Syracuse, NY: Syracuse UP, 1962.

"Johnson, Andrew." *World Book Encyclopedia*. 1960 ed.

Kennedy, John F. *Profiles in Courage*. New York: Harper, 1956.

Krug, Mark M. *Lyman Trumbull, Conservative Radical*. New York: Barnes, 1965.

---. *Steps Toward Impeachment: Andrew Johnson on Trial*. Boston: Little, 1960.

Milton, George Fort, and Alvin Baker. *The Age of Hate, Andrew Johnson and the Radicals*. New York: Coward-McCann, 1930.

Ross, Edmund G. "History of the Impeachment of Andrew Johnson." *Forum* July 1895: 12.

United States in 1865. Map. New York: Rand McNally, 1953.

Discovery Exercise for Parenthetical Citations

DIRECTIONS: Consult the Discovery Exercise for *Works Cited* on page 344 for the information needed to complete this exercise. Put the following references into correct form for parenthetical citations, keeping them in their present order. Use the blank spaces provided for your answers.

1. Page 76 of reference #1. The title of the essay "Some Thoughts on Dramatic Structure" is identified in the text of the paper. ______
2. Page 7 of reference #2. The critic is identified in the text of the paper. ______
3. Page 20 of reference #3. No bibliographic information is identified in the text of the paper. ______
4. Page 48 of reference #4. *Newsweek* magazine is identified in the text of the paper. ______
5. Pages 92 and 93 of reference #6. No bibliographical information is identified in the text of the paper. ______
6. Page 214 of reference #7. Only the author of the book is identified in the text of the paper. ______
7. Page 71 of reference #1. The author is identified in the text of the paper. ______
8. Page 36 of reference #9. No bibliographical information is identified in the text of the paper. ______
9. Pages 35 and 94 of reference #10. The title of the magazine article is identified in the text of the paper. ______
10. Page 320 of reference #12. No bibliographical information is identified in the text of the paper. ______
11. Page 72 of reference #13. The title of the book is identified in the text of the paper. ______
12. Page 32 of reference #3. Eliza Johnson is quoted in the pamphlet. No bibliographical information is identified in the text of the paper. ______
13. Pages 112 to 113 of reference #14. No bibliographical information is identified in the text of the paper. ______
14. Page 173 of reference #6. The editors of the book and the author they quote are identified in the text of the paper. ______

STUDENT SAMPLE—Term Paper

Read the following selection, and note how each part of the assignment is presented: prospectus, title page, outline, text with parenthetical citations, and list of works cited.

Complete the blank prospectus sheet at the end of the chapter as a beginning step in your research project. Be sure to receive your instructor's approval before proceeding to the next step.

Attach both Prospectus and the Term Paper Cover Sheet to your finished assignment.

PROSPECTUS FOR TERM PAPER

Name John Smith Class: 11 MWF

1. Topic: ESP (extrasensory perception)
2. Working { statement of purpose ☐ / thesis statement ☒ }

to investigate ESP and draw conclusions as to its possible existence

3. Aspects to be considered:

types of ESP
supports for ESP's existence
criticisms and negatives about ESP

4. Working list of 8 sources:

Author	Title	Publication Information	Date
S. Holroyd	Psi and the Consciousness Explosion	NY: Taplinger	1977
R.A. McConnell	ESP Curriculum Guide	NY: Simon	1971
D.E. Carr	"The Forgotten Senses"	Psychology Today 31-32, 61, 63	June 1979
D.S. Rogo	Parapsychology: a Century of Inquiry	NY: Taplinger	1975
	"Parapsychological Phenomena, theories of"	Encyclo. Britannica	1974
J.B. Rhine	Extrasensory Perception	Boston: Bruce Humphries	1964
I. Stevenson	Telepathic Impressions	Charlottesville: UP of Virginia	1970
J.L. Randall	Parapsychology and the Nature of Life	NY: Harper	1975

Instructor comments and/or suggestions:

Interesting and controversial topic.
Sources should be more up to date and come from a variety of sources.
Try an interview.

MS/RW
(Instructor approval)

3" from top

Uncommon Sense ← centered

5" from top

by

John Smith

centered and double spaced

Professor Jones

English 1

May 15, 1986

centered and double spaced

3" from bottom

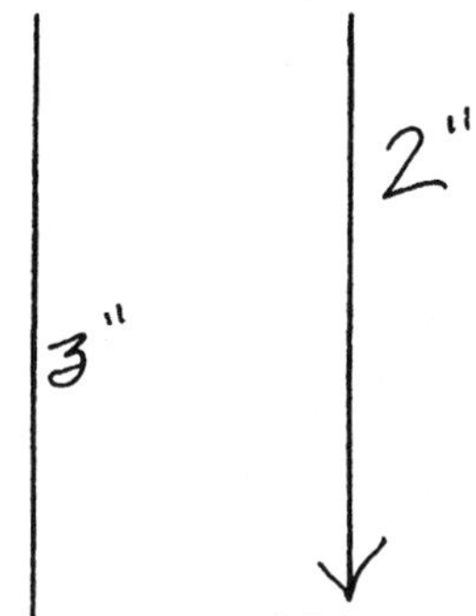

Outline

Thesis Statement: Extrasensory perception appears to be real and should be studied at length in order to better understand the relationship of mind and space. This paper will examine some of the more common forms of ESP, criticisms of its existence, and evidence to support its credibility.

I. Introduction
   A. History of ESP
   B. Problems with studying ESP
   C. Thesis statement
   D. Enumeration

II. Forms of ESP
   A. Precognition
      1. Definition
      2. Problems with precognition
      3. Everyone has precognitions, but difficult to accept
   B. Clairvoyance
      1. Definition
      2. Unlike precognition or telepathy
      3. Energy theory
   C. Mental telepathy
      1. Definition
      2. Zener cards
      3. Mathematical probability for success
      4. Mathematical probability for failure

III. Criticisms of the existence of ESP
   A. Criticisms of precognition
      1. Undocumented evidence--no proof
      2. Partial truths of evidence
      3. Inconsistent interpretation of evidence
   B. Criticisms of clairvoyance
      1. Difficult to accept energy theory
      2. Inverse square law
      3. Clairvoyance not affected by inverse square
   C. Criticisms of telepathy
      1. Early testing was poorly controlled
      2. Experimenters lead subject
      3. Statistics poorly applied
         a. Upton Sinclair tests
         b. Results by-product of unscientific techniques
      4. Better methods today

1"

IV. Evidence to support credibility of ESP
   A. Precognition
      1. "Train-dream"--undocumented
      2. Precognition usually negative
      3. "Empty-chair" experiment--documented
   B. Clairvoyance
      1. Swedenborg case
      2. Picture cards--unknown to subject or tester
      3. Possible influence of telepathy
   C. Mental telepathy
      1. Supporting evidence
         a. Tests of George Zirkle
         b. Long-range tests
         c. Why long-range scores are higher
         d. Illness affects scores
         e. Drugs affect scores
      2. Alternate form of telepathy testing
         a. Why better than card guessing
         b. More desire to know picture

V. Conclusion
   A. Hard to accept ESP
   B. ESP must exist
      1. Much positive data
      2. May further help people

Uncommon Sense

From the Greek oracle of Delphi to the modern carnival card reader, psychic phenomena have intrigued, baffled, and frightened people. However, little is actually understood about the various forms of extrasensory perception. Since the study and testing of the "sixth sense" have not been completely standardized and perfected, the traditional scientific community, as a whole, does not put much faith in its existence. Many times, as is the case with some ESP research, the scientist does not view the facts with an objective eye. Instead, personal bias, conjecture, and faulty reasoning combine with and cloud reality. However, the research conducted by Joseph Bank Rhine, a leader in the study of ESP, and others indicates that some type of human psychic ability does in fact exist. Extrasensory perception appears to be real and should be studied at length in order to better understand the interactive relationship of mind and space. This paper will examine some of the more common forms of ESP, criticisms of its existence, and evidence to support its credibility.

While there are many forms of extrasensory perception, the three most common are precognition, clairvoyance, and mental telepathy. The Encyclopaedia Britannica defines precognition as "the perception of some future event, which may be an act, a thought, or an emotion" ("Parapsychological Phenomena"). In other words, an individual purported to have powers of precognition thus has the ability to predict the future. As stated in the book Psi and the Consciousness Explosion, there are significant difficulties with accepting the validity of precognition: "It is easier to believe that information can be received paranormally from other minds or even from material objects than that it can come from the future" (Holroyd 86). Nevertheless, precognition is the most widely reported form of ESP. Virtually everyone has had a dream or thought that later physically occurred. However, because of preconceived notions of the linearity of time and space, most people who have a precognitive experience do not consider it important. If the individual were to believe in precognition, he might also reason that he does not possess freewill.

Another form of extrasensory perception is clairvoyance. Clairvoyance, formally called spontaneous clairvoyance, is, as researcher Paul Krafchik states, "The ability to perceive a mental picture of persons, objects or events at a distance" (3). Unlike pure telepathy, a mental image is not transmitted by a human sender. Unlike precognition, the event occurs at the same time that it is being visualized in the mind. Thus, the theory supporting the existence of clairvoyance must evolve out of the idea that for an event to occur, there must be a release of energy. The energy somehow transmits itself, sometimes over vast distances, into the clairvoyant's mind. Dr. Krafchik summarizes this hypothesis in a somewhat idealistic manner: "The occultists believe, as modern scientists do, that energy does not die, but remains forever and thus could be detected by the clairvoyant individual" (3).

The most feasible type of extrasensory perception is mental telepathy. Pure telepathy is defined by Joseph Rhine as "extrasensory perception of the mental processes of another person. 'Pure' refers to the absence of objective representation of the mental act or image which might permit of clairvoyance by the percipient" (xi). However, most experiments testing telepathy are not pure in design. Instead, a sender picks at random one of five different symbols (cross, star, circle, wave, and rectangle) which are pictured on cards. The cards, also known as Zener cards, come twenty-five to a pack or test. The number of symbols and cards in a test makes it easy for the experimenter to determine the success or failure ratio of the person being tested. The book *Extrasensory Perception* illustrates the use of mathematical probability with regard to card guessing: "I have been able, by adhering to the use of five simple card-figures, to keep the probability of success by pure chance at 1/5 for each trial" (Rhine 40). Consequently, a test of twenty-five cards should produce, on the average, five correct answers or twenty percent correct answers. Consistent test results above the odds of chance may indicate telepathy. Similarly, Rhine explains the great odds against consecutive correct answers: "Where a straight run of consecutive successes is to be evaluated for anti-chance probability, simply raising 1/5 to the power equal to the number of consecutive successes gives the value desired" (40). The formula $1/5^x$ (x = the number of guesses), when applied, is a good indicator of the difficulty in achieving success with the Zener cards when not aided by telepathy. The numbers become important when compared to actual test results. Because many people experience some type of paranormal activity that cannot yet be scientifically explained, these forms of ESP cannot be completely dismissed.

However, many criticisms of the existence of extrasensory perception continue to be expressed. For instance, the undocumented accounts of premonition are unacceptable to the traditional scientist. The scientist requires proof, but generally speaking, the person claiming to have predicted the future usually lacks proof to support the claim. The alleged evidence may also be falsified or may only contain partial truths. For example, "Suppose that there are 20 runners [in a horse race]; if 100 people report dreaming the correct winner but 1,900 dream the incorrect winner, then clearly there is nothing to be explained" ("Parapsychological Phenomena"). Unfortunately, only those people who dream about the winner report their experience. Thus, inaccurate conclusions are drawn. A second major criticism of precognition focuses on the interpretation of the laboratory test results. A report by Sara Feather and Robert Brier says, "[T]he results checked by the assistant showed above-chance scoring, those checked by the experimenter showed below-chance scoring, and the difference was statistically significant" (129). Therefore, reports and test results must be viewed with a certain amount of skepticism.

Similarly, criticisms of clairvoyance abound. Most notable is the difficulty in accepting the idea that the energy created by an event or object is able to project itself, through space, as a unified whole. Logically, it seems that energy would immediately expend itself and, while in the process, change form. Assuming that the energy created by an object could remain whole and organized, its energy should dissipate during the travel. However, as the noted researcher J. B. Rhine states, "The only way in which we can suppose a law of inverse squares to apply here, as in wave mechanics, would be to suppose some very strong compensating factor to be present . . ." (129). For example if the distance between a flashlight and the object it illuminates is doubled, the intensity of the light is quartered. Contrary to fact, clairvoyant images do not seem to suffer from the law of inverse squares. Thus, the evidence supporting clairvoyance often contradicts established physical properties.

Criticisms of mental telepathy are aimed almost entirely at testing procedures and the applicability of statistics. First, during the early stages of research, the conditions under which testing took place were not well controlled. On occasion, the researcher would lead the subject, whether consciously or subconsciously, to the desired answer. Facial expressions, hand gestures, and body movement, on the part of the tester, could very well have influenced the receiver's answers.

Similarly, statistical analyses in the past were poorly applied and often suspected of inadequacies. For example, the results achieved by Upton Sinclair, as recorded in the Mental Radio, seemed to prove that the ability for telepathic drawing exists (122-7). Sinclair and his wife, whom he believed to have psychic ability, spent three years and made almost three hundred tests before concluding the experiment. Sinclair rated just over seventy-five percent of the tests as totally or partially successful. But the favorable results obtained by the Upton Sinclair tests were, in all likelihood, a by-product of wishful thinking, tester influence on the subject, and a lack of experimental control. The same tests performed today would not have such a positive outcome. Statistical and procedural methods, however, are no longer considered flawed. According to the Encyclopaedia Britannica "the former [experimental design] has been investigated by the American Psychological Society, the latter [statistical analyses] by the American Statistical Society, and neither society made any adverse criticisms" ("Parapsychological Phenomena").

Just as the methods for testing mental telepathy have become more scientific, so much undocumented and some documented evidence support the existence of extrasensory perception. Of course, in order to be labeled as official, the precognitive experience must be recorded before the foreseen event actually occurs. However, almost every premonition that takes place is only known by the one person and perhaps immediate family or close friends. A dream, related by Dr. Walter F. Prince, is a good example of an undocumented spontaneous occurrence of precognition. Dr. Prince was awakened by his wife one night when she noticed that he was having a nightmare. He then recounted in great detail his dream to Mrs. Prince. Specifically, Dr. Prince told his wife about a two-train collision, including the setting, the type of wreck, the people involved, and the happenings after the accident. His premonition, on most points, became reality several hours later, approximately seventy-five miles from his home (Carr 32).

It should also be noted that premonitions are usually negative in content. As Stuart Holroyd theorizes, "Precognitions of disaster or death outnumber precognitions of happy events by four to one . . . and occur within a few hours or days of the events precognised" (89). Another example of precognition, tested under controlled conditions, was conducted by Eugene Osty, a French psychical researcher. Osty, along with a clairvoyant named Ludwig Kahn, produced many successful tests in precognition. One such was called the "empty-chair" experiment in which Kahn would predict the height, sex, age, and general information about persons who would later occupy a given chair or area (Holroyd 112). The information was recorded and then compared to actual findings. Often, the tests were quite convincing, though never conclusive.

While instances of precognition are difficult to substantiate, many cases support the existence of clairvoyance. One of the most popular proofs of clairvoyance comes by way of Swedish philosopher Emanuel Swedenborg. While at his home in Goteborg, Sweden, Swedenborg visualized and described, to numerous witnesses, in exact detail, a fire which was raging in Stockholm, some three hundred miles away. He was also able to report when the fire ceased. This event occurred in 1759, well before any form of instant, long-distance communication was possible. A few days later, a message arrived of the fire, the details of which coincided with Swedenborg's description (Krafchik 3). Laboratory tests of clairvoyance also indicate its possible existence, though the results are far from convincing. Picture cards, commonly found in other areas of ESP study, may be employed in a test of clairvoyance. Ideally, the symbol pictured on each card is not known by either the subject or tester. If the individual controlling the experiment concentrates on a particular card, the procedure may be erroneously influenced by telepathy. The use of "double-blind" experiments, however, has allowed for more accurate testing.

The area of mental telepathy has been studied by administering many hundreds of thousands of card tests, many with startling results. Studies conducted at Duke University on a subject named George Zirkle produced many theories concerning telepathy (Rhine 121). To begin, it appears that distance has little or no influence on telepathic ability. In fact, in Zirkle's case, telepathic powers were slightly enhanced by the greater distances. Through thousands of tests, Zirkle demonstrated the insignificance of distance and physical barriers. He consistently scored better than fifty percent correct, whether in the same room as the sender or separated by several walls.

Rhine summarizes by saying,

> [O]ne who is a considerable distance from the agent [the agent sends the mental images] tends to relax those sensory processes commonly depended upon for perception and utilizes the process

> of extrasensory perception the more; also, the rational judgment realizes its own uselessness and ceases to obstruct the ESP function; the result is better abstraction and concentration. (140)

Conversely, sickness tends to lower card-guessing scores. Zirkle is reported as having lost a degree of telepathic power during a period of illness: "This is a drop of 6.3 [Zirkle, who when healthy averaged 14.9 'hits' per 25 attempts, dropped to 8.6 per test] per 25, a highly significant value, and it leaves little question that, directly or indirectly, such illness is a condition very inhibitory to ESP" (Rhine 127). In similar fashion, depressant drugs, such as sodium amytal, tend to decrease scores, while caffeine and other stimulants make the telepathic responses less predictable. The fact that telepathy can be influenced by varying conditions indicates that some telepathic process is taking place.

A more stimulating and creative form of testing for telepathy is desired by some researchers. As ESP authority John L. Randall explains, "Some psychical researchers have criticized Rhine's methods on the grounds that card guessing is a boring procedure, bearing little or no resemblance to the emotionally-rich situations of everyday life in which spontaneous ESP seems to occur" (80). Thus, an alternative test for telepathy, though not widely used, employs telepathic drawings. This is also known as "free-response" experimentation. The goal is for the subject of the test to sketch a drawing, from mental images, of an unknown target picture. To do so, ESP course advisor R. A. McConnell believes that there must be a desire to know the picture: "This [accurate guessing] may be through the personal meaningfulness of the target, or because of a wish to please the experimenter, or as an expression of desire for achievement, or because of any sufficiently strong factor" (54). Equally important, the subject must be relaxed, in a good mood, and free from external thought. Thus, some evidence supports the concept of mental telepathy.

In conclusion, it may reasonably be said that the concept of extrasensory perception presents numerous scientific and logical problems. K. Ramakrishna Rao, author of Experimental Parapsychology, accurately writes, "[I]t is true that psi phenomena [ESP] seem to blatantly conflict with some of the basic assumptions on which our belief systems are founded" (4). However, much of the data which support ESP suggests, almost without doubt, that some form of paranormal activity occurs within the human mind. The voluminous information collected and analyzed, especially with regard to mental telepathy, is quite thorough and convincing. Thus, the complete understanding of precognition, mental telepathy, and clairvoyance may someday help to revise and expand the physical laws which guide people and nature.

Smith 10

Works Cited

Carr, Denise E. "The Forgotten Senses." Psychology Today June 1979: 31 +.

Feather, Sara R., and Robert Brier. "The Effect of the Checker on Precognition." Progress in Parapsychology. Ed. Joseph B. Rhine. Durham, NC: Parapsychological, 1971. 121-35.

Holroyd, Stuart. Psi and the Consciousness Explosion. New York: Taplinger, 1977.

Krafchik, Paul. "Clairvoyance." A Complete Course in Parapsychology. Sherman Oaks, CA: American Parapsychological Research Foundation, 1972. 1-17.

McConnell, Robert A. ESP Curriculum Guide. 2nd ed. New York: Simon, 1971.

"Parapsychological Phenomenona, Theories of." Encyclopaedia Britannica. 1974 ed.

Randall, John L. Parapsychology & the Nature of Life. New York: Harper, 1975.

Rao, K. Ramakrishna. Experimental Parapsychology. Springfield, IL: Thomas, 1966.

Rhine, Joseph B. Extrasensory Perception. Boston: Bruce Humphries, 1964.

Sinclair, Upton. Mental Radio. Springfield, IL: Thomas, 1962.

PROSPECTUS FOR TERM PAPER

Name: ______________________________ Class: ______________

1. Topic: ______________________________
2. Working { statement of purpose ☐ / thesis statement ☐

____

____

3. Aspects to be considered:

____

____

____

4. Working list of 8 sources:

Author	Title	Publication Information	Date

Instructor comments and/or suggestions:

____
(Instructor approval)

Name: ____________________

Date: ____________ **Class:** ________

TERM PAPER COVER SHEET		
Structure/Ideas	+	________
Usage/Mechanics	−	________
Total		________

Checklist:
☐ Title Page
☐ Outline
☐ Text
☐ Parenthetical Citations
☐ Works Cited
☐ Prospectus

Structure and Ideas **(300 points)**		
INTRODUCTION (eight to ten sentences):		
title; opening sentences, background information	30	________
statement of purpose or thesis statement + enumeration of subtopics (aspects)	15	________
BODY (ten to twelve paragraphs):		
topic sentences = transition + reference to purpose or thesis + subtopic (aspects)	10	________
sufficient development of paragraphs	120	________
appropriate use of source material (at least fifteen quotations)	20	________
CONCLUSION (at least five sentences):		
implications and significance of purpose or thesis	15	________
TERM PAPER:		
logical order of ideas and correct reasoning	30	________
effective style = tone + diction + sentence structure + coherence	30	________
source material: at least fifteen quotations and/or paraphrases	30	________
TOTAL	300	________

Usage and Mechanics **(minus points). See Correction Symbol Chart.**		
Usage: adj; adv; agr; awk; col; dm; frag; mm; ref; rep; shift; verb; ww; / /; ¶	−3 ea.	________
Mechanics: abbr; apos; cap; lc; p; ro; sp; ∧	−1 ea.	________
Citations and Works Cited: errors in format and punctuation	−1 ea.	________
Each Works Cited entry less than required minimum	−5 ea.	________
Total	−	________

CHAPTER 16
Handbook

The Handbook is a short presentation of the basic grammatical and mechanical information you will need in the preparation of your essays. The emphasis is placed on sentence writing and combining rather than on memorization of facts and rules. It is separated into four major sections.

Parts of speech, the first section, briefly reviews basic sentence parts, modifiers, and connective words. Every time you write, you should consult the lengthy list of transitional expressions grouped according to the relationships they convey. The second section, **sentence structures,** presents the basic sentence patterns and techniques for expanding them by modifying, coordinating, and subordinating. Each concept is accompanied by exercises to develop your skill in sentence combining. **Mechanics,** the next section, reviews the major rules of punctuation, capitalization, and spelling. A list of 350 often misspelled words is included for your study and convenience. A short exercise completes this section. The last part of the Handbook is **usage**. The major errors of fragments, misplaced modifiers, faulty pronouns and agreements, shifts, and faulty parallelisms are illustrated and then corrected. A short discovery exercise reviews these common problems. The Handbook concludes with a discovery exercise requiring the rewriting of a paragraph containing flaws in sentence structure, mechanics, and usage.

PARTS OF SPEECH

A practical approach to grammar is to understand the parts of speech according to the function they have in a sentence. Knowing the interrelationship of the elements in a sentence is essential to purposeful and imaginative writing.

Noun	Adverb
Pronoun	Preposition
Verb	Conjunction
Adjective	Interjection

These eight parts of speech are grouped into basic sentence parts, modifiers, and connective words.

Basic Sentence Parts

1. Noun
   - names a person, place, thing, action, idea, animal, or quality
   - pluralizes with **s** or **es**
   - frequently preceded by noun determiners: `a, an, the`

   Types of nouns:

   Proper—names a particular person, place, or thing: `Jane Brown, Chicago,` <u>`The Lord of the Rings`</u>

   Common—names an unspecified person, place, or thing: `girl, city, book`

   Types of common nouns:

   Abstract—names qualities or characteristics of people, places, or things: `strength, splendor, magnificence`

   Collective—names groups or collections of persons, places, or things: `jury, mall, herd`

2. Pronoun
   - substitutes for a noun (antecedent)
   - shares with its noun number (singular or plural), gender (masculine, feminine, or neuter), and person (first, second, or third)

   Types of pronouns:

   Personal—refers to person, place, or thing

Case	1st person		2nd person		3rd person	
	singular	plural	singular	plural	singular	plural
Subjective	I	we	you	you	he, she, it	they
Possessive	my mine	our ours	your yours	your yours	his, her, its, hers	their theirs
Objective	me	us	you	you	him, her, it	them

Relative—takes the place of a noun in the part of the sentence (the clause) it introduces
—joins and relates that part to the rest of the sentence

`who, whom, whose, whoever, whomever`—used for people

`which, whichever`—used for objects, animals, and ideas

`that`—used for people, objects, animals, and ideas

Indefinite—refers to persons, places, or things not specifically identified so does not take the place of a particular noun

all	each	many	several
another	either	neither	some
any	everybody	nobody	somebody
anybody	everyone	none	someone
anyone	everything	nobody	something
anything	few	nothing	

3. Verb
   - expresses action or being; indicates the time (present, past, or future) when the action occurs. A word without time sense is not a verb.

Principal Parts (regular)

present stem (infinitive)	to + verb	to paint, to take, to send
past tense	verb + ed, en, t	painted, taken, sent
present participle	verb + ing	painting, taking, sending
past participle	verb + ed, en, t	painted, taken, sent

Types of verbs:

Transitive—has an object

`The child hit the ball.`

Intransitive—has no object

`Dogs bark.`

Linking—connects what comes after it with the noun in front of it

`The teachers are parents.`

—is usually a form of the verb "to be"

Auxiliary or helping verb—assists the main verb in expressing meaning more precisely

auxiliary + main verb = verb phrase

auxiliaries: forms of **to be, to have, to do**

shall, will **may, can** **might, must**

could, would, should

main verbs: when used with an auxiliary are usually the present or past participle

verb phrase: **is + driving = is driving**

has + walked = has walked

should have + eaten = should have eaten.

Tense

present **I paint. I am painting. I do paint.**

past **I painted. I did paint. I have painted.**

future **I will paint. I will be painting.**

Modifiers

4. Adjective
   - describes, limits, determines, or shows possession in nouns and pronouns
   - answers the questions how many? how much? which one? what kind?
   - is placed as closely as possible to the word it modifies
   - occurs in one of only three locations; cannot be placed in any other position but can be shifted from one of these three positions to another
     —directly before the noun or pronoun
     —directly after the noun or pronoun
     —directly after a linking verb

   descriptive —**green sofa, tall building, soft pillow**
   limiting —**two cats, that book, some people**
   determining —**a dog, the boats, an apple**
   possessive —**my room, child's shoes, flowers' petals**

5. Adverb
   - describes verbs, adjectives, and other adverbs
   - answers the questions how? where? when? why? under what conditions? to what extent?
   - is flexible enough to be placed in different parts of the sentence
   - often ends in **ly**

adverb with verb—moved quickly
adverb with adjective—very comfortable chair
adverb with adverb—ate too slowly

Connective Words

6. Preposition
   - shows the relationship of a noun or pronoun to another word in the sentence; creates a prepositional phrase

   preposition + object = prepositional phrase

   to + the sky = to the sky (with noun)
   between + them and me = between them and me (with pronoun)

   - is used in a phrase as an adjective or adverb

   noun
   adjective prepositional phrase—counselors from camp

   verb
   adverb prepositional phrase—arrive in the evening

   Frequently used prepositions:

above	behind	for	over
about	below	from	to
across	between	in (to)	under
after	beside	of	until
around	by	on	up
at	down	out (of)	with
before			

7. Conjunction
   - joins two words, phrases, or clauses

   Types of conjunctions:

   Coordinate—joins elements of equal importance
   and, but, for, nor, or, so, yet

   two words—cats or mice
   two phrases—up the street and over the hill
   two clauses—The father bought the horse, but the child did not like it.

   Subordinate—joins two clauses of unequal importance

   Frequently used subordinators:

after	before	that	when
although	how	though	where
as (if)	if	until	while
because	since	what	unless

   If it rains, we will not be able to leave on our vacation.

8. Interjection
   - used rarely in formal writing
   - expresses emotion or emphasizes an idea
   - followed by an exclamation point or comma

   Wow! That was an excellent paper

Transitional Expressions

These words and phrases can be adverbs, prepositions, or conjunctions. The expressions emphasize the coherence or the relationship of ideas in a passage. Transitions clarify ideas and focus the reader's attention.

ADDITION

again
also
among many others
and
and then
another
besides
both
equally important
even so
finally
further
futhermore
in addition (to)
in the next place
in the second (third, etc.) place
interestingly enough
it is also interesting to note that
it must be added
just as
last, lastly
let us continue
let us now turn
likewise
moreover
my last point
next
nor
not only . . . but also . . .
one of the best examples
second, secondly
so are
to consider another phase of the issue
too

CAUSE

as, as it were
because (of)
for
for this reason
inasmuch as
it all depends upon
one cause of
one factor leading to
since
the next event leading to

COMPARISON

again
also
comparatively
inasmuch as
in comparison
in like manner
in the same way
in some respects
just as . . . even so . . .
like
like all others
likewise
parallels also appear
parallels between
similar, similarly
the . . . is closely parallel
to compare

CONCESSION

although
although it does not seem logical (true) at first
even if
even though
inasmuch as
it must be admitted that
presumably
though

CONCLUSION/RESULT

according to
accordingly
after all
and so
an effect of
as a consequence
as a result
as shown by
consequently
final, finally
hence
in conclusion
in consequence of this
in that case
in the final analysis
it may be said
it remains to be seen
naturally

since
so
so it is clear (evident) that
so that
the fact seems to indicate that
therefore
thereupon
thus
wherefore
whereupon

CONDITION

if
if so
lest
on condition that
provided that
supposedly
supposing
unless
whether or not

CONTRAST

albeit
and yet
but
but instead
but rather
contrariwise
conversely
despite the fact
different from
even though
however
in contrast to this
in order to understand the difference
in spite of this
instead (of)
neither does
nevertheless
nonetheless
notwithstanding
on the contrary
on the one hand
on the other hand
or
otherwise
rather than
still
the counterpart
the difference between
there is a vast difference between
turning now to the other side
unlike
whereas
while
yet

EMPHASIS/INTENSIFICATION

above all
after all
best of all
certainly
doubtless
especially
I assume, suppose, believe, think
I might say
in any event
in every case
in fact
in my opinion
in particular
indeed
it is essential
it is important for us to remember
it is true
it seems to me
least
merely
most
no doubt
obviously
of course
one feels
perhaps
plainly
primarily
so to speak
to be sure
true, truly
undoubtedly

INTRODUCTION OF ILLUSTRATION/ EXAMPLE

first
for example
for instance
for proof
in order to prove (show, illustrate)
in that case
. . . is best illustrated by . . .
it is reminiscent of
my first point
one such
that is

to cite an example
to exemplify
to illustrate

PURPOSE

because (of)
for this purpose, reason
in order that
in order to achieve, prove, show, understand, illustrate, demonstrate
so that
that
to this end
with this object, goal

REPETITION

and so again
as has been noted
as I have said
as I implied earlier
I repeat
in other words
more and more
once more
to repeat

SPACE/DIRECTION

above
around
at one end
behind
below
closer
further
in front of
in the background, center, foreground
next to
on the inside, outside
on the one (other) side
on the right, left
on the top, bottom, side
to the right, left, side, center
under

SUMMARY

all in all
all these
although it may not be apparent, on consideration it becomes evident
basically
for all that
finally
generally speaking
in brief
in conclusion
in effect
in every case
in general
in short
in summary
in this discussion we have seen that
in truth
it is necessary to consider that
it may be said
last, lastly
let us note
on the whole
to conclude
thus far
thus we see
to sum up
to summarize
we now see

TIME/CHRONOLOGY

after
before
finally
first
immediately
next
now
suddenly
then
until
when

SENTENCE STRUCTURES

The effective combination of different grammatical patterns creates variety and interest in writing. A range of these structures, along with tone, diction, and coherence, constitutes style.

Basic sentence
Expansion by modifying
Expansion by coordinating
Expansion by subordinating
Achieving sentence variety

BASIC SENTENCE (also called kernel sentence, simple sentence, main clause, independent clause)

- is a group of words presenting a single complete thought
- is composed of two basic elements: subject + predicate
- ends with a period, question mark, or exclamation point
- **Subject:** the naming part of a sentence—a noun or a pronoun
- **Predicate:** the telling part of a sentence—a verb and its completers (direct objects, indirect objects, subject complements—nouns or adjectives)

Sentence = Subject + Predicate (Verb + Completers)

Fundamental Patterns

Subject + Intransitive Verb

`Crowds gathered.`

Subject + Transitive Verb + Direct Object

`Dancers buy slippers.`

Subject + Transitive Verb + Indirect Object + Direct Object

`The pitcher threw the player the ball.`

Subject + Linking Verb + Subject Complement

`Dolphins are intelligent.`

EXPANSION BY MODIFYING—adding words that describe or limit the basic sentence elements

a. **single-word adjectives and adverbs**

adj / adv.

`Fish swim.` → `Colorful fish swim quickly.`

b. **transitional expressions**

transition

`The lawyer could not be reached.` → `The lawyer, however, could not be reached.`

c. **prepositional adjective and adverb phrases**

adv. / adj.

`Students write essays. During the semester, students in English classes write essays.`

EXPANSION BY COORDINATING—joining (compounding) two or more elements (words, phrases, or clauses) of equal importance with a coordinate conjuction; repeating the same grammatical pattern to achieve parallelism

Types of coordination:

a. **compound subjects**

`A movie or a play is my favorite form of entertainment.` (no comma between compound subjects)

b. **compound predicates**

`The children swam in the ocean and played games at the beach.` (no comma between compound predicates)

c. **compound modifiers:**

coordinate adjectives—two adjectives modifying a noun equally; to determine coordination, place **and** between them or reverse their order; one comma required to separate

The dark, dreary day finally ended.

consecutive adjectives—two adjectives modifying the same noun differently, especially if one is derived from a noun; no comma required

My light blue car is faster than frustrating public transportation.

adverbs and prepositional phrases

The ice skaters glide smoothly and easily around the rink or around the lake.

d. **items in a series**—three or more words or phrases; commas required to separate items including the one which is followed by a coordinate conjunction

The grocery cart contained vegetables, fruit, meat, and milk.

During our last vacation, we traveled on the train, in the car, and on the boat.

e. **appositive**—renaming, identifying, and explaining one noun with another noun or noun phrase; commas required to separate it from the rest of the sentence when it is free or nonrestrictive

appositive

I finally met my next door neighbor, a retired police officer.

appositive

The school fund-raiser, a one-hour jogathon, collected money for new gym equipment.

f. **compound sentence**—two independent clauses written as one sentence; punctuation required to separate equal clauses; incorrectly punctuated compound sentence is a run-on

Subject + Predicate, coordinate conjunction Subject + Predicate

The parents were angry, but the children refused to help.

Subject + Predicate; Subject + Predicate

The meal was delicious; however, we ate too much.

The cat meowed; the dog barked.

Discovery Exercises for Modifying and Coordinating

I. DIRECTIONS: Add the grammatical patterns specified to the sentences below. Do not change the basic sentence patterns. Use correct punctuation where necessary.

1. Add a single-word adjective and a single-word adverb to each sentence.

   Cars require maintenance. ______________________________

   ____

   Crime destroys property. ______________________________

   ____

2. Add a transitional expression to each sentence.

Term papers take effort. ______________________________

____

The telephone is a modern convenience. ______________________________

____

3. Add one adjective prepositional phrase and one adverb prepositional phrase to each sentence.

Grocery shoppers can save money. ______________________________

____

The guests arrived. ______________________________

____

4. Add a compound subject to complete each sentence.

______________________________ attend the movies often.

______________________________ deliver the newspapers.

5. Add a compound predicate to complete each sentence.

The election ______________________________

____

The educational system ______________________________

____

6. Add an independent clause to each sentence; use a different form of punctuation in each.

Riding a bicycle requires coordination ______________________________

____

My favorite dessert is chocolate cake ______________________________

____

II. DIRECTIONS: Combine the following groups of sentences according to the specific grammatical pattens identified. Do not eliminate any vital information. Use correct punctuation where necessary.

1. Combine by making coordinate adjectives.

The house in Virginia is very large. It is stylish and attractive.

____

The marketing report surveyed cosmetics. It was overdue and overbudget.

____

2. Combine by making two sets of consecutive adjectives.

Their silk clothing is dirty. It needs machine washing which is special.

____

____

The recreational vehicle was new. It traveled on mountain roads that were steep.

____

____

3. Combine by using compound adverbs and compound prepositional phrases.

   The horses trotted along the bridle path quickly. They also went over the bridge noisily.

   ____

   ____

   The cook skillfully put the food in the oven. Carefully the cook placed the food in the refrigerator.

   ____

   ____

4. Combine by putting items in a series.

   The skills involved in soccer are knowing how to pass and kick the ball. A player also has to be able to shoot accurately at the goal.

   ____

   ____

   Traveling to foreign places is very enjoyable because one sees new sights and meets new people. In addition, one can also buy unusual souvenirs and eat unfamiliar foods.

   ____

   ____

5. Combine by using an appositive.

   Wordsworth was one of the first English Romantic poets. He wrote *Lyrical Ballads* and *The Prelude.*

   ____

   ____

   San Francisco is a small cosmopolitan city. Like Rome, it is built on seven hills.

   ____

   ____

6. Combine by making compound sentences; use the two different forms of punctuation.

   Gilbert and Sullivan wrote many popular operettas. Their most famous one was *H. M. S. Pinafore.*

   ____

   ____

   The dogs whined at the door. We would not let them in.

   ____

   ____

EXPANSION BY SUBORDINATING—joining two elements (phrases or clauses) of unequal importance with a subordinate conjunction or a relative pronoun; using dependent clauses, verbal phrases, and absolute phrases

Types of subordination

a. **dependent clause**—a group of related words with a subject and predicate; functions as a single part of speech—adverb, adjective, or noun; forms a complex sentence when combined with an independent clause; not a sentence

Types of dependent clauses:

1. **adverb dependent clause**—begins with a subordinate conjunction, is able to be placed in different parts of the sentence

Subordinate conjunction + Subject + Predicate

• requires a comma when it comes before the independent clause:

After the dinner was over, the group went to the theater.

• requires no comma when it comes after the independent clause:

The group went to the theater after the dinner was over.

• requires commas before and after when it comes between the subject and predicate of the independent clause:

The group, after the dinner was over, went to the theater.

2. **adjective dependent clause**—begins with a relative pronoun which may be the subject or object of the dependent clause; must be placed as closely as possible to the word it modifies; punctuation depends on whether or not the clause changes the meaning of the sentence; to determine punctuation, read the sentence with and without the clause

Relative pronoun + (Subject) + Predicate

• **nonrestrictive (free)**—requires commas before and after when the clause is unnecessary to identify the specific person, place, or thing being discussed; adds additional information; does not change the meaning of the sentence when the clause is removed

My mother, whom I love, will visit next week.

My friend bought a sheepskin rug, which is made of wool.

A package arrived for Leslie, who lives next door.

• **restrictive (bound)**—uses no commas because it is necessary to identify more specifically the person, place, or thing being discussed; is not additional information; changes the meaning of the sentence when the clause is removed

My cousin whom I love will visit next week.

My friend bought a suit which is made of wool.

A package arrived for someone who lives next door.

3. **noun dependent clause**—begins with a relative pronoun or a subordinate conjunction; functions as a subject, object, or object of a preposition; requires no commas because it is a necessary part of the sentence

Relative pronoun + (Subject) + Predicate

- subject: That the flowers will die eventually is obvious.
- object: I did not know that I was going to arrange the flowers.
- object of preposition: I gave the pencils to whoever needed them.

b. **verbal phrase**—a group of related words without a subject or a predicate; functions as a single part of speech—adjective, noun, or adverb; derived from the present participle (**ing**), the past participle (**ed, en, t**), or the infinitive (**to** + verb) of the verb; not a sentence

verb phrase = auxiliary + main verb

were + going (present participle)
have + gone (past participle)

Subject + verb phrase = independent clause (sentence)

The students were going.
The students have gone.

verbal phrase = participle **or** infinitive

going (present) to go (infinitive)
gone (past)

Subject + verbal phrase = fragment

the students going
the students gone
the students to go

Types of verbal phrases:

1. **adjective verbal phrase**—uses present participle, past participle, or infinitive form of the verb; must be placed immediately in front of or after the noun it modifies; requires a comma when it precedes the main clause; requires commas before and after when it follows the noun and adds extra information; requires no commas when it follows the noun and is necessary to the meaning of the sentence

Running down the street, the water caused huge holes.

The water running down the street caused huge holes.

Written by Charles Dickens, A Tale of Two Cities is a novel about the French Revolution.

A Tale of Two Cities, written by Charles Dickens, is a novel about the French Revolution.

The chef baked the cake to serve at the birthday party.

The dress to be worn at the wedding is finished.

2. **noun verbal phrase**—uses the present participle or the infinitive; functions as a subject, object, or object of a preposition; called a gerund; requires no punctuation

   • subject:

   Present Participle

   Swimming in the ocean can be dangerous.

   Infinitive

   To write a poem requires skill.

   • object:

   Present Participle

   The members of the sports club loved skiing in the Alps.

   Infinitive

   The pianist wanted to give a concert.

   • object of preposition:

   Present Participle

   They passed the test by learning all the rules.

3. **adverb verbal phrase**—uses only the infinitive; requires a comma when it precedes the main clause

   Adjective

   The Smiths are next to play tennis on the first court.

   Verb

   To improve their golf game, the couple went to a golf clinic.

4. **absolute phrase**—a group of words with a subject followed by modifiers or a verbal; modifies the rest of the sentence but is not linked to it by a subordinate conjunction or the preposition **with;** requires one comma to separate it from the independent clause

   Her hands cold and numb, she pulled on her fur-lined gloves.

   The day being almost over, we prepared to leave for home.

Discovery Exercise for Subordinating

DIRECTIONS: Combine the following groups of sentences by leaving one clause independent and by subordinating the others as dependent clauses, verbal phrases, and/or absolute phrases. Do not eliminate any vital information. Use correct punctuation where necessary.

Example: The centers of the blossoms show color.
The petals drop from the fruit trees.
The petals cover the earth with colors.
The colors are pink and white.

Absolute Phrase

Sentence 1 The centers of the blossoms showing color, the pink

Subject — Verbal Phrase — Predicate

and white petals, dropping from the fruit trees, cover the earth.

Dependent Clause

Sentence 2 `While the centers of the blossoms are showing color,`

Subject Predicate — Dependent Clause

`the pink and white petals cover the earth as they drop from the fruit trees.`

1. Numerous proposals have been introduced into Congress.
   The proposals involve the way the President and Vice-President are elected.
   These proposals call for change.

   ____

   ____

   ____

2. Adam Smith was leading the first organized economic movement.
   This movement intended to liberate the individual from the government.

   ____

   ____

   ____

3. We drove to the theater to see the play.
   I was full of questions.
   I had never been to a play before.

   ____

   ____

   ____

4. Adam Smith wrote The Wealth of Nations.
   Then the term capitalism was nonexistent.
   He wrote instead of the "natural order of liberty."

   ____

   ____

   ____

5. The conquest of Mexico was an easy battle for the Spanish.
   The Spaniards had advantages of firearms and horses.

   ____

   ____

   ____

6. The paint was pigment mixed with egg.
   The paint was pale in color.
   The paint dried instantly.

   ____

   ____

   ____

7. Underdeveloped countries do not have enough capital and technology.
They cannot compete with other countries.
They have tc sell their labor and natural resources as cheaply as possible.

8. In the fourteenth century a small tribe of Incas rose from obscurity.
They created the mightiest empire of ancient America.

9. It was a crisp and sunny morning.
The frigid sea breeze nipped at my face.
I steered my fishing vessel toward the mighty ship.

10. One tribe of Latin American Indians was the Mayans.
They settled in the central part of Mexico.

11. I looked up with a squint.
I could see the tattered remains of canvas sails.
The sails were dancing feverishly like ghosts in the wind.

12. The motor boat chugged away.
The crashing of waves roared loudly.
The invigorating scent of the sea salt infiltrated the air.

ACHIEVING SENTENCE VARIETY

Combining several thoughts effectively in a single sentence gives writing vitality and style. The three principal ways of expanding the basic sentence are by modifying, coordinating, and subordinating. The following example shows how the same sentences can be combined in a number of different ways to vary the emphasis and make the writing more precise and mature. The exercise that follows this example will help you practice sentence variety.

Original basic sentences:

The Rosetta Stone was discovered in 1799 near the mouth of the Nile River.
It is an inscribed stone tablet.
The stone revealed the secret of Egyptian writing.
This secret had been lost for 1300 years.

Combination 1: compound sentence, appositive, adjective dependent clause

The Rosetta Stone, an inscribed stone tablet, was discovered in 1799 near the mouth of the Nile River; the stone revealed the secret of Egyptian writing which had been lost for 1300 years.

Combination 2: adjective verbal phrases

Discovered in 1799 near the mouth of the Nile River, an inscribed stone tablet called the Rosetta Stone revealed the secret of Egyptian writing, lost for 1300 years.

Combination 3: absolute phrase, adverb prepositional phrase, adjective dependent clause

The Rosetta Stone having been discovered in 1799 near the mouth of the Nile River, the secret of Egyptian writing which had been lost for 1300 years was revealed on this inscribed stone tablet.

Combination 4: adjective dependent clause, compound predicate, adjective verbal phrase

The Rosetta Stone, which is an inscribed stone tablet, was discovered in 1799 near the mouth of the Nile River and revealed the secret of Egyptian writing, lost for 1300 years.

Combination 5: adverb dependent clause, consecutive adjectives, adjective verbal phrase

Because the inscribed Rosetta Stone tablet was discovered in 1799 near the mouth of the Nile River, the secret of Egyptian writing, lost for 1300 years, was revealed.

Combination 6: noun verbal phrase, consecutive adjectives, adjective dependent clause

Discovering the inscribed Rosetta Stone tablet in 1799 near the mouth of the Nile River revealed the secret of Egyptian writing that had been lost for 1300 years.

Discovery Exercise for Embedding and Sentence Variety

DIRECTIONS: Combine the following groups of sentences by leaving one or two clauses independent and by embedding the others as modifying, coordinating, and subordinating constructions. Do not eliminate any vital information. Use correct punctuation where necessary.

1. The plants were covered with thorns.
   The plants were close to the edge of the cliff.
   The plants crept across the trails.
   The plants tried to reach the other side of the cliff.

   ____

   ____

   ____

2. The heroes and villains are unreal.
   The audience cannot relate the fictional experiences of these characters to reality.
   This task is one of the major functions of a play.

3. Howard Blair is an educator.
   He is a compassionate human being.
   He puts himself in the students' places.
   He experiences the same pains and frustrations as his students.

4. The electoral college system was adopted at the Constitutional Convention in 1787.
   The system was accepted.
   The system was not desirable.
   The system was a compromise.

5. No satisfactory definition of the concept of capitalism exists.
   In all probability, none will ever be agreed on.
   Capitalism itself means different things to different people.
   People have different ideas and different standards.

6. I was on my usual route that day.
   I had just rounded a piece of coastline.
   The coastline was treacherous and rocky.
   I happened upon an eighteenth-century sailing ship.
   The ship was remarkably preserved.

7. The ship's deck stretched ahead of me.
   The deck was lined on both sides with rusted cannons.
   The cannons were poised timelessly for a battle.
   The battle was never to materialize.

   ____

   ____

   ____

8. The Incas grew a large variety of crops.
   The Incas grew maize and potatoes.
   The Incas grew squash and beans.
   The Incas grew grain for herds of llamas and alpacas.
   The llamas and alpacas are members of the camel family.

   ____

   ____

   ____

9. My sadness was replaced by a smile.
   I realized that this glamorous lady of the sea would soon be at peace.
   I had been fortunate.
   I had spent a lovely last moment with her.

   ____

   ____

   ____

10. She helped me with my gear.
    She always did.
    She set my gear on the steps of my dorm.
    I unpacked my gear in my room.

    ____

    ____

    ____

11. This was my first airplane trip.
    I waited for take-off
    I sat rigidly in my seat.
    I tried to swallow the dryness in my throat.

    ____

    ____

    ____

12. I composed a song.
    The song was about medieval Europe.
    The song fulfilled the teacher's requirements.
    The song had a singable melody.
    The song had a logical progression of events.
    The song had reliable statements of fact.

____

____

____

____

MECHANICS

Observing the accepted practices in mechanics is a necessary part of effective writing.

Punctuation rules
Capitalization rules
Spelling aids and list

Punctuation Rules

End Punctuation [. ? !]

Every sentence must end with a mark of punctuation

- use a **period** at the end of sentences which make statements
- use a **question mark** at the end of sentences which ask direct questions
- use an **exclamation point** at the end of sentences which express surprise, disbelief, or other strong emotion

Comma [,]

Commas for coordination—one comma to separate equal elements

1. **Coordinate adjectives**
   - use "and" between adjectives } ← the test for coordinate adjectives
   - reverse order of adjectives }

   the dirty, dusty room
   the peaceful, intimate restaurant

   but **not**

   the little French figurine
   the fat white cat

2. **Items in a series**
   - use a comma between each element (word, phrase, or clause)
   - a, b, and c **or** a, b, c

   the ice cream cone, cake, and candy (words)

   The group walked to the store, to the movies, and to the library. (phrases)

   Jesse painted the fence, Maria replaced a window, and Ken repaired the roof. (clauses)

3. **Compound sentence**

   - use a comma and a coordinate conjunction **or** use a semicolon between the two independent clauses to avoid a run-on sentence

   Subject Predicate, coordinate conjunction Subject Predicate.

   > The students worked hard to edit their papers [, and] they submitted them with eager anticipation.
   >
   > The following week they were returned [, but] more the teacher considered them unacceptable.

   Subject Predicate ; Subject Predicate.

   > Buying a used car is a risky venture [;] a wise buyer needs knowledge and help.
   >
   > The heavy rains washed away the hillside [; however,] they did not damage the house.

Commas for subordination—one or two commas to set off unequal (less important) elements

1. **Introductory dependent clauses, lengthy prepositional phrases, and verbal phrases** (as modifiers)

   > Although the driver asked for help, no one paid any attention. (dependent clause)
   >
   > In the early hours before dawn, a lone dog howled softly. (prepositional phrase)
   >
   > Drawn by four horses, the sleigh skimmed over the snow. (verbal phrase)

2. **Adjectives out of normal order** (following the noun)

   > The team, tired and weary, returned from its out-of-town game.
   > The cat, happy and content, purred loudly.

3. **Appositives**

   > A place of important historical interest is Philadelphia, the city of brotherly love.
   > John Keats, a late Romantic poet, wrote many beautiful odes.

4. **Sentence interrupters**—transitional expressions

   > Mixing colors, moreover, is an important step in creating an artistic canvas.
   > In conclusion, the report was not adequately prepared.
   > Her efforts, I feel, will be rewarded.

5. **Nonrestrictive modifiers**—clauses and phrases that add extra information to the sentence

   > My grandmother, whom I love, has gone away.
   > Bob Brown, working forty hours a week, has little free time for hiking.

6. **Speaker in direct quotation**

   > The critic said, "The book effectively develops its thesis."
   > "The paper," the teacher said, "is due tomorrow."

7. **Dates and addresses and geographical names**

   > On Sunday, June 1, 1982, the young couple will marry.
   > They will live at 1527 Main Street, Centry, California.
   > Pearl Harbor, Hawaii, has a memorial to the sailors of the USS Arizona.

8. **Direct address and interjections**

`Mother, may I go to the movies tonight?`
`Oh, that was a delicious meal.`

Semicolon [;]

- to separate independent clauses not joined by a coordinating conjunction
- to separate items in a series if one item has internal punctuation

`Buying a car is necessary; one needs both time and money.`
`The pet store had a big, strong Labrador; a petite, fragile poodle; and a fluffy Persian cat.`

Colon [:]

- to separate a complete introductory statement from a formal list, a formal statement or quotation, or an explanation
- never follows a verb

`The stationer ordered a month's supplies: paper, ink, pens, rubber bands, staplers, and glue.`

Italics and Underlining [italics in printed works and underlining in handwritten or typewritten papers]

- to identify numbers as numbers, letters as letters, words as words

three <u>4's</u>, six <u>A's</u>, the word <u>wisdom</u>

- to indicate titles of books, magazines, movies, plays, newspapers, journals, and recording albums

<u>A Tale of Two Cities</u>, <u>Newsweek</u>, <u>Gone With the Wind</u>, <u>Death of a Salesman</u>, <u>Los Angeles Times</u>

- to identify foreign words and phrases

<u>adios</u>,
<u>raison d'être</u>,
<u>non sequitur</u>

- to identify names of ships, trains, aircraft, spacecraft, and works of art

<u>USS Arizona</u>, <u>Oriental Express</u>, <u>Air Force One</u>, <u>Discovery</u>, <u>Guernica</u>

Hyphen [-]

- to join two or more words acting as a single adjective before a noun
- to divide words of more than one syllable at the end of a line
- to form compound words from twenty-one to ninety-nine and fractions

Dash [—]

- to show abrupt change in thought or inclusive page numbers
- to emphasize additional, unnecessary material

Parentheses [( )]

- to set off comments and explanations that are incidental to the main idea

Brackets [ ]

- to set off material inserted in a quotation and to replace parentheses within parentheses

Quotation marks [“ ”]

- to set off direct quotations and dialogue

Place comma and period inside end quotation mark. `"Please go," she said. She said, "Please go."`

Place colon and semicolon outside end quotation mark. **Byron wrote "She Walks in Beauty"; Keats wrote "Ode on a Grecian Urn."**

- to enclose titles of short works: poems, essays from newspapers, journals, magazines, and anthologies, short stories, chapters, songs, reviews, television or radio shows, encyclopedia entries, editorials, and lectures
- to set off words used in a special way

Apostrophe [']

- to indicate possession in nouns and indefinite pronouns (except for personal pronouns)

singular noun + 's = singular possession

horse + 's = horse's saddle
someone + 's = someone's wallet

singular nouns ending in s + ' or 's = singular possession

Dr. James + ' or 's = Dr. James' house
Dr. James's house

plural nouns ending in s or es + ' = plural possession

birds + ' = birds' nest
Joneses + ' = the Joneses' car

irregular plural nouns put in plural form + 's = plural possession

child → children + 's = children's games
mouse → mice + 's = mice's cheese

- to indicate omissions in contractions and numbers

do not, don't
class of 1982, class of '82
they would, they'd.

- to form plurals of letters, numbers, abbreviations, and words as words

three <u>A's</u> and two <u>B's</u>, those <u>8's</u>, three <u>Ph.D.'s</u>, several <u>but's</u>

Capitalization Rules

1. the first letter of the first word of a sentence, a line of poetry, a direct quote which begins with the first word of a sentence

   Come in. "She walks in beauty." "How are you?" she asked.

2. titles before and after people's names

   Dr. Smith, Leslie Smith, Ph.D.

3. names of days, months, holidays

   Tuesday, May, Fourth of July

4. proper nouns, adjectives derived from proper nouns

   France, English

5. names of deities, religions

   Venus, Hindu

6. points on a compass when referring to a particular region

   North, West

7. names of specific periods or events in history but usually **not** names of centuries

   `French Revolution, eighteenth century`

8. names of organizations, institutions, political parties, government agencies

   `Salvation Army, Treasury Department`

9. specific course titles

   `Math 32, Accounting 2`

10. the first letter of the first word and the first letters of the major words of a title

   `"A Study of Dieting Fads"`

Spelling Aids

The inability to spell is not an incurable affliction. Improving spelling requires work, time, and patience. By learning the words in the spelling list at the end of this section, you can eliminate half of the spelling errors you now make. When you rewrite your papers, pay special attention to correct your original errors and not to misspell new words.

1. Test yourself on the words in the list in groups of 50 or 75. Have someone read the words as you spell them on paper. If you guess when spelling a word, make a note to study that word later because you are not sure of it. If you guess, you may be right one time but wrong the next time. Check over your list for misspelled or guessed words. Put these in a new list to study.
2. Add to the list words spelled incorrectly on any writing you have done. Add new words or terms from your reading. Keep the list current.
3. Invest in a hardback dictionary and use it regularly. For spelling improvement use the dictionary to learn more about these misspelled words: pronunciation, syllable breakdown, and meaning. The more you know about a word, the more likely you are to spell it correctly.
4. Study the misspelled words systematically.
   Pronounce the word aloud to fix it in your hearing memory.
   Look at the word carefully to fix it in your seeing memory.
   Write the word to fix it in your muscular memory.
5. Use additional memory devices when they are appropriate for difficult words.
   - pronounce a word the way it is spelled (but only for spelling purposes):

     `en vi RON ment`
     `bus I ness`

   - emphasize the problem area in a word by capitalizing it (but only for spelling purposes):

     `sepArate`   `existEnce`

   - find a word within the word and make a sentence with the two words to emphasize the proper spelling:

     `They RAN with perseveRANce.`

6. Use rules that apply to types of words.
   - form the plural by adding **s** to the singular but by adding **es** if the plural makes an extra syllable:

     `book, books; bed, beds`
     `church, churches; patch, patches`

   - **I** before **E**
     Except after **C**
     Or when sounded as **A**

As in **neighbor** or **weigh.**

I before **E:**	`believe, relief, piece`
after **C:**	`receive, deceit, conceive`
exceptions:	`weird, leisure, seize`

- double the final consonant before a suffix beginning with a vowel:
  when the word has only one syllabie or is accented on the last syllable
  when the final consonant is preceded by a single vowel

  `stop, stopped, stopping`
  `begin, beginning, beginner`
  `control, controlled, controlling`
  `occur, occurring, occurrence`

- do not double the final consonant:

  when it is preceded by a double vowel or two vowels

  `need, needed, needing`
  `treat, treated, treating`

  when the word is not accented on the last syllable

  `offer, offered, offering`
  `benefit, benefited, benefiting`

  when the suffix begins with a consonant

  `ship, shipped, shipping`

- change the **y** to **i** in words ending with **y** when a suffix is added, if the **y** is preceded by a consonant:

  `lovely, lovelier, loveliest`
  `copy, copied, copies`
  `try, tried, tries`
  `carry, carried, carries`

- do not drop the **y** before **ing** endings:

  `copying`
  `trying`
  `carrying`

- do not drop the **y** when it is preceded by a vowel:

  `play, played`
  `joy, joyous, joyful`
  Exceptions: `said, laid, paid`

- drop the **e** in words ending with a silent **e** when adding a suffix beginning with a vowel:

  `love, loving, lovable`
  `guide, guiding, guidance`
  `become, becoming`

  Exceptions: `changeable, noticeable, courageous`

- keep the **e** in words ending with a silent **e** when adding a suffix beginning with a consonant:

  `immediate, immediately`
  `force, forceful`
  `sincere, sincerely`

  Exceptions: `argument, truly, judgment`

- do not change the spelling of a basic word when adding the prefix **dis, mis,** or **un:**

```
dis + agree       =   disagree
mis + spell       =   misspell
un + necessary    =   unnecessary
```

350 Often Misspelled Words

accelerate
accidentally
accommodate
accompanied
accumulate
achievement
acquainted
across
address
advertisement
advice
aggravate
aggression
all right
allude
a lot
altogether
always
amateur
among
amount
apparent
appearance
appetite
approaching
appropriate
approximately
arctic
argument
around
arrangement
article
athletic
audience
awkward

background
barbarous
before
beginning
believed
benefited
breathe
brilliant
bulletin
buried
business

carrying
category
cemetery
changeable
chosen
clothes
coming
committee
comparative
competition
complement
compliment
conceive
conquer
conscientious
consider
continually
control
convenience
copies
corner
correspondence
course
courteous
criticism
curiosity

dealt
decision
defendent
definitely
definition
dependent
description
desirable
despair
desperate
destroy
devastating
develop
different
dining
disappeared
disappointed
disastrous
discipline
diseases
dissatisfied
dissipation
division
doesn't

eating
eighth
efficiency
eliminated
embarrassed
emphasize
environment
equipped
especially
exaggerated
excel
excellent
excitement
exhausted
exhilaration
existence
experience
explanation
extremely

familiar
fascinating
finally
flannel
foreign
formally
formerly
fortunately
forty
fourth
friend

gardener
generally
genius
glamorous
government
grammar
grievance
guard

handkerchief
handle
height
hindrance
hurriedly

ignore
imagination
immediately
implying
incidentally
independent
indispensable
intelligence
interesting
interfere
interpreted
interruption
irresistible
its
it's
itself

jewelry
judgment

knowledge

laboratory
laid
language
led
leisure
lightning
livelihood
loneliness
lose
losing

maintenance
mathematics
meant
medicine
middle
midpoint
midstream
merely
miniature
minute
mischievous
mysterious

naturally
necessary
negative
nevertheless
nickel
niece
ninety
ninth
noisily
noticeable
nowadays

obstacle
obviously
occasion
occasionally
occurred
occurrence
offered
omission
omitted
operate
opinion
opportunity
opposite
optimistic
original
outrageous

paid
parallel
paralyzed
parliament
particularly
partner
pastime
perform
perhaps
permissible
perseverance
persistent
persuade
phenomenon
physically
piece
pleasant
portrayed
possess
practically
preceding
preference
preferred
prejudice
preparations
principal
principles
privilege
probably
procedure
proceed
professional
professor
prominent
propeller
psychology
pursue

quantity
quiet
quite
quitting
quizzes

realize
really
received
recognize
recommend
re-define
reference
referred
relatively
relieve
religious
remembrance
repetition
resource
restaurant
rhythm
ridiculous

sacrifice
safety
satisfactorily
scarcely
schedule
second
secretary
seems
seize
sense
separate

sergeant
severely
shining
siege
similar
sincerely
sophomore
source
sparse
specimen
speech
stopped
strategy
strength
strenuously
stretched
studying
succeed
successful
superintendent
supersede
suppress
surely
surprise
symbolism
synonym

tastefulness
technique
temperament
their
there
they're
though
through
tobacco
together
too
toward
tragedy
transferring
tremendous
tries
truly
twelfth

undoubtedly
unnecessary
until
usually

valleys
valuable
varieties
vegetable
vengeance
vertical
very
view
vigorous
village

weather
weird
well-liked
well-made
well-planned
whether
whole
wholly
who's
whose
women
wonder
worrying
writing
written

Discovery Exercise for Mechanics

DIRECTIONS: Correct the mechanical errors in the following sentences.

1. Form a nouns singular possessive by using 's.
2. Remember that her's, it's, their's, your's, and our's have no apostrophe for possession.
3. In sentences paragraphs essays and books commas keep a string of items separated.
4. It's necessary to separate equal coordinate adjectives with a comma.
5. Do not write a run-on sentence for you must punctuate properly.
6. The rule about the colon is: the colon comes only after a complete clause to introduce a quotation a list of items or an explanation.
7. Do not use commas, which are not necessary.
8. When writting be sure to spell corectly.
9. Words interrupting the flow of the sentence however are set off by commas.
10. When a less important idea precedes the main part of the sentence a comma is needed.
11. Quotations the teacher said should be set off with quotations marks.
12. In English we capitalize and italicize the titles of books like gone with the wind.
13. It is a well known but much abused rule that a hyphen joins two words acting as a single adjective before a noun.

14. Semicolons sometimes separate two independent clauses at the end of the second clause a period is required.
15. An appositive a word which renames a noun requires commas to set it off from the rest of the sentence.

USAGE

The rules and principles of grammar must be followed for correct writing. Errors in these areas weaken the effectiveness of a paper by destroying its coherence, causing lack of clarity, and distracting the reader's attention from the ideas.

Errors:
- Fragment
- Modifier mistakes: dangling, misplaced
- Faulty pronoun reference
- Faulty agreement: subject-verb, pronoun-noun
- Shifts: person, number, tense, tone, mood, voice
- Faulty parallelism

1. **Fragment**—a part of a sentence, such as a phrase or dependent clause, written as a sentence

    `Fishing in the mountain stream.`

    `The person who moved in next door to me.`

    Avoid by having each sentence contain at least one subject and one predicate not introduced by a subordinating conjunction or relative pronoun.

    `Fishing in the mountain stream requires expensive equipment.`

    `The person who moved in next door to me owns two dogs and two cats.`

2. **Modifier mistakes**
    - **Dangling modifier**—an adjective verbal phrase that refers to the wrong noun or pronoun in a sentence and makes an illogical statement

      `After driving fifty yards, the trail opened up to a rocky beach.`

      `To lose weight, a good diet must be followed precisely by the dieter.`

    Avoid by reconstructing the sentence in one of two ways: add a subject and an appropriate form of the verb to the adjective phrase or make the subject of the main clause the word that the phrase modifies.

    `After we drove fifty yards, the trail opened up to a rocky beach.`

    `To lose weight, the dieter must follow a good diet precisely.`

    - **Misplaced modifier**—an adjective or adverb word, phrase, or clause that is needlessly separated from the word it modifies

      `They even sleep during the movies.`

      `The shopkeeper gave oranges to the children with pits in them.`

      `We bought jewelry at a store in a resort area which cost forty dollars.`

    Avoid by placing the modifier as close as possible to the word it modifies. The sentence can be rearranged without having to be reconstructed.

```
They sleep even during the movies.
The shopkeeper gave oranges with pits in them to the children.
At a store in a resort area, we bought jewelry which cost forty dol-
        lars.
```

3. **Faulty pronoun reference**—a pronoun which does not refer clearly to the noun (antecedent) it is replacing because the reference is divided or vague; weakens a paper's coherence

- **Divided** (two possible noun references)

```
The teachers told the students that they will have to leave class
early.
```

Avoid by reconstructing the sentence to make the pronoun clearly refer to only one noun.

```
The teachers said that the students would have to leave class early.
```

- **Vague** (no specific noun reference)

```
Steering a bicycle mainly involves eye and hand movements and dis-
tance judgment; a child finds this (it) very hard at first.
```

Avoid by changing the pronoun to a noun.

```
Steering a bicycle mainly involves eye and hand movements and dis-
tance judgment; a child finds these tasks very hard at first.
```

4. **Faulty agreement**

- **Faulty subject-verb agreement**—a verb that does not agree with its subject in number

```
The subject of my essays are usually my personal experiences.
```

Avoid by making the verb agree with its subject and not with the intervening object of the prepositional phrase.

```
The subject of my essays is usually my personal experiences.
```

```
There is several basic reasons for having a physical examination every
year.
```

Avoid by recognizing inverted sentence order where the subject follows the verb.

```
There are several basic reasons for having a physical examination
every year.
```

```
My favorite snack are potato chips and pretzels.
```

Avoid by making the verb agree with the subject of the linking verb, not the complement (noun in the predicate).

```
My favorite snack is potato chips and pretzels.
```

- **Faulty pronoun-noun agreement**—a pronoun that does not agree in gender or number with the noun (antecedent) it replaces

```
While a person is sleeping, their unconscious mind stays awake.
First, one has to decide what kind of horse they want.
The walls looked as if every visitor had left their signature.
```

Avoid (except in informal usage) by having a singular possessive pronoun refer back to a singular unspecified noun or singular indefinite pronoun.

```
While a person is sleeping, his unconscious mind stays awake.
First, one has to decide what kind of horse he wants.
The walls looked as if every visitor had left his or her signature.
```

A common way to avoid using the singular masculine pronoun (or the awkward combination of masculine and feminine pronouns) to refer to both male and female is to make the noun or pronoun plural.

```
While people sleep, their unconscious minds stay awake.
First, people have to decide what kind of horse they want.
The walls looked as if many visitors had left their signatures.
```

5. **Shift**—an unnecessary and illogical change in point of view involving person, number, tense, tone, mood, voice

- **Shift in person**

```
The bison has two long horns, and its chin is tucked into his chest.
We picture this symbol of perfection and wonder what one would ask this
tree if it could talk.
```

Avoid by deciding on first, second, or third person for the entire passage and being consistent. First (I and we) and third persons (he, she, it, and they) are preferable in semiformal writing.

```
The bison has two long horns, and its chin is tucked into its chest.
We picture this symbol of perfection and wonder what we would ask this
tree if it could talk.
```

- **Shift in number**

```
The corporation has major economic problems that they must solve.
```

Avoid by deciding on singular or plural and being consistent.

```
The corporation has major economic problems that it must solve.
```

- **Shift in tense**

```
The look on the coach's face was blank as the team finally gives up
trying to win.
```

Avoid by deciding on present or past tense and being consistent.

```
The look on the coach's face was blank as the team finally gave up
trying to win.
```

- **Shift in tone (diction)**

```
People who try to get back at their nasty neighbors are misguided rep-
robates.
```

Avoid by consistently using diction appropriate to the formal, semiformal, or informal level of language. The semiformal level is preferable in most writing.

```
People who take revenge on their unpleasant neighbors are misguided.
```

- **Shift in mood**

```
Instructors can use various methods to teach singing. Use a tape ma-
chine to record students' voices.
```

Avoid by using either the mood of statement or the mood of command ("you" implied).

> Instructors can use various methods to teach singing. Teachers can have a tape machine record students' voices.
>
> OR
>
> Use various methods to teach singing. Have a tape machine record students' voices.

- **Shift in voice**

> *Subject (doer) Object (receiver)*
> We visited Australia last summer, [active voice]
> *Subject (receiver) Object of preposition (doer)*
> and the trip was enjoyed by us. [passive voice]

Avoid by placing in the subject position of both clauses the doer of the action and by putting in the object position the receiver of the action. The active voice is stronger and more effective in writing and, therefore, preferable. Be consistent.

> *Subject (doer) Object (receiver) Subject (doer)*
> We visited Australia last summer, and we enjoyed
> *Object (receiver)*
> the trip. [active voice]
>
> OR
>
> *Subject (receiver) Object of preposition (doer)*
> Australia was visited by us last summer, and the
> *Subject (receiver)*
> trip was enjoyed. [passive voice]

6. **Faulty parallelism**—two grammatical constructions (words, phrases, or clauses) that express equal ideas in differing structures; weakens a paper's coherence

> *adjective adjective noun*
> The artist was sensitive, compassionate, and a fine intellect.
>
> *infinitive gerund*
> I like to swim at the beach, hiking in the mountains, and
> *gerund*
> fishing in the lakes.
>
> *independent clause dependent clause*
> The tour spent the day sightseeing and where they shopped for souvenirs.

Avoid by putting equal ideas in identical grammatical constructions. Join words with words, phrases with phrases, and clauses with clauses.

> The artist was sensitive, compassionate, and intellectual.
>
> I like swimming at the beach, hiking in the mountains, and fishing in the lakes.
>
> The tour spent the day where they saw the sights and where they stopped for souvenirs.

Discovery Exercise for Usage

DIRECTIONS: Correct the usage errors in the following sentences.

1. Just between he and I, I should know my prepositions.
2. Do not break sentences. In two. Remember the rule. About fragments.
3. Verbs has to agree with its subject.
4. Each pronoun agrees with their noun reference.
5. A writer must not shift your point of view.
6. Always try to lay off slang expressions.
7. In my opinion, I think that students when they are writing shouldn't get into the habit of using too many unnecessary words that they don't need in order to convey their idea.
8. Clichés can weaken your train of thought.
9. When writing verbal phrases, an effective sentence should not use dangling modifiers.
10. Pronouns in sentences are weak unless they refer to specific nouns.
11. Equal ideas should be put in the same grammatical construction: words with words, using phrases with phrases, and to join clauses.
12. Properly placed modifiers give ideas to the readers with concrete details.
13. A pronoun must replace a particular noun; this makes the writing clear.
14. When you write an essay, make sure the verb tense did not shift.
15. Students should use the active voice of the verb in their writing; on the other hand, shifting to passive voice should be avoided by them.

Discovery Exercise for Sentence Structure, Mechanics, and Usage

DIRECTIONS: Correct the paragraph below. Make the sentence structures more varied and interesting by using the expansion techniques of modifying, coordinating, and subordinating. Correct all mistakes in mechanics and usage.

From the passed two decades the United States have spent billions of dollars on an agressive space program. It goes without saying that the program has produced significant results. The most noticable contribution by the space program is advanced technology. Scientific research has come up with new methods of measurement and analyzing. Satellites can now affectively predict and evaluate the weather, beaming down pictures and informative data. Bouncing radio waves off of satellites, the field of communications have been enhanced. Meanwhile back on Earth, seismic analysis has also been improved by the same devices used to measure and recording earthquakes on the Moon. Productivity in the government and business sectors moreover have gotten up to higher levels. Computer systems developing to control the voyager space probes. These computer systems have new applications in the industrial world. America national defense has been complemented by fancy weaponry. Missle guidence and tracking systems are much more affective now then there obsolete predecessors. New forms of propulsion have also been adopted at the armed forces. In the medical sector, some of the most beneficial rewards of space program research can be found in this day and age. New life support systems have save countless lifes, experiments with the human body in space has showed up many unknown facts. This has provided us with instruments that measure stress and behavior patterns. There is also qualitative methods to study and in understanding the bodys smallest components. Last but not least medical solutions in the field of disease treatment have been updated by discoveries of Radiation healing. The Shufflecraft will be launched later this year. A new decade of space exploration will begin. Our quest in space must continue. Our progress must move forward. For all Americans the fruits of their investments have, are, and will continue to be realized.

Index